NOTRE DAME HIGH SCHC
NILES, ILLINOIS

WITHDRAWN

W9-DEU-206

A CATHOLIC VISION

A CATHOLIC VISION

Stephen Happel and David Tracy

FORTRESS PRESS   **PHILADELPHIA**

270
H252

NOTRE DAME

MAR 1 9 1984

LIBRARY

NILES ILLINOIS

WITHDRAWN

COPYRIGHT © 1984 BY FORTRESS PRESS

All rights reserved. No part of this publication may be reproduced, stored in a retrieval system, or transmitted in any form or by any means, electronic, mechanical, photocopying, recording, or otherwise, without the prior permission of the copyright owner.

———

Library of Congress Cataloging in Publication Data

Happel, Stephen, 1944–
  A Catholic vision.

  1. Catholic Church—Doctrinal and controversial works—Catholic authors—Addresses, essays, lectures.
2. Catholic Church—History—Addresses, essays, lectures.
I. Tracy, David. II. Title.
BX1755.H26 1984   282   83–5687
ISBN 0–8006–1719–3 (pbk.)

———

K110E83   Printed in the United States of America   1-1719

CONTENTS

FOREWORD

A *Catholic Vision* by Father Stephen Happel and Father David Tracy is the second in the triad of books that Fortress Press is presenting of succinct, scholarly expositions of three major American religious faiths: Judaism, Catholicism, and Protestantism. It was preceded by Rabbi Howard R. Greenstein's *Judaism—An Eternal Covenant,* and the series will be completed by *Protestantism—Its Modern Meaning,* now being written by an eminent churchman.

As the editor of these books I am grateful to both Happel and Tracy, for they have opened wholly new worlds to me, a non-Catholic, and have made me acutely aware not only of the spiritual, cultural, and intellectual legacies bequeathed to us over nineteen centuries by this major sector of Christendom, but also of the gigantic efforts now under way by the Church of Pope John Paul II to face the problems of today's world.

At the same time I am impressed by three other aspects of *A Catholic Vision:* first, the eloquent yet restrained affirmation of Catholicism, its venerated traditions and contemporary messages; second, the solemn but muted note of acknowledgment of an indebtedness to Judaism, mother faith of Christianity, coupled with an implicit reproach to their fellow Catholics, both past and present, for their persecution of the Jewish people; and third, the confession that Protestantism in its infinitely varied forms is an inevitable outgrowth of a Catholicism that had allowed its intellectual strength to wane and its spiritual powers to diminish. This treatment is truly "catholic" in the full sense of an oft-misunderstood word, for its catholicity lies in its universal, all-embracing outlook.

A *Catholic Vision* reminds us of the richness of the Catholic Tradition, the wealth of wisdom it bespeaks, and its hospitable outreach to other Traditions, especially Judaism and Protestantism, in appreciation of their distinctive truths. For example, the treatment of the Protestant Reformation is high-minded and objective, and Catholicism is not portrayed as blameless or without fault. Also, the

Counter-Reformation is presented in a clear, dispassionate, unbiased fashion. Finally, the authors critically note some of the present-day trends within Catholicism and are clear and candid in their comments on the contemporary Catholic scene.

As Fathers Happel and Tracy say so aptly in their preface, their experiences as priests and teachers have also been "catholic," for the juxtaposition of their rural and urban posts in these past years deepen their insights and embody their faith.

I am happy to have had a part in the inception, the formation, and the development of this distinguished work. I, a Protestant, have grown in mind and spirit with *A Catholic Vision*.

I am indebted to Fathers Happel and Tracy for their gift of *A Catholic Vision*, a new and fresh perception of our ecumenical faith.

June 1983   Carl Hermann Voss

Carl Hermann Voss is Ecumenical Scholar-in-Residence for the National Conference of Christians and Jews.

PREFACE

The following essays in collaboration have a somewhat lengthy history. Begun in 1969 by David Tracy, they have been revised, to be taken up finally by Stephen Happel in 1981–82. Yet they would never have been completed except for the constant vigilance of their (more than) editor, Carl Hermann Voss. His ecumenical concern oversaw the project through multiple shifts in geography, scholarly attention, and personal trials. This book owes its existence to his dedication.

Over the years, however, partners in dialogue have engendered new thoughts, turned to different projects, and become interested in specialized issues. The political and religious situations have drawn the participants to more immediate topics. In such an environment, collaboration means many things. Two people have obviously worked together, contributing their judgments about Catholicism, negotiating compromises where disagreement was inevitable, shaping a whole which belongs to both of us together and to neither of us separately.

Beyond this, however, a deeper common effort emerged. Once teacher and student, we are now colleagues in an academic community. Since at this writing one of us is a professor in an urban university, the other a teacher at a seminary and pastor of a rural parish, we have for long spoken to the widely varying publics (academic, confessional, and societal) that join our religious world. As members of diocesan presbyterates (Bridgeport, Connecticut and Indianapolis, Indiana), we are convinced of an ecclesial responsibility to manifest God's Word to modern society.

From within our respective fields of vision, we have hoped to write a book that will appeal to literate inquirers—those who are surveying one of the major understandings of Christianity. The volume, however, is not a scholar's history, a specialist's position on the nature of the Church. It is not a catechism of Catholic doctrine or a systematic treatise on theological ideas.

We have written a rhetorical invitation to the meaning of Catholic life. Taking from other writers information about dates and places, interpretations concerning particular episodes, and judgments on individuals, movements, and their purposes, we have woven together materials which display designs of value to believer and nonbeliever alike. Like all rhetoric, however, our presentation involves partial argumentation and selective examples, though we believe that what is incomplete here can be described more fully, argued perhaps more cogently, and envisioned in more partisan fashion in other works. Here we have a story of what has been "going forward" during the formation of the Catholic tradition.

The view of the Church which follows can be only a single frame of a developing picture, the final composition of which awaits Divine action. If we awaken interest in what this Church may have to say to our world, if we can offer to the many honest searchers for meaning a hope that here there is some significant value, if we show believers that trusting their own story can revitalize their beliefs, then we shall have succeeded. We shall have encouraged others to share with us a Catholic vision which continues to inspire our faith, to nurture our hope, and to enable our love in a world which sorely requires all three.

Stephen Happel   David Tracy
St. Meinrad School of Theology   The Divinity School
St. Meinrad, Indiana   The University of Chicago

Advent, 1982

ACKNOWLEDGMENTS

To accomplish our task, we were grateful for the willing help of Ephrem Carr, Cyprian Davis, Colman Grabert, John Huckle, and James Walter, each of whom contributed clarity of thought and correction of fact. Jackie Culpepper, Ava Gehlhausen, Shirley Kurtzhals, Shirley Risinger, and Andrew Wimmer provided inestimable technical assistance. Irena Makarushka completed the careful index. The errors that remain, the choice of particulars through which we have chosen to see the whole—all these continue to be our own. The volume is dedicated to our nieces and nephews, brothers and sisters with whom we have learned Catholicism and who will in turn continue that Tradition in their actions and speech.

WHAT IS CATHOLICISM?

> Glory be to God for dappled things—
> Gerard Manley Hopkins (1844–89), "Pied Beauty"

Catholicism is a classic. Some would say, of course, that like a dinosaur, it should remain a museum piece to spark the brushfires of the child's imagination about the past. Others speak of it as though it were a laboratory specimen to be preserved so that its analyzed entrails might foretell the exact detail of our religious future. Still others read its story from cover to cover, find a quaint dust jacket, and believe that they can place it back on its shelf, going about their religious business without further attention to its program.

But a true classic will allow none of these dismissals of its power. An authentic artifact provokes those who would ignore it, piques the interest of those who wish to examine it disinterestedly, and surprises those who think they have it easily labeled. Michelangelo's *Pietà* is such a stunning work of art; so are Cervantes's *Don Quixote,* Palestrina's *Motets on the Song of Songs,* Shakespeare's *King Lear,* and the Monet *Water Lilies.* There are authoritative people, such as Joan of Arc or Thomas Jefferson; events such as D-Day in Normandy or Brutus's killing of Caesar; architecture like the Taj Mahal or the cathedral at Chartres; even places of natural beauty like the English Lake Country or the Grand Canyon.

Such persons, places, and things startle us by their continuing need to be experienced, understood, absorbed into our lives. They compel us into arguments with those who disagree with us (for example, about the meaning of Adolf Hitler or Franklin Roosevelt); they sometimes frighten us by their power over us (like the nuclear bomb); or they console us through remembered pleasure and anticipated comfort (like a favorite piece of music). They cannot be heedlessly discarded whatever we think, feel, or do.

Catholicism cannot be ignored. Whether we are one of those who detest it because we think it a monolithic tyranny or whether we welcome it as the most varied interpretation of the Christ-event, we cannot but be impressed by its amazing energy. No one who witnessed any of Pope John Paul II's tours of Poland, the United States, or Middle and South America can deny the extraordinary appeal this man's religious Tradition generates. No one who anxiously watched television after he was made the victim of an assassin's bullets can disregard the emotional value for which he stands. The papal role in the contemporary Catholic Church is a powerful witness to the strength of this religious Tradition.

But the present pope of Polish background is only one surprise among many in recent years in the Catholic Church. What once seemed a stolid, squatting giant has suddenly been transformed into a corps de ballet—a troupe of multicultural dancers who do not always seem to follow the same choreographer. Yet the diversity that is more obvious to us now, due to contemporary communications, can be turned like a telescope onto the history of Catholicism as a whole. Looking back through the centuries, we find armadas and rosaries, councils and inquisitions, medieval crusades and papal pleas against the nuclear arms race, revolutionary clerics and military chaplains blessing battleships. Catholicism is all of these and more.

It is *more* because if all these differing realities were simply relayed to us as so many beads on a string, they would not disclose the religious energies that generated all these events, peoples, and things. For Catholicism is not simply a cultural classic of the first order: it is a *religious* standard. Religious events or people claim to speak not about a part of reality, but about the Whole. They prod us into dialogue with that Whole; they disclose the one Voice without which we cannot hear our own words; they proclaim themselves as the gift of that Speaker within all languages.

Religion discloses this ultimate mystery through the experiences of death, estrangement, the absurdities of existence, the trust or wonder invited by the world, the simple sense of "something more" to reality, and the experience of a love which knows no restrictions or conditions. This experiential focus will determine the particular symbols, stories, or themes in which authors embody their religious meaning. But in each case, on the other side of death and sin, a sense of the uncanny or all-consuming love appears as the gifted dimension of life.

That graciousness may threaten our authenticity or confirm our moral generosity—but it stubbornly refuses our attempts to limit its scope or power. It commands at the same time that it frees. Catholicism is that sort of religious classic. Throughout its history, it could rarely be ignored.

CATHOLICISM AS A CLASSIC

Catholicism is nothing without its history. Its religious understanding of Christianity is wedded to its own experience as the presence of the original event of Jesus. Not only is it based upon the one crucial moment of the life, death, and resurrection of Jesus of Nazareth as portrayed in the Jewish and Christian Scriptures, but it believes the history of its own community to be the preservation and *re-presentation* of his transforming presence.

Re-presentation will always mean the making present of a reality that occurred uniquely in the past, disclosing in the present the core or essence of a particular event, recognizing God's universal Presence in time and space. The substance of Catholicism is presented again in each age—but always embodied in new events and people. The authentic religious experience does not simply repeat itself, but appears in newly divined circumstances as the same God in different presentations.

The Christian Scriptures look to specific years (about 6 B.C.E.– 33 C.E.)[1] in an out-of-the-way place (Palestine) in the Roman Empire as decisive for all times and places. The Gospels do not pretend to be historical or biographical in the same way we ordinarily take those words. They are interpretations of the significance of Jesus' life and death for the early disciples of Christ—a bold announcement inaugurated by faith in a living Lord risen from the dead. And because these convictions about Jesus are clothed in religious symbols, stories, and concepts which were vibrant for first-century Jewish or Hellenistic audiences, they remain far from us in place and time. But we have the uncanny sense upon hearing these texts that the events are of earth-shattering importance—to be left aside only at the peril of our whole being. God acted here in history; he can be spurned only out of ignorance or malice.

CATHOLIC HISTORY: TRADITION

Catholicism's perennial vigor is due to its belief in that particular history and its own ability to embody that original event. It is in and through the history of its successive transformations that Catholics find the meaning of their religion. By interpretations of the past and ongoing anticipations of the future, Catholics commit themselves to the re-presentation of their Lord. This living frame of reference the Catholic calls *Tradition*. Removed from the rituals, texts, persons, and institutions which continue to present that Tradition, Catholics feel lost, dislocated, exiled. Catholics are at home in history.

Recent Catholic theology, philosophical as well as biblical, has focused on the ideas about history which join the parts of this book. They are drawn from the heart of Jesus' preaching: the coming of the Kingdom of God into world history. As an academic subject, it has been called *eschatology* (from the Greek *eschata* meaning "last things"), since it dealt with the final events of the cosmic process. More recently, however, eschatology has included the broader meaning of Jesus for the history of our world in all its dimensions.

This religious sense of history has not always been the center of Catholic theology; and the path to change has not always been easy. It will be helpful for us to recall here some of the factors which have shaped this shift in Catholic thinking—particularly since they affect this book.

Shaping Our Destiny

There is first a widely recognized move from classicist to historical consciousness.[2] Since the nineteenth century, we experience ourselves as the shapers of our own lives. Not only do we pass through history, but we are made by that history. The past weighs us down or liberates us; the future pushes us forward or into shock; and the present is a moment of decision, of the possible rejection or acceptance of past and future.

Not only need we not always be the way we were, but it might be critical enough to make a revolution in the present so that we can live a completely different future. The political revolutions of 1776 in the colonies of England in North America and of 1789 in France liberated the personal power of individuals and classes to think that the world could be other than it was. And even if in our revised history the darker side of each revolution has tempered the original enthusiasm, these events still appeal to us, telling us that there can be something *new* if we help it to happen.

Science and Religion

But this shift from a consciousness which thought of the world, peoples, and the social order as necessary and unchanging occurred first among scientists. It was Aristotle, then Newton, who studied the world for its abstract, eternal laws, convinced that they were tapping the unmoving structures of reality. Contemporary scientists, however, have more modest goals. They inquire into what is probable, what can be empirically verified. Instead of searching for *the* essential, changeless universe, we are content to live with the best scientific opinion.

Christian theology is disciplined reflection upon religion in a specific culture. As a result, it is affected by the notions about thinking held by scientists and philosophers of culture. Through the framework of a changeless science, our ancestors could experience the harmony and power of the world as a religious event. But one of the prime goals of modern science was the harnessing of nature for practical purposes. Early scientific experiments such as those concerning gases were tried so that eventually their power might be made to work for us. Technology has always been an intertwined means and end in modern science.

As a result, nature is no longer so alien to us. It may still provoke awe, as for example when Mt. St. Helens erupts; but it does not invite us to the same religious experience of eternity. We are stirred by the thrill of scientific discovery, by the impact of political events, by the marvel of international communication, and by the tragedies and successes of forming human community. We can only recover the religious meaning of nature through the discovery of the transcendent value of the transitory, the historical.

Historical Overload

New cultures are born in our midst and the oldest ones die or are exterminated by industrial "progress." What happens in Nigeria can be seen simultaneously in New York. At the same time that we are exploring other planets and planning journeys to the moon, we wonder somewhat breathlessly whether we can halt the destruction on our own planet. Constantly bombarded by these phenomena, we have begun to feel not only how fleeting our experience is—but also how much the sheer weight of data in our computer banks oppresses us. Our identity escapes us in all the diverse demands of modern culture. If our ancestors could say, "The more things change, the more they stay the same," we can no longer fully believe that.

THE HISTORICAL NATURE OF FAITH

The historical dimension of modern experience has forced the leading minds in Christian communities to employ scientific methods for the study of their own past. Through these critical investigations, we have come to understand and interpret the Christian experience itself. Results have confirmed the deeply temporal nature of our New Testament faith. The Jewish and Christian God is not primarily a deity of nature or of nature's unchangeable laws. Rather God is One who acts in time, who leads people through history. God is that One who encounters men and women exhausted and exhilarated by events and draws them toward love through just such times and seasons. It is this living God of promise and of hope to whom Jews and Christians pray and for whom Jews and Christians search again in this century. If we are to discover our God at all, we must find the Divine Presence in the public stories of peoples, nations, and churches.

Our immediate past has made Christians' involvement in history even more compelling. No sooner did the soothing, ultimately deadly optimism of nineteenth-century Europe collapse in the dreadful trenches of World Wars than Christian theologians began to wonder how theology could live so comfortably with the myths of progress (and so later with the unspeakable horrors of Nazism). The knowledge of change, of the constantly shifting human condition, drew

Christians inward. Turning from the public world of nature, education, and politics, fearful of confronting what they could not control,
they valued the private loyalties, the familial virtues, and the intimate
loves. This can and did lead to insularity, isolationism, narcissism,
and a mere nostalgia for the past. But it was easier to live inside the
Church than to bear the crushing controversies of war, nuclear arms,
the depletion of resources, and the economic exploitation of Third
and Fourth World countries. Christianity was reduced to a "private"
classic, a cultural Church that had forgotten its own past. But its
religious power has stubbornly refused suicide.

Catholicism sometimes retreated into the privatized world of personal piety; but its commitment to its own public institutional face
has more often prohibited neglect of the world. Some may not have
agreed with Pius IX's rejection of contemporary values (*Syllabus of
Errors,* 1864), Leo XIII's support for the just wage (*Rerum
Novarum,* 1891), Paul VI's understanding of marriage and contraception (*Humanae Vitae,* 1968), or his judgments on private
property (*Populorum Progressio,* 1967); but over the last one hundred years, the Catholic community has juxtaposed itself to culture
with intransigent opposition, hearty acceptance, or critical persua-
siveness.

American Catholics have been forced by the cultural acceptance of
abortion, the public defense of the wars in southeast Asia, or the
support of authoritarian regimes in South and Middle America to
reexamine their own complacent histories. Catholics know that their
fears and hopes are shared by commentators in the United States as
well. Assassinations, attempted and achieved; race riots; uncon-
trolled inflation; severe unemployment among minority groups;
foreign policies that ignore human rights—each in its own way has
pushed Catholics into a new search for the God of their history. It is
no pastime of the ivory tower.

UPDATING THE CHURCH

The Second Vatican Council (1962–65), called by Pope John
XXIII, gathering all the Catholic bishops of the world to "bring [the
church] up to date" (*aggiornamento*), encouraged Catholics to rethink and relive the relationship between themselves and their cul-

tures. *The Pastoral Constitution on the Church in the Modern World* (1965) announced that the "joys and the hopes, the griefs and the anxieties of the men of this age, especially those who are poor or in any way afflicted, these too are the joys and hopes, the griefs and anxieties of the followers of Christ. Indeed, nothing genuinely human fails to raise an echo in their hearts."[3]

This deepened sense of our own world, the sharpened tools of historical criticism, the alienation from nature as a vehicle for religion, and the overarching shift in the classicist notion of an unchanging science have challenged Catholics to reenvision their own community. For the Roman Catholic Church is not meant to be merely one more institution standing with equal dispassion alongside the other institutions of our society.

Whatever concrete structures the Church has, or has had, have been intended to serve the proclamation of the New Testament history. The structure has meant to be a reflection of a living, continuous community of ritual, morality, and doctrine. We cannot naively identify this concrete Church through the ages with the full realization of the New Testament Kingdom of God. Rather, the Church knows itself to be the servant of that approaching Kingdom, obedient to its Word and committed to the faithful sowing of that Word in the soil of history. "The Church seeks but a solitary goal: to carry forward the work of Christ Himself under the lead of the befriending Spirit."[4]

Once we realize this, the Catholic Tradition becomes less important institutionally, but more significant religiously. The Church can be experienced as the *community* of those awaiting God in history. Indeed, it is precisely this experience of God's Future communicated to those who wrote the New Testament and to the figures who followed in the history of Catholicism which forms the *community* of eschatological hope.

The Church for Catholics is primarily an event, not a thing. It is the place where all peoples communally may celebrate the Good News of God's actions for all. It is the space where we allow ourselves to be judged by the demands of a genuine religious life. It is—at its best—always reforming itself, "always living and always young," as Pope John XXIII stated in his convocation of the Second Vatican Council. The Church "feels the rhythm of the times and . . . in every century beautifies herself with new splendor, radiates new light, achieves new conquests, while remaining identical in herself, faithful to the divine image impressed on her countenance by her Spouse, Who loves her and protects her, Christ Jesus."[5]

OUR PROJECT

It is this *cumulative* identity of the ecclesial community that this book hopes to outline. Neither of us as the authors of this book pretends to be a historian; both of us believe that it is possible to interpret the life of the Church in such a way that the ongoing story of the community can enlighten the religious meaning of our wider culture.

As a cumulative experience, Catholicism has often been accused of being totalitarian or uncritical of its own history. In the chapters that follow, we hope to provide a largely *typological* interpretation of Catholicism. It is like tracing the major events of particular ages on sheets of transparent plastic and placing them one on top of the other so that at the end we can look through the centuries and see the overlapping identity. For Catholicism's history, like that of an individual, can be secured only at the end; and the end is God's work, not ours.

Throughout our study, we will indicate some of the demands made upon the New Testament experience by events and issues within and without the Church. In doing so, we do not think that the Christian experience was collapsed into contemporary cultural demands. We simply believe that religious values and norms must be embodied to be seen and heard. As a result, it is only as the centuries move on that some subjects even appear on the scene. For example, the whole notion of *eschatology* (Jesus' meaning for human history) is largely a nineteenth- and twentieth-century interpretive tool. That does not mean that people did not think of historical events or of the end times until then, only that it became an explicit subject for investigation at about that time.[6]

Catholic identity is a constantly emergent sense of new experience, and how that newness may be confronted, absorbed, and Christianized. Catholics believe in the development of ever new events happening to all those who share God's promise of redemption. This means that not only in the past, but in the present and the future, the message of Jesus Christ will initiate ever remarkable and radically wondrous possibilities.

The story of these experiences for Catholics—past and present—will be our concern in the remainder of this book. Religious people ask: "What is the meaning of the Whole?" "Is it possible to be responsible for our lives in the face of death?" The community's struggles with and answers to those religious questions unroll as the story of Catholicism. The authentic responses to the questions embodied in the people, places, and things which appear in its history manifest themselves as the servant of the Kingdom, as the shining sacrament of his Presence.

NOTES

1. In deference to our Jewish, Islamic, and Buddhist coreligionists, we will not employ A.D. (in the year of the Lord) and B.C. (before Christ), but B.C.E. (before the Common Era) and C.E. (Common Era).

2. Bernard Lonergan, *Method in Theology* (London: Darton, Longman & Todd, 1972), 2, 29, 301–2, 305–19.

3. "Pastoral Constitution on the Church in the Modern World," *Vatican Council II: The Conciliar and Post-Conciliar Documents,* ed. Austin Flannery (Northport, N.Y.: Costello, 1975), 903–5.

4. Ibid.

5. "Humanae Salutis," December 25, 1961, in *The Documents of Vatican II,* ed. Walter Abbott (New York: Guild Press, 1966), 706.

6. See fig. 1, p. 183 for an image of the fields of theology as they emerged throughout Catholic history.

2

THE EMERGENCE OF
CATHOLIC CHRISTIANITY (I)
Images, Symbols, and Stories:
New Testament Catholicism

> Son of God, have pity on us
> And do with us according to thy kindness,
> And bring us out from the bonds of darkness:
> And open to us the door by which we shall
>   come out to thee.
> Let us also be redeemed with thee:
> For thou are our Redeemer.
> And I heard their voice;
> And my name I sealed upon their heads:
> For they are free men and they are mine.
> Hallelujah.
>
> Anon., *Odes of Solomon* (about 150 c.e.)

Christian identity began in Galilean images and stories opposed by
Jews and Greeks alike. Yet by the early fourth century, it had the
tolerance, then approval, of the Roman Empire. The known world
heard the Gospel proclaimed. What had provoked this amazing
growth? What are the crucial elements in the original experience that
encouraged the event of Jesus of Nazareth to take the shape of a
transracial, transnational community? The transformation of a
Jewish movement into the categories of the Greco-Roman world is in
many ways a most distinctly Catholic development. For "Catholic"
means, first of all, "universal."

During the first three centuries, emerging Catholicism was a complicated affair. What is clear, however, is that imperial citizens, in
accepting those whom they formerly persecuted, introduced their
own cultural experience into Christianity. How Christians rebuilt
that culture into Catholic truth is the subject of this and the two
following chapters.

11

THE PATTERNS OF NEW TESTAMENT EXPRESSION

Let us probe more deeply in the Christian Scriptures themselves to communicate a basic, recurring pattern within the plural expressions that interpret the classic event of Jesus. Since we are concentrating on a Church which defines itself in terms of history, we should meditate a few moments on time itself.

Apprehending Time

Each one of us would like to capture a moment or two in our lives. We never want to repeat the ordinary, boring minutes but rather the cheerful times. All too often, we remember being jailed behind the bars of unpleasant, even tragic, hours. Yet what we discover is that in no way can we isolate atomic moments, embalming them so that they can be viewed in the round, pinned to a piece of cardboard like a butterfly. Time continues to live in us. There are no disconnected moments, only a series of presents which contain within them the shadings of memory, custom, and education, and the hoped-for projections of fears, desires, needs, and plans. The present is thick, pregnant with the children of our past and heavy with the adolescents and adults of our future.

Sometimes we find that the past dominates the present moment, so powerful is our memory. Whole societies can be entranced with their own pasts, as in the United States when the Revolution of 1776 or the Civil War are recalled. The past can also cripple our actions in the present: for example, when we remember the guilty time of our betrayal of a friend. Often the loss of someone we love virtually stops all motion, making our lives vibrate to the tunes of pain and grief.

The future can also drag us unwillingly from the present. Occasionally our daydreams, our projects, our images for economic success or societal utopia seize us with such passion that the immediate context dissolves. Our daydreams become nightmares, visions of nuclear desolation and corpselike certainty. The present recedes into dreadful fascination with a future over which we have little control.

Gabriel Garcia Marquez's *One Hundred Years of Solitude* epitomizes our contemporary attitude toward time. In Macondo, a tropical Brazilian *Erewhon*, time crystallizes into a multifaceted jewel, a phantasmagoric dream, in which we see the ancient colonial decades and Indian magic through an enigmatic prism of present and future. We are never quite certain in what part of the time machine we have arrived. The bizarre effect of this novel reveals our present in which stone-age nomadic cultures abut urban villages like Brazilia. It is as though the whole history of our world were suddenly simultaneous—the past and future concentrated into a distilled present whose liquor we can drink with our morning news.

Biblical Time

But so it has always been with the classic documents of our Tradition. Time comes alive in their present as a memory which shadows us now and as a future which sometimes hectors us when we least expect it. The same was true with the community of Christians when they lived, wrote, and dwelt within the Scriptures. The images which dominate the New Testament—the Kingdom of God, the heavenly Jerusalem, the mustard seed, the pearl of great price, and preeminently the stories of the cross and resurrection—have shaped the Church's memories and anticipations.

Sometimes the presence of the Risen Lord has so overwhelmed believers that they can but sing, pray, and prophesy. Speaking their own words, but caught up in the presence of the Divine, they cry out with God's voice. For the prophets it was a matter of being addressed by God in the very moment of their own speaking.

Remembering their origins, communities celebrated the Lord in ritual, preaching, and sacrament. From this strong sense of God's presence came stories about the past of their God. The narrative traditions were embedded in a dialogue with the Risen Christ. Believing themselves Jews for whom the Messiah and his age had come, they related their founding event to those who would listen. Building upon the covenant given to Abraham, Isaac, and Jacob, they knew their Lord to be the *already* of a Kingdom which had *not yet* come, the first fruits of those who would enter the Holiness of God. It was not an uprooting of the promises made to Israel, but a new grafting to the Ancient Vine of David.

But sometimes the community became so frustrated that their only religious option longed for the future when God would right all the social and personal wrongs of the present. During this messianic age, the humble Prophet crucified like a thief would reveal himself as the Lord of glory.

Catholic history is founded in this New Testament experience of

13

the *prophetic,* the *traditional,* and the *apocalyptic* (named for the Greek word for revelation). One or another of these moments has always shaped Catholic life, like an idea in the mind of a sculptor. Occasionally the conversation among these temporal moments has been a debate or even a battle. But what has marked Catholicism most is its yearning to encompass all partners in a creative dialogue. When the attempts have failed, Catholicism has cheated itself of its own universality.

The Prophetic Word

In our Jewish heritage, prophets are those for whom God is so real and powerful a presence that they cannot *but* use their tongues as though they were burned by a fiery coal. Nothing—honor, fame, career, money, even life itself—means more than being aflame with God's power of proclamation. All the usual distractions of life are only so many temptations away from the consuming presence of Yahweh. Whether it is manifesting God's presence through some symbolic action (as Isaiah did by walking through Jerusalem naked! Isa. 20:2ff) or preaching in fierce rhetoric the judgment of God's coming victory over the evils of sin, the prophet can do no other.

Jewish and Christian prophets proclaim the thrust of God's Kingdom into our world. In a series of startling figures such as Isaiah, Jeremiah, Amos, Hosea, Ezekiel, John the Baptist, and culminating in Jesus of Nazareth, the Christian Tradition is claimed by the Word of God. Each individual, in his own particular voice, manifested the presence of God to and in the people. By threatening military defeat (Jer. 1:14), by an overwhelming welcoming love for the sinful (Hos. 1:2), or by demanding repentance because the axe was laid to the root of social evil (Matt. 3:9–10), every prophet announced that life without God was vanity and illusion. The past and the future seemed relatively unimportant as long as people would hear God's voice in the *now.*

But the qualifier "relatively" is vital since no authentic Christian or Hebrew prophet ignored the past or neglected the future of God's salvation for the people. The prophets' present understanding and awareness of God allow them to absorb the traditions of their people and to await the future as the action of God alone. In fact, the very authenticity of prophets is bound up in their ability to reinterpret the nation's past in continuity with God's present word and to anticipate with singular vision what God has prepared for the world.

It is not so much that prophets "foretell" the future as that they are so committed to the truth of God's present that their words as God's words sow the seeds of the authentic future. Ralph Waldo Emerson once remarked: "An institution is the lengthened shadow of one man." Such individuals found communities by their forthright speech and we call them prophets. These are the creative, originating heroes and heroines of faith.

For Christians, such an individual was Jesus of Nazareth. The *presence* of God manifested in his actions and words was so powerfully transforming that all later Christian prophets speak in *his* name. He alone makes their prophetic comments a possibility. Our expectations of life—security, comfort, happiness—are shattered when we are faced with this eschatological Prophet who faithfully lived the final power of God even in death itself. God's voice disclosed in Jesus constantly drives Christians into a world that needs to be reformed according to Divine love. The witness that believers give is modeled upon, rooted in, and empowered by this Divine Man, this human Face of God.

The Traditional Story

But a heightened sense of the presence of the Lord, an intense awareness of a transforming energy, can also be present in the memories of the community. For the events of Jesus' life, death, and resurrection need to be told and retold as witness to his prophetic ministry. The stories of his existence which we call the Gospels (*Euangelion*—the Good News) were written to preserve this dangerous memory.

The memory about Jesus is dangerous because it constantly calls into question the status quo. These Gospels, reflecting the concerns of various Christian communities, offer comment upon, and application to, the foundation times of the Churches. They proclaimed the continuity of Jesus' presence in the history of the believing communities. They made it clear that it was God who was acting in Jesus; it was God who was calling believers to witness by service to the world and loving generosity to one another.

The language of Jesus' story, therefore, became the paradigm for the common life. His prayerfulness (the "Our Father") was the prayer of the Church; his Tradition of learning (the Hebrew Scriptures—the "Old" Testament) became the interpretive categories of the "New" Covenant made by God. All Christians could have Christ's meaning available to them in prayer, worship, sacrament, the gifts of leadership and office, creedal doctrines, and the narratives of the Good News.

Some of the genius of Catholicism lies in its ability to live what is possible for men and women as they are. Although not everyone is given the strength to be prophetic, all are called to be religious. Catholics can live holy lives by belonging to that community, the Church, which keeps the dangerous memory of its religious origins not just intact, but always renewed through Word and sacrament. The interplay of prophets, office-holders, ordinary pray-ers, visionaries, preachers, and thinkers, in which each accomplishes his or her unique witness to Christ *is* the rich strength of the Catholic Church.

In the New Testament itself, this development can be seen in "emergent Catholicism"—the growth of offices such as deacon, presbyter, and bishop who govern the community, protecting it from errors of content in the memory of Jesus (1 Tim. 3:1–13, Titus 1:5–7). The experience of doctrinal confession discloses a somewhat different world from that of the prophetic witness. There is an emphasis upon the information of our confession; the shock of Jesus' proverbs, parables, and sayings about the End Times has shifted toward specific applications, moral prescriptions, and clear beliefs. It is an honoring of the everyday character of the religious enterprise, the manifestation and proclamation of God's presence in Jesus' daily gift of table fellowship to outcasts and ordinary sinners.

This traditional Catholic manner of remembering the vitality of Jesus is in fact a social and intellectual fence around the original witness. It is a hedge against forgetting. But that does not mean that it is somehow a secondary element in the New Testament experience.

The institutional forms of office, doctrine, gospel, or ritual are the authentic presence of the risen Lord. If they seem less intense, that is due more to our human tendency to screen out their conversation with prophetic charism, the tension of symbols, and the ecstatic prayer of longing for God. In dialogue with these elements in the

New Testament, Catholics believe that each authentically re-presents the Christ event.

The Apocalyptic Vision

In addition, however, to the prophetic and traditional elements in the Christian experience, there is a third factor which looks more directly toward the future. It is the apocalyptic, named for the Greek word meaning revelation (*apocalypsis*). It is a name usually given to the final text in the New Testament, the Book of Revelation.

Apocalyptic literature is provoked in times of utter crisis (for example, during persecution or social destruction). When the world seems ready to implode, apocalypse announces the coming Reign of God, the victory of Divine Presence over evil. It does so through dreams, visions, and symbolic descriptions of warfare between good and the powers of evil.

The apocalyptic thread in the New Testament is a major theme in Jesus' own proclamation of the coming reign of God. The Son of Man will judge the living and the dead at the End Times. The seer of the Book of Revelation expects a new heaven and a new earth after the conflicts and persecutions which will anticipate the end. The apocalyptic visionary always throws a challenge at the community, a rebuttal to any complacency which has crept into its experience. The *real* hope for the Churches is not their mediations of Jesus through texts, offices, or rites; rather the true future is God's in Christ. The vision constantly corrects all other expressions of Christian meaning, for everything is risked on the future.

We tend to think of individuals who constantly expect the reversal of common hopes and dreams as too pessimistic, too other-worldly. But events themselves can provoke this shift in religious awareness. There are times in history—the period 200 B.C.E. to 100 C.E., during which the stories of the New Testament took place, is one of these—when prophets are rare, traditions in question, and the present is riddled with calamities. Then only God's future seems to have any significance. One's hope—that God will remain faithful to the world—requires trust in a future that God alone controls and transforms all history.

Early Christians, during the decades of ecclesial formation and particularly with the destruction of Jerusalem (70 C.E.), sensed such an apocalyptic moment. Only the Father of the Lord Jesus could save them from the Roman armies. It is not surprising that apocalyptic Christianity has recently revived in a world in which ordinary believers feel that their very daily lives have been snatched from their control. Wars and the rumors of war thrust Christians into a future known only to God.

No matter what we may think of the contemporary suffering of humanity and certain assessments that all mediations, religious and otherwise, have fallen short or even failed, we know that the apocalyptic response is an authentically religious one. We may find visionaries strange and seers all too fallible—but we know that they form one of the partners in the conversation of Catholicism. Without the criticism offered by those who can only see the *not yet* of God's presence, Christianity too easily forgets the dangerous character of its own past and lists becalmed in the ship of a complacent present.

Jesus of Nazareth provoked all three responses: the prophetic, the traditional, and the apocalyptic. In hymns, stories, sayings, letters, and theological meditations, the presence of this Jesus comes forward to encounter the believer. Now one temporal dimension, now another, will dominate. But each helped form the community of believers who followed the Nazarene. The Presence of God to and in the man Jesus—a Presence which for the Catholic *is* his Identity—proclaims him as Lord of all time: past, present, and future. His history is the model of individual and social stories; the history of his Presence founds the community of that Presence.

Saintly Heroes

We shall look at three early figures in Catholicism who tell us about its developments in the New Testament: Peter, Paul, and Stephen the Martyr. The character of later Christianity is clearly informed by these remarkable individuals.

Peter, Leader of the Twelve

We actually know very little about the life of Peter. Aside from his legendary background as a fisherman (Mark 1:16–18), we know only that invariably he is located first in the lists of the disciples (Matt. 10:2), and that he regularly took the lead, becoming the mouthpiece for the Twelve, as when he says that they could not leave

Jesus (John 6:66–69). At Caesarea Philippi, his confession of Jesus' Messiahship earned him the name Peter and a role of authority in the coming Kingdom (the keys to the palace—Matt. 16:13–20).

Peter was, however, a thoroughly "ordinary" individual, whose enthusiasm (John 18:10) and subsequent denial of Christ during his passion and death (Matt. 26:33f) signify his utterly human abilities. According to the Gospel of Luke (Luke 24:34), he was granted a special appearance of the risen Christ; and this conscious awareness made him the first preacher on Pentecost (Acts 2:14–41), a miracle worker in the name of Jesus (Acts 3:1–10), and a speaker before the Sanhedrin (Acts 4:1–21).

Early traditions placed Peter's death in Rome during the persecution after Nero's burning of the city (65 C.E.). It is as saint and martyr, and as first missionary apostle of Rome, that Catholic Christians honor Peter as the first pope. This great man, so fallible, so faithful to the Lord, so relatively obscure, still seems to capture the imagination of Christians. For Peter is honored as that rarest of religious phenomena: a holy leader whose humane moderation, whose "common touch," created a powerful Tradition. It is to just such a figure that Pope John XXIII (1958–63) appealed when he established a Secretariat for Promoting Christian Unity (1960) and had the Catholic Church represented at the World Council of Churches (1961). When Pope John Paul II tapped his foot during a rally with youth in Yankee Stadium in New York City (1980), Peter's missionary and prophetic humanity was again announced.

Paul, Apostle to the Gentiles

Peter's great counterpart and occasional antagonist (Gal. 2:6–9) is Paul, or Saul of the tribe of Benjamin. Paul remains to historical eyes the most forceful personality in early ecclesial life. If Peter's great claim is to be the founder of an ecclesiastical Tradition, Paul's untiring gift of his person in missionary journeys, in writing letters (or epistles), and in producing a theology that justified his turning to Gentiles to fill the ranks of Christians marks him as the co-Apostle of the founded Church.

But Paul was not always an Apostle, that is, one sent to preach the Good News and to found Christian communities. He had been a persecutor of the Christian Jews; and only after an intense experience of conversion (Acts 9:1–19, 22:5–16, 26:12–18), in which he saw the Risen Lord in his persecuted followers, did he choose to devote his life to Christianity. He was baptized and retired to Arabia for solitude and prayer. Three years later he returned to Damascus and Jerusalem.

The Christian community at Antioch sent him on the first of his missionary journeys. Throughout his life, he traveled ceaselessly and tirelessly preached the Gospel throughout the Mediterranean world. He seems to have died in Rome during the persecution of Nero (about 65 C.E.) in which Peter himself was killed.

In the letters to various Churches Paul founded or visited, we have the first great Christian theology. For he labored at that crucial problem of the early communities, the relationship between the Christ and Jewish religious life under the Law. In his confrontation with Peter (described schematically as the First Council of Jerusalem in Acts of the Apostles 15), Paul won Gentile converts the right to neglect certain prescriptions of Jewish ceremonial and religious law. For example, circumcision was no longer required of the baptized Christian male.

Yet Paul says later (Rom. 9:1–5) that he would even be willing to be separated from Christ if his own brothers, the Israelites, could be reconciled. "Theirs was the adoption, the glory, the covenants, the lawgiving, the worship, and the promises; theirs were the patriarchs, and from them came the Messiah" (Rom. 9:4–5, NAB).

For Paul, Christian Gospel had liberated us from the Law by a sheer gift of God's grace. In Christ, the world's purpose finds its goal (Phil. 2:6; Col. 1:15–17). He is the Lord of a new humanity which replaces the old Adam of our failures. One need no longer be under the power of sin, since a new energy, an enabling gift, has entered our world in Christ's death and resurrection. Through baptism we receive and confirm this gift (Rom. 6:3–6) and accept God's own Spirit whose charity binds the common herd into a community of Churches. The signal action of this community is the great Thanksgiving, the Eucharist (1 Cor. 10:16–21; 11:20–34), in which the one sacrifice of Jesus is remembered and re-presented. But all this is to see but darkly; one day we shall see our God face to face (1 Corinthians 13).

Paul's ability to view the past event of Jesus' death as present and to proclaim it, his conviction that this risen Presence would soon return, and his knowledge of the human heart in all its stark confusion has allowed him to confront each age of Christians. The literary and religious power of his letters has founded prophets, theologies, and Churches. Without his prophetic vision, Christians could have confined themselves to the original Semitic experience and ignored the ethical responsibility to the *not yet* character of the future coming of the Lord.

Stephen, the Martyr

At Paul's origins stands Stephen's murder. For while still a persecutor of Christians, he is said to have tended the garments of those who stoned Stephen. Stephen was probably a Hellenistic Jew who was chosen as one of Seven to serve tables in the Jerusalem community (Acts 6:5). He cared for the needy, preached the Gospel, and performed miracles, earning the hostility of the local non-Hellenistic population. In the beautiful homiletic set piece recorded in Acts 7:2–53, Stephen recalls all of Israel's history as leading to *the* Prophet announced by Moses, one Jesus who was killed on a cross. For his preaching efforts, he was made the first Christian martyr.

Before he died, however, he saw the glory of God returning (Acts 7:54–56) and Jesus at God's right hand. As he died, he forgave his enemies as did his Lord before him. It was this intensity of vision that forced him from the present into God's future for him.

Peter, Paul, and Stephen, woven together by God in coincidence, conflict, tragedy, and glory through their allegiance to Jesus, demonstrate the contrasting diversities of the founding preachers of Catholicism. For while Paul discloses the burning genius of the fiery preacher and Stephen the socially committed, culturally complicated visionary, Peter displays our steady common humanity. Tradition, prophecy, and apocalypse disclose the intertwining truths of Catholic history. From Jesus, the source, spring Catholic claims to the universe of time and space; in Peter, Paul, and Stephen and a constant current of others flows the abiding history of Catholicism, diversity in unity.

FURTHER RELATED MATERIAL

For a helpful introduction, employing some of the literary-critical methods of interpretation present in this book, see Norman Perrin, *The New Testament: An Introduction* (New York: Harcourt Brace Jovanovich, 1974) and for historical-critical background, see Robert M. Grant, *A Historical Introduction to the New Testament* (London: William Collins Sons, 1963). For various understandings of Jesus in the New Testament, see Gunther Bornkamm, *Jesus of Nazareth* (New York: Harper & Brothers, 1960); Reginald Fuller, *The Foundations of New Testament Christology* (New York: Charles Scribner's Sons, 1965); Edward Schillebeeckx, *Jesus: An Experiment in Christology,* trans. Hubert Hoskins (London: William Collins & Co., 1979) and *Christ: The Experience of Jesus as Lord,* trans. John Bowden (New York: Seabury Press, 1980); and Bruce Vawter, *This Man Jesus: An Essay Toward a New Testament Christology* (Garden City, N.Y.: Doubleday & Co., 1973). Sections of Hans Küng's *On Becoming a Christian,* trans. Edward Quinn (New York: Doubleday & Co., 1976), 145–165 are also useful.

3

THE EMERGENCE OF CATHOLIC CHRISTIANITY (II)
The Search for Unity

My Redeemer, redeem me for I am yours;
  from you I came forth.
You are my mind; bring me forth!
You are my treasure-house; open for me!
You are my fullness; take me to you!
You are my repose; give me the perfection
  that cannot be grasped.
  Anon., "Gnostic Prayer of the Apostle Paul" (about 200 c.e.)

It required a lengthy time, at least two hundred years, before Christians began to define themselves according to the writings they had received from their founders. Only between the late second and fourth centuries did a canon, or rule of approved books, come into general use. Early Christian controversies over what exactly constituted an authentic interpretation of the Christ-event were manifold. To understand the development of Catholicism, it is central to our story to have some knowledge of these early movements and the attempts by theologians, churchmen and women, prophets, and martyrs to state *who* the Church was. The directing impulse was not so much to exclude people or interpretations, but rather to care religiously for the truth of the originating event.

We have looked at the primarily Hellenistic forms of Christian experience which emerged in the New Testament literature. But there were at least two other major interpretations which vied with the present canon of Scriptures: specific Semitic forms, generally called Jewish-Christianity, and a largely Greco-Roman religious expression, Gnosticism.

Broadly speaking, we might say that Hebraic or Semitic Christianity did not wish to stress the distance of Christians from Jews which resulted from the Roman destruction of Jerusalem (66–70

23

C.E.) and the expulsion of the adherents of Jesus from the synagogues (70–100 C.E.). Gnostic thought pushed the message of Christ in the direction of cultural identity with the seemingly larger Hellenistic world outside Palestine. Between these two "movements," Christians defined a Tradition offering both criticism of culture and refinement of religious identity. It is this integrated Tradition that is the ongoing history of Catholicism.

JEWISH-CHRISTIANITY

For many years orthodox Jews and believers in Jesus as Lord shared the same general Semitic institutions and literature. Jewish society at the time of Christ was flexibly complex, consisting not only of Pharisees (an austere party which believed in resurrection of the dead and retribution in the next world), Sadducees (strict interpreters of the Mosaic Law), and Essenes (an ascetic, highly organized community in the desert), but also Zealots (anti-Roman agitators), collaborators like the tax collectors, and various Jews of the Diaspora in cosmopolitan cities like Alexandria.

From all these strands, Jean Daniélou and other scholars have isolated Semitic interpretations of Jesus. Jewish-Christianity began as a reforming interpretation of Judaism, but eventually broke its boundaries. Using experiences from the Hebrew Scriptures and apocalyptic literature, it developed a set of organizing images, a narrative to deal with the origins of evil in the universe and the unique event of Jesus. Jesus, the glorious angel of Yahweh, head of the archangels, the very Name of God and preexistent Covenant, redeemed us from the demons of the world by descending into Sheol to preach deliverance to the dead, then ascended into the heavens of God. His cross extended his arms in cosmic hope to all directions of the compass. Raised into the air, Jesus released his Spirit upon all who gazed upon him, recognizing him as Lord.

Using these physical, cosmic pictures, Jewish-Christians stressed adherence to the original Mosaic revelation in the Law, distrusted Paul's grafting of the Gentiles onto Jewish stock and preferred to think of Christ as the Prophet inspired by the Spirit of God. Essentially a conservative Christianity, anxious not to lose its Semitic roots, it branched out toward the East, establishing flourishing centers especially around Edessa and Antioch.

Although there flowered in the third and fourth centuries authentic Semitic theologies in Aphraat (about 260–345) and Ephrem the Syrian (306–73), later stress on the preservation of the Hebraic stories drew these strains into controversy with more Hellenistic Christian language. These believers were ethically austere, often apocalyptic in preaching and uncompromising in their devotion to the Galilean Jesus who had saved them. One of the most ancient forms of our Eucharistic prayer, The Liturgy of Addai and Mari, derives from this Tradition. The earliest important version of the Gospels, the *Diatessaron* (150–60 C.E.), compiled by Tatian (about 160), was a life of Jesus sewn together from all four Gospels. These Christians and their less orthodox relatives continued to inspire converts well into the fourth century.

GNOSIS: PASSIONATE WISDOM

Other groups also assimilated Jesus into their religious and cultural traditions. A deeply Hellenistic movement is called Gnosticism, after the Greek word (*gnosis*) for knowledge. Its origins are controverted and obscure, some authorities maintaining that it appeared prior to Christianity, others contending that it was its product or that of apocalyptic Judaism, still others assuring us that it can be found in early dualisms of the gods of light and darkness. With the discovery of a library of Gnostic texts in Egypt (Nag-Hammadi), we have better information.

A movement of religious combinations, Gnosticism contained elements of Hellenistic Judaism, Babylonian astrology, magic and fatalism, the emerging mystery cults to the gods and goddesses of vegetation, as well as the story and message of Jesus. Gnostics generally thought of Jesus as one who brought them a saving knowledge of God, the true meaning of the world. He came from the purely spiritual fullness of God's power through layers of cosmic confusion to free us from our imprisoned flesh.

The *Hymn of the Pearl,* heavily influenced by Gnosticism, tells the story of a king's son who was sent to Egypt to find the pearl of great price. He arrived only to find the Great Serpent coiled about it in the sea. Having stopped at a local inn, he changed clothes, so that he would not appear strangely dressed. When offered wine he became intoxicated and fell asleep. Awakened by a letter from his royal parents, he returned to his duty. He conquered the serpent, obtained the pearl, and regained his homeland, discarding the garments he received for clothing of transcendent beauty.

This basic story of mission, confusion, recovery, and homecoming became an elaborate system of thought under certain thinkers, such as Valentinus (about 136–165 C.E.). The king's son was sent on an errand of mercy and salvation, only to fall into human existence, a drowsy, drunken state. Lost in forgetfulness he was reminded of his call only by knowledge from another world. As a saved savior he must shed the psychic and physical envelopes which have weighed him down in his journey toward authentic existence.

The descriptive poetry and passionate prayers still have power to alert the inner eyes of consciousness. With the addition of some ritual elements and flexible ethical behavior, Gnosticism maintained a deep hold on Christians. It remains a contemporary possibility where the adage, "Knowledge gives virtue," or even better, "Self-knowledge grants salvation," is still believed.

These conflicting interpretations, together with those we now think of as orthodox, created resounding questions for the growing Christian communities. If this world is an evil one, how is it possible that a good God made it? What is the Christian's relationship to the culture of this age, until Christ returns? If sin is merely ignorance, a mistake or fate, then how do we live as saved? How is Christ uniquely different, if the world keeps going on as before? If God is completely nameless, then how do we know what the relationship of Jesus is to God?

The various answers to these questions created two kinds of crises which were intertwined. What sort of difference did Jesus make and who was he that he made that difference? And how does the community decide which are appropriate and adequate expressions of that difference? The answers to both these questions (the first, a question of *identity;* the second, the authority of certain *forms*) produced Catholicism.

EARLY CATHOLIC RESPONSES

For models of early Christian responses to the complicated questions of faith, we will focus upon some sharply etched representative documents and figures. There were beautiful Jewish-Christian texts like the *Didache* (about 60–117 C.E.), which described a Way of Light and a Way of Death, providing a Church order for its community (rules on fasting, prayer, baptism, the Eucharist, and how to deal with prophets, bishops, and deacons). Then there was Marcion (about 160) whose speculations about the God of Love present in Jesus forced him to reject the Hebrew Scriptures and their inferior Creator God. Marcion found that the Pauline letters supported his understanding of Christ's ransom from the fickle God's hold upon us; he also rejected all the Gospels but Luke's. He was successful enough that it became necessary to say which *were* the authentic texts upon which the community depended and in which it found its identity.

A Prophet

Justin Martyr (about 100–165 C.E.) began searching for God, as he related in his *Apology* (about 155), through pagan philosophies. The Stoics failed to tell him who God was; the Peripatetics said they would tell him, if he offered them money; the Pythagoreans wanted him to learn music, astronomy, and geometry first. Then Justin discovered the prophets and met the friends of Christ—and thus became a "true philosopher." Because Christians showed no fear in the face of violent death, Justin thought their religious posture must be worth investigation.

Taking the philosophical principle of the *Logos* (a rational and physical structure of cosmic order), Justin identified the fullness of this Reason with Christ.[1] The seed of the Logos was scattered in all human beings, making truthful pagans into Christians before their time. But Christ under his own rational power became the suffering servant, thus fulfilling the prophecies made about him. Justin had a principle (*Logos*) of continuity and discontinuity which he could apply to the Christian event. Moreover, the language of the Johannine Gospel about the Logos becoming flesh confirmed Justin's interpretations. Everyone shared rational words; only Christ Jesus himself was the complete word of the Godhead.

A Traditionist

Irenaeus of Lyons (about 130–200) attacked Gnosticism directly. He did so by stressing not a speculative system, but what could be called common sense. What was plainly visible, understandable, and audible was the rule of authentic interpretation. Christ was the recapitulation of all religious history, the coming to a head of God's utter love for the world.

Against Marcion, Irenaeus claimed only one God, creator and redeemer; against the Gnostics, he maintained both the goodness of the world and the origin of evil in human beings. Only an authentic Tradition and a creedal formula would protect the community from blatantly stupid formulations. So he appealed to his discipleship under Polycarp (about 69–155), the Bishop of Smyrna, who in turn was a pupil of John and "the rest of those who had seen the Lord." Heretics were the inventors of the new; what came from the original event through morally upright and community-approved leaders was authentic.

A Visionary

Besides Justin the prophet and Irenaeus the traditionist, there was also a visionary, whose writing, *The Shepherd of Hermas* (about 140–55), was ranked for many years with the Gospels and Letters of Paul. He received the vision of an elderly woman, the Church, who proclaimed that unless those who had fallen aside in recent prosperous times repented, they would be excluded from the coming Kingdom.

In the *Shepherd's* vision, the contemporary conscience of the Church unfolded. Neither entirely good nor evil, it needed a second plank of safety for the shipwrecked, a saving repentance from God after baptism. The author's perspective was that of an ordinary Christian, a freed slave who married, became a merchant, and lost his savings when his children denounced him during the recent persecution. Hoping against hope, he encouraged all God's children to return—no matter what their betrayals of the Master. But the time was short. God's future was breaking in.

THE TWO WAYS:
INTRINSIC AND EXTRINSIC RULES OF FAITH

It was precisely during the period of these three theologians—Irenaeus, Justin, and Hermas—that the church first identified its boundaries. Were the Gnostics really Christians? Are we so universal, so catholic, as to accept all understandings of the Christ-event? Can we reject the Hebrew Scriptures? On what grounds do we find our continuing identity in them? The answers given to these questions followed the two basic threads offered by Justin, Irenaeus, and Hermas: the authority of Apostolic Tradition and the ability of the Scriptures to explain both Christ *and* contemporary culture.

The canon, or rule of Scriptures, developed only slowly as an external norm for deciding what was an authentic Christian text and what was not. Justin Martyr was the first to appeal to written Christian texts, although others had quoted sayings and stories about Jesus. The ultimate authority of the religious book was that it reflected God's intentions for our world in Christ (2 Pet. 1:19–21). But it was only with the various collections of texts and their consequent community-founding authority that arguments could be made from them.

Eusebius (about 260–340), the historian and Bishop of Caesarea, provided a scriptural list approved by the Eastern Churches with which he was familiar. The Emperor Constantine (+337) used this catalog to offer fifty copies of the Bible to the Churches of Constantinople. This combination of ecclesial identity and political approval seems to have settled the matter, though it was Athanasius (about 296–373), the Bishop of Alexandria, and fighter for orthodoxy, who provided the final accurate listing in 367.

What seems like an arbitrary decision to limit the books which Christians could read during prayer and upon which they might reflect for moral and religious identity was not really capricious. Unified missionary efforts, internal instruction of those to be baptized, confusing interpretations of various factions, and finally persecution from secular authorities until the early fourth century forced upon the developing communities the need to determine their boundaries.

Although a variety of interpretations of Jesus was possible, not all could be sustained if the Tradition was to exist as a true unity. These approved texts became the foundational documents of the new Church. Their authority derived from a close connection with those who knew the Lord.

But there was always a requirement to see the external principle of authority as an internal event as well. The event of Jesus and the texts to which Justin appealed interpreted the culture in which he lived. There was an intrinsic principle through which God encountered the world, participated in it, and transformed it. The Christ-event was the true philosophy, the authentic Word to the world, not only because its texts came from an authentic past, but also because they could be found in the meaningful present.

Authority and measured cultural embodiment were the prophetic responses to the crises of early Christian identity. These two ways of governing and controlling the nest of images surrounding Jesus continue to be the main moments of Catholic religious life.

ORIGEN, FIRST SYSTEMATIC THEOLOGIAN

The most important attempt to achieve a coherent theological unity for Christianity in the early years was offered by Origen (about 185–254) in Alexandria. As the head of a school for catechumens (Christians preparing for baptism) and its primary instructor at an early age, he found it necessary to organize Christian theology in all areas. Consequently, his work fell into many categories. He determined accurate scriptural texts through the Hexapla or six-columned book which provided four translations of the Hebrew Scriptures. He wrote homilies and commentaries on all the Scriptures and composed the first treatise in systematic theology.

In *On First Principles* (220–30), Origen provided his synoptic vision of the universe with Christ as its center. These catechetical instructions, heavily influenced by his training in middle Platonic philosophy, investigated all reasonable opinions and provided consistent, clear arguments about the whole of Christian belief. Deeply conscious of the intellectual and moral weight Christ could have for the educated world, Origen mastered the range of scriptural data, organized available images and opinions, weighed conflicting interpretations, and constructed viable positions which he constantly revised.

The success of Origen's work can perhaps be seen by the fact that in the Eastern Churches, about every one hundred years after his death, there was a condemnation of one or another of his opinions. Origen preached, wrote, and taught at a time when Christian identity was still fluid. But he, above all, granted that his understanding of Christ was limited and that it could be corrected by further logic and Christian experience. In the end he believed that it was not knowledge but the power of God's grace enabling the will that saved us. "Mere clarity in stating the truth," he said, "will not suffice to move the human heart; words must be beautiful by grace."[2]

The prophets of early Christianity were those who spoke for unity: a unified interpretation of the past and a cogent understanding of the contemporary. They called for adherence to a Tradition which had emerged from Jesus and for a unity of intellectual, religious, and, ultimately, political culture which would protect and further the Christ-event.

THE NONBELIEVER'S REFUSAL: PLOTINUS

Their success may be seen in the response of the philosopher Plotinus (205–70 C.E.) who rejected Gnostic myths as well as the stories of Christian redemption. It was all so much confusing legend. Thought could lead to the Divine One; contemplation of Unity would bring personal and cosmic integration. Knowledge was not a matter of some blunt instrument handed to the spirit to travel back to Unity; rather it carefully criticized the options offered in our world, accepting or rejecting as occasion warranted.

But Plotinus's analyses, subtle, mystical, occasionally sublime, fell afoul of the problem of evil. For him evil in our world was a mere defect, a crack in the mirror of images we see, nothing for which we are particularly responsible, nothing which we can effectively overcome—except by philosophy. Samuel Taylor Coleridge reminded us well over a hundred years ago that philosophy would save only the few. Thought, critical and serious, is too difficult for the many; and the "most appropriate language of Religion" is imagination, the "poetic connection." What is needed is too awesomely important to be "trusted to the Stumblings and alternate Pro- and Re-gression of the growing Intellect of Man."[3]

Irenaeus, Justin, Hermas; the prophets, traditionists, and apocalyptic visionaries of Catholicism trusted to the unifying, transforming power of the Cross of Christ. Only that would make the world whole; only that would make the world one.

NOTES

1. *The Second Apology,* 2.10, in *Writings of St. Justin Martyr,* trans. Thomas B. Falls (New York: Christian Heritage, 1948), 129.

2. *Against Celsus,* chap. 6.2, as translated somewhat poetically in Jean Daniélou, *Origène* (Paris: Table Ronde, 1948), 112.

3. *The Philosophical Lectures of Samuel Taylor Coleridge,* ed. Kathleen Coburn (London: Pilot Press, 1949), 396.

FURTHER RELATED MATERIAL

For useful introductions to Semitic Christian thought forms, see the classic Jean Daniélou, *Theology of Jewish Christianity,* trans. John A. Baker (London: Darton, Longman & Todd, 1964) and his more general survey *Gospel Message and Hellenistic Culture,* trans. John A. Baker (Philadelphia: Westminster Press, 1973). For Gnosticism, see Robert Grant, *Gnosticism and Early Christianity* (New York: Columbia University Press, 1959) and Hans Jonas, *Gnostic Religion* (Boston: Beacon Press, 1963). For the entire period, see the analyses of Johannes Quasten, *Patrology,* 3 vols. (Utrecht-Antwerp: Spectrum, 1966—), Jaroslav Pelikan, *The Emergence of the Catholic Tradition* (Chicago: University of Chicago Press, 1972), and Robert M. Grant, *Early Christianity and Society* (New York: Harper & Row, 1977).

4

THE EMERGENCE OF
CATHOLIC CHRISTIANITY (III)
A Stable Social Reality

> The banners of the king advance,
> The mystery of the cross shines forth,
> On which the founder of our flesh
> Was suspended as from a gallows.
>
> O blessed tree whose limbs
> Supported the price of the planets!
> O balance prepared to price the corpse,
> You snatched the spoils from Sheol!
>
> Venantius Fortunatus (about 530–609),
> "Vexilla Regis Prodeunt."

The poet Venantius made his fortunate entry into what is now France in the late sixth century. Having completed a pilgrimage across the Alps to the shrine of Martin of Tours (+397, a bishop who had been proclaimed holy not by martyrdom but through a life of good deeds), he settled near Poitiers. He could not return to his own lands near Venice because the barbarian Lombards had invaded. Entering the service of Radegunde (518–87), the former wife of the Merovingian king Clothaire I (497–561), now a deaconess and foundress of a monastery of nuns, Venantius was first steward, then priest/chaplain of the community. Eventually he was elected bishop of Poitiers.

In 569, Radegunde received for her convent a portion of the Cross of Christ, found by Helen (about 255–330, the mother of the Emperor Constantine [+337]). Venantius composed a hymn ("The Banners of the King Advance") which has been part of Catholic worship ever since. Despite the barbarian incursions and the collapse of the remnants of imperial civilization, Venantius envisioned the once rejected Criminal's cross conquering the entire earth.

In the late sixth century, after the fall of the Roman Empire (476), it must have been difficult to believe that Jesus was Lord of the earth.

But in Venantius's own story there are the elements which, by the ninth century, would stabilize Western society into the new order which we now call Christendom. It was constructed from the hymns of poets like Venantius, the generosity of barbarian women like Radegunde, Roman familial government like Martin's, and the arbitrary military loyalties, oppositions, and religious sensibilities of various emperors, kings, and queens. In this cultural melting pot a new material was forged to support the religious quests of Catholic Christianity.

The Edict of Toleration (313 C.E.) agreed upon by the Eastern and Western emperors at Milan created a new situation for Christians. No longer would they be persecuted by governmental authorities. How would they take responsibility for their faith without a constantly hostile environment?

In this chapter we will describe some of the fundamental elements of Western Christianity: the earliest commentators on Scripture and society, known as the "Fathers" of the Church; the meetings, called synods and councils, held to sort out complicated cultural and religious questions; the development of unified symbols of worship; and the volcanic islands of monastic stability.

Each had to reflect upon serious issues.

Who belongs to this Christian movement?

What are the criteria for telling the difference between Gnostic, Jew, pagan, and Christian?

Is it a matter of the right doctrine (ortho-doxy) or of correct behavior (ortho-praxy)?

What are the rules for establishing unity within the community's diversity?

Will the rules developed in the second and third centuries (apostolic Tradition and theological principles of unity) be sufficient now that Christianity is an approved religion?

Venantius Fortunatus, like all the "antennae of our race" (Ezra Pound), anticipated that a successful, or at least an adequate, embodiment would be discovered.

THE FATHERS OF THE CHURCH: AUGUSTINE

In the earliest days of the Churches, it was clear who belonged. It was always those who were willing to lay down their lives (John

15:13–14) in martyrdom. So we have the official court proceedings against Justin (+165) and eyewitness accounts of Polycarp (+156) or Felicity and Perpetua, Africans condemned at Carthage (+203).

Ignatius of Antioch (+107), the Syrian bishop of Antioch, early successor to Peter, requested on his journey to Rome that his martyrdom not be stopped. He wished to be "ground by the teeth of wild beasts, that I may end as the pure bread of Christ."[1] Ignatius combined a severe Christocentric mysticism with uncompromising concentration of Church order as a way of re-presenting that authentic Christ. For this martyr that person was *catholicos,* that is, universal, catholic, who surrounded the bishop standing in the place of the Heavenly Father. The bishop was the responsible teacher, the unifier in truth, and the presider at worship.

It is this integration of religious interiority and external order that characterized the begetter of Western Catholicism, Augustine of Hippo (354–430). Without his concern for personal salvation from sin, his attempt to understand God's grace in individual life and universal history, his theology of Church and sacrament, his scriptural sermons and commentaries, there would have been no medieval Christendom and most assuredly no Reformation in the sixteenth century. With Augustine, we have a full exposition of the crucial relationship between institutional holiness and prophetic Church.

Unlike some of the more remote religious ancestors of our tradition, Augustine told his own story. His autobiographical classic, *The Confessions,* inaugurated an entire genre of literature: the introspective memoir which made unified sense of a lifetime's cultural and psychic change.

As a youth, Augustine tried whatever experience was available to an energetic North African male. Although he received a Christian familial upbringing, he drifted from it during his education in rhetoric at Carthage. There he took a mistress to whom he was faithful for fifteen years and by whom he fathered a child. He prayed: "Grant me chastity and continence, but not yet!"[2] He shifted his intellectual and personal interests successively toward Ciceronian philosophy, Manichaeism (a dualist Gnosticism), agnosticism, then Neoplatonism. He left northern Africa, traveled to Rome to open a school of rhetoric, departed there in anger, and located in Milan where he came under the influence of Ambrose, its bishop (about 339–97), who was known for his intelligence, holiness, and especially for his eloquent preaching. In all this he was unsatisfied. "Our hearts are restless till they find rest in Thee."[3]

His turn to God in Christ was swift and stunning. Though intellectually convinced of the religious value of Christian teaching, he was offended by its poor Latin; moreover he could not see the Christ beyond his moral blinders. In emotional and intellectual upheaval, Augustine sat in the garden of the house weeping. Overhearing children playing a game and calling to each other "Take and read; take and read," he opened the New Testament and his eyes fell upon this passage: "Let us behave with decency as befits the day: no revelling or drunkenness, no debauchery or vice, no quarrels or jealousies! Let Christ Jesus himself be the armor that you wear; give no more thought to satisfying the bodily appetites" (Rom. 13:13–14, NEB).

From that moment until his death, Augustine astonished the world: as bishop of Hippo he showed unusual skill and pastoral concern; as the first great synthetic Western theologian, he founded almost all areas of Western Christian philosophy and theology. This required not only an understanding of his own dreaded call to holiness, but also a vision of universal history under God's gracious assistance.

In the end, he says, one can dwell in only one of two cities: that of God, the way of charity and love of the Other for the Other's sake; or the city of human endeavor, a way of selfishness and self-seeking importance. Civil government, personal gain, and individual needs are valuable only insofar as they embody the City of God; otherwise they are merely sin. There can be no neutral acts in our lives.

Augustine spoke for the Pauline priority of God's love, his gracious assistance in human life. Whether it was in the controversy with the Donatists (a North African separatist group who argued that Christians who had lapsed during the persecutions should not be readmitted to communion) or with Pelagius and his followers (who stressed human ability to acquire virtue), Augustine argued for God's primary claim upon all reality. We are free because God has freed us; without Divine love, we would drift into sin. The sacramental life of the Church occurs because God acts in worship, not because we win Divine favor through our prayer.

In effect, both Donatists and Pelagians said that the public life of the Christian community (whether baptism or office) was human work, the achievement of men and women. If Christians were not inwardly holy, then the external actions of the community were void, without religious meaning. Augustine argued that the Church and its primary realizations, the sacraments, were the medium of God's activity. "The divine excellence abides in the sacrament, whether to the salvation of those who use it right, or to the destruction of those who use it wrong."[4]

The very holiness of God was mysteriously mediated through the historical, sacramental life of the Catholic community. "The Eucharist is our daily bread; but let us receive it in such a way, that we may be refreshed not in our bodies only, but in our souls. For the power which is apprehended there is unity, that gathered together into His body, and made His members, we may be what we receive. Then will it be indeed our daily bread."[5]

This mixture of interior conversion and external loyalty did not always cohere well in Augustine's understanding of Christianity. But it provided the vocabulary and the grammar of an entire age. He taught Western Christians to take the journey within—the search for God's Kingdom of truth inside themselves. From this, he constructed a theology which was willing even to probe the very mysterious Triune divinity itself.

Every great Christian renaissance—the twelfth–thirteenth centuries, the Reformation, even the contemporary existentialist revivals—has returned to Augustine as a prophetic model of how to reflect honestly and deliberately upon Christian life.

COUNCILS AND SYNODS: JUDGMENTS OF TRUTH

The meeting of Christian experience with the Greek and Roman world gave rise to a number of new and previously unexplored possibilities. Hellenistic Christians, confronted by their cultural heritage in philosophy, art, and science, questioned the Scriptures through logic, metaphysics, aesthetics, and physics.

We have noted how difficult it was for Augustine to accept the New Testament simply because of its poor Latin translations. He felt required to seek the interior message that was embodied in the inelegant style. Others besides Augustine were compelled to ask in what way the eternal, unchangeable, all-powerful Father could become flesh, limited, changing, and death-ridden. How was Jesus both divine and human simultaneously? These questions preoccupied Christians throughout the first six to eight centuries.

How did one reconcile the statements by Jesus which said: "I and the Father are one" (John 10:30, RSV), and the "Father is greater than I" (John 14:28 RSV)? Articulated judgments concerning the conflicts provoked by faith in Christ emerged in two stages which centered around the worldwide or Ecumenical Councils of Nicaea (325) and Chalcedon (451). The doctrinal and ecclesiastical decisions announced there constitute Catholic Tradition to the present day.

Schools of Interpretation

In the earliest Christian Churches there appeared two principal schools of thought about Christ which colored all intellectual and political discussions. The School of Antioch heard the Scriptures with a literal ear. Its reflections tended to follow Aristotle (384–322 B.C.E.) and to focus upon the historical nature of the text. Interpreters did not look for a hidden mystical meaning in the text, but for the sense intended by the author. As a result, they almost always emphasized the humanity of Jesus. In the controversies about the identity of Christ, they stressed the dual character of Jesus' Presence—his divinity and humanity—having little philosophical language available to disclose their unity.

The School at Alexandria, on the other hand, took its philosophical categories from Plato (427–347 B.C.E.) and Neoplatonic philosophers such as Plotinus (about 205–70 C.E.). In reading the Scriptures they stressed the allegorical, moral, and mystical meanings deep within the text. Above all, the believer had to recognize God's action in human history and his disclosure of himself in Jesus. This emphasis upon the divinity of Jesus tended to obscure his human experience, so that in more heterodox moments theologians like Apollinarius (310–90 C.E.) said that all the highest human faculties were simply replaced by divinity in Jesus. So just as Antiochenes stressed duality, Alexandrines preached unity and identity.

We do not need to rehearse the often difficult Greek philosophical, theological, and political debates of the period to see that crucial issues were at stake for Christian life. Beneath all the high words, the sometimes virulent attacks, the generous gestures, and the malicious deeds lay one question: Do the scriptural stories and theologies announce in Jesus salvation from death, sin, and failure? If Jesus was not divine in a human way, or human in a divine way, then our faith is in vain. The categories of these centuries were regularly metaphysical and philosophical; the issue was existential reconciliation or separation from God.

Putting the Question: Arius and Apollinarius

Arius (about 250–336) formulated the question so sharply in Alexandria that no one could ignore it. For him, the Logos who became flesh (John 1:14) was a creature, a better than human but not quite completely divine being. Arius's interpretation succeeded, not only because of his personal asceticism, popular preaching ability, and political connections, but because it seemed utterly logical. To be both human and divine required a bit of both mixed together. In this way, God could still remain sovereignly free, unchanging, and eternal while humanity maintained its qualitative difference as limited, sinful, and historical.

Apollinarius, Bishop of Laodicea (about 310–90), was an ardent anti-Arian. He proclaimed the divinity of Christ without qualification. There was certainly no moral development in Christ. Humanity and divinity were united in him. Therefore Apollinarius argued that although Christ had a human body and soul, he had only a Divine Spirit, the Spirit of the Word. This argument against Arius was disastrous. For if Christ was not completely human, then how could he be a true example for us? How would he have redeemed all of our human reality?

Athanasius and Conciliar Judgments

The great figures of the Eastern theological Tradition, such as Athanasius (about 296–373), argued otherwise. For him, Jesus was both fully human and fully divine—however philosophically illogical that might seem. But how can One who is unbounded be born in a womb? How can one who is so sincerely human—compassionate, crying, eating, and drinking—be divine *precisely in* that humanity?

For Catholic Christians these issues were articulated into official positions called doctrines between 325 and 681. The two principal councils were the first and fourth of six. Called by the Emperor Constantine, the Council of Nicaea (325) solemnly declared that the true belief of Christians was that Jesus Christ as Son of God was equal to (of the same substance—or in Greek, *homoousios* with) God the Father and Holy Spirit. The Christian God was One and Triune simultaneously. At Constantinople (381), further clarification concerning the Holy Spirit was added; and it fathered the Nicene-Constantinopolitan Creed (the so-called Nicene Creed) which is prayed by Catholics each Sunday. The fourth ecumenical council, Chalcedon (451), declared that Jesus Christ was truly human and truly divine, that the one person of Christ existed in two natures.

Neither doctrine stopped theological discussion; indeed, if anything, they pushed it forward. They provided a non-Scriptural language which re-presented to Greek (and Latin) culture the same message as the New Testament. Repeating the New Testament stories did not solve the question Arius asked; finding a new set of words in which to proclaim Christ to another culture did.

Mind had asked a question: "Is he or is he not a creature?" Reason deserved a religious answer commensurate with its intelligence. Jesus was a part of our real world; so was his salvation. It had either made a difference to that one world or it had not. The Councils maintained that Catholic Christians could not retreat to a private religious world to nurse their personal symbols, nor could they be parents of some divergent logic which operated in religion and not in the world at large. However hard it might be, the Christian would be required to find an adequate embodiment of Christian faith in the articulated beliefs of particular ages.

WORSHIP: THE PLACE OF BELIEF

The familiar Catholic blessing "In the name of the Father and of the Son and of the Holy Spirit" and the gestures of touching the forehead, the chest, and shoulders symbolize something very important. For just as surely as they announce the central belief of Trinitarian experience, they are also worship, the experience of prayer. The doctrines of Catholic Christianity, whether intellectual or ecclesiastical, were born in address to the Father of the living Jesus.

Prosper Tiro of Acquitaine (about 390–463) canonized this important ecclesial principle. "The law of worship establishes the law of belief."[6] In the reports of the major Councils we have just mentioned, this was most certainly the case. The Fathers of the Councils appealed at Nicaea to the baptismal liturgy to justify their expression of Trinitarian faith. It was because the community baptized through triple immersion in the name of Father, Son, and Spirit that the Creed confessed God as triune. At Chalcedon it was the simple fact that Christians prayed *to* Christ as well as *through* him that convinced the bishops and theologians that Jesus could be confessed as both divine and human. We would not blasphemously worship a creature.

The sacramental life of the Christian community was a way in which it was catholic. The common gestures, the common Gospels proclaimed at worship, the eating and drinking in memory of the Lord Jesus defined Christians throughout the empire, despite cultural, gestural, or linguistic differences. So Pliny (62–113), the governor of Bithynia (northwest Asia Minor), wishing to confirm his persecution of Christians, wrote about their gathering at dawn before the workday to worship.

In early years both the one who presided and the prayers said at the main service of worship differed from place to place. But by the mid-second century (for example, in Justin Martyr), there was considerable structural analogy from one Church to another both in order of worship and the leaders of prayer. The combination of readings from the New Testament, prayers for the living and the dead, acceptance of gifts (both bread and wine or food and monetary offerings for the poor), the great thanksgiving prayer including the memorial of the Lord's final supper, a common "Our Father," and the breaking and distribution of the sacred Bread and Wine to those present were all constants in both Eastern and Western liturgies of the Eucharist (after *Eucharistia,* the Greek word for thanksgiving). Such communion was a sharing in the Body of Christ, as Augustine had stated.

But the Body of Christ has many members (1 Cor. 12:12–31), not all of whom accomplish the same tasks. St. Paul's images and the growth of the community prompted individual Churches to adopt an organization which would pattern their experience of worship and culture. Catholics modeled their ecclesiastical experience more and more upon a stratified civil government. With the acceptance of Christianity as a legitimate religion of the empire, the local "overseer" or bishop assumed not only the role of chief presider at worship and authentic interpreter of doctrinal discussions, but became a sign and hierarchical bond of political unity as well. As it became more and more difficult for the local bishop to preside over worship in outlying districts, he appointed priests, that is, presbyters, to take his place. The common gesture of inauguration for such specialized ministries in the Church was the laying on of hands.

Both belief and Church order emerged from worship. The need to clarify the symbolic expressions of the community issued in the Councils and creeds. The requirement to structure social prayer created normative offices in the community. These Hellenistic developments of doctrine are particularly Catholic. Such reformulations make utterly clear that the Catholic Tradition is an organic history, adapting to new situations without losing its roots in the original experience of Christ. The type of its identity is preserved, even if the form changes.

The intensely personal preaching and theology of Augustine and other fathers, the development of a canon of authentic scriptural texts, the discernment of right teaching in the doctrines of councils, and the achievement of structurally analogous forms of worship and Church order provided the marks of the Catholic Church at the conclusion of the sixth century when Venantius Fortunatus made his pilgrimage to Gaul. There was a recognizably universal community of believers which had grappled creatively with the dying culture and attempted to transform it through an extraordinary program of personal and societal evangelization. To sustain its identity, Christianity asserted itself as part of an edifice of classical life whose achievements it recognized, whose sins it deplored, and whose political government it used to spread the Gospel. The story of Jesus was becoming the foundation stone of an entire civilization.

But in the fifth and sixth centuries, the old Roman traditions were collapsing. Christians were taking control of various political offices because the old apparatus at the edges of the empire was disintegrating. Before we can understand that distinctively Catholic culture called medieval Christendom, we must examine an important prophetic movement. It is a place where the tradition of texts, the prophetic missionary, and the proclamation of the apocalyptic Heavenly Jerusalem met—the movement called monasticism.

THE PROPHETS OF EARLY MONASTICISM

Every religious impulse has its ascetic or rigorist movements. So there are solitary hermits in Buddhism and Hinduism, philosophical ascetics such as Pythagoras (about 570–496 B.C.E.), and the Essenes (about 100 B.C.E.–200 C.E.) in Judaism. The origin of Christian ascetic movements seems to have been in Egypt where solitaries (called in Greek *monachos,* monks) went to the deserts in their quest for religious unification, coherence, and integrity. From earliest days, such hermits lived celibate lives. Following Paul's dictum that it was better not to marry due to the coming Day of the Lord (1 Cor. 7:25–40), monks struggled for an undivided heart, for simplicity of spirit in anticipation of the Parousia (the glorious return of Christ).

With the persecutions of the Emperor Decius (250–51), the crisis in the fervor of the Christian community became acute. Monasticism spread in response as an escape from lax or lapsed believers in urban areas and as an attempt to recover the original dedication of Christian missionaries, martyrs, and apostles.

In the *Life of Antony* (about 251–356), Athanasius (about 296–373) praises this Egyptian ascetic who gave away his goods and property in addition to his right to marry. The holiness of Antony's hermitlike life attracted followers who gathered around him in an ordered community of work and prayer.

Pachomius (about 290–346), a former soldier, founded a monastery at Tabennisi in the Thebaid near the Nile about 320. He developed an austere rule for his community; yet before he died, he ruled as *abbas* (abbot) over nine foundations of men and women. He believed that his coenobitic (i.e., communitarian) monasticism recovered the "apostolic life" of the early Christian community (Acts 4:42–47) in which prayer, property, and possessions were ideally held in common.

Basil the Great (about 330–79) provided the common rule for most urban monastic foundations in the Eastern Empire. The rule of charity was paramount. As he said: "If you live alone, whose feet will you wash?" While strict poverty, chastity, and obedience to an abbot were required, hours of liturgical prayer, manual labor, and even the education of children in schools attached to the monasteries were encouraged. The poor were always to be welcomed. This communitarian experience disclosed the presence of the Heavenly City on earth.

By the early fifth century there were so many Latin Christians in Eastern monasteries that it became necessary to provide a rule in their vernacular. An Eastern monk, John Cassian (about 360–435), brought Egyptian monasticism to the West near Marseilles. Out of his years in the East he wrote *The Institutes* and *Conferences,* which record the ordinary rules of community life and the various hindrances to perfection.

Benedict of Nursia (about 480–550) retired to a cave at Subiaco in Italy, but as a hermit he attracted religious disciples who eventually founded a monastic community at Monte Cassino (about 525). The *Rule of St. Benedict,* which draws from Cassian, Basil, the desert monks, and Augustine, but especially from the New Testament, provided a prudent, humane, common life. He wished to found a "school of the Lord's service." This has become through the centuries the charter document of all later monastic experience in the Western Catholic Church.

THE CATHOLIC COMMUNITY

The influence of monastic life in the Church cannot be neglected. Its emphasis upon simplicity, self-discipline, and the meditative reading of the Scriptures and the Fathers plus a strong centralized government around an abbot inaugurated an extraordinary gesture of stability in the chaotic Western world. The radical demands of the cross and resurrection had met the need to remain within one's social environment in a holy way.

In the early Church, martyrdom was an obvious sign of membership in the definitive religious community. Now the struggle to develop concrete incarnations of holiness in an empire which permitted and even encouraged Christianity had become the Church's most important task. The early prophetic and even apocalyptic strains of the Christ-event kept solidifying into Tradition and custom. How was this original event to be kept authentic?

The early conflicts of the believing community through their resolutions in doctrine, creed, office, sacraments, Councils, and most of all through their creative theologians, provided evidence of the electricity transmitted in Jesus of Nazareth. In a sense, if the prophetic character of the event had *not* become Tradition in a series of religious institutions, it would not only have died; it would have given evidence simply of its ultimate bankruptcy as a religious enterprise.

The early Church was not simply a *gnosis,* a knowledge or a speculative theology. To be Catholic, to be faithful to the radiance of that astonishing Jesus, Christians were forced to examine not only the limits of the intellectual interpretations of its message, but also the practical, quite ordinary implications of holiness. For creeds, doctrines, and theologies were only one side of the ecclesial reality. Sacrament, the offices of bishop, priest, deacon, and deaconess were the social embodiment of the interior horizon envisioned by all believers.

Monasticism is a fruitful place to conclude this brief description of the marks of Catholic Christianity. The monks and women religious of East and West were utterly seminal in the stabilization of the interior, as well as exterior, elements in the Church. Their fundamental thrust toward the interiorization of the Christian message, coupled with the sacramental, liturgical, and governmental externals, made them a magnetic force in evangelization. And although the tensions between the visible and invisible aspects of Catholic existence have remained throughout its history, no one can refuse to see in this central institutional expression elements of prophetic proclamation, apocalyptic withdrawal, and purification encapsulated in a Tradition of prayerful meditation and cultural preservation. The dangerous memory of Jesus of Nazareth—his table fellowship with the poor and the outcast, his disclosure of God's gracious love—was being transmitted to the future.

NOTES

1. Letter to the Romans 1.2, 2.1, 4.1, in *The Apostolic Fathers,* trans. Francis X. Glimm, Joseph Marique, Gerald G. Walsh (New York: Christian Heritage, 1947), 108.

2. *Confessions of St. Augustine,* VIII.7, trans. J. G. Pilkington, in *Nicene*

and Post-Nicene Fathers, ed. Philip Schaff (New York: Charles Scribner's Sons, 1902), 124.

3. Ibid., I.1, p. 45.

4. On Baptism against the Donatists, see III.10.15, in *Writings in Connection with the Donatist Controversy,* trans. J. R. King (Edinburgh: T. & T. Clark, 1872), 62.

5. Sermon VII on Matthew 6, in *Nicene and Post-Nicene Fathers,* VI:282.

6. *Indiculus,* chap. 8 in *The Teaching of the Catholic Church,* ed. Josef Neuner, Heinrich Roos, and Karl Rahner (Staten Island, N.Y.: Alba House, 1966), 376.

FURTHER RELATED MATERIAL

There are three fine books on St. Augustine among the many: Peter Brown, *Augustine of Hippo: A Biography* (Berkeley and Los Angeles: University of California Press, 1967); Eugene Teselle, *Augustine the Theologian* (London: Burns & Oates, 1970); and G. Van der Meer, *Augustine the Bishop* (New York: Harper & Row, 1965). For conciliar history, see G. L. Prestige, *God in Patristic Thought* (London: SPCK, 1969); for a theory of what was going forward during the period, see B. J. F. Lonergan, *The Way to Nicea: The Dialectical Development of Trinitarian Theology* (Philadelphia: Westminster Press, 1976). On the developments in worship, Gregory Dix's *The Shape of the Liturgy* (London: A. & C. Black, 1970); and on monasticism, Helen Waddell, *The Desert Fathers* (Chicago: University of Chicago Press, 1958); or better, but less available, Derwas J. Chitty, *The Desert a City* (Oxford: Basil Blackwell & Mott, 1966) and Lowrie J. Daly, *Benedictine Monasticism: Its Formation and Development through the Twelfth Century* (New York: Sheed & Ward, 1965), and the historical introduction to *RB 1980: The Rule of St. Benedict,* ed. Timothy Fry (Collegeville, Minnesota: Liturgical Press, 1981), especially 3–151.

5

THE TAMING OF EUROPE (692–1073)

> Franks, Romans and all believers
>   are immersed in misery and great distress.
> O my sorrow!
> Infants, the old, grand prelates, and mothers
>   weep at the loss of Caesar.
> O my sorrow!
> Never shall the rivers of tears cease,
>   for the whole world laments the death of Charles.
> O my sorrow!
> Common Father to all: orphans and widows,
>   wanderers and maidens.
> O my sorrow!
> Christ, you who govern the armies of the skies,
>   In your kingdom grant rest to Charles.
>
>   anon., from *A Solis Ortu* (800–900)

There is a capital sculpture in the eleventh-century atrium of the church at Saint-Benoît-sur-Loire in which two large creatures vie for control over a doll-like figure suspended between them. The being on the left is scaly of face, swathed in flaming skins, with a bloated countenance perched on a heavy body, legs planted firmly on the pillar below. His leechlike mouth remains eternally open, prepared to suck in whatever might feed his master's appetite, while his eyes stare resolutely toward the earth. Hovering over the pillar the seraph on the right enfolds his invisible torso in neatly pleated drapery which repeats the pattern of his wings. His face is long and narrow, crowned with Roman curls, jeweled with wide eyes directed toward the heavens. His mouth smiles. In between lies poor humanity. Blank-eyed, staring eternally forward, neither right nor left, up nor down, the figure is naked, distended in the arms by the tension of enormous powers beyond his control. He is caught—and the centuries have taken away his mouth. Is the creature screaming in terror at its predicament or comforted, knowing that the angel has cupped his right hand in blessing over its head?

Struggle may be the operative word for the early Middle Ages and its Church. Human ambiguity and the paradox of experience sometimes seemed overwhelming. And if the Catholic Church had found the basic instruments of religious cultivation in its doctrines, creeds, ordinations, and sacraments, the fields in which it tilled regularly resisted or grew strange hybrids which eventually required serious weeding.

AN OVERVIEW—THE PAINS OF GROWTH

This period (692–1073) begins with strife between the Eastern and Western branches of the Church and ends with two churches and a war between ecclesiastical and civil society in the West. At the Council called Quinisext (692), East and West diverged over largely disciplinary matters (such as celibacy for the clergy, the Lenten fast, and the primacy of Constantinople or Rome). Religious and civil politics occasionally divided the churches governed from the seats of the Eastern and Western Empires through 1054, when the two episcopal sees condemned each other.

This breach between Greek-speaking and Latin-speaking Catholicism formed the Greek Orthodox family of Churches. The excommunications (prohibiting intercommunion among Churches along with other legal consequences) were lifted only in 1965 when Pope Paul VI and the Patriarch Athenagoras embraced in Jerusalem.

In 1073 Hildebrand (about 1021–85) was elected as Pope Gregory VII. Convinced of the West's need for internal moral reform, he attempted to extricate the secular from the religious duties of Catholicism. Papal government was centralized and augmented. The High Middle Ages, to be assessed in the next chapter, had begun.

The world of early medieval Catholicism was confused. There were further invasions into the old boundaries of the Western Empire. Islam and Constantinople both had more sophisticated levels of culture. Moreover, the population of the West was thin, growing only slowly until about 1300; nonetheless, agriculture continued to lag behind the enlarging market for goods and food until the early 1200s. Multiple local lords claimed property, the only stable currency. In the midst of this stood the Church, claiming allegiance to a Lord whose rule was meant to extend over all powers and over all commercial goods. How was this community of believers to assert the transcendent goal *within* the early medieval experience? It chose social order and religious law.

With the assistance of certain spectacularly successful princes, the Church struggled for its catholicity by contributing to the building of a stratified ecclesial and secular society. This social order is known as *feudalism,* a system of allegiances originally meant to stop petty wars and vicious vendettas. Sometimes it succeeded; often it failed— allowing the Church to slip itself into the arsenal of princes or prelates who were quite willing to use divine legitimation for their own personal gain.

But we must begin where we earlier concluded—with monasticism. As the world approached the end of the first millennium, its theme was order and unity—which could too easily translate into servile obedience to one's superiors and a uniformity of expression.

MONASTIC MISSIONARIES— THE PROPHETS TO PEOPLES

Monks may have wanted to establish a permanent Heavenly City on earth; but within one hundred years of Benedict's major foundations, Irish and English missionaries were making pilgrimages from their communities to evangelize the barbarian continent. Celtic missionaries like Columbanus (about 543–615) and Gall (550–645) planted islands of stability among the barbarians of Gaul, Switzerland, and Italy. These austere missionaries brought with them a love of learning and the desire for God.[1] The schools of writing and textual preservation at St. Gallen, Bobbio, and Luxeuil founded some of the most famous continuing libraries in Europe.

Boniface, Apostle of Unity

The Celtic Church in England had been largely destroyed by the Saxon invasions during the fifth century. Yet rapidly, Saxon monks like Willibrord (658–739), a native of Northumbria, followed the same paths as their Celtic forebears.

The greatest of these missionaries was Boniface (680–754), or Wynfrith as he was originally known. Unsuccessful in Frisia, he went to Rome where he was given papal authority to preach in Germany.

His courage in chopping down the oak dedicated to Thor transformed him into an invincible hero. Here was no weak word-man,
but an engaging, muscular personality, absolutely dedicated to the
single cause of preaching the Gospel of Christ. His mission was to
found bishoprics and monasteries in Germany, to establish settled
ecclesiastical points from which the Church could radiate its catholicity.

Boniface combined in himself Latin and barbarian cultures and
offered a clear identity to his converting Christians. He searched for
intercultural answers to the problems of relatives' marriages, the
validity of sacramental life performed by false, heretical, or even evil
priests, and the social order of government and Church.

His solutions were important. "It is our earnest desire to maintain
the Catholic faith and the unity of the Roman Church. As many
hearers or learners as God shall grant me in my missionary work, I
will not cease to summon and urge them to render obedience to the
Apostolic See."[2] Boniface, through cultural training and religious
conviction, evangelized the Saxons with Roman art, language, literature, and traditions. To overcome the fragmentation which he saw
among the barbarians and to establish the Gospel, he implanted
uniform doctrines and morals.

One and the same faith was always believed everywhere, as Vincent of Lérins (+ about 450) said. Christianity was identical from the
beginning, and what better place to find the origin of that unity than
in Rome where Peter and Paul were martyred? Boniface's extraordinary success at establishing ecclesiastical provinces served only to
prove the point. Barbarians were interested in the civilizing influence
of the Roman Church.

The Apostles of the East

This interpretation is born out in noticing, by way of contrast, the
two great missionary brothers to eastern Europe, Cyril (+869) and
Methodius (+885). They translated the Scriptures and liturgies into
early Slavonic, inventing an alphabet for the purpose (Cyrillic).
Although Cyril is buried in the Roman Church of San Clemente,
Latinizing missionaries north of the Alps were not at all pleased with
their efforts, so much so that at one point Methodius was imprisoned

by German bishops for two years. Nonetheless, Slavonic continued to foster not a Latinized barbarian culture, but a vernacular expression of Christian Greek culture. It was this Christian culture which spread in the tenth century to the lands governed by the Rus.

These missionary efforts would have been fruitless without military and governmental support. An instance of this can be seen in the Arab incursions across the Pyrenees as far north as the Loire River just south of Paris. In 732, Charles Martel (about 690–741) defeated the Saracens at Poitiers in pitched battle. Without the peace created by the empire and an unqualified allegiance to it, Boniface's attempts to frame laws and provinces for the Church would have been in vain.

The Public Consequence of Sin

Public law and evangelical precept met in the Christian experience of sin. For despite the fact that the monastic missionaries wished to be absolutely faithful to the practice of the Roman Church, they introduced into the continent a private form of penance. Since *Hermas* it had been possible to have a second chance after baptism, but in a purely public fashion, by joining the ranks of penitents— wearing special garb, separating oneself from other Christians, and living a thoroughly ascetic life until death. Before the fourth century some sins were for all practical purposes "unforgivable" (apostasy, adultery, and murder).

Celtic and English Evangelizers brought with them the monastic practice of constant examination of conscience and the confession of faults to one's religious brothers. They enshrined this penitential practice in books of tariff penances which informed the priest what to impose upon the lax Christian. For example, for a monk, drunkenness required 30 days of penance, while for a priest or deacon, 40 days. Fornication with a virgin brought one year of strict penitential discipline; but intercourse with a married woman required four years. There were even penances for theft, murder, and heresy— sometimes up to twenty years of penance.[3]

What became important in this civilization of barbarian society was that religious actions had real consequences in the world. One was separated by fasting, habits of marital abstinence, and prayerful practices from those one knew and loved. Penance became compatible with certain forms of barbarian law in which one must "pay back" one's harm to another by a reparation fee (*wergeld*). If one sinned, one paid a spiritual restoration.

Later it became possible to ameliorate or even cancel penance through a financial gift which mandated prayers said at a particular monastery. Wealthy (or particularly military) princes began to found monasteries *before* they went out to do battle, just in the event that they might offend in some religious fashion. Society was beginning to fuse into unity—but not always to the benefit of the Gospel's confrontation of human values.

THE CONSOLIDATION OF TRADITION:
SOCIETY AND CHURCH

The Carolingian Renaissance

King of the Franks and the Lombards, first ruler of the Holy Roman Empire, Charlemagne (742–814) governed both Church and state with grace, intelligence, and power. When he died, many looked at the Carolingian Renaissance of culture and governmental solidity as the ideal. The cathedral at Aachen, built between 796 and 804, modeled Ravennese mosaics for the northern kingdoms. Its octagonal dome towered over the countryside; God and king were praised together under the magnificent circular lights suspended from its center.

By title, of course, Charlemagne was only ruler of the state. But in his various capitularies (church regulation issued as civil laws) he centralized the patterns for ecclesiastical reform. The General Admonition of 798 mandated a school for every cathedral Church, annual visitation of bishops to the Churches of their dioceses (in conjunction with a civil governor to ensure that the bishop did his duty), a standardized religious instruction for all the baptized, the imposition of the Rule of Benedict upon monasteries in the kingdom, and tithes to be given to the Church. Charlemagne appointed almost all bishops and abbots directly and regularly disposed of ecclesiastical property as though it were the crown's. By various synods of bishops, he was described as the "devoted defender of holy Church" (Capitulary of 769), God's official, the Lord of the Church in the kingdom, the rector of the Church, priest, and king. In his circle of intimates, where classical nicknames prevailed, he was known as David the King.

After Charlemagne had stabilized the Italian political situation and confirmed Leo III (795–816) in his election, the pope crowned him Roman Emperor, Augustus (800). The pope then knelt and offered him homage, separating himself from his Byzantine loyalties. This gesture of the pope's severed Charlemagne's political ties with the Eastern Empire for some time; only in 812 did the Greek Emperor recognize this German as Emperor of the Western Empire.

Papal and Imperial Politics

Within one hundred years of Charlemagne's death, however, a synod of bishops near Laon (909) announced: "The world is full of lechery and adultery, churches are robbed and the poor are oppressed and murdered." As Church and state marched toward the end of the first millennium, they found themselves locked in a struggle of imperial proportions. For just as the classical culture of Rome believed there was really only one culture, normative for all times and places; so too its inheritors, whether Church or state, were convinced that only one institutional tradition could be supreme. Thus in the same fashion that Charlemagne consolidated political power, ecclesiastical powers attempted unification of Church under the government of Rome.

The regularly confused politics of Italy constantly encouraged papal-imperial confrontations. By mid-eighth century, there was a developing papal duchy surrounding Rome. At the same time, the last Merovingian king of the Franks was interned in a monastery; and Pepin the Short (714–68) took an oath (754) to protect the pope against the Lombards in the North.

A document, originating in the Frankish church and called the "Donation of Constantine," appeared, purporting to give the pope primacy over the major sees of the East (Antioch, Constantinople, Alexandria, and Jerusalem) and dominion over Italy. Within 100 years the text found its way into the Pseudo-Isidorean Decretals compiled near Le Mans or Tours. These collections of canons, letters, and laws were largely forgeries; but during the entire Middle Ages they were thought to be genuine both by proponents and opponents of papal hegemony.

Despite the attempts to make ecclesiastical life orderly, there were bizarre moments. The mid-ninth to the mid-tenth century is known by historians as the "obscure age" of papal history. One macabre example will suffice. Various successors to Charlemagne's children claimed Italian political loyalties. Pope Formosus (891–96) granted the imperial crown to a count of Spoleto of French lineage. He and his son's oppressive rule prompted the pope to ask the German king to establish order in Italy. The German king responded, took Rome, and received the imperial throne, but was stricken by paralysis before he could control the city and provinces. His seven-year-old son reigned briefly (900–911). Formosus's successor as pope held office for only two weeks; the next pope, Stephen VI (896–97), an enemy of the Franks, had the body of Formosus disinterred, stripped, and mutilated at a synod. He passed judgment upon the corpse as invalidly elected, annulling all the laws and orders conferred by him. Stephen was strangled in prison during an uprising; two years later his synodal laws against Formosus were repealed. The incident speaks for itself.

Only with the rise of the Ottonian dynasty (936–1000) in Germany did the Church begin to forge some independence from local Italian politics. Bishops and abbots became princes of the imperial realm, more able by their civil status to wrest independence from local lords and landowners. Monastic foundations were exempted from local taxation and made subject to the pope himself, thus giving them important leverage in the struggle for free expression of the Gospel.

Beautiful Letters

These centuries are murky, "dark" in many ways. Yet while the larger civil and ecclesiastical conflicts were engaged, monks were quietly preserving antiquity's religious and secular manuscripts. Without their excruciating effort, we would have no access to classical culture. Barrel-vaulted churches with Romanesque arches were constructed, solving serious architectural problems. The schools Charlemagne founded under Alcuin of York's (735–804) tutelage diminished clerical illiteracy and fostered a literary language with an accurate scribal orthography.

Extraordinary religious poetry in the vernacular, such as the Old English *Dream of the Rood* (about 750) or the Old Saxon *Heliand*

(*Savior,* about 800), was composed describing Christ as the primary prince to whom we owe allegiance and the apostles as his faithful vassals. Going against the grain, they counsel humility as virtue in the authentic Lord and love for one's enemies. During the same period monastic foundations such as Gandersheim (Saxony) or Nivelles (Belgium) increased, offering women access to educational emancipation. Biblical commentaries were fostered by theological controversies of the period ultimately culminating in a *General Commentary* (or *Glossa Ordinaria*) on the entire Bible which could be used as a basic textbook for lectures in the schools.

The Heroes of Memory

Three important thinkers of this period consolidate an important element in medieval life. The philosopher Boethius (about 480–524) translated and commented upon Aristotle's works on logic and grammar, wrote a brief theological work on the Trinity, and described in *On the Consolation of Philosophy* the way of the human soul to wisdom. Written in prison, this book converted many Western religious to the way of philosophy as well as to Christianity.

Bede the Venerable (about 673–735), a Northumbrian monk, is the Father of English Church history. His *Ecclesiastical History of the English People* evidences his genius as a historian, gathering information from firsthand witnesses when possible, weighing authorities, and sorting likely from unlikely events.

John Scotus Eriugena (about 810–77), in a treatise on nature, attempted to reconcile Neoplatonic physical cosmology with Christian creationism. His belief in the unity of the Genesis accounts and classical culture is shown in his translations of the mystical writings which went under the name of Dionysius. These works stressed the union of the Christian soul with God in wordless and imageless wonder and affected all later religious thought and liturgical practice.

Each of these thinkers patterns perhaps *the* important trait of medieval thought—the security of having reflected previous Tradition. Bede, Boethius, and Eriugena quote authorities, whether philosophical or religious, to prove their point. Their greatest horror in many ways was to be "new," original, separated from the Tradition from which they emerged. Despite their own considerable abilities at synthesis, they preferred to think of themselves as craftsmen, carefully tooling already tried materials into excellent shapes and designs. From the debris of cultural and political morals, religion, and statecraft, they hoped to preserve the truth from the transient errors of the present in much the same way that their contemporaries shaped gilded shrines for the bones or relics of holy men and women of the past. Without this connection with days gone by, one was lost. The thinkers' careful retention of antique polished jewels helped restore faith in a future which seemed confused and offered some glimmer of hope in their present.

THE CRISIS OF THE FUTURE:
THE COMING OF THE MILLENNIUM

Crisis produces apocalyptic writings. It is no surprise that the struggles for power and identity in the early Middle Ages called upon that critical New Testament grammar of religious possibilities. Surely the victorious Son of Man would return to cleanse his community of the buyers of ecclesiastical offices, murderers of the innocent, and knightly despoilers of the countryside.

The medieval figures whom we must briefly mention could not ignore the perilous times. They criticized their contemporaries in the light of God's universal plan for history. The conversion of the Roman Empire, the invasions of Islam, the developing centralized papacy, the closure of one thousand years of Christian history—each provided a nodal point around which visions clustered. While philosophy dealt with the universal eternal laws of time and space and the institutional traditions focused upon preserving the past, apocalyptic writing of the period offered believers and thinkers a way of locating the specific events and cultural shifts of the present within a history directed by God's victorious justice and liberating love.

Papal Foreclosure

Curiously enough we may begin with Pope Gregory I (590–604). Son of a senator, he sold his property, becoming first a monk, then a deacon of Rome, diplomat to Constantinople, and pope. He fostered liturgical reform, including support of the music known as plainsong or Gregorian chant. Gregory was a masterful preacher and spiritual guide. His pastoral rule for bishops became a handbook; his commentary on Job a mine of practical moral judgments and ethical theory. As administrator, he challenged barbarians and emperors and sent missionaries to England.

But amid all this remarkable constructive activity, Gregory believed that society had little future. "Cities are destroyed, armed camps overturned, districts emptied of people, the earth reduced to solitude. . . . Let us despise with all our being this present—or rather extinct—world."[4] Gregory was convinced that the terrors of the present—climatic changes, wars, famines—were signs of the times, the presage of the judgment of God.

Cultural Confrontations

The Eastern Empire shared this pessimistic vision. A seventh-century Syrian author (Pseudo-Methodius of Patara) anticipated a last world emperor who would vanquish the invading Moslems. There was to be no collaboration with these children of Ishmael and no reliance upon weak rulers for assistance. Only God would suffice.

Where culture clashed with culture, schemes of eschatological conflict flourished. In an Old High German relic of the ninth century, Elijah meets the Antichrist, that mysterious figure (with origins in 2 Thess. 2:6–7) who would appear before the End to torture the earth. Elijah's wounds in this battle would make the mountains catch fire, destroy the trees, and dry up the waters. Even the bonds of tribe and nation would break down.

Abbot Adso (910–92) shifted the scene of the final warfare between good and evil from either Constantinople or Rome. The conquering emperor, the one in whom we hope for victory over the Antichrist, would be the king of the Franks. After terrifying trials this ruler would govern Christ's empire, travel to Jerusalem, and put aside his scepter and crown on the Mount of Olives. The Antichrist would be killed by the humble power of the Lord Jesus alone. The time for this judgment is the present.

CONCLUSIONS

These negative visions of the world gained inflated currency as the millennium approached. Abbo of Fleury (about 945–1004) remarked that he had heard a sermon as a young man which proclaimed that "as soon as the number of a thousand years was completed, the Antichrist would come and the Last Judgment would follow. I opposed this sermon with what force I could."[5] But rumor continued to thrive. What is one to make of these developments? Are they in some way religious? How are they Catholic?

The pain of religious incarnation in various cultures is acute. It is not accomplished without false starts, blind alleys, and the corridors of power. The early Middle Ages knew only one normative society, the decaying Roman Empire, a government in which religion supported the state and state was founded upon religious ritual, order, and narrative. The struggles between Church and empire upon which we now look with somewhat bemused or belligerent antipathy for their seeming venality, collusion, and neglect of the Gospel may in fact reflect something more important.

For without the attempts by the Church to establish itself as an independent political enterprise, it might have been swallowed completely by the maw of the state. Papal and episcopal politics were regularly an attempt to maintain maneuverability within an increasingly narrowed situation. While that does not condone evil, it helps explain some history. Church without property in early feudal society was a Gospel without independence. It became a court jester, supporting the prince in good or bad policy, telling only occasional ironic tales to tweak the conscience of the powerful. And though this was sometimes the case during this period (and others we shall study), even spectacular failures witness, by contrast, the fundamental goal of Catholicism—the embodiment of the Gospel in all phases of human life.

Whenever Catholic Christianity combined the prophetic missionary spirit of Boniface, the reforming instincts of the Tradition in Pope Gregory, and the constant criticism of the present of an Adso, then the Gospel manifested itself. Church could proclaim support and consolation for the troubled and offer confronting transformation for the sinful and oppressed. When the three moments of Catholicism lost their ability to speak to one another, the dominance of Tradition, prophecy, or apocalyptic visions regularly sent the contemporary culture marching against imaginary enemies or into secluded complacency. That these latter possibilities did not dominate the Catholic Tradition will be seen in the ongoing vigor of the intellectual, spiritual, and political traditions of the High Middle Ages.

NOTES

1. Jean Leclerq, *The Love of Learning and the Desire for God,* trans. Catherine Misrahi (New York: Mentor, 1962).

2. *The Letters of St. Boniface,* trans. Ephraim Emerton (New York: Norton, 1976), 79.

3. Theodore's Penitential, in *Councils and Ecclesiastical Documents Relating to Great Britain and Ireland,* ed. Arthur W. Haddan and William Stubbs (Oxford: At the Clarendon Press, 1964), 3:173–190.

4. Bernard McGinn, *Visions of the End: Apocalyptic Traditions in the Middle Ages* (New York: Columbia University Press, 1979), 62–81.

5. Ibid., 89.

FURTHER RELATED MATERIAL

On monastic theology, one of the finest introductions is Jean Leclerq, *The Love of Learning and the Desire for God,* trans. Catherine Misrahi (New York: Mentor, 1962). R. W. Southern's *Western Society and the Church in the Middle Ages* (Baltimore: Pelican, 1972) emphasizes the social, political, and economic dimensions of the period. Francis Oakley's *The Medieval Experience: Foundations of Western Cultural Singularity* (New York: Charles Scribner's Sons, 1974) stresses the relation of European life to especially non-Western medieval cultures. Bernard McGinn, *Visions of the End: Apocalyptic Traditions in the Middle Ages* (New York: Columbia University Press, 1979) recovers a too frequently neglected aspect of medieval life.

6

THE CULTURE AND
CRITICISM OF CHRISTENDOM (1073–1453)

> Born to us, He gave Himself as neighbor;
> At table, He gave Himself as food;
> By dying, He gave Himself as ransom;
> As King, He gives Himself as crown.
> O Saving Victim!
> You open the gate of heaven.
> Hostile wars press us.
> Grant us strength; bring us help.
>
> > Thomas Aquinas (about 1225–74), from
> > "Verbum Supernum Prodiens."

A period drama in the history of Catholic Christendom occurred at Canossa in the Apennine mountains during January 1077. There Henry IV, emperor of Germany (1056–1106), clothed in the hair shirt of a penitent, knelt shoeless at the gate of a castle, pleading with Pope Gregory VII (1073–85) for release from the ban of excommunication. After three days of prayer and penance Henry was absolved by Gregory and admitted to the Sacrament of the Eucharist. The struggle between empire and Church was decided in favor of ecclesiastical control. Or was it?

The complicated civil machinations which preceded and succeeded this supposed snowy scene actually left Henry with an empire he might otherwise have lost. For in March of that same year, German princes, unhappy that Henry had been released from excommunication, elected a brother-in-law as king.

These sliding loyalties originated in Gregory's attempts to reform the Catholic Church. For the Middle Ages (previously considered a halfway house between Roman antiquity and its humanistic revival in the Italian Renaissance) was a period of struggling reform movements. The successful ones regularly made use of legal and institutional aids to press their claims, electing to high office those who could call the Church to its originating evangelical values.

Medieval Christendom was an uneven ballet among the institutions of empire, priesthood, and academy (*imperium, sacerdotium,* and *studium*). When they moved as partners, there was cultural uniformity, graceful steps which won admiration and participation from all alike. Even while they bickered, limping and staggering, the dancers refused to choose other participants, counting upon their genuinely singular culture to sustain the meaning of their ungainly slips of intelligence, conscience, and power.

During the period when rising technological advantages, burgeoning agricultural plenty, and architectural or sculptural creativity expanded the medieval world, challenges to its cultural unity emerged both without and within. In 1453, the city of Constantinople fell into the hands of the Moslems and the Byzantine Empire died. In the early sixteenth century, Martin Luther's (1483–1546) call for reform of the Church may have echoed earlier voices; but his refusal to allow civil sovereignty over evangelical piety ended the unity of religion and society. Christendom was dead.

The development of Catholic Christianity during these four hundred years is a fascinating story. Uniformity to the culture of Rome predominated as both an ideal and energetic program; yet there remained within the traditional institutions windows to the Church's prophets and visionaries. There was in fact no top-heavy superstructure of boring scholastics and inquisitorial priests, but a genuinely creative tension of architectural forces which vaulted the medieval world into the Christian future.

EMPIRE, CHURCH AND ACADEMY—THE IDEAL OF CULTURAL UNIFORMITY

Attempts to preserve the tradition of the Gospel regularly assumed the form of a promotion and defense of the papacy during the High Middle Ages. The episcopacy of Rome rapidly became the feudal keystone in a hierarchically stratified organization. Just as the differing ministries of priest, reader, cantor, and deacon had collapsed into the single role of priest-celebrant at Eucharistic worship because of scarce liturgical books, so the pope came to be seen as the highest authority within the community, including in his person all the subsidiary ranks of the clergy and laity.

Sacerdotium: The Church as Public Authority

Gregory VII (1073–85) began his reforms of the Church with the Lenten Synods at Rome (1074–75). Noncelibate clerics were forbidden to exercise ecclesiastical roles; laymen and women were encouraged to shun them. Simony, the civil sale and acceptance of religious office, was prohibited. Gregory was unbending: "The Lord did not say, 'I am tradition,' but 'I am truth.'"[1]

Freedom for the Church meant for Gregory separation of ecclesial office from civil entanglements. To free the Church required the extrication of his own power from societal encroachments. A document found among Gregory's letters illustrates this well: "The pope can be judged by no one; the Roman Church has never erred and never will err till the end of time; the pope alone can depose and restore bishops; . . . he alone can revise his own judgments; . . . he can depose emperors; . . . all princes should kiss his feet; . . . a duly ordained pope is undoubtedly made a saint by the merits of St. Peter."[2]

Many of these extravagant claims have their origin in the forged *Donation of Constantine* (see chap. 5); nonetheless they announce an extraordinary proposal for the supreme power of the papal office. Gregory's prohibition of civil nomination for, and investiture in, ecclesiastical office stemmed from his assurance of his own religious dominance. The kingdom of Christ superseded all others.

This claimed and largely achieved primacy of the "Petrine" authority always remains ambiguous in Catholic history. Contemporaries often experienced medieval popes as a voice of religious authority, however much they spoke in the tones of political force. For us, it is easy to lose perspective since we are accustomed to forms of Christianity other than Catholicism. Moreover, attracted to the more humane papal role of recent years, we find the prestige and imperial authority of the medieval popes unpleasant at best, unevangelical at worst.

Gregory could see no way to establish the autonomy of the Gospel without the political legitimacy of episcopal and papal authority. In essence, the vast religious community of medieval Europe practically justified many of his policies. By supporting the establishment of a caste in the celibate clerical bureaucracy, he provided an ecclesial work force divorced in principle from civil control. At its best it could challenge the world's leaders and peoples without indebtedness for food, clothing, or salary; at its worst it merely set up an alternate secular mode, complacent in its own ecclesiastical luxuries.

Imperium: The State as Religious Force—
The Crusades and the Inquisitions

The almost incredible mixture of power and Gospel in Gregory, and in the even more famous Innocent III (1198–1216), is obvious to us in both the Crusades against Islam and the Inquisitions against heretics and Jews in the Western Church. The Crusades were nine "holy" wars, stretching from the eleventh through the thirteenth centuries, meant to liberate Palestine and its inhabitants from Islamic overlordship and cultural domination. They were the attempt to impose Western cultural supremacy upon the Eastern Church, Empire, and nonbelieving lands. Their combination of venality and grace, of Gospel and military power, promoted papal authority and served neither Church nor state very well.

If the Crusades were the Church's "external arm" to achieve cultural uniformity, the Inquisitions (lasting from the twelfth through the fifteenth centuries) were its arm to corral the inner cultural and religious dissidents. Any doctrine that did not cohere with the orthodox tradition was proscribed. This included the beliefs of Jews and Moslems as well as heretical Christian doctrines. Confiscation of property, imprisonment, branding, banishment, and even the death penalty were used to ensure compliance. It is said that under Tomás de Torquemada (1420–98), Grand Inquisitor for Isabella of Castile (1451–1504) and Ferdinand of Aragon (1452–1516), some twenty thousand Jews, Moslems, and heterodox Christians were burned by the state.

These sinful horrors of the medieval spirit, however, were not a function of faith, but an excess of devotion to a single cultural ideal. No contemporary Catholic would defend the papal ascendancy, crusading conquests, or inquisitorial strategies against all non-Western, non-Romanized believers. To understand in this case is not to absolve; responsibility for brutality cannot be erased by locating procedures inside historical eventualities. The coercive use of force lodges as a dangerous memory of human suffering which cannot be forgotten except at the price of further inhumanity. Like a chastened individual, the Catholic Tradition must repay the faults of sinners in its past by championing justice for the oppressed in its present.

The High Middle Ages believed that there could be only one civil culture with one religious force, just as a body could contain only a single animating soul. What had been bequeathed by the early Middle Ages as a vibrant prophetic attempt to enliven culture by faith grew into an unwieldly adolescent of uncertain parentage and an adult of fierce, unholy demeanor. It was a religious internationalism which could embody itself solely through a uniform religious and civil practice.

Studium: The Academy as Theologian

An intellectual development made possible by Christendom remains a vital force in contemporary Catholic life—academic theology and the university. The theoretic and systematic achievements of medieval canon lawyers and theologians provided an extraordinary intellectual support for, as well as criticism of, the public institution. In thinkers such as Thomas Aquinas (about 1225–74), Bonaventure (about 1217–74), Roger Bacon (1212–94), and Raymond Lull (1235–1316), as well as in lesser known men and women, intellectual classics transcended the doctrines of the age.

Conflicting Legal Interpretations

Ivo of Chartres (about 1040–1115) systematized the multiple collections of law that accumulated from the fifth through ninth centuries. Following him, Gratian (+1159), in his *Concordance of Discordant Canons,* provided a collection which until 1917 was the basis of all Catholic legislation. Gratian's style of reasoning combined a question, texts, and arguments for and against an answer and then reconciliation of disagreements. This scholarly comprehensive moderation established the shape of medieval scholastic thought.

Conflicting Biblical Interpretations

What the lawyers first accomplished appeared rapidly as a theological development. Just as the reflections on the earliest traditions had originated in the biblical images and stories, and doctrines had emerged to maintain the legitimate outlines of belief in a new culture, there was now a need to clarify just how these various understandings could be ordered.

Accurate readings of the biblical texts and consistent commentary were provided through the School of Laon (about 1100), when Anselm, Ralph, and Gilbert the Universal completed *The Ordinary Gloss (Glossa Ordinaria)* as a basic textbook for the monastic and cathedral schools. Stephen Langton (+1228) divided the books of the Bible into chapters and verses, a practice which made reference considerably simpler. His work, with small modification, is still in use.

The Thrust Toward System: Scholasticism

While the basic materials were being solidified, theologians, first in northern France, then in Paris and Chartres, attempted to order the Christian message into a system. In this they were dependent upon philosophic tools made available to them through the intellectual labors of Ibn-Sina (Avicenna, 980–1037), who combined Aristotelian and Platonic theories of knowledge in a religious context, and Ibn-Rushd (Averroes, 1126–98), whose creative commentaries upon the texts of Aristotle earned him the title "The Commentator." Western theologians had before them the examples of Origen (185–254), who used Middle Platonic thought to arrange Christian questions into a whole, and the descriptions of Pseudo-Dionysius (about 500), whose cosmological mysticism painted a symbolic picture of the universe.

The "masters of the sacred page" and their expositions of Scripture were thus succeeded by the theologians. Hugh of St. Victor in Paris (1096–1141) set for himself the goal of rewriting Augustine's whole project for the Middle Ages. Anselm of Canterbury (about 1033–1109), however, is the acknowledged father of Scholasticism. His philosophical argument for the existence of God still teases thinkers. God is that than which nothing greater can be thought. But to exist in reality is greater than to exist merely in thought. Therefore God must exist.

Such ingenuity encompassed the entire range of theological issues but especially those of salvation itself. Why *did* God become a human being? At the same time that he was extricating the Church from the power of his king, Anselm did not think it blasphemous to ask questions of God's Word and to construct intelligent answers.

He clearly believed that since God gave us both reason and faith, the two could not ultimately be in conflict. Life was a matter of "faith seeking understanding" (*fides quaerens intellectum*), a definition of theology as a discipline which has never been superseded.

The School of Chartres turned to questions of physics, culture, and religion. Could the literal meaning of the Bible be coherent with the physics available in Plato's accounts of the origins of the world (an earlier version of the creationism-evolution debates)? If natural causes will explain an event, must we appeal to God as cause?

Conservative Reaction

Such questions frightened some believers. For rather than supporting some extrinsically derived thought-system, these theologians marched around the edges of the empire of faith. Not all Christians wished to go further than the well-traveled pilgrimage routes; they preferred to have their ordinary sacramental companions and local authoritative assurances. This problem may be seen in a preeminent controversy between Peter Abelard (1079–1142) and Bernard of Clairvaux (1090–1153). Bernard speaks first: "[Abelard] points his mouth to the heavens and looks into the depths of God; looking back, he returns ineffable words not permitted a man to speak. Moreover, he has provided a reason for everything, even those things which are above reason, even against reason and against faith. . . . What could be more against faith than to refuse to believe whatever one is not able to attain by reason?"[3]

Monastic theology emphasized the experience of faith, not its rational interpretation. Its primary daily task was "divine reading" (*lectio divina*), which permitted assimilation of the biblical and theological tradition in a personal and communitarian fashion. Bernard himself thought the object of *theologia* (the logic of God) was to know Christ crucified; one could not achieve that knowledge without prayer and a considerable degree of humility. As a result of this theological process, we learn to love ourselves as God loves us. Rupert of Deutz (about 1075–1129) confirmed this in a sharp formulation: "Whatever can be thought up apart from sacred scripture or fabricated out of argumentation is unreasonable; and therefore pertains in no way to the praise or the acknowledgement of the omnipotence of God."[4]

Abelard, a brilliant and passionate teacher, developed a theological method which occasioned this abuse. Indeed he is the first thinker to use the word "theology" in its contemporary sense as rational thought about the Divine; before him, it had included prayer, sacraments, hymns—all religious expressions. In his *Sic et Non* (1121–22) he set an intellectual standard against which all later thinkers were required to measure themselves. Setting standards does not make a thinker popular—particularly when that thinker is as embroiled in moral and religious controversy as Abelard was. (We need only recall the story of his love for Heloise [1101–64] to be reminded of such arguments.)

The text of *Sic et Non* takes 158 questions left unanswered by the authorities and marshals the opposing viewpoints under them. In his introduction Abelard offers general rules for deciding which authority to follow, paralleling those of the canonists. The major conflict with opponents like Bernard is that he did not choose to resolve serious questions in a pious way. He let them simply stand. The authorities who conflicted were the traditional fathers of the community. Thus contemporary minds were setting themselves up as judges over their traditional past. For Bernard this was utter arrogance.

Aristotle's Assistance

Human pride in this case was leavened by the successive entries of the philosopher Aristotle into Western European thought. For before the twelfth century, there was only a meager amount of the thinker's works available: the *Categories* and *On Interpretation,* generally called the Grammar or Old Logic. But between 1140–60 Aristotle's *Sophistical Refutations* and the *Prior* and *Posterior Analytics* were translated, known as the New Logic or Dialectics. The majority of Aristotle's works, all those of strictly philosophical rather than simply logical interest (physics, psychology, metaphysics, ethics, and politics) were not translated until 1240–50.

Aristotle's analyses created a vast sea-change in religious circles. Thinking Christianity through Aristotle resulted in a more terrestrial, empirical, and scientific approach to God and God's dealings with human beings. What Bernard thought of Abelard can be encapsulated under those three adjectives: his theology was not sufficiently heaven-directed, spiritual, or homiletic. It could not be Christian. It was dependent on the first and second entries of Aristotle.

The inclusion of Aristotle's thought as a way of seeing the world thoroughly and scientifically with religious faith took some time. It was only as Catholics began to see religious benefits from it that such endeavors became more than merely suspect.

Teacher and Textbook

Peter the Lombard (+1159) helped in that process. For what Abelard left unanswered, Peter resolved. As a result his *Liber Sententiarum* (*Book of Sentences*, i.e., opinions) became a standard lecturing textbook for theologians well into the seventeenth century. He ordered all Christian questions around four basic topics: God; creation and the history of the world before Christ; the incarnation and redemption in Christ; and the sacraments and eschatology. Under those headings, he posed the various questions which were current, outlined the authorities for and against, and made a judgment about which were valid.

Like all textbooks, it had a common-sense approach; and common sense, while resolving many difficulties in our ordinary religious world, regularly leaves some assumptions unexamined. Yet its lucid organization, clear exposition, and ready answers made it a landmark in scholastic method. The question itself had become a tool of theological research; its resolutions depended upon the understanding of Christ and the cultural, intellectual embodiment attained by the thinker.

Thomas Aquinas

Although there were other scholastics during the "Golden Age" of the thirteenth century, none is the peer of Thomas Aquinas (about 1225–74). In the battle of authorities, Aquinas commented: "If the master determines the question by an appeal to authorities only, the student will be convinced that the thing is so; but he will have acquired no knowledge or understanding and will go away with an empty head."[5] Aquinas was on the side of "faith seeking understanding" through whatever scientific tools were available.

Aquinas noticed first that the objects of religion (God and the world in God) have a certain oddity about them. They are present, but not available to us in exactly the same way as other physical things. To provide a language for understanding them, we need a *meta*-physical language, a body of terms and relations which will help us distinguish the location of religion among other realities in our world. He found that theoretic set of terms in Aristotle's metaphysics. To understand the other pole of the gracious act of God's love, humanity, Aquinas reinterpreted Aristotle's rational psychological texts so that he could unravel the knowing process itself.

Religion was different from philosophy. Where the principles of reality presented themselves to philosophy after sometimes difficult thought, in Christianity the principles (namely God as Triune) revealed themselves. Theology for Aquinas was first of all God's own knowledge of himself. God alone knows who he truly is; for creatures to become aware of him, God must disclose himself to us. All knowledge about God, whether faith, theology (as the understanding of faith), or final union with God, is dependent upon the one Teacher. Theology is thus not geometry, whose principles can be discovered by reason itself.

If the science of faith becomes a habit or second nature to us, then we can depend upon our own intellect for some reasonable explication of religious faith. But even thought itself is affected by pride, so we require the assistance of the Holy Spirit to achieve true wisdom. Theology is not merely a speculative discipline. It includes both thought and action. Theology is directed toward the good and the beautiful as well as to what is true.

With this understanding of reason and faith, Aquinas wrote his *Summaries (Summae)* of theology. Now summary could be a misleading term, since what Aquinas prepared was a reasoned, systematic expression of the understanding that a scientifically trained individual might reach. Where Hugh of St. Victor might use symbolic language or Peter Abelard might simply set up oppositions to tease the mind, Aquinas marshaled all his forces. He knew the intellectual terrain, had clarified and distinguished the different types of personnel and material available, and pondered the tactics which would accomplish the goal. His *Summa* is rather like a strategic map of the Christian religious world. Those who wish to find their way a little can follow his lead; those who will complete the campaign must duplicate in their own experience of faith the relationships envisioned. It is a masterful achievement. All things come from the Triune God as origin and all things return to that God. The image of

God which was lost through sin after creation is regained as a likeness to God, a share in his divinity through the one Way: Christ.

A mind critical of the intellectual aspects of life might be tempted to think that nothing so scientific could really remain religious. Yet Aquinas not only thought, he also prayed, preached, and composed religious poetry. He was so profoundly moved by what was at stake in the Christian experience that he joined the new order of mendicant (begging) preachers formed by Dominic (1170–1221). He did not hesitate to reject his family's wealth and position in order to obey the Christian Gospel's command for simplicity and poverty. But at the same time he dared to employ in his own faith the pagan, worldly thinker Aristotle.

Universities as Religious Criticism

This was a world of university theology, an academic lever of criticism raised in support of, but sometimes against, the political and ecclesiastical institutions. The survivors of the old cathedral and monastic schools had banded together, drawn up constitutions, and obtained important exemptions which guaranteed the student body personal safety, administrative autonomy, exemption from taxation, and the right to confer teaching licenses.

From the late twelfth century, Paris developed a *universitas magistrorum* (university of teachers) which was given statutes by Pope Innocent III in 1215, primarily centered upon the faculties of theology, law, medicine, and the liberal arts. Chartered schools appeared all over Europe: Bologna (twelfth century), Toulouse (1229), Rome (1244), Naples (1224), and Salamanca (1243). But Paris remained the most famous for philosophy and theology; it numbered among its teachers Thomas Aquinas, Bonaventure, William of Auxerre (+1231), and a Latin Averroist named Siger of Brabant (about 1240–84). By the year 1300 there was an estimated student population in Paris of thirty thousand.

With scholastic thought, Christians had come of intellectual age. They had learned to live in the house of religion and understand its structure scientifically without trying to pretend that the mystery of God's grace in Christ would ever be exhaustively explained. With Scholasticism Catholics no longer felt compelled to choose between faith and reason. They discovered a way to distinguish these two central dimensions of their lives in order to reunite them in a single edifice of wisdom founded upon the Gospel.

Places of Prayer

Diversity collaborated to produce unity in high Gothic art as well. In 1231, at the same time that Alexander of Hales (+1245), a Franciscan scholastic of considerable merit, began the earliest *Summa,* the architect Pierre de Montreuil (about 1200–1266) conceived the new nave of the Church of St. Denis outside Paris. Just as Aquinas's *Summa Theologiae* hoped to include within its interpretation all elements of Christian experience and understanding, distinguishing, balancing, supporting, and eliminating the fruitless consequence, so the Gothic cathedral aimed at a totality. Chartres, dedicated in 1260, enshrined on its facade a sculptural program encompassing all time and space emanating from the dawn of the triumphal Christ. The plastic light from the brilliant windows wrapped the believer in an entire range of colors and shapes, tracing all the major themes of the Bible.

In the Middle Ages spirit met flesh in a most uncompromisingly ordinary fashion. For the shrines of medieval Christendom with their glowing jewels for windows and biblical inspiration housed a motley populace who arrived on pilgrimage to heaven. Perhaps nowhere for the English-speaking reader is this more evident than in Geoffrey Chaucer's (about 1343–1400) *Canterbury Tales.* For what Chartres was to French Christians and Campostella to Spaniards, Canterbury's shrine to the royal martyr Thomas à Becket (about 1118–70) was to English pilgrims.

Though unfinished, Chaucer's *Canterbury Tales* reflects that sophisticated knowledge of human beings which can combine compassion for weakness with irony over ideals unfulfilled, intelligent criticism of the goals of society with an intricate understanding of their interpersonal complexities. His pilgrims are monks who love hunting, prioresses who combine prayer and aristocratic manners, dignified merchants and not-so-stately or aristocratic cooks, millers, pardoners, and estate managers. The whole tapestry of medieval life is woven into his poetry; the figures are sprightly, the background filled with thousands of flowers.

But the keystone of medieval society was religion. So Chaucer, quite capable of attacking ecclesiastical abuse, described an ideal parish priest as rich in thought and work, patient, diligent, and devout. Instead of receiving tithes, he gave from his own substance to his parishioners. He did not think twice about criticizing the rich or powerful. As Chaucer says:

> But Christes lore, and his apostles twelve,
> He taught, and first he followed it himself.[6]

Chaucer knew both ideal and real; his art reflected reality, challenged it, and awakened the world to its own best possibilities.

The experience of turning the Tradition of Catholicism into a solid building to house the diversity of Christian prayer founded upon the Gospel was the project of medieval Christendom. The papacy, scholasticism, and civil government collaborated (in their best moments) to provide a unified Tradition of prayer, thought, and action which would incarnate again the event of Christ. Their achievements contained difficulties and limitations exploited later. But the vision and its not inconsiderable accomplishment in classics like Gregory, Aquinas, or Chartres should teach us something very important about the fierce conviction of Catholicism that the Tradition of symbols, sacraments, doctrines, institutional office, and intellectual endeavor can authentically disclose the Gospel of Jesus.

PROPHETS AND VISIONARIES:
BEGGARS AND PREACHERS

The counterpoint to the institutional Tradition in the Middle Ages is to be found in the rise of the mendicant or begging orders like the Franciscans and Dominicans. Men like Francis of Assisi (about 1132–1226), his more intellectual followers like Bonaventure (1221–74) or Dominic (1170–1221), and Robert of Molesme (about 1027–1111), who founded a strictly contemplative community, spoke for the edges of human experience, whether it was through their dedication to poverty, prayerful silence, or preaching to the remaining unchurched barbarians.

These communities of reform, though they seem marginal to us now, were each called to embody the radical demands of the Gospel. Indeed it is the very marginality of monastic life that Thomas Merton

(1915–68), a Trappist monk in Kentucky, saw as important to society. He spoke of the monk as one who stands on the edge between words and silence, between sociocultural construction and the evangelical values which must inform them, between action and contemplation. Such men and women are never escape artists, or bystanders; rather they always alert the Catholic Church to its common call to holiness.

Such prophets were paralleled by men and women like Joachim of Flora (1135–1202) or the author of *Piers Plowman* (about mid-fourteenth century) who through a steady application of the ideals of Scripture to their contemporary life startled the late medieval world from complacency. Seized by the pain of the shifting cultures of their day, they prompted traditions of thought which were revolutionary and radical.

THE DECLINE OF CHRISTENDOM AND
VISIONS OF UNITY

The Great Western Schism (1378–1417) occurred in the Catholic Church when French cardinals, having returned to Rome after residence in Avignon for many years (1309–77), elected an opposition candidate for pope (Clement VII, 1378–94). National feelings controlled the conflicts for almost forty years, with first one, then another pope claiming ascendancy. Some Christians knew a world in which there were always two, even three, popes. Some dioceses had two or three claimants for office. The luxury of the Avignonese papacy ceded to a dreadful collapse of Christian unity. There was a growing split between national consciousness and religious loyalty. Allegiance by baptism to the local Church was not necessarily support of the local or imperial prince; and political fealty might require opposition to the religious pretensions of a papal lord.

If, however, much of this controversy seems too refined in its enthusiasm to catch our interest, too complex in its loyalties to help us understand the Gospel, Dante's *Divine Comedy* does not. Dante Alighieri (1265–1321) described Christian life as a pilgrimage through three worlds: Hell, Purgatory, and Paradise. He was prophetic in his ability to incarnate Christian experience in the poetic language of his own people; he was traditional not only in founding a tradition of poetry and language, but in embodying the philosophical tradition of Scholasticism; he was apocalyptic in that he knew that only criticism of the present could afford glimpses of the future world that God offers.

Decline and vision marked the end of Christendom. The unanswered questions of the High Middle Ages, the relationship of civil and religious power, and, even more fundamentally, the nature of Christian salvation seethed at the surface, boiling over into the passions of the Reformation.

By the end of the Middle Ages these issues polarized the situation. Either faith or reason, religion or Scholasticism; either our works or God's grace, merit or redemption; either the literal meaning of Scripture or allegory, fact or fiction; either popular sovereignty in aid of the rising national states or the authority of an international prince, whether emperor or pope.

Decade by decade, the traditional bridges which had integrated each pole into a common vision of society, Church, and God's love were disintegrating. It was as though a river which Christians knew over generations had changed its shoreline, and only gradually did everyone realize that the old bridges would no longer transport people where they wanted to go. The classic roads remained; but the language of a *Summa,* a Gothic cathedral, even a *Divine Comedy* seemed antiquated, rather unsafe, misplaced since the banks of the river had changed. Where was the bridge-building expert in this crisis of Christendom?

NOTES

1. Quoted in Francis Oakley, *The Medieval Experience: Foundations of Western Cultural Singularity* (New York: Charles Scribner's Sons, 1974), 34.

2. Gregorii VII Registrum, *Monumenta Germaniae Historiae,* Epistolae Selectae, ii, ed. E. Casper, pp. 201–8 as cited in R. W. Southern, *Western Society and the Church in the Middle Ages* (Baltimore: Penguin Books, 1972), 102.

3. Letter to Pope Innocent, No. CXC in *Works of St. Bernard,* ed. Jean LeClerq and H. Rochais (Rome: Cistercian Editions, 1977), 8:17–18.

4. *De Omnipotentia Dei,* chap. 27; *Patrologia Latina,* ed. J. P. Migne (Paris, 1854), CLXX, col. 478.

5. *Quodlibetal Questions* IV, question IX, article XVIII.

6. General Prologue, Geoffrey Chaucer, *Canterbury Tales*, 2:528–530 in *The Works of Geoffrey Chaucer,* ed. F. N. Robinson (Boston: Houghton Mifflin, 1961), 22.

FURTHER RELATED MATERIAL

Much has been written on medieval universities, theologians, and politics. A delightful introduction to university theology is Helen Waddell's *The Wandering Scholars* (Garden City, N.Y.: Doubleday & Co., 1961). An important series of essays, though difficult, is M-D. Chenu, *Man, Nature and Society in the Twelfth Century* (Chicago: University of Chicago Press, 1967). David Knowles's *The Evolution of Medieval Thought* (New York: Vintage, 1962) almost bristles too much with names, places, and ideas while Étienne Gilson's classic *History of Christian Philosophy in the Middle Ages* (New York: Random House, 1955) can occupy the very serious student of the period. James Weisheipl's biography of Thomas Aquinas, *Friar Thomas d'Aquino: His Life, Thought and Works* (New York: Harper & Row, 1974), is excellent along with the classic M-D. Chenu, *Toward Understanding St. Thomas* (Chicago: Regnery, 1964).

7

THE CRIES FOR
REFORM AND THE RISE OF
RELIGIOUS SUBJECTIVITY (1400–1622)

> Why are the times so dark,
> Such that no man knows another?
> For governments meander, as we see,
> From bad to worse without recourse.
> Times past seemed so much better.
> Who reigns? Sadness and annoyance!
> Neither Justice nor Law walk the streets.
> I do not know where I stand.
>> Eustache Deschamps (1346–1406)[1]

After a lengthy debate with his conscience, Martin Luther (1483–1546) knew where he stood—captive to the Word of God. "I cannot and I will not recant anything, for to go against conscience is neither right nor safe. God help me. Amen. Here I stand. I cannot do otherwise." Thus sharply is Luther's speech reported before the Catholic Emperor Charles V (1500–1588) and his electors at the Diet of Worms (1521). The wandering Church and society of the fourteenth century, tortured by wars, political hatred, and lack of confidence in its own confessions, had coalesced through a new energy. But there was an enormous ransom paid for this new direction—nothing less than the division of Western Christendom.

No single origin can be named. The events issued from knotted ropes of sincere religious motivations, civil opportunism, and cultural determining factors far beyond the participants themselves. The quiet reasoners and prudent administrators who could conduct the choruses of prophets or visionaries against the solo voices of Tradition were not heard. At the conclusion of the sixteenth century the oratorio of medieval Christendom had grown discordant.

Required by custom to fight their battles as a secular state, popes, cardinals, and bishops financed their political causes through the religious "goods" available to them. Bishoprics and indulgences were sold to the highest bidder. Simultaneously, a rising nationalism among the emergent states of Europe harnessed religious reform movements and drove them to their own ends. A Church less closely connected with Rome meant a Church more subject to local civil control. Nor was it easy for rulers in need of money for consolidation of power to ignore the extensive economic holdings of the Church, especially those of the monasteries.

Yet the religious impulse for reform was dominant, if not always heeded. Jan Hus (about 1372–1415) remarked: "I desired in preaching to obey only God rather than the pope or the archbishop and the rest of the satraps opposing the word of Christ."[2] Hus's combination of anger and religious zeal won him a heretic's death at the Council of Constance (1414–17).

The passions produced by the visible corruption of the traditional instruments of spirituality cannot be easily measured. The ideals announced by the sacramental spectacles of the Church were separated from ordinary Christian lives. The visionary Joachim of Flora (about 1132–1202) believed that in the age to come, the primary participants would be monks and friars—not married men and women. Religion had become something to watch from afar—rather than a prayerful event common to baptized participants. Its application to the lives of believers focused upon the historical past of Jesus' life, rather than upon contemporary ecclesial achievement.

Yet by the end of the sixteenth century, Christianity had finally reformed itself into two competing branches: Protestant and Catholic. Only with the discussions for reunion in our own time (the ecumenical movement) have the two arms of Western Christianity viewed the turmoil of these years with less distorted vision. Though faithful to their own traditions, Catholic and Protestant historians of this century, humbled by the knowledge that angry arguments have only contributed to a belittled Christian Gospel, now read and write with historical rigor and ecumenical compassion.

The modern meaning of Catholicism cannot be understood without reference to the questions, concerns, and passions of Protestant reformers. The reformulation of the Catholic Church after the division of Christendom, although coherent and consistent with its previous Tradition, has been affected by the sometimes peaceful, sometimes violent conversations with its familial relations.

THE NEED FOR REFORM

Reform is a critical principle in human affairs—a negative reaction to what speciously passes for truth, justice, or love. The popular fervor of the late Middle Ages was a passion for the sensible, whether sacred or profane. Some relatively brief, largely benign examples may show what we mean.[3]

Peter of Luxembourg (1369–87) cultivated hardship. He wanted to preach the Gospel; his parents opposed it, so he became an eccentric ascetic instead. As William James was to say of a later figure: "In this poor man, we have morbid melancholy and fear, and the sacrifices made are to purge out sin and to buy safety."[4] Unwashed, sickly, covered with lice, Peter copied his sins in small notebooks. At his death, an entire chest of small scraps (kept for his confessor) was found. A bishop at fifteen, then a cardinal, Peter's case for canonization was assured at death—since all the lords of France testified to his sanctity *and* to his devotion to the French pope in the Great Western Schism. His holiness was witnessed concretely—by his healing of tournament wounds, the resurrection of a steward struck by a thunderbolt, and the salvation of the Duchess of Bourbon from two weeks of labor pains.

This example of the "underwitted saint" (as James might have called him) should be paralleled by the chronicler's description of the Great Entrance of Louis XI (1423–83) at the time of his coronation (1461). The historian speaks of "three very handsome girls, representing quite naked sirens, and one saw their beautiful, turgid, separate, round, and hard breasts, which was a very pleasant sight, and they recited little motets and bergerettes." Such nude spectacles were not uncommon during the entire century.

The late Middle Ages needed visible evidence of the meaningfulness of life. Sacramental piety focused on a growing devotion to the presence of Christ in the Eucharistic Supper. Although the Feast of Corpus Christi (the Body of Christ) had been ordered part of the universal religious calendar by 1264, it was the fourteenth century that tells us about the Sacrament reserved in the hand of a silver statue of the Virgin Mary, placed above the high altar.[5]

Nor was this grasping for the concrete Divine limited to the visual. Medieval preaching required the startling sensible example to ensure effectiveness. The Archpriest of Talavera, Alfonso Martinez de Toledo (1398–1466/70) details human avarice and lust through copious earthy stories.

> I knew one such whose house was always full of this nonsense, an old hag of seventy. I saw her hanged from the balcony of a man she had murdered by applying poison to his armpits; and they also hanged her by the neck at the door of a matron that she had killed, and burned her later for a witch at Caned, outside the city; nor was she saved by the great favor she enjoyed with many gentlemen.[6]

There was a constant need to reify the religious impulse.

Perhaps it is this somewhat fleshy sedimentation that accounts for the uncompromising venality of so many Renaissance and early Reformation popes. One cannot but be scandalized by the paradox of religious sentiment, artistic splendor, and vulgar opportunism. In the nepotism of Innocent VIII (1484–92) for his illegitimate family, the bribed election and open concubinage of Alexander VI (1492–1503), Julius II's (1503–13) military programs, and the cultured laxism of Leo X (1513–21), we see the squandering of centralized papal power on debauchery and personal ambition. Their lethargy, avarice, and politically self-serving prudence, though sometimes exaggerated by Reformers' polemics, did not rise above the same vices in their secular contemporaries. Hilaire Belloc (1870–1953), that most Catholic historian, remarks that because they had not returned to their evangelical origins, the external organizers of the Church had failed to "capture the spiritual discontent and to satisfy the spiritual hunger of which these errors were the manifestation."[7]

THE CENTERS OF OPPOSITION

Three movements contributed to the critique of religious arrogance and corruption: *conciliarism* in ecclesiastical polity; *nominalism and Ockhamism* in academic thought; and *humanist scholarship* in religious piety. Each was a profoundly dialectical move within Catholic experience; each suspected the reigning common sense of having tipped the incarnational balance of the Gospel on the side of secularizing leaden weights. Although we can only briefly indicate the issues raised by each complex development, we must do so to set the stage for Luther's dramatic entrance.

Conciliarism—The Pride of the Papacy

Conciliarism wished to vest the ultimate authority of ecclesial life in a general council. Its theory began simultaneously with the rise of papal power but grew in cogency during the Great Western Schism. Because the Council of Constance (1414–17) was largely successful in its attempts to end the Schism, the fathers decreed reforms which entailed periodic general councils to settle ecclesiastical affairs. But these largely died in the later administration of reforms which were to be settled through rather weak concordats between the papacy and national groupings. In 1460 Pius II (1458–64) prohibited all appeals from papal decisions to general councils.

Ockhamism—The Arrogance of the Academy

If conciliarism was a plea for decentralization of authoritarian rule in the Church and release from supranational taxation, nominalism was a critique directed at the arrogance of reason in matters of faith. William of Ockham (1285–1347), though perhaps not strictly a nominalist himself, emphasized that our knowledge can be only of the singulars in the empirical world. Thus without divine revelation we would never know any intrinsic connection between the world and God. Ockham's anger was directed against all those intermediaries who pretended to assume responsibility and knowledge of the divine plan. His philosophical, or perhaps better said, logical, positions were meant to preserve the sovereignty of God's free action from any limitations imposed upon that absolute power by overweening Scholasticism and politics.

Humanism—The Hubris of Religious Abstraction

Medieval piety stressed the accumulation of ascetical merit and passive participation in sacramental spectacles. It was criticized by those who emphasized mystical religious experience, by those who sought a "modern piety" (*devotio moderna*), and by historical and biblical scholars.

Luther's personal anxiety for salvation appeared within a Tradition of mystics who, like Meister Eckhart (1260–1327), presented religion in a deeply affecting German. For Eckhart, to live as God does meant to be utterly selfless, without possession, separated from the idols we have of self, world, and God. Along with John Tauler (about 1300–1361), Henry Suso, (about 1295–1366), and others, Eckhart preached a return to interiorized religious development.

This homiletic invitation was encouraged further by a movement of lay-centered piety founded by Gerhard Groote (1340–84). The Brethren of the Common Life, living a quasi-monastic communitarian life in Deventer, The Netherlands, were never meant to be clerics. They were contemplatives who continued their ordinary vocations, only later establishing schools where a general education was offered without fee. Numerous reformers such as Pope Hadrian VI (1522–23), Gabriel Biel (about 1420–95), and Nicholas of Cusa (1401–64) came through their doors. But perhaps the brother with the longest popular history was Thomas à Kempis (1380–1471), whose small work, *The Imitation of Christ,* has taught Catholics for centuries how to seek perfection by putting on Christ as a model of life.

It is from these religious circles that there emerged humanist scholarship such as that of the eternally intriguing thinker Desiderius Erasmus (about 1469–1536). A truly international scholar, he taught in Paris, Louvain, and finally housed himself in Basel with the printer Froben (about 1460–1527). Through this printing house, Erasmus provided the Western Church with its first critical edition of the Greek New Testament (1516). Prior to this the Church had been dependent upon Jerome's (about 342–420) Latin edition (the *Vulgate*). Only by returning to the authentic sources of Catholic Christianity could the Church reform itself properly. When at Thomas More's (1478–1535) home in England, Erasmus wrote *In Praise of Folly* (1509), a sharp diatribe against civil and ecclesiastical abuse. But despite his constant arguments against pious confusions, religious lukewarmness, and institutional stupidity, Erasmus could not envision a separated Church as a Gospel value.

The criticisms of the Church from within its ranks should have provided the ferment for a revitalization of the community. Although there were many figures like John Gerson (1363–1429), doctor of theology, chancellor of the University of Paris and untiring champion of reform, others possessed a fundamental failure of vision. The divisive reform of the early sixteenth century was an inability to reenvision the world after all the criticisms (conciliarism, nominalism, humanism). No one seemed capable of seeing how the prophetic, visionary, *and* traditional moments of Catholic life could be encompassed within a single polity.

No one really wanted the somewhat elderly gentleman whose irascibility, incorrigible behavior, and inflexible character made him seem incapable of recovering his religious youth. Many no longer believed that he could remain a member of the family as it met new crises, faced new problems, and learned new skills. With the Catholic partners in earlier fertile dialogue now insulated from one another by anger and political protectionism, there was scant opportunity to forgive the sins of the old Church or welcome anything but the rival siblings of the new.

PROPHETIC QUESTIONS

It is appropriate, but inadequate, to describe the major Protestant Reformers briefly. Since this is the story of Catholicism, we can only barely indicate some of the questions and concerns raised by major figures and leave further explication to others. The danger is oversimplification; but if the questions raised are taken as the fruit of the Reformers' lifelong quests for religious understanding, the desire for civil and ecclesiastical justice, and hope for gradual change dashed, then we will have been mildly successful.

We may take as representative three men: Martin Luther (1483–1546), Ulrich Zwingli (1484–1531), and John Calvin (1509–64). If the first was a religious prophet and the second a rather radical political visionary, the third was a consolidator of the new Tradition.

Martin Luther

Luther's questions emerged from his own acute struggle with the absolute graciousness of God's love over all attempts by human beings to justify themselves. Can anyone merit or earn God's grace? This believer in the monastic experiential Tradition responded with a thundering "No." In his three reforming treatises of 1520 (*To the*

German Princes; On the Babylonian Captivity of the Church; Concerning the Freedom of Christians), he appealed to civil authorities to take ecclesiastical reform into their own hands: to forbid taxation by Rome, to abolish the celibacy of the clergy, to disallow religious orders' exemption from local rule, and to reformulate the internal religious policies of worship and morality. All religious answers must conform to the norm of the gracious Word of God as found in the Scriptures.

Ulrich Zwingli and Thomas Münzer

Ulrich Zwingli carried the reformed position one step further: "There is no vehicle necessary for the Spirit."[8] All concrete manifestations of Christendom (whether sacramental, institutional, ascetical, or artistic) were divorced from the inner life of the believer. If Catholic critics were concerned that Luther's position would favor a personalized private conscience, they knew that Zwingli's preaching was even more dangerous. Pictures were removed, images smashed, Eucharist was limited to a few times a year. But the Zwinglian question still haunted European Reformers: Which mediations of God's grace are authentically Christian? Are *any* to be preferred to the internal witness of the Spirit?

Zwingli's religious radicality was paralleled by his political involvement. He sought independence from papal intervention for Swiss cantons. He is rivaled only by Thomas Münzer (about 1490–1525) in his engagement for civil freedoms. "Don't put up any shallow pretense that God's might will do it without your laying on with the sword."[9] Münzer's armed insurrection to establish a Christian millennial age was stopped when Luther invited the German lords to crush the Peasants' Revolt (1525). The unthinking brutality of powerful institutions begot the power of thoughtless violence.

John Calvin

But Zwingli's and Münzer's underlying problem with the old Christian polity remained. How do we establish a Christian civil government? Is there a public form to Christian love? John Calvin attempted to reconstitute Christendom as a fragment of itself in Geneva. He hoped to revive Christian life by imitating the ancient Church. His *Institutes of the Christian Religion* grew from a small catechism into a grand Protestant *summa* of theological synthesis in which the sovereignty of God's wisdom and love elects some to share in divine glory. Calvin's combination of a helpful ecclesiastical order, sharply defined scriptural exegesis, notionally distinct doctrinal positions, and deep religious conviction made his interpretation of the Reform necessary in a situation in growing need of organization. Calvin carefully, though sometimes ruthlessly, institutionalized the reforming Tradition.

THE REFORM OF TRADITIONAL CATHOLICISM— THE COUNCIL OF TRENT

If the prophets and apocalyptic visionaries had largely separated themselves from the ecclesiastical authority, what did the institution have to say for itself? Traditional Catholicism, prodded by the growing external forces of reform, and pulled, sometimes quite reluctantly, by its own ardently loyal leaders, haltingly reconstituted itself, a fragment of a whole and reestablished an alternate Christendom to Lutheran, Calvinist, and Zwinglian Churches.

As the most clearminded Catholic reformers knew, only a general council could revive the religious dry bones. Yet just as Luther could not ignore the German princes in his quest for religious freedom, so Catholic need for religious reform was not the sole consideration in the calls for and against a general council. Too many kings and petty princes wanted not so much to reform Rome as to embarrass their secular rivals, the Renaissance popes and their changing allies. The popes wanted reform, but only if their civil independence was maintained. Fortunately the council overcame political opposition, and Pope Paul III (1534–49) called for an extraordinary gathering of theologians, bishops, cardinals, and national representatives in December 1545. The Council begun at Trent was to survive eighteen years of intensive, if necessarily sporadic, labor, three major sessions, and five popes.

Its final results were mixed in character, but were without doubt in the reforming Tradition. On the negative side, the Council of Trent did not achieve—in fact, it did not even attempt what had by then probably become an impossibility—reunion with the Protestants. As a result of this failure, many of its decrees and canons were so critical of Reformers' positions that they ensured that the break would be irreparable.

But positively, Trent made impressive gains since Catholic reformers carried the day. There were remarkable men, such as Gasparo Contarini (1483–1542), who worked tirelessly for reunion; Jerome Seripando (1492–1563), general of Luther's former religious community and chief representative of Augustinianism at the council, and Reginald Pole (1500–1558), archbishop of Canterbury, who led the council in its earlier sessions. In the last session, Charles Borromeo (1538–84), of considerable acumen in Scripture, doctrine, and religious education, directed the council's carefully worded, lucid statements on the whole range of Catholic disciplinary and doctrinal questions.

The Council formulated a view of justification by faith that asserted God's prior Word of love before, during, and after our human choice to love God; but it did so in the context of a scripturally based and nuanced understanding of human development and change. We are saved by and in Christ. All subtle attempts to vitiate human responsibility or divine love, whether by negating human choice (Luther) or by exalting it to self-salvation (Pelagius), are rejected.

Simultaneously, practical reforms were issued. Where the Protestant reformers focused on raising the religious literacy of the ordinary Christian, Catholic Tradition leveled its primary broadsides at the disciplinary life of its Church leaders. Seminaries for the education of clerics were to be formed in all major dioceses to ensure that future priests and bishops would be religiously formed, intelligent speakers for Catholicism. Readers in Scripture were appointed, the duties of preachers outlined, the obligation of bishops' residence in their dioceses and their moral and religious competences set forth. Clerical celibacy was upheld, dueling forbidden, and religious orders of men and women reformed. These practical directives eventually issued in the form of a Catechism, a revised Book of Prayer (the Breviary) for clergy and religious, and a Missal and Ritual regulating the sacramental usage of Catholic communities.

Doctrinal decrees on the sacraments, the meaning of the presence of Christ in the Eucharist, Original Sin, marriage and ordination, the authority of the biblical text, and penance were promulgated. In short, there was not a single area of ecclesiastical life that was not touched by the conciliar fathers. They demanded that the theological sources of the Tradition (the Scriptures, earlier doctrinal positions, and medieval Scholasticism without its later accretions) ensure solid but renewed foundations for a reforming community of believers throughout the world. Trent achieved continuity with its past, yet not at the price of repression or separation into fragments.

This stable, uniform culture provided the energy and daring for three extraordinary movements within reforming Catholicism: the rise of activist mystics in Spain; the emergence of the prophetic "armies of God" in the Jesuits, Ursulines, and other local missionaries; and a combination of Church and academy strengthening the revival, indeed, the flowering of Catholicism in the seventeenth and eighteenth centuries.

MYSTICS, MISSIONARIES, AND PERFECT SOCIETIES

What was inaugurated and consolidated by the Council of Trent became much of the substance of the Catholic Church as we have known it prior to Vatican Council II (1962–65). For some 350 years, the art, piety, theology, mysticism, and anti-Protestant polemics of the Catholic Revival marked Christian life. Certainty, caution, and security were the forces at work. It was safer to remain within the fortress of one's Church than to make excursions into theological or religious *terra incognita*. Catholics looked at the splitting seams of the Protestant cloth and huddled triumphantly within the organizational tent of the old renewed Christendom.

Mystics—The Experience of God

In its search for its own origins, the Catholic community focused upon the very religious subjectivity that had animated Luther. In figures like Teresa of Ávila (1515–82) and John of the Cross (1542–91), Catholics maintained that the existential moments of evangelical conversion can and should be found in dialogue with the Tradition. Both figures combined heroic practical sense with shrewd judgment and religious conviction. John's vernacular poetry and theological reflections and Teresa's holy common sense and deep interior life helped form a culture hungering for a language in which to speak of the delicate maneuvers of the spirit in its loving search for God.

Missionaries—The Edges of Ecclesial Life

But the Catholic Revival was meant to convert not the cloistered religious, but the populace. It trained clergy in seminaries, ran schools of religion, gave parochial missions to develop the life of the local community, and established general educational endeavors. Some, especially congregations of women, nursed the sick, founded schools, and performed the charitable and social works left unaccomplished by disbanded or lax monastic communities.

Men and women like Philip Neri (1515–95), Angela de Merici (1474–1540), Francis de Sales (1567–1622), Vincent de Paul (1581–1660), and others cared for pilgrims and convalescents, ministered to galley slaves, founded orphanages, and worked in the local parishes, transforming each particular situation by their charitable, ascetic lives. In their differing ways and cultures, they achieved that personal blend of humanism and Christian grace for which the reforming fathers at Trent had striven. We recognize in Francis de Sales's *Introduction to the Devout Life* not so much austere and grand mystical raptures, but a sure insight into the lives of ordinary men and women. Philip Neri and Vincent de Paul are not fierce and startling prophets, but they remind us that those who dare to become saints need not lose their humanity in the process. When the Revival fostered such domestic virtue, it had succeeded.

But the most notable community of reformers was the Society of Jesus. Ignatius of Loyola (1491/95–1556), its founder, was a military man who, while recuperating from a war wound, experienced a religious conversion. His company of religious soldiers intended to reform the Church internally through education, the frequent use of the sacraments, and missionary preaching. At his death, the Compañia de Jésus extended from Brazil to Japan with over one hundred houses and well over a thousand members. In the chivalrous zeal of Ignatius, Jesuits strove to conquer the world for Christ.

Because their work was always at the edges of ecclesial life, whether in non-European lands (as with Francis Xavier [1506–52] in Sri Lanka, Goa, China, or Japan; with Isaac Jogues [1607–47] among the Hurons and Iroquois of North America, or José de

Anchieta [1553–97] among the Paraguayan Indians) or in polemic disputations with Protestants in Europe, they were always controversial figures. Yet it was not force which succeeded; well-educated teaching and fiery religious preaching were their weapons.

A Perfect Society
One God, One Church, One Culture

If religious fervor was the ultimate origin of the quest for ecclesiastical reform in both its Protestant and Catholic forms, the Catholic community built up its new separated identity through instruments peculiarly its own. By the continued use of Latin in worship, Catholics distinguished their sacred ritual from profane vernacular cultures; nonsacramental devotions, such as the rosary and other private prayers, filled the gap between popular religious instinct and official services. If Protestants would deny the incarnational mediations of Christian faith by an emphasis upon the overpowering graciousness of God, then Catholics would stress the sacramental, ecclesiastical, juridical, hierarchical, and cultural instruments of Divine Presence.

Polemics made Catholic theologians and preachers defensive. Watchdogs of confessional purity, such as the Holy Office (begun 1542) or the Index of Forbidden Books (1557–1966), condemned opinions and made believers cautious. Consolidation of position on the safest territory possible was the plan. Somewhat surprisingly, such strategies produced creative theologies.

In two figures we have a paradigm of this development. Melchior Cano (1509–60), a Spanish Dominican, provided the internal argumentation by which theology was largely known well into this century. Robert Bellarmine (1542–1621) offered a rationale for the structure of the post-Tridentine Church which, with some significant additions, has persisted through the Second Vatican Council.

Cano categorized the various sources of theology (Scripture, Tradition, reason) so that they could be given priority and rank in theological discussion. Appeals to Scripture and Tradition were paramount; then followed the interpretations of the universal Church, councils, decrees of the Roman See, the Fathers, and Scholastics. Only then could one appeal to the "foreign" sources for proof: natural reason, philosophy, historical examples, and personal witness, in descending

order of importance. Then the Catholic thinker could make a judgment concerning the certainty or probability of the results, and a
pious reflection might be added to aid devotion.

This rather dry formulation was primarily an appeal to authority
which Thomas Aquinas would have thought the weakest link in the
chain of religious argument. Cano gave the impression that the truth
of Catholic faith could be achieved without reference to believers'
conversion in community, their prayer and worship, or their moral
authenticity in public life.

What Cano developed for a hierarchical method in theology
Bellarmine offered as a stratified version of the authorities in the
Church. Thomas Aquinas could assume a Church with a body of
Tradition stretching back to the apostles; for Bellarmine, that was
precisely what was contested. Since individuals could now decide
whether to belong to the Catholic Church or to a Reformed Tradition, it had become necessary to offer some understanding of Catholicism's legitimacy. What duties were now required of those who
belonged? How were we to know the true Church of Christ's
Gospel?

Bellarmine provided a solution by maintaining that the Church as
a divine gift must necessarily reflect the most perfect of societies—a
monarchy. Since it has a single authority, with guaranteed unity of
allegiance, uniform adherence, and coherent beliefs, it must be the
best of social bodies. The visible society of the Church required just
such a central authority to ensure its identity. Catholics could always
be marked by their loyalty to this one regime, disclosing their faith
among the hostile religious differences of the world. Nonbelievers
would always know this group by its universality (catholic), fullness
and variety of believers (holy), its strict continuity or succession from
the apostles (apostolic), and the uniformity of its members with the
pope (one).

Although Bellarmine helpfully categorized ecclesial life in a period
of confusion, what disappears from his view are the plural cultures in
which Catholics live and work. In emphasizing papal unity, he
neglects any semiautonomous agents in the Church (councils,
bishops, or theologians) and grants them little influence. In this
Church, prophets are not likely to be accepted as authentic speakers
of the charisms of the Spirit.

Now by the time this vision of the Church had taken hold in the Catholic community, it only paralleled the experience of absolutism and the divine right of national monarchs. In one sense Bellarmine provided a path by which the Catholic Church could play a social role independent of the civil rulers with whose limitation of the human rights of their subjects it often disagreed. Just as the Christian community had assimilated Jewish presbyteral government, Roman judicial procedures, feudal fealties, and imperial trappings to leave itself room for social independence, so now it began to find its alignment alongside monarchical nation-states.

In each era, however, the Church has always risked losing its identity in the particularities of the period in which it has found itself. That it has not remains a testimony to the dialogue engendered by its prophets and visionaries. With some of those voices now in alternate versions of Christendom, whether at Wittenburg, Utrecht, London, Edinburgh, or Geneva, this self-critical discussion became a rivalry among brothers and sisters, a competition for the testament of a seemingly absent Father. The unfinished conversations of those days continue to plague us.

DANGLING CONVERSATIONS
OF RECONSTITUTED CHRISTENDOMS

Christians of various confessional Traditions are now left with an accumulation of questions which cannot be ignored. What had been open, if contested, issues in a united Church had now become controversial arguments from authority dividing parties and Churches. Questions in one area became suspicions in another. Theologians condemned spiritual enthusiasts; ecclesiastical leaders feared theologians and peasant believers alike; believers thirsted for the Spirit and were afraid of being given a stone by clergy and thinkers together.

Yet in such a thin environment, the Catholic Revival reasserted certain principles of Christian life contravened by the Protestant Reformers. There was an *intrinsic relationship* between God's grace in redemption and the life of God given in creation (humanity was not depraved, but seriously flawed by sin). The sacred and the profane could not be separated as absolutes (government

and Church must both reflect evangelical values). And the sacramental life of the Church was an authentic continuation of Christ's
redeeming Presence (Christ's gift of the Spirit was a *visible Presence*). The stress on the mediations of God's grace and love was
authentically Catholic, a universal remembrance of the Christian
Tradition.

But any number of matters were posed and left unanswered or
answered too hastily and therefore unsatisfactorily. How is this gift
of God's grace stated in a new pluralist cultural situation? How is the
Bible at once the Church's book and the religious formation of
believers? The Christ-event is surely normative for the entire religious Tradition: social, institutional, and political. How is he also an
existential moment in the hearts of believers such that it does not
overturn the social government of Christian life? Must the prophetic
and traditional always be in opposition?

The problem is that the partners of this dialogue had separated—
unwilling to stay in the same room to talk to one another. It is
fruitless hindsight to say that had the elements of power and money
not been involved, dispassionate conversation might have ensued.
That is naive. For Christian discourse is also about fiscal and political
economy. The belief of Christians is that they can handle the
snakelike social praxis of the world as well as their own interior
religious experience. Here both sides failed with disastrous consequences for all. The rare individual in this period who understood all
the factors of the disintegrating medieval world, burgeoning early
modern polities, and the religious ardor of believers did not often
find a conversation partner. Lecturing the Reformers or Catholic
Revivalists is condescending; answering their unanswered questions
in the present may become a blessing.

ANTICIPATIONS OF A FUTURE WORLD

A final sacrament of the Catholic resolution of religion and culture
during this period can be seen in the ambiguous role missionaries
played in the expanding European economies and colonial governments. After the Treaty of Tordesillas, administrated by Alexander
VI (1492–1503), Spanish, Portuguese, and Italian preachers traveled with the military conquerors of each country to Brazil, the
Caribbean, Africa, the Far East, and the Americas. Wherever the

colonizers ruled, churches were founded, schools were established, even universities (Mexico, 1544) were inaugurated.

The underlying assumption of this colonial missionary effort was that Christendom (whether Spanish, Portuguese, English, Italian, etc.), the best form of religious and political belief, should be given to all. Missionaries baptized entire populations of natives whose understanding and appropriation of Catholicism can have been only minimal at best.

There were exceptions of course—individuals like Bartolomeo de Las Casas (1474–1566), who worked tirelessly against the slave trade, pleading persistently for the equality of the native populations with the Spanish colonizers. An even more stunning example can be found in Mattheo Ricci (1552–1610), Jesuit missionary to China, who spoke and wrote classical Chinese, dressed as a mandarin, learned Asian science, and presented the Christian Gospel as the fulfillment of Confucian wisdom.

What the Jesuits in China understood was that the universality of Catholicism was not an abstract unicultural religious expression. Rather it required accommodation (as they called it) to the indigenous language, mores, and previous beliefs of the people. In this century we find that an enlightened view, but the controversies that it raised in Catholicism were significant. To permit other cultural expressions of Christianity was to admit diversity into the Gospel of Christ. The Gospel of Christ was not to be compromised with the "barbarism" of the "unenlightened."

The fundamental question raised by the Reformers was evangelization. Does the Gospel have only a single cultural shape? Can it be expressed with a range of legitimate doctrinal, ethical, and ecclesiastical positions? Can differing existential embodiments of Christian language, literature, art, and polity subsist side by side without competition, subjugation, mutual syncretism, or bored tolerance?

Where the Christendom of the High Middle Ages had disintegrated into the fragmented Churches of the Reform, whether Catholic or Protestant, each was forced for a time to rethink its identity as *the* authentic heir of the Christian Gospels. Yet when each had strengthened its ecclesiastical bulwarks against external Christian neighbors, it discovered that the pluralism without only registered a pluralism of cultures within the walls. External war had become internal strife.

NOTES

1. French text quoted in Johan Huizinga, *The Waning of the Middle Ages* (Garden City, N.Y.: Doubleday & Co., 1954), 36.

2. "To John Bradaček and the People of Krumlov," in *The Letters of John Hus,* trans. Matthew Spinka (Totowa, N.J.: Rowman and Littlefield, 1972), 53.

3. See Huizinga, *Middle Ages,* 185–86, 315–16.

4. William James, *The Varieties of Religious Experience* (New York: Collier Books, 1961), 242.

5. Edmund Bishop, *Liturgica Historica* (Oxford: At the Clarendon Press, 1962), 449–50.

6. *Little Sermons on Sin. The Archpriest of Talavera,* trans. Lesley Byrd Simpson (Berkeley and Los Angeles: University of California Press, 1977), 158.

7. Hilaire Belloc, *Europe and the Faith* (New York: Paulist, 1930), 211.

8. *Fidei Ratio* (1530), excerpted in *Documents Illustrative of the Continental Reformation,* ed. B. J. Kidd (Oxford: At the Clarendon Press, 1911), 474.

9. Norman Cohn, *The Pursuit of the Millennium: Revolutionary Messianism in Medieval and Reformation Europe and its Bearing on Modern Totalitarian Movements* (New York: Harper & Row, 1961), 256.

FURTHER RELATED MATERIAL

No one reads quickly through the Reformation. Josef Lortz's important study, *The Reformation in Germany* (New York: Herder & Herder, 1968) is in two volumes, but crucial. Less demanding surveys can be found in Owen Chadwick, *The Reformation* (Baltimore: Penguin Books, 1964); John Dolan, *The History of the Reformation* (New York: Mentor-Omega, 1967); and Steven Ozment, *The Age of Reform: 1250–1550: An Intellectual and Religious History of Late Medieval and Reformation Europe* (New Haven: Yale University Press, 1980). For descriptions of the final period of medieval decline, see the entertaining, if somewhat depressing, Johan Huizinga, *The Waning of the Middle Ages,* (Garden City, N.Y.: Doubleday & Co., 1954). On the Catholic Revival, see A. G. Dickens, *The Counter Reformation* (New York: Harcourt Brace Jovanovich, 1969) and J. C. Olin, *The Catholic Reformation: Savanarola to Ignatius Loyola; Reform in the Church, 1495–1540* (New York: Harper & Row, 1969).

8

CATHOLIC ISOLATIONISM: THE ALTERNATE CULTURE (1630–1789)

> But reverend discipline, and religious fear,
> And soft obedience, find sweet biding here;
> Silence and sacred rest, peace and pure joys,
> Kind loves keep house, lie close, and make noise,
> And room enough for monarchs, while none swells
> Beyond the kingdoms of contentful cells.
>
> Richard Crashaw (1613–49), from "Description
> of a Religious House and Condition of Life."

When Ulrich Zwingli (1484–1531), the Swiss Reformer, visited the pilgrimage Church of Einsiedeln, he was shocked at its trivializing levity and superstition. Less than two hundred years later, Caspar Moosbrugger (1656–1723), an art-loving brother of the same monastic community, designed (1719–23) a decorated Baroque masterpiece to enshrine Catholic triumph. As one enters the square, the grand scale and palatial character of the façade displays itself chastely in gray-green stone. But upon entering the octagon which begins the nave, the believer is captured by the elaborate ornament and stunning frescoes completed by the Asam brothers (Cosmos, 1686–1739, and Egid, 1692–1750).

The viewer makes common cause with what seems to be a fellow pilgrim looking into the dome, his stucco foot firmly planted on the very top of a pillar. What the suppliant sees is an uncountable multitude of earlier believers: shepherds and sheep, angels and saints in the open air, spiraling toward the manger in Bethlehem. Above this incarnation, in the center, is the Father of Lights—located in the intensely serene brightness of eternity.

Catholic baroque art stressed the unity of earth and heaven. The believers' faith draws them from what is seen to the Unseen, from the heard to the Unheard, from what is tangible to the God who always escapes human grasp. These monuments present a regularly placid (occasionally stolidly triumphal) face to the world—yet entrance into their space proclaims a power not their own, seducing the

95

believer through sheer multiplicity of detail into a rapture of divine love.

The conspicuous contrast reflects the life of seventeenth- and eighteenth-century Catholicism. The problems caused by the Reformers were by the 1700s largely internalized, not solved. Controversy had made the Church prudent in securing a seemly façade; the discussions of Catholic piety, theology, and discipline took place behind closed doors whenever possible. The marketplace was neglected.

Isolated by political power when hegemony in Europe passed to the northern countries, Catholicism began to turn Roman insularity from an external requirement into a cultural policy. The once vibrant Catholic spirit neglected, even opposed at times, the rise of the European scientific spirit. To be "enlightened" did not mean to be baptized as it once had, but to be free of authoritative, ready-made religious solutions. Catholic intellectuals retreated into narrower familial concerns without prophecy, without vision.

A historian of cultures might view such a withdrawal as a necessary stage in the recurring cycles of all religious development. Just as it is essential for the individual to return to the affective comfort of family and friends to restore energy and accept healing for the larger tasks of work, country, and society, so too Catholicism required a retreat. But the creative, even daring, approaches which Catholicism brought to its former situations contrasted sharply with the parochial views which developed from the end of the Thirty Years War (1648) until the French Revolution (1789).

During this phase Catholicism seemed to be more defensive, less secure than at any time in its past. Despite the Baroque ornamental devices, Catholic portraits appeared somewhat drab and lackluster. But the Church was not without its prophets and saints or its moments of beauty and valor. In providing an alternate culture to the more powerful outside world, it produced a set piece which has lasted well into this century.

THE CRISES WITHIN

Gallicanism

France, proud of its title "eldest daughter of the church," tenaciously, even brutally, held to its religious identity when its powerful neighbors had turned to the Protestant Reform. When Jacques Bossuet (1627–1704), the great court preacher and bishop, wrote his *Discourse on Universal History* (1681) for Louis XIV (1643–1715), he pressed the specifically religious claims made by God on rulers of nations.

> They neither control the configuration of circumstances that was bequeathed to them by past centuries, nor can they foresee the course of the future, much less control that course. All this is in the hands of Him Who can name what is and what is yet to be, Who presides over all the ages, and Who knows in advance what will come to pass.[1]

Nonetheless, Louis XIV used the Catholic Church as a substantial cannon in the French arsenal of political independence, authority, and power.

This political union of Catholicism and French national interest provoked the first great internal crisis during this period. Labeled Gallicanism, it revealed French pretensions to, and accomplishment of, an international hegemony. For many centuries, to be "civilized" meant to speak, write, and (often enough) think French thoughts. When the political centralization of Louis XIV's power turned to religious matters, it expressed itself in the affirmation by the French clergy (at the instigation and support of Bossuet) of the *Four Gallican Articles* (1682). They asserted that the king, not the pope, had authority in civil affairs and that general councils must consent to, or deny, contested papal judgments. Although the *Articles* were denied by Pope Alexander VIII (1689–91) in 1690 and retracted by the king himself in 1693, they were taught and promulgated in France for a decade. The question of the rights and privileges of the French national church continued to bedevil theological and political interchange for almost a century.

What remains distressing about such in-house investigations is that they diverted the best minds of the era into problems more ecclesiastical than theological. Studies into the nature of the Church's evangelical role in the wider world and the implications of justification and grace for society were shunted to one side, while interminable arguments took place concerning the appointment of French bishops and the administration of theological seminaries. There is little doubt that Gallicanism intensified French Catholics' temptation toward cultural withdrawal. The twentieth-century loss of the "working-class Catholic" in France has its origins much earlier than this era.

Jansenism

Simultaneously, a graver, more lasting internal debate appeared in the form of Jansenism. Named after Cornelius Jansen (1585–1638), a professor at the University of Louvain in Belgium, the movement focused French discussion upon a significant, if probably insoluble, theological issue. It reopened the Church's reflections on the nature of justification: "How is the Christian saved by God in Christ?"

Jansen returned to Augustine for his answers; and, in a lengthy, posthumously published text (the *Augustinus,* 1642), he defended what he believed to be the Bishop of Hippo's position. Most would now agree that Jansen was neither entirely faithful to his mentor nor to the difficulty of the problem itself. He gave such an exclusive prominence to God's activity in every action that the reality of human freedom was placed in jeopardy.

It is not likely that this question will ever be completely resolved. The *Decree on Justification* from the Council of Trent asserted that God's loving grace is always a gift, always prior to our own acceptance—but that our acceptance is also always and in all ways free. Theologians realize that this *is* the mystery of divine-human interaction—and that to locate the disclosure of the gift is the fundamental task, not to *explain* the event exhaustively. But theologians always have a tendency to want to unpuzzle the world, just the way any thinker does—and Jansen was no exception.

Jansen's French followers were determined to reform ecclesiastical life. They were keen, ambitious, subtle, and stubborn, convinced that any yielding to human ability in this matter was tantamount to blasphemy. In 1643, Antoine Arnauld (1612–1694), a priest of the community of Port-Royal near Paris, wrote a small text, *On Frequent Communion,* which severely criticized the practice, emphasizing the sinfulness of believers and their need for the correct interior dispositions to be truly Christian. On the one hand, Arnauld's practices fostered a prophetic grasp of the reality of the gracious God in an authentically Christian life; on the other, they favored a gloomy, austere opinion of human possibilities and a distrust of the ordinary sacramental life of believers.

The result was a division of French Catholicism into Jansenists and more traditional Catholics led by the Jesuits. Some, like Molière (1622–73) in his play *Le Tartuffe* (1669), satirized religious pessimism and false asceticism. But the Jansenists had a literate sympathizer in Blaise Pascal (1623–62), who was both repelled by the superficiality of Catholic textbook morality and attracted to the severe demands of Jansenist piety.

In the *Provincial Letters* (1656–57), Pascal exposed the immorality of simplistic ethical complacency and caricatured Jansenism's opponents. So brilliant were his polemics and his literary style as a controversialist that European Jesuits remained stigmatized as dangerous laxists and devious politicians.

The religious fervor of Jansenism did not last. Because its legacy was not the joyful experience of Francis of Assisi, the activist piety of Teresa of Ávila, or the benign wisdom of Philip Neri, it could not be successful in its attempts to reform Catholic morals. On the contrary, Jansenism's negative tone gave the very word "Jansenist" the popular meaning of a narrow moralism peculiar to certain Catholic populations. Cornelius Jansen, Blaise Pascal, and many others strove to be prophets; but the Jansenist Catholics peopling the novels of François Mauriac and Graham Greene regularly witness to a more defeatist vision of human nature.

Quietism

If Jansenist asceticism promoted a task-oriented religiosity, Quietism did the precise opposite. The founder, Miguel de Molinos (1628–96), recommended in his *Spiritual Guide* (1675) that the religious individual must achieve the silence of complete contemplation, even at the price of annihilating personal projects, ritual and ascetic practices, or resistance to temptation itself. The soul must be indifferent to everything but God.

Molinos's stress upon the terrifying and fascinating call to holiness (*Mysterium tremendum et fascinans*) captured the fervor of many contemplative women whose spiritual lives he directed. When these religious sisters discarded their private devotions, refused to recite public prayer, and generally disturbed discipline in their communities, Molinos was condemned. Throughout the process of imprisonment, trial, and judgment, Molinos remained submissive and undisturbed.

Molinos's doctrine spread to France through the conferences and letters of Jeanne Marie de la Motte-Guyon (1648–1717), who taught that believers must cultivate complete indifference toward God, excluding even the thought of reward or punishment. Upon meeting her in 1688, François de Salignac de la Mothe Fénélon (1641–1715), archbishop of Cambrai, missionary to French Protestants, and tutor to the grandson of Louis XIV, began a long controversy with Bossuet on the questions of grace, free will, and the interior life of the spiritual person. Bossuet somewhat peevishly accused Fénélon of being an enthusiast, little better than a heretic. After a bitter quarrel, Roman authorities intervened at the king's request. Fénélon's positions were termed rash and liable to cause scandal. The archbishop acquiesed without reservation.

By emphasizing the demands of God's invitation, Quietism deepened the Catholic Revival at a time when the European Church required considerable religious conversion; but its attack on public activity of all kinds encouraged the same withdrawal from broader cultural pursuits that Gallicanism invited and Jansenism supported. These prophetically inspired movements could not reform a Catholicism which further divided itself in self-examination.

Politics

By order of the Queen Mother of France, Catherine de' Medici (1519–89), well over five thousand Protestants were slaughtered on St. Bartholomew's Eve (24 August 1572). It was only a symbol of the civil and theological battles undertaken by bishops, kings, and assembly to secure an absolutely integral national identity and to suppress religious diversity. In England, the national or Anglican church (1533), initiated by Henry VIII (1491–1547) to establish his Tudor dynasty and consolidated under Elizabeth I (1533–1603), tolerated a range of religious expression which erupted into civil war (1642–48) between Anglican Royalists and Puritan Roundheads under the leadership of Oliver Cromwell (1599–1658).

But in Germany the savage Thirty Years' War (1618–48) pillaged and depopulated entire independent principalities. French political strategy continuously encouraged the intervention of foreign mercenaries, turning a weak neighbor into a limping enemy.

During these wars, Catholic and Protestant ecclesiastics fought for control of old territorial boundaries through the military remainders of their dynastic, familial, and political ambitions. The Peace of

Westphalia (1648) ended the war, returned property rights of both parties to 1618, balanced imperial electors between Catholics and Lutherans, and granted mutual toleration and political equality to all parties. No one was satisfied, and neither religious group could claim anything but a worried, bored exhaustion.

After the Peace of Westphalia, German Catholics strengthened the revival of their religion in their own lands. Popes of the period shifted support among kings and emperors to achieve political leverage and support for Catholics in the civil wars in the north. When the popes' civil power declined, they were obliged to attend to their ecclesiastical possessions in Italy (the Papal States) as a way of preserving their own independence. Even though their moral authority increased, due to the election of worthier candidates, they found themselves capable only of inviting or persuading civil powers to participate in political quarrels.

THE CRISIS WITHOUT

The self-isolation and insulation by others of Catholic piety, political identity, and theology made the Church particularly unprepared to face the most important moments of the early modern world. If the plunder of buildings, the wounds of war, and the snatching at sterile authority seemed to be the immediate problems to be healed and restored, the long view of Catholic identity required that more patient, more attentive medicine be given to the discoveries of modern science and the surgeries wrought by the Enlightenment.

Revolutionary Science

The English historian Herbert Butterfield has remarked that the scientific revolution "outshines everything since the rise of Christianity and reduces the Renaissance and Reformation to the rank of mere episodes, mere internal displacements, within the system of medieval Christendom."[2] As Butterfield phrases the matter, picturesquely but accurately, this new mode of Western thought required people to don new thinking caps.

We have grown so accustomed to our scientific garments that we forget how truly novel they were in the European world. The epic adventure of modern science controverted the geopolitical centrism of the European West, overturned Aristotelian physics as its normative self-explanation, and reexamined, then discarded, large elements of the culture formed from Greco-Roman and ancient Hebrew ingredients. If we are to understand ourselves in the present or appreciate the vast difference modern science brought to all religious traditions, including the Catholic one, we must understand the nature of this contemporary journey.

Galileo Galilei

The easiest way to convey the difference between the old and the new attitudes toward the experience of our world is to focus upon the melancholy tale of Galileo Galilei (1564–1642) and his tangled relationship with the Church at Rome. In Padua, where he taught for eighteen years, Galileo improved the telescope and revolutionized astronomy, leading him to agree with the theories of Copernicus (1473–1543), who had hypothesized that the earth moved about the sun. For Copernicus, this theory best explained the data of variations in seasons, the movement of the planets, and other astronomical phenomena. Galileo, with his telescope, provided the empirical evidence for the claims—and it is this which placed him in contest with the Roman Inquisition.

Galileo was forbidden to teach or defend the Copernican position because it was "philosophically foolish and preposterous and, because contrary to Scripture, theologically heretical." Galileo kept silent for a time (some fifteen years), but shortly before his death he spoke again and was condemned.

Galileo's insistence upon a new method lay at the heart of the seventeenth-century conflict between religion and science. Religious thinkers of that time knew only two major approaches to the question of truth: the *authoritative* (i.e., God's Word in the Scriptures and the Tradition of the Church) and the *philosophical* (i.e., the largely deductive, metaphysical methods of Greek philosophers and medieval Scholastics). To argue for an *experimentally rigorous verifiable method* was a radical departure; it struck a major blow at the intellectual certitudes of the day.

Galileo's "compositive" and "resolutive" method (as he called it) was not, however, a mere piling up of particulars. Rather he argued from mathematical hypotheses through verifying experiments. It was his belief that mathematics analyzed the very structure of things; to be scientific was to be in contact with what was real. This shift in empirical seeing, inductive thinking, in experimental knowing itself, was intensified when the results called into question not only the received natural science of the ancients (Ptolemy [the second-century C.E. Greco-Egyptian astronomer] and Aristotle), but even the view of the world held through the prevailing literalist understanding of the Scriptures.

The Inquisition's triumph over Galileo (only examined by the Roman Curia again in our times) was a Pyrrhic victory. Not only were Galileo's methods valid and his scientific conclusions vindicated, but all attempts to contain the empirical method only isolated the Catholic Church further from future intellectual currents.

What so frightened the religious officials of Galileo's day can now be seen as a complicated question, but a false dilemma. Science as a careful, empirical, inductive, and verifiable procedure is a sure way of discovering the truth about reality. Religion, disclosing the ultimate meanings of our human experience, remains the surest way to embody, apprehend, and understand the *limits of* all reality and the *limits to* all possible experience. Contemporary scientists and religious believers understand and accept what could not be seen three hundred years ago: that there need be no real clash between authentic science and authentic religion.

Blaise Pascal

Pascal's (1623–62) preeminence is not due to his literary abilities in the Jansenist crisis but rather to his capacity for combining mathematical skills and religious fervor. The reader of his *Pensées* (1670) can recognize a transparently honest spirit caught between the two contending factions of his (and his age's) life—science and religion. He was unwilling to forego either, wishing to remain faithful to the scientific methods of his day, while reminding his contemporaries that "the heart has its reasons which reason knows not at all." Wisdom sees the brilliance (*éclat*) and the reverence (*vénération*) due to both Archimedes and Jesus Christ.[3]

Pascal might have found a way to transform the tensions between science and religion into a new cultural synthesis; but the incontrovertible fact is that few listened. As a result, the continued conflicts forced men and women to choose sides; rarely was it possible to achieve both an authentic scientific attitude and continue within a personal confessional Tradition. In the many grand "ifs" of history, we may wonder what Catholic history "might have been" had it been able to heed the thinking of such eminent Catholics *and* scientists.

The Enlightenment—The Rise of Rational Religion

What was in the seventeenth century a movement of scientists, a theoretic method, and a set of practical procedures printed a cultural currency of uncertain denominations for the eighteenth century. Religious insecurities and a general skepticism toward authority, rhetorically inflated during the religious wars, funded attempts to bank religion and culture on reason rather than *any* contentious religious Tradition.

The Enlightenment, as Immanuel Kant (1724–1804) summarized it at the end of the century (1784), was our release from "self-incurred tutelage"—the willingness to become autonomous, leaving behind authorities of religious or cultural dogma and claiming personal freedom. It was a moral ideal of knowledge. To be free risks stepping away from our cherished, self-supported beliefs and to test their meaning and truth by the experiments of reason.

So the Enlightenment concerned itself with the various authorities which required reexamination: *textual authority* like the Scriptures; *confessional Traditions* like Lutheranism or Catholicism; *philosophical assumptions* and *principles* like those of Aristotle; and finally *religion* itself. There was science and there was superstition: the first was critical; the second mere belief, general consent, and tired custom—the authority of the masses.

Kant prodded:

> It is so easy not to be of age. If I have a book which understands for me, a pastor who has a conscience for me, a physician who decides my diet, and so forth, I need not trouble myself. I need not think, if I can only *pay*—others will readily undertake the irksome *work* for me.[4]

Dispassionate Enlightenment would demystify priestcraft and superstition, political tyranny and personal illusion. Reason should triumph.

Textual Slavery

The conflicts over how to read the Bible began when Richard Simon (1638–1712) published his *Critical History of the Old Tes-*

tament (1678). Whether the book was the *Iliad* or the *Pentateuch,* the analysis of the genuine, "critical" text was the same. Simon carefully and simply (in French rather than Latin) showed how the biblical text was altered over the centuries by various authors and later scribes.

Though Simon wished to show Protestants how the Tradition of a text was essential for validation of the Word of God, he ended by calling into question the authenticity of the Hebrew, and later the Christian, Scriptures. The "authority" of superstition would be overcome by sheer attention to the certain facts of the biblical text.

Reaction was swift. Simon was expelled from his religious community, his book banned by the French Royal Council, then later (1683) placed upon the *Index of Forbidden Books.* Bossuet, ever ready to take on controversy, argued in his *History of the Variations of Protestant Churches* (1688) that authority was the only true principle upon which Church could be based. The constantly splitting sects of non-Roman confessions were not simply due to matters of taste, but to a shift from the very unified essence of Christianity itself.

Political Infamy

But European consciousness was changing. Difference was no longer automatic heterodoxy from the received, authentic religious identity; pluralism could be enriching. Believing what one was told without examination was not the ideal. Nowhere can this doctrine be seen more clearly than in that figure who dominated the French Enlightenment, the extraordinary François Marie Arouet (1694–1778), whose pseudonym was Voltaire.

Voltaire is no unworthy exemplar of the entire age. He combined all the virtues and all the limitations of an exciting period. He was witty, polished, liberal, antiecclesiastical. As an author, he is now remembered for his *Candide* (1759), a satirical description of the classical metaphysician's "best of all possible worlds." As a counselor and *philosophe,* he argued for freedom and justice in a world still largely enslaved politically and ideologically.

But this giant of literature, art, and religious toleration also displayed some of the least attractive qualities of the times: an enormous vanity; a failure to separate the abuses of Catholicism from its religious values; and an inability to distinguish between wholesale attack on religious institutions and their gradual, careful reform. He praised the Quakers and Unitarians, but the first for their pacifism, the second for their rationality. The true value of religion was its anticipation of reason. "Every sensible man, every honorable man, must hold the Christian sect in horror."[5]

Since atheism seemed only to beget societal confusion, Voltaire encouraged a minimal loyalty to the religion of reason—Deism. In this intellectual surrogate for confessional Traditions, God appeared as a classic watchmaker who wound up the spring of the machine, set the whole world ticking, and then remained absent in the background without intervention in free human affairs. Christians, protesting Catholics maintained, could not accept *this* God as their own.

Religious Serfdom

Thomas Paine (1737–1809) combined pamphlets in favor of revolutionary independence from the King of England with rational freedom from religious subservience. In *Common Sense* (1776) he argued that though we are all "children of the same family," God wills that there should be a diversity of religious opinions among us.[6] Any priestcraft which counters the ideals of the French Revolution had to be destroyed, announced *The Age of Reason* (1793).

A publicist rather than an original thinker, Paine composed direct prose which addressed ordinary individuals. It frightened many; it exhilarated others. Though Jesus was a virtuous and amiable individual, it was curious to Paine that the Christian Church could so easily spring from pagan myth.

> A direct incorporation took place in the first instance, by making the reputed founder to be celestially begotten. The trinity of gods that then followed was no other than a reduction of the former plurality. . . . But when . . . one part of God is represented by a dying man, and another part, called the Holy Ghost, by a flying pigeon,[7]

our credulity is stretched beyond limit. Christianity can only be an "engine of power" by which avaricious priests enslave people through their appeal to a derogatory notion of divinity.

Paine's opposition to religious confessions, however, was due not simply to their overweening authority, but also to their method of theological thought. It was not scientific; it had no data; it demonstrated no conclusions. It is the "study of nothing." Science and religion cannot share the same bed.

A God who encouraged human freedom combined with a strong skepticism concerning the miraculous content of revealed religion made Deism a haven for those, like Voltaire and Paine, who believed that social anarchy would ensue under later materialist thinkers like Denis Diderot (1713–84), Jean le Rond d'Alembert (1717–83), or Paul-Henri d'Holbach (1723–89). Deism, a kind of civil religion, provided distance from historical religious expressions, left the authority of religion to survive in the individual intellect, and offered flexible standards for judging ecclesiastical expressions. It may well be true, as recent interpreters maintain, that the religious instincts of Voltaire and his colleagues were not as nonexistent as some of their opponents would have us believe. It is no less true, however, that the reckless and corrosive nature of their "enlightened" criticism succeeded in separating true religion from true science for several hundred years.

A Plea for Tolerance

Gotthold Ephraim Lessing (1729–82), the most representative figure of the German Enlightenment, became librarian to the Duke of Brunswick at Wolffenbüttel and began to publish fragments of an unpublished work by Hermann Samuel Reimarus (+1769). Reimarus's attacks on scriptural events (the Exodus, the resurrection narratives, etc.) and his plea for tolerance of the Deists encouraged Lessing to appeal to an inner truth which undergirded all specific confessional beliefs. "The written traditions must be interpreted by their inward truth and no written traditions can give the religion any inward truth if it has none."[8]

Lessing's allegiance to religion was more a faith in inner religious optimism. It is "enough if men hold on to Christian love; what happens to the Christian religion does not matter." In *Nathan the Wise* (1779), the protagonist of the drama appeals for tolerance of all religious differences. Jews, Moslems, and Christians are each partial realizations of the one religious truth that exceeds each historical form. Only through common suffering and dialogue will the characters learn their universal humanity. "Now, let each one emulate the other, in affection untouched by prejudice."

Authority stultifies; authority destroys independence; authority, whether in Scripture (with Simon, Paine, and Lessing), in politics, (with Paine and Voltaire), or in religion itself requires criticism. It demands the autonomous mind of the selfless investigator who is willing to weigh all possible evidence and judge for himself or herself. In such a world, born of the scientific revolution, tolerance of difference was crucial; intolerance, bred by the fissiparous politics of religious wars, had only grown into an inhuman ogre whose existence in fairy tales could be fantasized, but whose cancerous existence in the body of the nascent culture must be excised.

CATHOLIC THEOLOGY
AND THE MANUALS OF CERTITUDE

Catholics read the relentless attacks of Voltaire or Paine and the more gentle remonstrances of Lessing with the eyes of those seeking certitude, assured and secure in their own religious political positions. Questions produced doubts; doubts, divisions. And although some rulers, notably the Empress Maria Theresa (1740–80) and her son Joseph II (1780–90), administered ecclesiastical and educational reforms in their Catholic realms, the Church retreated further into a ghetto.

Doctrinal orthodoxy was pronounced in orotund rhetorical tones based upon a textbook theology which distilled into clear, distinct conclusions an essentialist Catholicism. Such analyses ordinarily began not with a question (as in Aquinas), but with a position, a thesis. One defined its terms, indicated the status of the proposition (of defined faith, only proximate to faith, etc.), noted any adversaries, and then proved the thesis by appeal to specific texts of Scripture, the Tradition, and correlative doctrines. Theology was a proof for the already-held doctrines of belief.

In ethical analysis, Catholic consciences were formed according to the established principles, customs, and rules of belief. It was an ethics of obedience in which no one should act without certainty of motive or the objective knowledge of the good. Ambiguity was to be avoided at all costs. Elaborate rules of discernment which helped the believer to establish the most probable authority were developed. And in Catholic seminaries, endless cases were presented to prepare future priests for all the possibilities in which principles might be contravened.

This formal theological organization held sway in Catholic seminaries well into the twentieth century. It emphasized certainty, universality, abstract reason, and propositional knowledge. But the high degree of abstraction, the controversies within theological circles, and the rigorist doctrinal and ethical positions left the mass of the Catholic population largely untouched. Since theology did not function as an engaged critique of the symbolic, gestural, and ethical lives of Catholics, it is not surprising that the proponents of Jansenist or Quietist piety were successful.

But the disparity between popular piety and theological criticism is in many ways a direct product of the years of the Reformation. The emphasis by the Reformers on the clarity and integrity of the Word of God and their relative disapproval of medieval sacramental life produced a reaction in Catholic life. On the one hand, there was a constant stress on the visual, sacramental aspects of ecclesial life; on the other, a deliberate attention to the catechetical instruction and doctrinal purity of believers. The Enlightenment milieu fostered further refinements in propositional form; and reformed religion, whether Catholic or Protestant, became largely an elitist affair.

So just as an almost Cartesian (after René Descartes, the philosopher, 1596–1650) theology survived into this century, so too did Catholics stress dependence upon papal authority as the primary formation of conscience, the extrasacramental piety of novenas in honor of particular saints as models of behavior, parochial missions or revivals, a growing devotion concerning Mary, the Mother of God, and an emphasis upon the adoration of the reserved Presence of Christ in the Eucharistic Bread.

These developing sensibilities were the popular Catholic response to the failure of theologians, Catholic philosophers, and institutional representatives to wrestle more creatively and more tellingly with the giants of early modern science and Enlightenment. For the modern meaning of Catholicism is as much a product of ordinary Catholic believers as of an institutional Tradition.

Separated by a strictly Catholic culture, insulated from the ever-widening circles of attack, Catholics could better negotiate some inner peace—but a religious peace bought at a level of religious coinage which contemporary believers find largely uninteresting and at a price which made their currency unusable in the rapidly changing world. Private piety and public isolation did not ready the Catholic opera of sensibilities to greet the revolutions of the late eighteenth century.

REVOLUTION AGAINST RIGIDITY—1789

The attacks of the Enlightenment philosophers upon the political and religious tradition were largely intellectual, since it was not until the end of the eighteenth century that the Age of Enlightenment gave way to an Age of Revolution. Inspired by the revolt of the British colonies in America (1775–83) and by Enlightenment critiques of monarchical injustices, the French raised the standard of full and complete revolution (1789) against their hierarchical society. The story of this monumental shift in society is best told in a history other than a chronicle of Catholicism, but the Church was deeply affected by its results.

Catholics fell on both sides of this greatest of divides. For those who chose support of the revolutionaries, this was a providential event. So determined had the most "Catholic" of monarchs been to extend his absolute and "divine" power to the lives of his subjects that the Church itself was seriously weakened and in many ways was subjected to the crown's whims. In such a situation many agreed with the anonymous French observer who wrote: "God saved the Church by sending the French Revolution to destroy princely absolutism." But most official Catholic representatives could not greet the revolution and its demands with anything but horror and condemnation.

So began one of the most critical struggles in the self-understanding of Catholicism. On the one side stood those revolutionary Catholics who accepted even the brutal, violent history of the age as an instance of God's judgment upon the rulers of their society and as an opportunity for human beings to link the battle for freedom with the quest for universal love. It would presage a new

Catholic Revival, a cultivation of democratic community. On the other side, there converged the "conservative" forces of Catholicism, already exhausted by internal crises and external battles with "godless" science and the vultures of the Enlightenment. Their solution was to retreat further into Catholic culture, the perfect society with its clear and distinct truths, its absolute moral rules, and its sure authoritarian political structure. Even though the initial promise of the French Revolution disintegrated rapidly into the despotisms of violence, war, and the Napoleonic order, the Catholic Church of the nineteenth century remained polarized between these progressive and conservative parties. The questions raised by the Reform concerning individual piety and personal conscience, by science and its quest for an empirical validity of knowledge, and by the Enlightenment on the philosophical value of historical differences would not be ignored.

NOTES

1. Jacques-Bénigne Bossuet, *Discourse on Universal History*, trans. Elborg Forster, ed. Orest Ranum (Chicago: University of Chicago Press, 1976), 375.

2. Herbert Butterfield, *The Origins of Modern Science, 1300–1800* (New York: Free Press, 1966), 7.

3. Blaise Pascal, *Pensées* XII, 793, in *Pensées et Opuscules,* ed. Leon Brunschvicg (Paris: Hachette, 1971), 696–97.

4. Immanuel Kant, "What is Enlightenment?" in *History,* trans. Lewis White Beck, Robert E. Anchor, and Emil Fackenheim (Indianapolis: Bobbs-Merrill, 1963), 3.

5. Peter Gay, *The Enlightenment: An Interpretation. The Rise of Modern Paganism* (New York: Vintage, 1968), 391.

6. Thomas Paine, *Common Sense,* ed. Nelson F. Adkins (Indianapolis: Bobbs-Merrill, 1953), 41.

7. Thomas Paine, *The Age of Reason* (Secaucus, N.J.: Citadel, 1974), 53–55, 187.

8. G. E. Lessing, *Lessing's Theological Writings,* trans. Henry Chadwick (Stanford, Calif.: Stanford University Press, 1957), 15–18.

FURTHER RELATED MATERIAL

For a general introduction to this complex political period, see Gerald R. Cragg, *The Church and the Age of Reason, 1648–1789* (Baltimore: Penguin Books, 1966). Ronald Knox's sometimes slanted book *Enthusiasm: A Chap-*

ter in the History of Religion with Special Reference to the Seventeenth and Eighteenth Centuries (New York: Oxford University Press, 1961) is still useful for recapturing the flavor of popular religion. Paul Hazard's *The European Mind, 1680–1715,* trans. J. Lewis May (Harmondsworth, Eng.: Penguin Books, 1973) offers the classic intellectual overview of the shifting consciousness of the period. Peter Gay's *The Enlightenment: An Interpretation—The Rise of Modern Paganism* (New York: Vintage, 1968) outlines the more important figures. For the best overview of the rise of modern scientific method and its consequences, see Herbert Butterfield, *The Origins of Modern Science, 1300–1800* (New York: Free Press, 1966).

9

THE CHALLENGE OF HISTORY (1800–1900)

> Oh, what a shifting parti-color'd scene
>   Of hope and fear, of triumph and dismay
> Of recklessness and penitence, has been
>   The history of that dreary, life-long fray!
>   John Henry Newman (1801–1890),
>   from "The Dream of Gerontius"

Igor Stravinsky (1882–1971), composer and conductor, locates the change from Johann Sebastian Bach (1685–1750) to Richard Wagner (1813–83) in the experience of dissonance.[1] In Bach the music regularly resolves its dissonant, clashing sounds into the peace of harmonic order; in Wagner dissimilar tones emancipate themselves, thrust their harsh distensions independently toward the ear, grip the listener with at once a nostalgia for the old repose and a yearning for some future musical meaning. The transcendent became no longer the symmetrical arrangement of parts in an architectural whole, but the concurrence of discrete individuals jostling for simultaneous unity.

At the beginning of the nineteenth century, music still fit the old forms, but at its conclusion, musical form itself became a problem. Opera no longer fit the stage of its origins, symphonies sounded formless to the uneducated ear, and sonatas became the irregular, effusive phantasies of the composer. Musical pieces required larger complements of instruments, orchestras became bigger and louder, performances reached for more populous audiences.

Catholic identity underwent just such a transformation. The interwoven texture of melodic individuals, the instruments of communication, and the counterpoint to the political difficulties of the era originally seemed to fit within the old, rigorously formal shapes of ecclesiastical life. After the French Revolution (1789) and its initial shock to the Church's too easy liaison with monarchical or imperial absolutists, the clashing strains provoked the institution to return to its old nostalgic harmonies.

113

The major and minor conflicts that compose nineteenth-century Catholic experience lead directly to our contemporary problems. What had once in the eighteenth century been an angry attack by those outside the community upon those inside its walls became a duel within the ecclesiastical house itself. There were those who labeled themselves "liberals." They believed that it was possible to include the Reformers' notions of religious experience, the scientists' methods of knowing, and the philosophers' invitation to tolerance and political freedom within the Church without destroying it. But those who called themselves "conservatives" heard no hope of internal harmony, convinced the newer distensions were only the old heretical ones. Let us briefly examine this contrast through two important instances: *The Syllabus of Errors* (1864) and the journal *L'Avenir* (*The Future*), published by Felicité Robert de Lamennais (1782–1854).

In the *Syllabus,* we have an example of the flight from the contemporary world advocated by some conservative ecclesiastics. It stated that the Roman pontiff need not reconcile himself to "progress, liberalism, and modern civilization." In eighty propositions, it condemned all the movements contemporaries thought forward-thinking. It epitomized in its ill-fated tone a peculiar characteristic of the century's expression of Catholicism.

In previous chapters, we have traced traditional, prophetic, and apocalyptic strands of the Catholic Church in a variety of different ways. During these troubled years a strange blending of the traditional and the apocalyptic took place, evidenced in many of the official documents of the Church such as the *Syllabus.* "Conservatism," in its best sense, draws strength for the present from its memories of God's actions. It conserves and preserves the cognitive, ethical, and affective center of what religious men and women have experienced in their heritage. But during this century conservatives did not merely remember creatively, they judged and often condemned what did not fit their notion of Tradition.

The first half of the century appeared to hold better hopes. De Lamennais and the journal *L'Avenir* crusaded for an alliance between the Church and democratic freedom. He preached a society in which liberties of speech, press, and religion would guarantee the necessary Catholic principle of freedom. These "pilgrims of God and liberty" (as they called themselves) supported the growing revolutionary movements in Europe (Belgium and Poland), and warned that union of Church and state was not necessarily in believers' best interests.

De Lamennais's pleas went unheard. Successive papal decrees in the 1830s told Polish, Belgian, and Irish Catholics to support their local Protestant governments. De Lamennais's own positions were officially rejected in 1832. While the popes frequently intervened in local disputes in place of lower authorities, they sought "balance" between the competing factors in political problems. This search for balance regularly placed the administrative authority not so much in creative response to past traditions but in a simple repetition for the sake of future preservation. Balance, though often our common-sense method for handling ordinary affairs, is simply insufficient as a Gospel response to civil and religious crisis.

Catholic theological and ecclesiastical oscillations in the nineteenth century do not make easy reading. Despite political complexities which lasted through the dissolution of the Papal States (1870), there were public signs of a future Church struggling to enter the twentieth century. Indeed some of the movements, such as the revival of Thomas Aquinas, which struck contemporaries as repetitions of the past, actually helped Peter's alternately enthusiastic and lukewarm Church lurch its way into the modern world.

FACING THE MODERN WORLD

Preliminaries: Hume and Kant

The first cannon-burst against nineteenth-century theology was really fired by David Hume, the Scottish philosopher (1711–76). Hume's conviction was that all knowledge is ultimately derived from experience. There is no innate information (idea) which precedes our perception of things. We receive sense impressions from which we derive ideas, rather like a faded copy of the original. The mind is simply unable to frame significant concepts about matters that cannot in principle be experienced.

What room does this leave for religion? Not a great deal. Claims made about miracles as proof for confessional belief or about the order of the world and a Divine Cause are improbable at best. Since matter-of-fact experience is our sole source of knowledge, what we *know* is that nature is uniform, regular, and that miracles violate the laws of nature. It can never be *reasonable* to accept miraculous events; other explanations which have their psychological origin in experience would be more sensible. Nor does the utter order of the world necessarily speak of a God beyond the world or of the Christian God, since there is evil as well as order, suffering as well as joy. The Principle who constructed this world need not be perfectly good and surely is not perfectly powerful.

Hume's radical skepticism raised these same problems for any reality that escapes sensible perception. So not only questions like the existence of God, but the immortality of the soul and the freedom of the will were also at stake. Any philosophical, scientific, or religious language that required metaphysical statements, positions that at once met the world of experience but transcended it, were suspect.

Immanuel Kant (1724–1804) set out to answer Hume's objections. Hume woke him from his "dogmatic slumber." In a series of three major works, the *Critiques of Pure Reason, Practical Reason,* and *Teleological Judgement* (and Taste), Kant tried to refound science, morality, religion, and aesthetics on certain grounds. He asked not only "*What* do we know?" but "*How* do we know what we know?" The answer to this second question limits the answers possible for the first.

Kant postulated knowing faculties of sensibility, understanding, and reason. Sensibility perceives the particular data of experience; understanding provides the intellectual schemata or mental equipment (so to speak) by which one may sort out through concepts what one is knowing. These categories are purely formal, that is, they do not give us information, but only provide the proper frames through which we can combine sense data intelligibly. Reason secures the categories of the understanding by means of principles which Kant calls Ideas. These Ideas are the immortality of the soul, the freedom of the will, and the existence of God.

Now if we try to prove the reality of these Ideas through our experience, we fall into complete contradiction. We can just as easily disprove the existence of God as prove it. The same is true for the permanent unity of the psychological subject and the freedom or determinism of the human will. But we know that these formal ideas

116

regulate our whole way of being. We act as if they were the case; indeed, we must live *as though* we were free, a psychological identity—and *as though* God exists.

Kant believed that through his understanding of scientific (or pure) reason, he had provided a symmetry with moral (or practical) reason. Knowing and doing were correlative; but actions were dependent upon the free choices, the risks of belief that something which is the case for me should be that way for all.

Kant viewed aesthetic judgments as a third sort of human option. On the basis of particulars, we judge that something is beautiful not to everyone's taste but that everyone who sees this particular art object will operate with the same imagination and emotive force.

Kant's three critiques tell us something about nineteenth-century theology. In attempting to answer the criticism of David Hume, theologians went through each one of the doors which Kant opened. There were those who disagreed with Kant, trying to locate religious notions in the realm of speculative reason. Some agreed with Kant that religion was primarily an ethical matter, unprovable by rational endeavor. Still others identified religion with the aesthetic and emotional. Catholics opted for all of these in one form or another to understand their faith.

Religion as Moral Reason—Georg Hermes

Georg Hermes (1775–1831) tried to make Catholic theology credible in terms of Kant's notions of scientific certitude. Since God is the most important "object" of religious knowledge, surely we must know for certain that he exists. Redesigning Catholic philosophy, Hermes attempted to show that God could be seen as the absolute Condition for the achievement of any reasonable moral action. If we are going to fulfill our moral obligations, then we must trust in God's authority, which permits us to be certain in our actions. Otherwise, we would be acting in doubt.

Though Hermes realized that his apology for Catholic faith did not look like the old arguments based upon miracles and God's Word, he would not have expected the condemnation of his positions which occurred after his death. Pope Gregory XVI (1831–46) saw only that the act of faith itself was a gift of divine grace, not a reasonable addendum to our achievement of practical affairs.

Religion as Aesthetic Trust in the
History of the Kingdom

The shift in English poetry between Alexander Pope's (1688–1744) heroic couplets and Percy Bysshe Shelley's (1792–1822) lyrics cannot be more obvious. What before had been reason, discipline, and polished manners became expressive passion, eccentric genius, and conventionless freedom. As Samuel Taylor Coleridge (1772–1834) put it: "Deep thinking is attainable only by a man of deep feeling." The poetry, music, and prose of the Romantics—and their theology—were meant to ignite the world. Their inspiration and optimism were inaugurated in the American, then in the early days of the French, Revolutions. As William Blake (1757–1827), the poet and artist, has it in *The Marriage of Heaven and Hell* (1790–93): "Exuberance is Beauty."

German Catholic and Protestant theologians, under the spell of Romanticism, shifted their horizons from the rational and universally demonstrable to the affective and the particular. They embraced both sides of historical studies with passion. The upper blade of the scientific scissors demanded that they think the continuities of past data, searching it for clues to patterns; the lower blade required the recovery of exact facts separated from fable. The first mode of thinking permitted new ways of thinking around or beyond Kant so that the meaning of Christian faith could be reestablished; the second provided accurate data so that theories about faith could never become abstract or unrelated to the actual Tradition.

Johann Sebastian von Drey (1777–1853) and his students boldly undertook to think through the particulars of the Christian Scriptures and Tradition to the meaning of a historical faith. Unlike Hermes's rationalism, Drey's analyses took the Romantics' notion of the universe as an organic developing whole and applied it to Christian revelation. God's creation of the world was his loving disclosure of himself. God's Kingdom is an evolving idea, revealed at the beginning of everything. Social and historical, this idea comes to conscious expression in the Church. The bearer of God's revelation in the present is therefore the growing, changing, social history of humanity, progressively unfolding itself until God gathers the Kingdom into himself. All visible manifestations of ecclesial life are signs,

118

symbols of this generous communication of Love. Faith was not irrational, but a reasonable confidence in God's action in history and society.

Historians like Johann Joseph Ignaz von Döllinger (1799–1890) and Lord Acton (John Emmerich Edward Dahlberg, 1834–1902) believed that the introduction of historical-critical methods could only benefit Catholic self-understanding. Their emphasis upon the tools of research, the hard work of manuscript recovery, the critical analysis which distinguished fact from legend assumed responsibility for the traditions of scholarship begun by the French Benedictines of St. Maur in the seventeenth century and canonized by Leopold von Ranke (1795–1886). To discover what actually happened as opposed to what people thought might have happened requires the skill of a detective and the surgeon's delicate scalpel. Every cherished body of belief which undergoes the suspicions of historical criticism finds the operation painful.

Acton and von Döllinger, however, saw the historical sciences as a "trusty ally." They believed that the actual data of history would bear witness to the truth of Catholic positions. If history did not, then the positions themselves required reconstruction. Acton wrote,

> We are bound to see that the laws of true reasoning and of historical criticism are not tampered with; it is by them only we can know in their reasonableness and integrity the doctrines which have been revealed and developed in the process of history.[2]

Later nineteenth-century controversies required both von Döllinger and Acton to step back from their strenuous matchmaking between contemporary science and the Catholic Tradition. Both continued to believe that the forceful history of truth was the only authentic victory of faith.

Neo-Scholasticism

By midcentury, the strength of the Romantic theological movement had been spent in Catholic circles. Simultaneously, the Middle Ages had been discovered (especially by the English essayists and critics John Ruskin [1819–1900] and William Morris [1834–96]). Here was a premodern society in which thought, action, and religion made a coherent social pattern. Interest in medieval philosophy and theology followed in the attempt to find answers to (what seemed the rational subjectivism of Kant, the relativism of historically minded theologians, and the political criticism of progressives.

The Jesuits were in the forefront of this recovery of the past with their restoration (1814) after political suppression in 1773. Men like Joseph Kleutgen (1811–83) used political power and the Society's organs of communication (the Roman College, now the Gregorianum, and the journal *Civiltà Cattolica*) to foster the replacement of all modern systems of philosophy or theology with the study of Thomas Aquinas.

Kleutgen's opposition to newer theologies turned on the belief that contemporaries confused or intermixed the act of faith and the role of reason; the action of God's grace and independent, though subordinate, value of nature; and the interdependent coprinciples of soul and body. Theologies such as Drey's which believed that the movement of history was at once God's action *and* human choice were immediately suspect, though his particular opinions were never condemned. The rationalism of Hermes, however, proved to be a confused mixture of faith and reason. Reason and faith, nature and grace, body and soul were not opposed to each other; but in each case, the second contrary was only a helpmate to supernatural values.

Kleutgen's recovery of the Aristotelian bases for Aquinas's theories of knowlege (epistemology) permitted him to develop a knowing subject who was capable of metaphysical arguments for the existence of God *and* a sure knowledge of ethical judgments based upon the natural law. Contemporary thinkers had either rejected Divine Presence on the basis of sense (empiricism, e.g., Hume) or immanentized Divine Presence in a pantheist subject (idealism). An authentic Aquinas would permit not only a true theory of knowledge (*how* we know), but also a metaphysics (*what* we know), guaranteeing a society of secure moral roles.

Kleutgen's presentations were overwhelmingly successful. Although we know now that his understanding of Aquinas was rather defective, nonetheless, he had given Thomism an intellectual respectability it had probably never had before. He had shown that spirituality, practice, and truth were a religious unity which should not be divided in the contemporary world. His positions would be emended, contradicted, and surpassed; but he provided the base for the rich reinterpretations of Aquinas by Étienne Gilson (1884–1978), Jacques Maritain (1882–1973), and Joseph Maréchal (1878–1944) as well as the contemporary analyses of Karl Rahner (b. 1904) and Bernard Lonergan (b. 1904). The future was in the seeds of the past.

POPE PIUS IX—THE PAPAL STATES AND VATICAN COUNCILS

Pope Pius IX (1792–1878) began his pontificate in 1846 as a reformer in the lands under his civil jurisdiction. He granted amnesties, proposed economic reforms and social changes which widened electoral representation. He was determined to strengthen the dilapidated state bequeathed to him by Pope Gregory XVI (1831–46) or the puppet state which Napoleon I (1769–1821) had wrested from Pius VII (1800–1823). With this history, it is not surprising that the existence of the Papal States seemed, even to some liberal Catholics, an essential instrument for the independence of the head of the Catholic Church.

Over the period of a year, Pius granted more and more authority to democratic bodies subordinate to the papacy until, in 1848, he granted a new constitution making himself, in effect, a limited ruling monarch. In April, however, he refused to allow papal troops to join the Catholic King of Piedmont-Sardinia in a war against Catholic Austria; and shortly thereafter terrorists assassinated his prime minister in Parliament. Pius fled to Naples in disguise, returning only when French troops occupied Rome. This military security remained in the city from 1849 until 1870, when their removal occasioned the takeover of the Papal States by the forces of Italian unification. Pius remained intransigently opposed to any compromise with modern democratic ideals.

During the last two decades of his pontificate, Pius turned to "spiritual" affairs where his strong conserving voice was not always reactionary. He erected new dioceses and restored the episcopal hierarchies to England (1850) and Holland (1853). But his two major successes were the proclamation of the doctrine of the im maculate conception of the Virgin Mary (1854) and the decrees o the First Vatican Council (1869–70).

In the proclamation of 1854, centuries-old devotion to the Mothe of Jesus, which had grown largely without any official ecclesiastica discussion since the Council of Ephesus (431), received institutiona approbation, support, and correction. Pius, encouraged by the bishops whom he had consulted and by Catholic piety, declared Mary's immaculate conception a dogma, that is, an official belief o the community. The theological meaning of the dogma was stated clearly. Mary, because of her office and role as the Mother of Jesus was conceived without the sin (Original Sin) which is the heritage o all human beings. This did not mean that Mary had been raised to the level of Redeemer; but that as the Mother of the Redeemer, she shared beforehand in the grace of his life and work. Her own concep tion and birth were quite normal; the statement was a religious, not a biological, one—that Mary is the first of the redeemed; that indeed if she is not the ultimately faithful disciple, pondering all things in her heart, not one of us can be.

The culminating accomplishment of Pius's reforming conser vatism is far more important for the Catholic world—the first gen eral council of the Church since Trent (1545–63). Its dogmatic constitution *Dei Filius* (*Son of God*) recalled Catholics to their scholastic heritage, best described as a middle course between the theological temptations of fideism (faith alone without, or in opposi tion to, the use of human reason) and rationalism (reason alone without faith). The council fathers reminded their contemporaries that, at least since the time of Anselm of Canterbury (1034–1109), the Catholic ideal for theology must include both faith and reason.

Reason provides *some* understanding of the mysteries of faith, partially from analogues in the natural world, partially from com parison with other beliefs of the community. Catholics must con tinue to be "pilgrims in this mortal life, not yet with God; 'for we walk by faith and not by sight'" (2 Cor. 5:7, NAB). Art and science, with their own methods and principles, contribute to this life of faith; and authentic art or science can never really be in opposition to faith.

The most controversial conservative document of the Council, however, is that concerning the infallibility of the pope in matters of faith and morals. There were, of course, political undertones to the decree. Pius IX had centered loyalty to the Church more and more upon allegiance to the papacy; political events demanded it, according to his mind. Nor was it possible for him or his opponents to see a distinction between his role as sovereign of civil territory and servant-head of the Church. Civil war against the pope was destruction of his spiritual authority.

The internal dissension between liberals and conservatives in the Church repeated itself in their attitudes toward the papacy. Some, usually called the Ultramontanes, claimed extravagant power for the papal office. Strong support of the papacy in France went along with strong opposition to civil control of the Church. There was a bizarre coherence between thinking of Pius IX as "the most enlightened sovereign of the age" (as one London newspaper phrased it) and the "vice-God of humanity" (as a French bishop remarked). One Italian Ultramontanist described it this way: "When the Pope thinks, it is God who is thinking in him."[3]

These extravagances, seemingly so blasphemous now, were not isolated. Opponents before and during the Council felt that it was utterly inopportune, though not perhaps inaccurate, to describe the pope as infallible. They generally feared the particular sort of infallibility which might be defined.

The Council, however, was not a rubber stamp for the thoughts of Pius IX. It is now clear that there was quite adequate time for nuanced discussion and moderate revision of the decree on the Church and infallibility which ultimately emerged from the Council halls.

The doctrine of infallibility reasserts the belief that God will not let the Church be led into major errors on basic questions of faith and morality. As a result, solemn pronouncements upon urgent matters of faith and morals by a pope, when he speaks not as an individual but for and to the universal Church, cannot be erroneous. It is thus the charism (or spiritual gift) and power of teaching that is protected in this dogmatic statement of the council. However, not all papal teaching is protected, only the teaching on issues of consequence in faith or morals.

Vatican Council I represents a high point of traditional Catholicism in the nineteenth century. The development of more far-reaching Catholic reforms lay ahead, for the prime issue continued to be the separation of most Catholics from the wider culture of political democracy and contemporary science. Pius himself seems to have understood that an era was passing. Shortly before his death, he is reported to have said:

> I hope my successor will be as much attached to the Church as I have been and will have as keen a desire to do good: beyond that, I can see that everything has changed; my system and my policies have had their day, but I am too old to change my course; that will be the task of my successor.[4]

THE PROPHETS OF THE FUTURE

Change came swiftly. European Catholicism saw a shift to the forces of liberalism at the highest level. Upon the death of Pius IX in 1878, Cardinal Gioacchino Vicenzo Pecci (1810–1903), formerly a student of Jesuit Neo-Scholasticism and papal diplomat to Brussels, London, Paris, and Cologne, was elected as Leo XIII. Making use of the enormous prestige gained in the Catholic Church by the emphasis upon the role of the pope, Leo wrote significant letters, encyclicals, outlining creative resolutions to the interchange between Church and world (*Immortale Dei*, 1885) and describing the freedom of citizens in republics (*Libertas Praestantissimum*, 1888) and in Christian democracies (*Graves in Communi*, 1901). He established the return to the authentic texts of Thomas Aquinas as the proper educational tool for theological students (*Aeterni Patris*, 1889) and encouraged the critical study of the Bible (*Providentissimus Deus*, 1893). He opened the Vatican archives to historical research (1883) and established a Biblical Commission (1902) to deal with questions of interpretation by a committee of scholarly peers. As Leo stated: "The first law of history is to dare not to lie; the second is not to fear to speak the truth—and to leave no room for prejudice." Probably his most renowned encyclical, however, is *Rerum Novarum* (1891), which comments on the social, religious, and political value of labor, property, government, and industrial society. This letter established a program of social reform which has been reiterated to the present by continuing papal support.

Just as one prophet of future Catholic life was an Italian pope, the other was an English cardinal, a convert from the Church of England. John Henry Newman (1801–90) reflects the creative stature and shifting energies of nineteenth-century Catholicism perhaps better than any other. As he himself put it: "To be human is to change; to be perfect is to change often."

Newman's own life made this ideal concrete. As an Anglican clergyman, he quickened the reforming tempo of the Church of England through the Oxford Movement (1833–45). As a Roman Catholic priest, he helped, by his own historical research, to promote a needed awareness of the biblical and patristic origins of the Catholic Tradition. As an Englishman, he brought the British empirical, scientific, and historical traditions into contact with continental Catholicism. As a thinker and believer, he made it clear that he could not and would not leave aside anything that was fundamentally human in his presentation of faith. And finally, as one of the foremost prose writers in his century, Newman created a style which could communicate to all readers the meaning of a life spent in search of religious values.

In his *Essay on the Development of Doctrine* (1845), Newman outlined how history and critical historical research itself can be aids to the understanding of changing beliefs. As his intellectual interpretation for becoming a Catholic, the *Essay* described how the Church had changed throughout the past and how believers can only anticipate that it will continue to do so in the present and the future.

The Newman one remembers most winningly is the quiet, stringently honest, straightforward man whose autobiography, *Apologia pro Vita Sua* (1864), registers all the thoughtful tensions and affective paradoxes, the religious heights of conversion and the depressive depths of sin that an individual can undergo in the quest to be both modern and Catholic. In his *Essay in Aid of a Grammar of Assent* (1870), Newman's mature reflections on the relation between faith and reason provide an analysis not of concepts nor of abstract truths, but of the act of faith itself. What are we doing when we believe? Is it a contemporary possibility?

Newman comprised in his life and understanding of that faithful life the three major concerns that had occupied most of nineteenth-century Catholicism: *who* the believer is (subjectivity); *how* the

125

believer comes to faith (history); and *why* the believer should trust the Christian faith as socially, philosophically, and politically credible (reason). Newman's original contributions to these questions of theology, culture, philosophy, and history were not always appreciated by Catholics in the nineteenth century. Somewhat suspicious of his arguments, they could not have guessed that in 1879, Leo XIII would grant Newman the cardinalate. There is here no finer symbol of Newman's achievements as an individual believer or of the success of the progressive forces whose triumph he represented in the Catholic Church.

HEARING THE STRAINS OF FUTURE HARMONIES

The nineteenth-century Catholic experience ended in quite another key than it began. From Napoleon's hegemony over Pius VII to Leo XIII's invitation to the modern world is a shift in form. The contrasts and dissonances with the powerful position of papal authority transformed themselves into a chorus of praise with conservative dissidents. The century's Catholic history seems to the uninitiated or uninterested much like a later symphony of Anton Bruckner (1824–96)—lengthy, formless swells of passion, sharply broken by reasonable melodies lasting but a moment, alternately loud, then soft, ending rather then concluding.

But the century's Catholic identity is merely complex. The polarizations at its beginning—either the modern world or the Church; either critical history or the Bible; either democratic freedom or papal authority; either the philosophy of the human subject or objective beliefs—did find their positive resolution in prophetic figures such as the early Lamennais, von Döllinger, Acton, and Newman—and curiously enough in Neo-Scholastics like Kleutgen and popes like Leo XIII. It is in those dramatic figures, and many others whom we have not named, who were willing to risk scientific history in their faith and to embody action based upon history, science, and faith, that a vision of a Catholic Church in the twentieth century was achieved.

NOTES

1. Igor Stravinsky, *Poetics of Music,* trans. Arthur Knodel and Ingolf Dahl (Cambridge, Mass.: Harvard University Press, 1979), 33–42.
2. Lord Acton, *Essays on Church and State,* ed. Douglas Woodruff (New York: Crowell, 1968), 273.
3. See Cuthbert Butler, *The Vatican Council, 1869–70,* ed. Christopher Butler (Westminster, Md.: Newman, 1962), 44–62.
4. Alec R. Vidler, *The Church in an Age of Revolution: 1789 to the Present Day* (Baltimore: Penguin Books, 1968), 153.

FURTHER RELATED MATERIAL

Stephen Neill's, *The Interpretation of the New Testament 1861–1961* (New York and London: Oxford University Press, 1966) chronicles nineteenth- and twentieth-century biblical developments affecting theology. Paul Tillich (*Perspectives on 19th and 20th Century Protestant Theology*, ed. K. Braaten [New York: Harper & Row, 1967]) and Karl Barth (*Protestant Theology in the Nineteenth Century* [Valley Forge, Pa.: Judson, 1973]) offer contrasting Protestant understandings of the development of the period. Catholic theology of the period is excellently presented in Gerald McCool, *Catholic Theology in the Nineteenth Century: The Quest for a Unitary Method* (New York: Seabury Press, 1977). The political and religious grid is admirably described in E. E. Y. Hales, *Pio Nono: A Study of European Politics and Religion in the Nineteenth Century* (Garden City, N.Y.: Doubleday & Co., 1962), while Cuthbert Butler, *The Vatican Council, 1869–70,* ed. Christopher Butler (Westminster, Md.: Newman, 1962) offers a still helpful view of the previous Vatican Council. Mark Schoof's *A Survey of Catholic Theology, 1800–1970,* trans. N. D. Smith (New York: Paulist, 1970), while sometimes spotty and episodic, nonetheless describes the major figures. A. R. Vidler's *The Church in an Age of Revolution: 1789 to the Present Day* (Baltimore: Penguin Books, 1968) overviews the whole. An intellectual vision of the entire period is best presented with added bibliography and helpful questions in James C. Livingston, *Modern Christian Thought from the Enlightenment to Vatican II* (New York: Macmillan Co., 1971).

THE CREATORS OF
TWENTIETH-CENTURY CATHOLICISM (I)
Europe: Prophets from the Past,
Pastors for the Future

> It is done.
> Once again the Fire has penetrated the earth.
> Not with the sudden crash of thunderbolt,
> Riving the mountain tops:
> Does the Master break down doors to enter his own home?
> Without earthquake, or thunderclap:
> The flame has lit up the whole world from within.
>> Pierre Teilhard de Chardin (1881–1955),
>> from *Hymn of the Universe*

Our world is made of images—moving pictures, video recordings, photographic reprints. We fix on film certain ways of seeing, knowing something or someone. We still the mobile present into a past we can detach from a book, an album, and handle or repeat it—sometimes with loving care, sometimes with desire, occasionally with fear and hatred. Pictures, as Susan Sontag has noted, have become a defense against our anxieties about the transience of things and friends, a tool to establish control.[1] If we have in our possession birthday pictures of our children for the first fifteen years, if we have family Christmas ensembles imprinted on paper, then we control the change in our children and the divisions in our families in the present. We can look in on a time in which we once were "all together."

If our overview of the history of Catholicism—of its prophets, apocalyptic visionaries, and proponents of Tradition—is seen as merely a lengthy group portrait of our occasionally inept, sometimes saintly, even brilliant ancestors, then we have failed. For the modern meaning of Catholicism must be a *cumulative* presence of questions, heroes and heroines, texts and places which continue to surprise the Church with its active memory.

The contemporary shape of the Church attempts to come to terms with its own universality, its own catholic nature. If in the post-Reformation period the Church saw itself providing a uniform cultural alternative to the confusions, disagreements, and anger of early modern societies, it now recognizes that universality will require not an abstract unique culture, but a strong network of interlocking cultural expressions of Christian spirituality, action, and beliefs. It is a vocation to the concrete Catholic incarnation of the Gospel, whatever the cost to itself.

Thus there remain those who continuously propose the Tradition, and their extraordinary gift to the future was the Second Vatican Council (1962–65). There are the prophets who constantly call the Church to social justice, political freedom for the oppressed, food for the hungry, and they come regularly from those countries where former colonial powers were once exploitive. Then there are the visionaries—those who can see only God's future in a world dominated by the threat of nuclear war, a population explosion with its consequent crises of food, resources, and international terrorism.

In the three chapters that conclude our survey of Catholic identity, we will discuss these people, places, and things in a sequence that begins in Europe where the Tradition recently has been so brightly refurbished and continues in the United States where the principle of religious freedom has been upheld. We will finish our journey in the world of Latin America, Asia, and Africa, where the future dreams of criticism and hope seem to lie. But our vision of the Catholic future begins in recovery of the Catholic past.

A QUESTION OF THE PAST:
REACTIONS AND RECOVERY OF OPINIONS

The Crisis of Modernity

When Pius X (1835–1914) was elected in 1903, this utterly pious man (later declared a saint [1954]) announced that in contrast to the politically and educationally progressive initiatives of his predecessor Leo XIII, he would "restore all things in Christ" (Eph. 1:10). His program for restoration included the growing involvement of lay Catholics in the missionary life of the Church, a new codification of Canon Law (the first since the Middle Ages), reforms of the prayer life and Eucharist of the Church—and the annihilation of Modernism.

Most scholars now agree that Modernism, defined by Pius's papal letters *Pascendi* and *Lamentabili* (1907) as a "synthesis of all heresies," was less a movement than a loose combination of individuals faced with the problems of modernity in the Catholic Church. They were concerned about the same range of questions as their "liberal" forebears (such as De Lamennais): the acceptance of historical-critical method in biblical research, the rigidity of the reigning scholasticisms, growing papal authoritarianism, and the Church's affiliation with repressive political regimes. But they combined these issues with a recognition that the religious experience of Christianity, precisely as *religious,* transcended all narratives, symbols, interpretations, institutions, and systems.

Even though critics of papal policy think the decrees were an extremely skillful articulation of the logical implications of contemporary ideas, most would agree that no matter how clever the construction, the reaction was hasty, regrettably defensive, and even panic-stricken. The primary error of Modernism, according to its opponents, was its reduction of religious truth to personal religious experience. Sacraments, dogmas, and hierarchy were dispensable expressions judged by the private needs of the individual. The encyclical saw the movement as a contemporary form of Docetism, an ancient heresy in which Christ did not so much *become* human with all its limitations as cloak his divinity in a discardable humanity.

Though upon occasion some Modernists were somewhat devious in the propagation of their ideas (through the use of pseudonyms), the suspicious reactions created as much of a crisis as the ideas themselves. A concerted effort was made in dioceses throughout the world to hunt out avant-garde thinkers, requiring candidates for ordination, seminary professors, and theologians to take an anti-Modernist oath. Schools of theology fostered stricter behavior and more rigid teaching called Integrism, which always harshly and loudly proclaimed its loyalty to the past. This sometimes hysterically reactionary element, with its pattern of spies and informers, remains a raw nerve in Catholic life to the present day.

Pius X sensed, rather than thought, that there must be a halt to scholarship before the Church was captured in images in which it could no longer recognize its continuity with its own identity. For the Modernists, the crisis was one of methods: of the Church's ability to adapt creatively to a new situation. What is the truth of the situation?

What did Modernists teach? We must look briefly at three individuals: Alfred Loisy (1857–1940), a French Scripture scholar; George Tyrell (1861–1909), a Jesuit theologian and essayist; and Friedrich von Hügel (1852–1925), layman, philosopher of religion, and theologian. The first two were excommunicated from the Church; von Hügel, though suspect, escaped censure.

Alfred Loisy—Biblical Critic

Loisy believed that his mission was to reconcile contemporary critical scholarship of the Bible with the essence of Catholicism. As a professor in Paris, he lectured against the factual character of the early chapters of Genesis. Dismissed from his professorship (1893), he wrote a response to Adolf von Harnack's (1851–1930) *The Essence of Christianity* (1900), which he saw as a "liberal" misreading of the New Testament. In his *The Gospel and the Church* Loisy argued that the most primitive Jesus-texts were the proclamations of the imminence of the kingdom, not the Fatherhood of God, the infinite value of the individual soul, and an ideal of ethical living, as von Harnack thought. This eschatological kingdom *had to give way* to the doctrinal institutionalizations of the Church. Jesus announced the kingdom; it was the Church that arrived.

This biblical critic thought of his position as an eminently pastoral defense of the Tradition through which the New Testament was written. Development was essential to the very existence of a Catholic community. Ecclesiastical formulas are not the object of faith, since only God himself, Christ, and his work can guide the contemporary Church.

Loisy's somewhat left-handed support for Catholic identity was received with suspicion. His assumptions that the Gospels were not historical biographies of Jesus; that they were only testimonies of belief by early communities; that Jesus' own consciousness of his mission was limited, even erroneous; and that doctrines are a change in the substance of the Tradition did not fit the prevailing understandings of Catholic experience.

George Tyrell—Mystical Doctrine

During George Tyrell's early years as a convert to Catholicism, he became an ardent disciple of Thomas Aquinas; but late in the century he came into contact with other philosophies. The conflict this produced caused him to reject all authoritarian forms of doctrine— but not to disavow Catholicism. The Modernist, unlike the liberal, adheres to both modernity and Tradition. "By the modernist, I mean a churchman, of any sort, who believes in the possibility of a synthesis between the essential truth of his religion and the essential truth of modernity."[2]

Tyrell, like Loisy, had a certain mystical temperament which believed that the practical return of the heart's love to God was more important than any theoretic or institutional formulation. Faith in the continuity of spiritual revelation precedes parables and facts. Institutions and constructs are symbols of the essentially transcendent religious ideal. When we read his remarks about the Church, we cannot help but think of later words by Vatican Council II. Tyrell states that Christ

> lives in the Church, not metaphorically but actually. He finds a growing medium of self-utterance, ever complementing and correcting that of His mortal individuality. . . . The Church is not merely a society or school, but a mystery and sacrament; like the humanity of Christ of which it is an extension.[3]

Friedrich von Hügel—Spiritual Teacher

Baron von Hügel was a philosopher of religion, a director of troubled souls, and an authority on mysticism with or without his Modernist connections. Born in Florence, educated in Europe, settling near London, he became the intellectual switchboard for the Modernist conversation. His distrust of Scholasticism was as profound as Tyrell's; he found it incapable of including the historical, the experiential, and the critical. His convictions concerning the use of biblical scholarship were just as severe as Loisy's. Yet he neither left the Church nor did the Church leave him. Why?

Von Hügel was absolutely convinced of the cognitive, even strictly metaphysical, element in every religious experience. He lamented the fact that his friends were non- or antiphilosophical. Doctrine was an integral moment of all experience, especially religious experience. Secondly, von Hügel was deeply attached to the institutional Church. The Catholic Church embodied for him the spiritual experience of humanity and his personal piety depended upon it. Finally, von Hügel was a diplomat, a master of European languages, whose ability and will to mediate among opposing parties no doubt reflected a certain mental ability which permitted his seeing many sides of an issue simultaneously.

Though von Hügel considered the papal decrees of 1907 deeply unjust, he also understood, particularly later in life, how unsatisfactory some of his friends' philosophical and ecclesial positions were. For him, Christianity was three interlocking, overlapping spheres: the mystical, the intellectual, *and* the institutional. None could be ignored except at the risk of losing Catholic identity.

The Modernists identified the problem facing the Catholic Church at the turn of the century as one of culture rather than of faith. It is also clear now that none of the participants had an adequate set of methods (philological, interpretive, historical, or metaphysical) to deal constructively with the problems they had isolated. Although their attempts to update Catholicism through scientific tools were urgently required, they often ignored authentic institutional elements of the past in their understanding of the present.

Painful as the Modernists' views were to the "official" Church, the conflict itself can be viewed historically as the final sour breath of nineteenth-century reactionary attitudes. Yet the consternation at the excesses of Modernists created an impasse in Catholic life, heightening the temptation to forget the claims modernity has on faith.

A Return to the Sources

Fortunately the heedless neglect of modernity, fostered by the squinting response of the papal office to Modernism, did not destroy the intellectual and religious quest of Catholic thinkers. From the end of the nineteenth century, partially due to the fear created by Integrist suspicions, intellectuals began gathering the evidence of the past which would develop in midcentury into a full reconstruction of Catholic life.

The *liturgical revival*, begun by Abbot Prosper Guéranger (1805–75) at the Abbey of Solesmes as a somewhat nostalgic return to medieval piety and music, rapidly gained intellectual and institutional weight through Pope Pius X's support. A largely monastic and Benedictine development under Lambert Beauduin (1873–1960), of

Mont César in Belgium, and Pius Parsch (1884–1954), an Austrian Augustinian canon, it stressed lay participation in worship and encouraged less-perfunctory performance of ritual. People joined in the Eucharist through dialogue and read translations of the liturgical texts while the priest prayed in Latin. Critical and historical studies by Louis Duchesne (1843–1922) and Fernand Cabrol (1855–1937) gave scholarly support to the movement of piety and reform.

The *biblical revival* introduced historical-critical and philological methods into the interpretation of the Christian Scriptures. Marie-Joseph Lagrange (1855–1938) founded the École Pratique d'Études Bibliques in Jerusalem (1890), writing commentaries on both Jewish and Christian Scriptures that rapidly became standard. In 1902, when Leo XIII established the Biblical Commission to promote and supervise biblical studies, Lagrange was made a member.

The *patristic revival* picked up the standard of the Maurists, Cardinal Newman, and Ignaz von Döllinger. It cataloged sources, established critical editions of texts, translated into vernaculars, distinguished legendary from factual narrative, and produced serious biographies. By individuals like F. X. Funk (1840–1907) at Tübingen, Heinrich Dénifle (1844–1905) of the Vatican Archives, Duchesne and his student Pierre Batiffol (1861–1928), Ludwig von Pastor (1854–1928), whose history of the popes became a critical norm, and Charles Joseph Héféle (1809–93), whose *History of the Councils* (1855–90) with its twentieth-century additions (1907–38) by Henri Leclerq (1869–1945) provided an accurate record of doctrinal change, the data of the Catholic Tradition were established with scientific rigor.

Nor did *philosophical studies* forget a return to their sources. Leo XIII's and Pius X's emphasis on Thomas Aquinas as the most important theologian entailed a new edition of his works and the creative recovery of Aquinas's thought in individuals like Joseph Maréchal (1878–1944), Jacques Maritain (1882–1973), Pierre Rousselot (1878–1915), and Étienne Gilson (1884–1978). The early works of the three most important Catholic systematic theologians of the mid–twentieth century were reinterpretations of Aquinas on epistemology and metaphysics (Karl Rahner [b. 1904]); on grace and human freedom (Bernard Lonergan [b. 1904]) and on sacrament (Edward Schillebeeckx [b. 1914]). Recent work has also rethought the place of other scholastics (for example, Bonaventure and Duns Scotus).

Two major nonscholastic philosophers have influenced twentieth-century theology as well. Through the concrete analysis by Maurice Blondel (1861–1949) of the human will and its inability to be entirely satisfied by particulars, Catholic theologians have been able to emphasize the experiential components of religious knowledge. In Gabriel Marcel (1889–1973), Catholics found a philosophy of existential and interpersonal encounter which validated the noncognitive, though not irrational, aspects of Christian life. These philosophers, by their emphasis on both metaphysical and existential aspects of existence, have proven helpful in going beyond the Modernist tendency to make theologians choose between being or person; philosophy or experience.

The easiest way to understand the basic thrust of this multidimensional movement of change after the Modernist crisis is to hear the French word that symbolizes the whole period from 1920 to 1960—*ressourcement*. The basic meaning of the word is *return*, but as a widespread recalling of the sources of Catholicism. Recalling becomes rehearing the original message; and Catholic *ressourcement* invoked critical investigation and reassessment of the present in the light of the past.

In these various scholarly revivals, Catholics joined their Protestant colleagues in the scientific study of the original documents of their beliefs. Not only did this collaboration provide the initial steps toward the healing of confessional differences, but it established a common thirst for authentic Christian service to the world. Analyses still produce disagreements, but rarely upon confessional loyalties. It has permitted forms of common worship which respect the present institutional disunity, but grant it no angry permanence. Catholics and Protestants have begun to remember a common Tradition.

THE EXISTENTIAL CRISIS— DEPRESSION AND WORLD WARS

The scholarly revivals, the ecumenical movement, and the encounter with philosophical theories all occurred during two brutal, devastating wars which framed a financially enervating depression. During such periods in an international community, one has the preservers and the risk-takers; those who would prefer to avoid conflict as well as those who would provoke it for the sake of polarizing the evangelical or demonic values involved. The official, institutional Church took both positions.

The underlying goal of every pope was to remain sufficiently neutral in political conflicts so that the charitable, social, educational, and religious endeavors of the Church might continue. Whether it was Benedict XV's (1914–22) neutrality and negotiations for peace, or Pius XI's (1922–39) concordats and treaties with Soviet, German, and Italian nationalist states, the practice of diplomacy with governments was not meant as approval, but as a political enablement for pastoral care. In the case of the Lateran Treaty (1929) with Benito Mussolini's (1883–1945) government, Pius XI wanted neither a simple identification with fascist policies and repression, nor utter antagonism toward governmental attempts at social and economic stabilization.

Yet when the German bishops asked for a papal encyclical on the problems of their Church, Pius responded with a vigorous condemnation of National Socialism (*Mit brennender Sorge, 1937*). No one may put state, government, national religion, or blood-race in the place of God. Shortly before he died, the pope repeated his summons to Catholics by recalling that in the Eucharistic Prayer we call on Abraham as the patriarch and forefather of all. "It is impossible for a Christian to take part in anti-Semitism. It is inadmissible. Through Christ and in Christ we are the spiritual progeny of Abraham. Spiritually, we are all Semites."[4]

The complexity of ecclesiastical response to totalitarian governments during the Second World War (1939–45) reflected the public diplomatic fears and the private charity of Pius XII (1939–58). As a former official representative in Berlin, he had protested bitterly (in some forty notes) on behalf of the papacy against Nazi persecution of Church and peoples. As pope, however, his careful, scholarly use of the international media (especially Vatican radio) proved too general, too abstractly principled to anti-German forces. Pius gave Vatican City passports to refugees, hostages, and Jewish detainees, housing them in extraterritorial Vatican buildings all during the war; but his lack of direct confrontation with Nazism contrasted too distinctly with the growing acerbic anger of Pius XI.

Like all diplomats, Pius XII seemed to believe that reasonable solutions were always possible. That such approaches were sufficient in the case of specific atrocities, like the deportation and holocaust of European Jews, is not only questionable but impossible. During the war, various Jewish groups thanked the pope for his interventions in the preservation of some four hundred thousand Jews from certain death. Yet in this era of precisely institutional responses, was that enough to claim loyalty to a Tradition engendered by Jesus of Nazareth?

Pius left the heroism of the institution to the corporate responsibility of national bishops and individual martyrs. And there were martyrs at all levels, individuals like Edith Stein (1891–1942), a Carmeline nun, philosopher, teacher, and writer, who was removed from her Dutch refuge to Auschwitz where she died in the gas chambers; or Maximilian Kolbe (1894–1941), a Polish Franciscan, who offered to replace a young prisoner who had a family. He died of starvation at Auschwitz. Even though Pius XII feared reprisals against Catholics in Germany and in occupied Europe, bishops like Michael von Faulhaber (1869–1952) of Munich and Clemens A. von Galen (1878–1946) of Münster publicly condemned euthanasia, concentration camps, imprisonment without trial, and confiscation of property. Priests like Rupert Mayer (1876–1945) maintained that a German Catholic could never be a National Socialist, spoke out, and received imprisonment as a response. Yet in the end, nothing is enough to remove the common responsibility of the Churches and Western Allies in not speaking earlier, with more forcefulness, and with greater effectiveness. We may not justify ourselves in the face of sin.

THE RISE OF A PROPHET—POPE JOHN XXIII

In the postwar years, Catholics needed a prophetic and dramatic figure, a new apostle who could communicate the progressive advancements of Church life in the face of the denials of war, depression, and death. One of the most amazing "accidents" of Catholic history occurred in the appearance of a prophet who was also pope, an authority who was servant.

Pope John XXIII (1958–63) was astounding by any standard. The style of Pius XII's government had been authoritarian and triumphal; in his later years, his considerable intellectual abilities waned and his native conserving *Romanità* could see no further than the crises of his early papacy. By contrast, John XXIII was Francis of Assisi raised to the role of Peter in the Church. His pontificate was brief; but when he died, the entire self-understanding of most Catholics had changed.

The impact of this pope was not so much that of intellect, though he had been a shrewd diplomat, nor of program, but of person. He appeared as a pastor and common father to all peoples of the world. His final encyclical, *Pacem in Terris* (*Peace on Earth,* 1963), was addressed to all men and women of good will. When he called together the few cardinals present in Rome for a meeting in January 1959, few realized how momentous his papacy would be. His agenda announced a few reforms and the calling of an ecumenical council. He saw its purpose as threefold: to link the bishops of the world to the pastoral responsibilities of the Bishop of Rome, to begin a reform or *aggiornamento* (Italian for "updating") of the Church itself, and to promote Christian unity. Pope John's personal attitudes were so outgoing that he could no longer maintain the policy of earlier Catholic withdrawal from contemporary intellectual and political life. Cardinal Montini, then archbishop of Milan and later pope as Paul VI (1963–78), remarked that it would be "the greatest Council the Church has ever held in the whole of the twenty centuries of its history. . . . Before our eyes, history is opening up enormous prospects for centuries to come."[5]

A NEW PENTECOST—
THE SECOND VATICAN COUNCIL (1962–65)

When the Council opened with a membership of approximately twenty-five hundred bishops and representatives of other Christian churches, the pope described the apocalyptic and condemnatory policy he hoped the fathers would repudiate. Those "prophets of doom" who saw in society only ruinous calamities should discover the "mysterious designs of divine Providence." Although the rejection of the old style of institutional distance to the world happened slowly, the Council did attempt to reshape the Church's pastoral role in an expanding culture. The declarations of the Council directed themselves to the reordering of Catholic institutional life, the relation of the Church to other Christians and nonbelievers, and to the world as a whole.

Inner Life: Worship and Collegiality

Through documents on worship, revelation, and the Church, the Council hoped to confirm the newly developing expressions of Catholic self-awareness. The *Constitution on the Sacred Liturgy* (1963) called for a simpler, more biblical worship which would engage the participation of the entire congregation. This was most clearly signaled in the return to the vernacular languages of believers, the removal of privatized prayers and merely ornamental gestures. It promoted the possibility of an utterly international style of indigenous liturgical evolution, reversing the uniformity which had so characterized the reforms dependent upon the Council of Trent.

Changes in worship were paralleled by a growing understanding of the Church itself. The *Dogmatic Constitution on the Church* (1964) and the *Decree on the Bishop's Pastoral Office in the Church* (1965), together with those on lay activity and priesthood, identified the Church as collegial (i.e., with an authority held in common, like a college). The Church has concentric circles of shared (or co-) responsibility among all members, with each member taking responsibility in his or her own way.

This notion of authority is strikingly different from that of a previous era in which the "common laity" were at the base of a pyramidal, layered communication that saw clergy (priests and bishops, then the pope) at the hierarchical apex. An ecclesial authority whose self-understanding had been largely *stratified,* that is, settled in ever higher and higher rungs of responsibility, was now describing itself as *differentiated* or dependent upon the differing competencies of the roles held in the community. The bishops saw themselves as completing the work begun at Vatican Council I when it defined the infallibility of the papal office. All authority in the episcopal office originates in Christ's death and resurrection as the service of redemption. Each bishop holds his authority directly from Christ's office, but in relationship to all others and to the primacy of the Bishop of Rome.

This technical, theological emphasis upon collegial responsibility has had important practical effects in Catholic communities. It has fostered the sharing of tasks and duties in national conferences of bishops; associations and senates of priests; evangelical, diocesan, and pastoral councils of laymen and women; and the local lay consultants called parish councils. The conciliar constitution led to a major decentralization of official authority and an increasing democratization of the Church (also with its consequent bureaucratization as well) on both the international and local levels.

The Council's ability to resee Catholicism in biblical and patristic images—the people of God, the Church as mystery, as sacrament ("a sign and instrument of communion with God and unity among all"), "holy, yet in need of purification," a prophetic and eschatological community—could not have been accomplished if it had not listened again to revelation itself (*Word of God,* 1965). The decree supported biblical scholarship, promoted the teaching of Scripture, and described revelation itself as God's disclosure of his own love, available in the faithful preaching of the prophets and apostles, crystallized in the Scriptures and Tradition which continue to interpret them.

Relations with the Future

In its four autumn sessions, however, the Council not only looked at reforms within the Church, but through its use of Protestant "observers" found ways to describe the common life of believers in the larger world. In the *Constitution on the Church* (1964) and the *Decree on Ecumenism* (1964), diatribe and the parochialism of withdrawal were decisively rejected for a fresh spirit of collaborative respect.

This new ecumenism was especially true for Catholics in relationship to their Jewish brothers and sisters. One of the darkest stains on the records of our Christian past has been the anti-Semitism which expressed conscious and unconscious motivations through harassment, persecution, and programs of racial destruction. The conciliar fathers made a first, if halting, attempt to atone for previous Christian sins of omission and commission by removing from Jews, as a people and as individuals, the charge of deicide (i.e., the killing of God). Efforts were made, though they were not wholly successful due to the opposition of Middle-Eastern Christians, to offer support for the national, political existence of Israel (established in 1948). "Spiritually, we are all Semites," as Pius XI had reminded us.

In two further documents, the *Declaration on Religious Freedom* (1965) and the *Pastoral Constitution on the Church in the Modern World* (1965), the Church declared its openness to the true values of contemporary modernity. Largely inspired by the writings of the United States Jesuit John Courtney Murray (1904–67), the *Declaration* affirmed the value of religious freedom for all people in all nations. The Church was not releasing individuals from their responsibility to be religious before God, but rather encouraging the free exercise of religion in every society. The dignity of the human person, proclaimed by Christian revelation, demanded it. But this *Declaration* merely confirmed what had been said in the *Church in the Modern World*—that the scientific search for truth, the political and social struggles for freedom and justice, the common striving of all human beings for a universal community have been embraced by the Church as *part of its own service* to the world. Christ's message is a transvaluation of the values of the world; the Church is his servant.

A Shift in Sensibilities

In the years that followed the Council, each successive pope has administrated the Church's heritage with renewed zeal. Paul VI continued John's gestures of openness to other Christian traditions, traveled widely throughout the world to show the Church's international character and its concern for justice. If his reforms of bureaucracy seemed too slow, his personal appointments to important posts and his increase of Third World representation balanced the delay. Recent popes have reduced papal pomp and circumstance, speaking no longer of *our*, but *my* positions in letters. Pope John Paul I (1978), during his brief time in office, rejected use of the tiara and described his first Eucharist as the inauguration of his ministry as supreme pastor rather than as a coronation. Papal coresponsibility meant service, not power.

These are shifts in sensibilities that the Council has promoted in Catholic life. The constant call by popes for social reform in recent encyclicals (*On the Progress of Peoples*, 1968; *The Redeemer of Humanity*, 1978; *Rich in Mercy*, 1980; *On Human Work*, 1981) repeats the demands of predecessors since Leo XIII for the valuation of individuals, the dignity of labor, and the political development of repressed peoples. Implementations of the internal affairs of the Conciliar renewal have been no less enterprising, particularly in the development of lay ministries (catechists, readers of Scripture, ministers of Eucharist to the sick, and in some countries a host of others).[6] The establishment of a portion of the clergy who are married (men who are permanently deacons) has made it possible for the Church to see that ministerial service in the Catholic community need not be limited to the celibate. Sufficient change has occurred so that in some places, women, particularly those from religious communities, administrate parishes, operate in marriage courts and diocesan chanceries, and establish effective political lobbies.

Catholic life since the Council has indeed changed—perhaps no more so than in the sense of individual conscience which has emerged—largely through the negative reaction of Catholics in developed Western countries to the papal letter *On Human Life* (1968). After considerable discussion, Paul VI decided to repeat previous teaching which prohibited the use of artificial contraception to limit births. Because some clergy anticipated a reversal and the post conciliar commissions divided their recommendations, many hoped for change. The pope could not see that a consensus had been reached and maintained the previous position. The international dissent was clearly audible. Recent studies indicate that Catholic couples and the priests who counsel them regularly disagree with the papal position. The delicate question of the moral teaching authority of the papacy and its weight for hierarchies and for individual Catholics is at stake.

For just as surely as it is possible to dissent from papal teaching on ethical matters in sexuality, so, too, Catholics may question positions on social justice, just wages, the dignity of work, and international cooperation. If, largely negatively, some Catholics discovered that their consciences were their own through *On Human Life,* what prohibits utterly subjective decisions in social, political, and international affairs? So Pope Paul VI's eloquent cry for peace at the United Nations ("war never again") will be rejected unless clear criteria for conscience, theological and personal dissent, and unquestioning adherence to authority are reexamined. Many national episcopal conferences as well as the International Theological Commission itself are engaged in just such discussions.

The problem of ethical and theological dissent reflects signs of an international community redefining itself in local terms. Pope John Paul II has praised the spiritual heritage of ancient cultures like the Chinese, recalling the work of adaptation carried on by Jesuits in the sixteenth century (February 1981). It is possible, he maintained, to be truly Christian and authentically Chinese, since the Church's call is to service and not political colonialization. Yet attempts by the Dutch bishops to develop multiple lay ministries for the local Church, out of necessity as well as policy, met with considerable papal caution for the preservation of clerical difference (January 1981).

The final moving images of Pope John Paul II remain something of a blur—imperishable energy which propels him away from Europe toward Middle and South America, Africa, Japan, Mexico, and the United States; a photomontage of a pope with native American headdress, sombreros, baseball caps, and sunburned bare head; a preacher whose affecting cry for land reform, redistribution of wealth for the poor, and the dignity of the human person focuses the attention of nonbeliever and believer alike; a simple faithful human being whose body bleeds with an assassin's bullet. Pope John Paul II is convinced that the energetic exercise of his moral authority is Christ's gift to the role of Peter's headship in the Church. He intends to use it to establish the Christian humanism of which his predecessor Paul VI spoke.

Sergei Eisenstein (1898–1948), the Russian film producer, director, and critic, has argued that the constant splicing of images into a montage, the sheer juxtaposition of different aspects of reality, creates not only a new truth, but simultaneously a way to the truth.[7] John Paul II, the first non-Italian pope since the Renaissance, with his gift for languages, by his pilgrimages to every land, wishes to comprise in himself the diverse character of contemporary Catholicism. Seeing him allows Catholics to envision the presence of their unity in Christ. This shift from an abstract, universally uniform Church to a community everywhere available in indigenized particular or local churches will require many decades of ecclesiastical leadership.

Councils are always ends as well as beginnings. This ingathering of Catholics concluded a lengthy historical development in which the community began to turn toward the contemporary world of enlightenment, revolution, and the sciences. It starts an era in which the Church must unlock the treasures of its beliefs, rituals, and moral principles for the individualized attention of a multiplicity of cultures without losing its identity as precisely Christian. There are, of course, signs that the fearful would prefer to return to the old uniform Christendom, however narrow and discredited in the contemporary world; but Catholics in the United States and in the Third World, who now make up by far the majority within the Church, preach in differing tongues. "You can't go home again," as Thomas Wolfe has told us.

Vatican Council II proposed a new image for the Church—a pilgrim people, who like their master, Jesus, have no place to lay their heads. The hope for the future of Catholics lies in their ability to see themselves on a journey toward the Lord who comes to greet them, not in waiting behind closed doors for his arrival. The New Pentecost has propelled the Church into a future from which there is no return.

NOTES

1. Susan Sontag, *On Photography* (New York: Farrar, Straus & Giroux, 1978), 9–11.

2. George Tyrell, *Christianity at the Crossroads* (London: Longmans, Green & Co., 1909), 5.

3. Ibid., 275.

4. J. Derek Holmes, *The Papacy in the Modern World* (New York: Crossroad, 1981), 116.

5. Ibid., 208.

6. See David Power, *Ministries That Differ: Lay Ministries Established and Unestablished* (New York: Pueblo, 1980).

7. See Sergei Eisenstein, "The Film Sense," in *Film Form and The Film Sense*, trans. Jay Leyda (New York: World, 1967), 32.

FURTHER RELATED MATERIAL

Besides texts mentioned in chapter 9, Alec Vidler's *A Variety of Catholic Modernists* (New York and Cambridge: Cambridge University Press, 1970) is insightful and largely fair. J. Derek Holmes, *The Papacy in the Modern World* (New York: Crossroad, 1981) is an excellent description of the period from the institutional perspective. An entertaining, informative reading of the developments of Vatican Council II may be found in Xavier Rynne (pseudonym) *Letters from Vatican City: Vatican Council II (First Session)* (New York: Farrar, Straus & Giroux, 1963). Avery Dulles, in *The Dimensions of the Church* (Westminster, Md.: Newman, 1967), gives helpful reflections on the Church from the point of view of the Council. The recent volume by the same author, *A Church to Believe in: Discipleship and the Dynamics of Freedom* (New York: Crossroad, 1982), offers comments on the problem of the teaching authority of the episcopal office and the work of theologians.

11

THE CREATORS OF
TWENTIETH-CENTURY CATHOLICISM (II)
The United States
and Religious Freedom

> Christ, fowler of street and hedgerow
> of cripples and the distempered old
> —eyes blinded as woodknots
> tongues tight as immigrants—
> takes in His gospel net
> all the hue and cry of existence.
> Heaven, of such imperfection,
> wary, ravaged, wild?
> Yes. Compel them in.
>   Daniel Berrigan (b. 1921), from "The Face of Christ"

In March 1788, Catholic priests of the former British colonies petitioned Pope Pius VI (1775–99) for a bishop. They asked that he have power in his own right, that they choose the city in which the diocese would be established, and that they elect by ballot the individual most qualified. In July their requests were granted. On 18 May 1789, John Carroll (1735–1815) became first Bishop of Baltimore by a vote of twenty-four to two. Carroll planned that all future ecclesiastical organization in the new country would be patterned on this first appointment. The experiment of the Catholic Church with modern democratic processes of government had begun.

When this bishop became head of the Catholic missions in the United States, his pastoral care extended from Maine to the Carolinas and claimed territory from the Atlantic seaboard to the Mississippi River. Yet this was only a portion of the diverse Catholic population that constituted the American Church. To the original Spanish settlements in the Southwest and on the Pacific coast were added the French and British fur traders and trappers of the Midwest; the English Catholics of Maryland and Kentucky from which

Carroll emerged; the Irish, Italian, and Slavic immigrants of the later urban expansions; the Ukrainians, Armenians, and Greeks, with their non-Western liturgical languages; and the black Catholic slaves and shareholders in the South. *Diversity* of class, race, country of national origin, language, and region of settlement has always marked the Catholic Church in the United States.

There have been three fundamental stages in the Catholic institutional development: from the colonial period through 1830; from 1830 to 1960, in which enormous immigration solidified into a common Church; and from the turbulent 1960s with the entrance of the Second Vatican Council (1962–65) until the present. A *startling rise in the Catholic population* from the colonial period (a mere .03 percent) until the present (over 20 percent) has also characterized Catholic history in the United States.

Despite the Church's origins in Europe, its financial and ecclesiastical support from Rome, and its youth (a foreign mission until 1908), it has developed its own temperament. Its internal experiment with democratic politics grew into problems with Roman authoritarianism in the later nineteenth century. Its distance from the colonial seats of government made its citizens pragmatic. They "made do" with solutions that poor communications, insufficiently educated authorities, and personal inadequacy required.

Moreover, they had to wrestle with the fundamental Enlightenment principles that guided the founders of the Republic. Benjamin Franklin (1706–90), John Carroll's political supporter, stressed the mundane virtues: thrift, hard work, prudence, honesty, and moderation. Individual initiative, joined in a government by consent, was the basis for progress. Thomas Paine (1737–1809), the religious and political journalist, proposed a reasonable religion and detected Christianity's superstition, cruelty, and rational incomprehensibility. Thomas Jefferson's (1743–1826) interest in Christian experience was largely through an adherence to a useful moral code from which the confessional controversies and supernatural events had been removed. George Washington (1732–99) announced to Joel Barlow (1754–1812), then ambassador to Tripoli: "The government of the United States is not in any sense founded on the Christian Religion."

Separation of Church and state and the consequent religious tolerance enshrined in the first amendment to the American Constitution of 1788–89 did not establish a particular confessional Tradition, but neither did it encourage any "godly" affiliations. The antagonisms which had animated Church-state relations in Europe were not officially condoned; yet attainment of a mutual respect among pluralistic Christian, non-Christian, and areligious traditions had to be achieved through the dialogue of a common history. American Catholicism has been "on its own." As John Carroll remarked in 1783: "In these United States our religious system has undergone a revolution, if possible, more extraordinary than our political one."[1]

CATHOLIC DIVERSITY—ALWAYS PRESENT

The diverse origins of the Church in the Americas have marked every successive generation of Catholics. There have remained Catholic Christians whose native language is not English, but some other European tongue: French, Spanish, Polish, Italian, Czech, Hungarian, German, or Portuguese. Each national group faced isolation from its cultural roots, the aggressive missionary character of previous landholders, and the internecine repercussions of European conflicts on this side of the Atlantic. The three major colonial groups, joined by the mid-nineteenth-century immigrants and their twentieth-century counterparts, arrived for somewhat different reasons—and their religious identity reflects these original goals.

The Spanish Conquerors

Church and state arrived together in 1493 when Puerto Rico was claimed by Columbus for the King and Queen of Aragon and Castile. While the soldiers' primary objective was exploitation of the soil's resources, especially precious metals, Franciscan missionaries settled stable villages in which largely nomadic native tribes could be socialized to European culture and religion through education, vocational training, and codes of manners. The attachment of local Indians to the missions varied; most were virtually indentured serfs, all were loyal second-class citizens of the crown. The most difficult problems for the missionaries were the constant threat of force used by civil authorities and the ugly moral example given by exploring adventurers.

What once was merely a survival of religious place names in the Southwest, Texas, and Florida (St. Augustine, 1565; Santa Fe, 1609), has become again a Catholic heritage with which to reckon. Legal and illegal Hispanic immigration from Mexico, Cuba, and strife-torn El Salvador and Guatemala; the Puerto Rican population in New York City and northern New Jersey; and the migrant laborers in almost all agricultural states have reestablished this once-strong colonial force. By the year 2000, it is estimated that Hispanic Catholics will comprise at least half the ecclesiastical population in the United States.

Growing numbers, however, are not the only factor. The deep sense in which religion, culture, and language are intertwined in personal and familial identity is quite distinct from the northern European voluntary experience of religious belonging. Yet prior to the appointment of Robert Sanchez as archbishop of Santa Fe (1974), there had been no bishops of Hispanic origin since colonial times—and little official interest in integrating this culturally distinct religious experience.

The Piety of French Explorers

The primary objective of the French who appeared in 1604 off the coast of northern Maine was to establish a fur trade. They were in constant opposition to the English merchants to the south who established rival military forts. The native Americans of the region (Mohawks, Hurons, Oneida, Algonquin, and others) were used in these European rivalries to brutalize one or another of the parties involved. Throughout the seventeenth century, Jesuits such as Isaac Jogues (1607–47) valiantly contributed their lives to missionary activity among the Indians.

Just as Franciscans followed the Spanish explorers, or led the way as did Junipero Serra (1713–84) in California, so the Jesuits collaborated with French expeditions in the Midwest. Jacques Marquette (1637–75) accompanied Louis Joliet (1645–1700) down the Mississippi River (1673); and in the early eighteenth century, New Orleans was founded as its port. The trade in brandy, prostitution, arbitrary treatment of Indians, and the immoral example set by European Christians made missionary work extremely difficult in French territories.

Yet the French factor in Catholic life remains more than in a few place names (Detroit, 1701; Vincennes, 1702). In this and the last century, farmers and traders immigrated into northern New England, increasing and solidifying what remained of the old French population. New Orleans continues to be a "Catholic oasis" in what are otherwise the largely Protestant southern states. Remainders of Jansenist piety, strong familial loyalties, and a certain anticlericalism born of the Enlightenment continue to perdure in this cultural segment of Catholicism.

English Dissenters

The Catholic most Americans remember is not Juan de Padilla (about 1500–1544), Spanish Franciscan missionary to Kansas and the first American martyr (1542–44), but the English Lords Baltimore (George, 1580–1632; Cecil, 1605–75; and Charles Calvert, 1632–1715). Exhausted by the wars and mutual persecutions of the Christian communities of Europe, these aristocratic settlers came to Maryland just as their Pilgrim, Puritan, and Quaker counterparts did—to seek religious freedom. They proved to be the earliest and most formative influence upon Catholicism in the United States.

The mixed religious situation of the English colonists included Calvinist and antipapal Protestants. They saw themselves as the New Israel, a missionary community between the vice of French Catholic marauders to the north and Spanish papist adventurers to the south. The classic by Nathaniel Hawthorne (1804–64), *The Scarlet Letter*, describes some of the moral and political conflicts in these colonies. Though martyrs to religious anger were rare, the anti-Catholicism that characterized European controversies continued to mark some strains of American Protestantism. Even in Maryland itself, it was only in the early years, when Catholics controlled the government, that universal religious toleration was permitted—in fact, permitted for the first time anywhere.[2]

Maryland, like all the English colonies, was not founded to provide financial support in gold or furs to the home government—but to offer ports in which exported goods could be sold. As the colonies became more prosperous, able to provide home-manufactured goods for their own purposes and less dependent upon Britain for the maintenance of money and population (women were always a scarcity in the early days), rivalries began to develop in the politically dependent relationship.

During the prerevolutionary years, Catholics by the name of Carroll in Maryland and Brent in Virginia were wealthy landowners, though Protestants were always in the majority in both colonies. In this agricultural society, priests and lay Catholics owned black slaves as early as 1634, continuing a pattern which only ceased after the Civil War of the 1860s. These families and their servants were served largely by Jesuits who numbered a little over twenty for the entire region. The city of Philadelphia provided Catholicism with its only urban home in the colonial period; its congregation numbered (1733–34) about twelve hundred Irish, English, and German parishioners.

Colonial Catholics found themselves on both sides of the controversy for independence—but primarily on the side of revolution. Charles Carroll (1737–1832), denied enfranchisement for his Catholicism, despite the fact that he was clearly the wealthiest individual in Maryland, nonetheless threw himself into the fight for freedom. As he said in his later memoirs: "When I signed the Declaration of Independence, I had a view not only of our independence of England but the toleration of all sects, professing the Christian religion, and communicating to them all great rights."[3] The city milieu of wartime Philadelphia offered some Protestants their first experience of Catholics who were not Spanish enemies.

In a manner which Europeans would have found almost unimaginable, American Catholics embraced the strict separation of Church and state as the surest way to guarantee both political and religious freedom. A pattern had been set: Catholics in the United States did not need to theorize about the values or faults of "secular" separation. Rather they lived it first; and through that experience, they found it both useful and providential for ecclesial growth.

An Immigrant Church

The nineteenth-century ecclesial narrative consolidated the gains of religious toleration won with the revolution and welcomed the millions of immigrants who arrived after 1830. Some of these groups were fleeing political and religious oppression. The Irish, for example, were leaving their native land, not only because of the potato famines (1820, 1845–49), but also because of the centuries-old repression directed against their national Catholic identity. German Catholics fled from the growing secularizations of Otto von Bismarck's (1815–98) unification of Germany (the *Kulturkampf* of the 1870s). At the end of the century (1880–1920), Italian, Polish, Hungarian, and Slavic Catholics poured into the Churches of the United States, well over a million people a year. Throughout the century, indeed even to the Second World War, the Catholic minority formed the laboring class and city dweller, the undereducated occupants of foreign ghettos.

Each successive group of immigrants met with some opposition not only from non-Catholics but from older established Catholic communities as well. Those of French and English origin had a major problem. How could a single society, a unified national religious body, really absorb such diverse, sometimes contradictory, cultural and ethnic elements into itself?

A successful integration, which simultaneously permitted the religious expression of cultural diversity, was the remarkable achievement of astute nineteenth-century American bishops. Their objective was twofold: to help disoriented peoples maintain their Catholic heritage within a pluralistic and regularly hostile Protestant society, and to enable them to respect, identify with, and preserve the values of an alien culture. Ecclesiastical, educational, charitable, social, and moral institutions became avenues for immigrants to maintain religious difference, to preserve cultural customs, and to achieve independence within a highly competitive political society.

The Expanding-Contracting Church

As early as 1829, American bishops announced the necessity of establishing schools to educate the young in literacy, morality, and faith. At the end of the century, such local parish education became a norm and the ideal: every Catholic child in a Catholic school. This extraordinary institutional commitment, unlike any other in the world, was initiated, supported, and maintained by the voluntary financial, personal, and political generosity of Catholics, especially religious women. In 1808, Elizabeth Ann Seton (1774–1821), the first native-born American to be declared a saint (1975), began a school for women in Baltimore; in Emmitsburg, Maryland, she and her small community opened the first free parochial school for both sexes in 1810. It was a prophetic way to begin the century, since it was this educational system that, until the last quarter of our century, has formed Catholic identity.

The institutional preservation of the religious Tradition was an authentic way of conserving the Catholic experience in a westward-expanding country. Bishops like Carroll of Baltimore; Benedict Joseph Flaget (1763–1850) of Bardstown and Louisville, Kentucky; Matthias Loras (1793–1858) of Iowa, Minnesota, and the Dakotas; Peter Kenrick (1806–96) of St. Louis; and the extraordinary Jean-Baptiste Lamy (1814–88) of Santa Fe, memorialized in Willa Cather's (1873–1947) novel, *Death Comes to the Archbishop* (1927), extended the organization of the Church well beyond the cities of the Atlantic.

Without this institutional protection, it is unlikely that the growing storms of anti-immigrant, anti-Catholic sentiment might have been weathered. The "American Experiment" of religious tolerance for all confessional Traditions was weakened by Protestant hatred for papist superstition and a nativist fear of foreign domination. Catholic leaders soon found themselves forced to organize their people economically and politically in order to counter the signs of the times: "No Irish need apply." Horace Bushnell (1802–76), author of theological liberalism among American Protestants, summed it up in 1847: "Our first danger is barbarism; Romanism next."[4]

The language of the age was violent and abusive. Nativist and American Republican ("Know-Nothing") Parties sprang up (1840–50) controlling both Philadelphia and New York. Priests were tarred, feathered, and ridden on rails; 6 August 1855 became Bloody Monday in Louisville, Kentucky, when some twenty people were killed and hundreds wounded. The strong political colors of anti-Catholicism faded in the more serious controversies over slavery, but Abraham Lincoln (1809–65) remarked late the same month: "As a nation we began by declaring that all men are created equal. We now practically read it: All men are created equal except Negroes. When the Know-Nothings obtain control, it will read: All men are created equal except Negroes, foreigners and Catholics."[5]

These struggles within the American Experiment made bishops extraordinarily cautious in their statements about the slavery question. Some (as for example, Martin J. Spalding, 1810–72, of Louisville) identified abolitionism with Protestant bigotry. Indeed, there was midcentury Nativist propaganda that described slavery as the "natural coworker" of Roman Catholicism.[6] But more often, the questions and answers of slavery were not focused by religious principles, but economic and geopolitical ones. Catholic theologians, like Francis P. Kenrick (1796–1863), bishop of Philadelphia, regretted the consequences of slavery but emphasized that the public law must be obeyed. Catholics wanted to fit into a society that was aggressively trying to reject them.

Despite the fact that Pope Gregory XVI (1831–46) had condemned the slave trade as evil (1838), Catholics in the larger cities who competed with blacks for low-paying jobs ignored the slavery question. Only rare individuals, like Archbishop John Purcell of Cincinnati (1833–83), issued a call for emancipation at an official level. After the Civil War, the Second Plenary Council of the American bishops in Baltimore (1866) decreed that freed slaves were to be evangelized. But it was because Pope Pius IX asked an English priest, Herbert Vaughn (1832–1903), to send the Mill Hill Missionaries to the United States that schools, parishes, and a seminary were finally opened. Augustine Tolton (1854–97), born a slave, was the first acknowledged black priest in the United States. Ordained in Rome in 1886, he was meant for Africa; but the Roman congregation returned him to the United States. Said the cardinal in charge: "America has been called the most enlightened nation. We will see if it deserves that honor." Tolton ministered as a priest in Quincy, Illinois amid some clerical opposition. He died in Chicago as a pastor.[7]

The cost of these early, dramatic struggles of institutional Catholicism in America was not inconsiderable. So committed were the energetic talents of its finest leaders to the task of survival that other more important issues (like the question of slavery) were simply left untended. American Catholicism proved itself utterly capable of practical institutional genuis—building hospitals, orphanages, schools, churches, and social organizations. But toward what end?

Was the Catholic Church in this country to remain forever a triumph of buildings and boundaries, institutionally powerful, but intellectually and prophetically weak?

THE BREAKDOWN OF CATHOLIC
DEFENSIVE POSTURE: PRESIDENT AND POPE

When Alfred E. Smith (1873–1944), governor of New York and presidential candidate for the Democratic Party in 1928, was defeated, it was widely believed by Catholics that it was due to the sharp rise in anti-Catholic bigotry during the campaign. This sometimes angry, often disappointed, defensiveness gave way only in 1960 when John F. Kennedy (1917–63) was elected by a narrow margin to the presidency of the United States. Catholics felt as though they had come of age.

To pry Catholics free from their "separate but superior" culture, however, it had taken participation in two World Wars, committed pastoral support during the Depression of the 1930s, and a general leveling of American social distinctions brought on by both events. Non-Catholics discovered that Catholics were committed to the historic separation of Church and state. Catholics began to see that it was possible to be progressive, tough, and pragmatic in politics. Defensiveness was needless.

The combination of John Kennedy's election (1960) and the election of John XXIII to the papacy at about the same time (1958) allowed Catholics to feel secure, expansive, and free to commit themselves to societal and religious change. As the conciliar documents emerged, Catholics were being asked to rethink their relationship to the Catholic culture which had nourished them, protected them, and built up their confidence in a pluralistic world. Religious freedom had a purpose—service of society. Catholics began to search their American past—not for institutional precedents, but for prophetic leaders.

AMERICAN CATHOLIC PROPHETS

American Catholics discovered that there was a long Tradition of men and women who were not quite willing to let institutional solutions settle public issues. Their attempts to mold a rapidly expanding, multinational Church should not so much be paralleled to the uniform cultural norm of the Carolingian or Constantinian Churches, but to the ensoulment of a quite new being.

Orestes Brownson (1803–73)

Brownson, a man of multiple literary talents and acerbic wit, found Catholicism after a lengthy trek through various American religious wildernesses. With his conversion at forty-one, he continued publication of the most original "personal" journal in Catholic history—*Brownson's Quarterly Review*. Although he was utterly convinced that the Catholic Church was the fulfillment of United States ideals, his criticism of parochial schools and immigrant Catholics, of despotic rule in the Papal States, his almost unique espousal of antislavery Unionism in 1860, and his hostility to Jesuits made his journal a constant source of irritation in midcentury Catholicism. Refusing either intellectual dependence or religious laxism, he spoke for both Catholic identity and democratic ideals in a period in which neither were honored.

Isaac Hecker (1819–88)

Hecker's personal religious quest led him through Ralph Waldo Emerson (1803–82) to a lecture of Brownson's which converted him to Catholicism (1844). Upon returning to the United States after his training by a German-speaking religious community, he traveled, successfully giving revivals. The community he founded, the Congregation of Missionary Priests of St. Paul (the Paulist Fathers), specialized in the communication of the Catholic experience in the United States. They founded the journal *Catholic World* (1865) and began a tract society which concentrated on appealing, intelligent, apologetic literature. In his own books (*Questions of the Soul*, 1855; and *Aspirations of Nature*, 1857), Hecker maintained his belief that Catholicism and democratic ideals could be synthesized.

John Ireland (1838–1918)

Ireland, the archbishop of St. Paul, Minnesota, spoke to French Catholics in mid-1892 with characteristic American optimism, enthusiasm, and activist concern. He urged priests to learn from their counterparts in the United States and leave their privileged positions to mingle with their congregations. Ireland rapidly found that his positions on the formation of conscience, the separation of Church and state, and the genuinely new legal experience of American politics were questioned. In 1897, when a French translation of Isaac Hecker's biography was published in Paris with an introduction by Ireland, it became the catalyst for a division of the French Church between republicans and loyalists.

In 1899, Leo XIII issued an encyclical (*Testem Benevolentiae*) which condemned "Americanism," warning against doctrines which came from the United States to Europe. As James Hennesey has remarked: "Something of a deep freeze set in, deepened further in the new century by Roman condemnation of Modernism."[8] But Ireland always remained a speaker for another way.

Prophets of Labor: John Gibbons (1834–1921) and John A. Ryan (1869–1945)

There can be no question but that American history would be different without the interventions of John A. Ryan and Cardinal John Gibbons of Baltimore. Just as the end of the nineteenth century saw Protestant theology writing and revising its social response to the Gospel in Walter Rauschenbusch (1861–1918), so Catholics could not ignore the political dimensions of squalor and oppression which accompanied the explosions of immigration and industrialization.

The Knights of Labor was the nation's first large union, founded by Uriah Stevens (1821–82) and headed after 1878 by Terence Powderly (1849–1924), a Catholic. Strikes and the Chicago Haymarket Riots (1886) frightened Catholics and Protestants alike. Through the support of Gibbons, the country's archbishops did not unilaterally condemn the movement as "socialist" or "communist"; and in a private visit to the Vatican, Gibbons assured Rome that its large Catholic constituency would not become radicalized.

Gibbons condemned child labor and urged the implementation of Leo XIII's encyclical *Rerum Novarum* (1890) on the living wage and just working conditions. With Ryan, Gibbons helped found the National Catholic War Council (NCWC) with its commitment to social and political action. After the First World War, the Council's commitment to social responsibility remained; and in 1919, it issued the "Bishops' Program of Social Reconstruction," written by Ryan. He advocated governmental employment offices, housing, pay scales, and an argument for a minimum wage. "Women who are engaged at the same tasks as men should receive equal pay for equal amounts and qualities of work."[9] He spoke in favor of industrial cooperation between workers and management. With some considerable difficulty, the Council became a permanent body of the American Church after the war: the National Catholic Welfare Conference (1922) and now the United States Catholic Conference.

When Franklin D. Roosevelt (1882–1945) was elected in 1933, Ryan welcomed the policies of the administration since they seemed to embody the very concepts of social justice for which he had argued. Ryan was at the NCWC from 1919 to 1945, and in charge of the social action aspects of the episcopal program from 1928. He never ceased to speak for social justice.

Dorothy Day (1889–1980)

If Hecker and Ireland spoke for American democracy and mystical Catholic freedom, Brownson for an intellectual Catholicism, and Gibbons and Ryan for labor, Dorothy Day spoke for the poor. On 1 May 1933, the first issue of the *Catholic Worker* was sold in New York City. In her religious autobiography, *The Long Loneliness* (1952), Day outlined the spiritual odyssey which drew her to Catholicism, despite her radical commitments to socialism, communism, and the American labor movement. It was only after meeting Peter Maurin (1877–1949), itinerant preacher for simplified life, justice, and community, that she saw how her commitments to social causes could be resurrected within the Catholic intellectual and religious Tradition.

With extraordinary dedication both to the institutional Church (the "cross on which Christ was crucified") and to the poor, Day inspired the foundation of Catholic Worker Houses across the country. They offer hospitality to all those who are in need. Day's contribution was not only to offer financial assistance, food, and clothing, but even the very privacy to which she might have been entitled. That was what it meant to share the life of the poor. As a pacifist, she condemned all wars, participating in antinuclear demonstrations even in her final years. Ever a pilgrim in United States middle-class society, she pricked consciences and provoked minds. Through the Catholic Worker houses traveled most of the Catholics of this century who have become conscious of their commitment to a new social order. For her, as for all the greatest of Catholic prophets, prayer and action were never separated because they proceeded from an undivided heart.

Journals, Monks, and Media

There were, of course, many other lesser-known prophets, such as Archbishop John Neumann (1811–60), now a saint (1977), who welcomed the Haitian black woman Elizabeth Lange (about 1810–89) when she began the first congregation of black religious to educate black children. Or Virgil Michel (1890–1938), a Benedictine monk of St. John's Abbey, Collegeville, whose publication *Worship* (originally *Orate Fratres*) was the focus for the liturgical movement and its link with the social action of Dorothy Day and John A. Ryan. Or Bishop John Lancaster Spalding of Peoria (1840–1916), who won his plea for the foundation of a national Catholic University in 1889 and opposed through the New England Anti-Imperialism League the colonial wars in the Philippines and Cuba.

When Fulton J. Sheen (1895–1979), later bishop and director of the national contribution to the worldwide Catholic mission effort (The Propagation of the Faith), called for a "Catholic Renaissance" in 1929, he helped awaken a sleeping giant, one whose institutional narcissism had made it more attentive to its own battles than others. From then until 1960, with Sheen's "Catholic Hour" (1930s–1950s) as companion, Catholics began reading more widely, writing more thoroughly about their past and present. They had as a widely recognized scholarly basis *The Catholic Encyclopedia* (1905–14). Journals like the nineteenth-century *Catholic World* (1865) were joined by the Jesuit-sponsored *America* (1909), the lay-controlled *Commonweal* (1924), and the scholarly *Theological Studies* (1940). The Catholic Historical Society (1884), the Catholic Biblical Association (1936), the Canon Law Society of America (1939), and the

Catholic Theological Society of America (1946) contributed to a significant maturation in Catholics' self-understanding.

Most prophets in American Catholic history were characteristically activists; but Thomas Merton (1915–1968), like the reluctant prophet Jonah, joined the others through becoming a contemplative monk, a Trappist at Gethsemani, Kentucky. After intriguing the country through his autobiography *The Seven Story Mountain* (1948), a chronicle of his wandering toward monasticism, he assimilated the Catholic religious and mystical Tradition and found his way into the silence of God. Upon "arrival," he discovered not only that others had preceded him, but that God turned him toward the problems of the social order that he had left. Prayer and silence offered him critical distance as well as the chance for complete immersion in civil rights, nonviolent pacifism, and antinuclear movements. "Today more than ever the Gospel commitment has political implications, because you cannot claim to be 'for Christ' and espouse a political cause that implies callous indifference to the needs of millions of human beings and even cooperate in their destruction."[10] Merton offered American Catholics a criticism of their complacency and a vision of a more compassionate world.

The Architect of Dialogue:
John Courtney Murray

The sages, soldiers of the ecclesiastical fortress, and holy men and women, by their dedication to the transformation of poverty, injustice, and cruelty, vocally propelled the Church into the center of public controversy. They were allowed to do so through the fundamental religious and secular freedoms that the United States permits. John Courtney Murray (1904–64) joined the progressive forces at the Second Vatican Council, not to baptize American experience nor to canonize assured results, but to confirm that the conversation would continue throughout the universal Church.

In the Council's *Declaration on Religious Liberty* (1965), the European community listened to the experience of one of its former dependent churches. Just as the Church must be free to serve Christ, so individuals must be invited, not coerced, into loyalty to the

Gospel. This fundamental freedom should be enshrined in civil constitutions and international agreements. This freedom cannot be abrogated without detriment to the glory of God.

RELIGION AND CULTURE—
THE POLITICS OF SECULARITY

The religious, civil, and intellectual dedication of American Catholics has continued in the world of post-Vatican II Christianity. The prophets of social reform, religious criticism, and activist involvement have not disappeared with the removal of the war in Vietnam (1962–75). American bishops themselves have spoken out on civil rights, racism, agricultural conglomerates, nuclear disarmament, the Appalachian poor, international politics, and welfare programs.

The genuinely conservative and authentically progressive forces in American Catholicism are now engaged in serious dialogue. Such debates are healthy; they indicate that values are at stake that control human lives. In just what direction this national discussion will turn is for the prophets to determine; that the Church is traveling is evident. Major religious movements which attempt to recapture the affective experience of Catholic life, like the charismatic renewal, the revival of Catholic ethnic consciousness and its frank avowal of cultural difference, the developing politics of lobbying groups like NETWORK or Right-to-Life, the shifting administrative patterns of diocesan life toward lay involvement, the lower economic support for the Catholic school system simultaneous with the rise in commitment expected of parish members—all these promise vibrant, energetic conversation within the American Church.

What they have in common is the attempt by Catholics in the United States to face the secularity of their environment. The concrete utility and versatile experience of the American Experiment continues to intrigue European Catholics. And if it has its blundering moments in a too facile approval of political opportunism (as in the anti-Semitism of Charles E. Coughlin [1891–1973], the radio priest of the 1930s), it nonetheless seems able to recover, by its very evangelical independence, a critical balance.

There can be little question that the most significant cultural force in our world is the spirit of modernity: the rational science born in the early modern period and the Enlightenment critiques of reason, history, politics, and religion. When these are combined with the industrial and especially electronic technology that dominates both recovery of the past and proposals for the future, the United States remains the place where this spirit manifests itself as a national destiny. Whether one is in rural America, the decaying cities of the old Northeast, or the rising population centers of the West and Southwest, the redistribution of wealth and welfare occurring in the United States reiterates in its geographical, political, and racial diversity the reigning international problems at the turn of the millennium.

Catholics in this country face this movement not as though it were an outside army with which they must contend by dint of arms, but as a force *within* their own self-understanding. They stand in a radically ecumenical fashion with all religious traditions in the world, whether Hindu, Buddhist, Jewish, or Moslem, and utter the fundamental religious question: Why be religious, Christian, at all? Can one be both committed to modernity and the Christian Tradition with intellectual clarity, personal honesty, and institutional humility?

Catholics refuse to collapse their experiential commitment to modern values into secularism—the ideology that *only* secular values are true. A mutually critical conversation between modernity and Christianity characterizes the contemporary situation. Having escaped the understandable but prolonged domination by European custom, the approach of American Catholics has become radical, though practical; theoretical, yet committed to experience; open and workable; long-range in its ideals, but pragmatic in its demands for explicit, short-range answers. This "realistic" approach to religious and secular affairs is not laxist complacency, bored capitulation, or angry separatism. It is the concrete attempt to find the *legitimate means* by which the evangelical seeds of the Spirit may grow in a new culture.

Pope John Paul II's visit to the United States (1979) highlighted both the radical diversity of the Church and its unity in the Gospel; its need to achieve a place for itself in the pluralism of American cultures and a critical distance in the formation of a new society.

163

Chastened by its participation in wars (like Vietnam) and rumors of wars (like Latin America), the Catholic Church's optimism about success has been dimmed, but not obliterated; its activism reshaped, but not erased. Its enthusiasm has diversified to represent the spectrum of its inner membership; its identity less adolescent, more mature.

The diversity no doubt seems chaotic to some—particularly to those for whom the uniform Catholic isolation of the past was home. But the pilgrim Church in this country, in keeping with its frontier spirit and the evangelical commands, has cast its lot with the vibrant conversation of the present in accord with the adage followed by Pope John XXIII: "In necessary matters, unity; on doubtful issues, liberty; but in all things, love."

NOTES

1. James Hennesey, *American Catholics: A History of the Roman Catholic Community in the United States* (New York and London: Oxford University Press, 1981), 4.
2. Ibid., 41.
3. Ibid., 59.
4. Ibid., 119.
5. Ibid., 126.
6. Ibid., 145.
7. Cyprian Davis, *The Church: A Living Heritage* (Morristown, N.J.: Silver-Burdett, 1982), 257–59.
8. *American Catholics,* 203.
9. Ibid., 229.
10. Henry Nouwen, *Thomas Merton, Contemplative Critic* (New York: Harper & Row, 1981), 57.

FURTHER RELATED MATERIAL

The best account at present of general American Church history is James Hennesey's *American Catholics: A History of the Roman Catholic Community in the United States* (New York and London: Oxford University Press, 1981). More general descriptions within the context of American Protestantism and culture may be found in Sidney E. Ahlstrom, *A Religious History of the American People* (New Haven, Conn.: Yale University Press, 1973) and Martin Marty, *Righteous Empire: The Protestant Experience in America* (New York: Dial, 1970).

12

THE CREATORS OF
TWENTIETH-CENTURY CATHOLICISM (III)
Third World Catholics:
Liberation for a Future

> I have looked upon a savagely potent countenance
> Of soft lines, of diverse directions.
> I have confronted it until it dissolved like cloud,
> And saw, behind, the true Countenance with no beginning or end.
>   Eduardo Anguita (b. 1914) from "El Verdadero Rostro"

Maps tell us where we are. We use them to show us how to find our
way to somewhere else. The first published maps from the European
colonial expansion placed the cartographer's native country in the
center of the earth with a distant, distorted Siberia, China, Australia,
and Oceania on the far right and Alaska to the far left. The Pacific
Ocean was divided.

These early drawings centered the world on its most important
population centers. But if we were to take seriously the changes in
demography since the sixteenth century, Rome and northern Europe
would no longer be the center of our space. Most of the human
beings of the third millennium will occupy an arc which extends
between South America to Africa through the countries of southern
Asia. Placing that crescent in the center of the map, Old Europe
would be on the left edges, New England on the right—and the
Pacific would have replaced the Mediterranean as the new inland sea.
Even now, well over 50 percent of the world's population dwells in
Asia, the new center of the known world.

Yet de facto shifts in population, as we know, are not necessarily
changes in power. The old East-West matrix of authorities still
dominates the economic and political structures of our world. Yet
the fundamental crises facing the construction of a global humanity
are now aligned along a North-South axis, where Europe, the United

States, and the Union of Soviet Socialist Republics comprise the North, and the southern hemisphere is the Third World.

The term "Third World" does not simply designate a region, but the economic, sociological situation of the massive numbers of people who live there. They are often resource-rich and finance-poor; they are exploited for their labor force, mineral deposits, or land and oppressed by oligarchic or multinational arrangements which preserve the status quo. Once dominated by European colonialism, they are now under great pressure from Soviet or American influence. In the wake of rising economic "development," they find themselves hostage to oil-producing countries (some developing nations themselves) who fuel their new factories. Economic imperialism has been no better than religious or nationalist colonialism. Resentment breeds anger and resistance; resistance breeds governmental instability and oppression; oppression breeds coups and revolutions.

What of the Catholic Church in this world of Asia, Africa, Middle and South America? As an explicitly international community, Catholicism sees the experience of these countries, however diverse, as a positive movement of the Spirit and waits to be taught their message. An explicit theology, rooted in the experience of suffering, poverty, and fear, has risen in the hearts and minds of Third World Catholics. It has stressed that God's future is with the poor and the disenfranchised. Catholics in countries of yellow, brown, red, and black peoples have become the visionaries of our religious future. European popes may have gathered a new Pentecost in the Second Vatican Council, and the United States bishops may have encouraged pluralism of expression, but the diversity of tongues that have responded is clearly from other worlds.

CATHOLICS IN ASIA—
THE MEANING OF TRANSCENDENCE

Asia is clearly the world's most religious continent. From its borders have emerged all three of the major world monotheisms, Judaism, Christianity, and Islam, as well as the major moral religions, Hinduism, Buddhism, Shintoism, and Confucianism. Asia contains 54 percent of the world's population, yet only 2.3 percent of it is Catholic. If we remove the Philippine peoples from that figure, then only .95 percent of the total belongs to the Catholic Church. Figures for the Protestant Churches are not significantly different.

In this least Christian environment, Catholics are largely a product of the evangelization efforts of Portuguese expansion. Their primary objective was to establish trading ports and protective fortresses, not to colonize inland territories. Catholics have maintained the same static presence, sponsoring schools and charitable institutions which house the poor and outcast. In India, conversion offered self-respect to the lowest castes and an exit to higher classes. In Japan, conversion meant incredible xenophobic persecution for two hundred years, rapid growth in the post-World War II period, and a 5 percent drop in the Catholic population every year since about 1960.

Why can Christianity not make a serious institutional or religious difference in East Asian life? Shusaku Endo (b. 1923), the Japanese novelist, remarks in *The Silence* (1969) that the religious vision of his nation is fundamentally different from that of the West—that it requires a vulnerable divinity whose compassion for human suffering and the ignobly oppressed appears as his most striking quality. The Christendom which transcends all countries and territories is fiercely powerful, proud, and demanding. The Christ Christians should witness is One who would have even denied his own divine mission out of love for bleeding humanity.

Others believe that it is the contemplation of Transcendence to which Christians must give testimony in their Asian missionary efforts. Like all Western activists, they founded schools, orphanages, and hospitals—important embodiments of the caring Tradition of Catholicism; but they failed to announce the gentle holiness that Buddhist monks proclaimed.

In no case is the witness of Asian Christians doubted. In Vietnam, during the long civil wars and struggles for independence, its Catholics were regularly persecuted; in Japan, Christians of all denominations were almost eradicated; and in China, there remained a nationalized Church after the 1948 Revolution, utterly dependent upon the state for survival, and an underground Catholicism of resistance to the government.

It is the *quality* of Transcendence to which Catholic Christians witness in East Asia that is at stake; it is the meaning of the Sacred announced by the Gospel of Jesus that requires new cultural delineation. But if the Church is to *listen* to the voices of Asian converts, it will hear new accents in its own understanding of God and the meaning of Christ. Catholics and Protestants in their common confrontation with secularization (now a prominent Japanese export) will comprise a new chorus.

AFRICAN CATHOLICS—THE JOY OF FAITH

Africa, although traveled by missionaries in the thirteenth century, remained largely a mystery to Europeans until 1900. The ancient Church of North Africa, which contributed so much in figures like Augustine (354–430) and Cyprian of Carthage (+258), was erased by the wars of Islam some four hundred years later. The colonial expansion of European powers carved the continent into areas of influence and exploited the population for the slave and ivory trades. It founded Catholic kingdoms like that of the native Affonso I (1506–45), whose realm stretched from the Atlantic to present day Kinshasa and south into what is now northern Angola. It is from this period that Christian symbols have remained an idiom of personal and social power in Zairean cultural heritage.[1]

No continent has been humiliated more than Africa through the colonial slave trade. The plight of millions in the Third World is riveted in the manacles which destroyed tens of thousands and imprinted scourges on the brains and the backs of Africans. Aimé Césaire (b. 1913), African politician and poet, states: "I am talking of millions of men who have been skillfully injected with fear, inferiority complexes, trepidation, servility, despair, abasement."[2]

Described in ethnological and exegetical nonsense as the accursed sons of Ham from the Book of Genesis (9:20–25), Africans can still feel their psychological servitude to missionaries. J. E. K. Aggrey (1875–1927) of Ghana cried: "My African people, we are created in God's image. They wanted us to think of ourselves as chickens, but we are eagles. Spread your wings and fly."[3]

In 1900, Africa contained two million Catholics; from 1952 until 1972, the African Church rose in population from twelve to thirty-six million believers. This missionary success seems to have originated not in colonial enterprise (it was a period of decolonialization) nor in stability of religious culture (it was the period of Vatican II), but in two other factors: the effectiveness of the missionary school and a deep religious predisposition of the African spirit.

Africa's Catholics embraced the conciliar *Constitution on the Liturgy* (1965) with enthusiasm, particularly its sections on cultural adaptation to local language, customs, and indigenous talent.[4] But the religious spirit of the people is not merely ritualistic; indeed, its deepest sense is of nature, the family, and tribal loyalty. The areas in which Catholicism has had its most difficult problems in evangelization in Africa are precisely those in which ordinary ecclesiastical law prohibited adaptation to cultural expression: polygamy and tribal initiation rites.

The original purposes of the missionary school, catechesis and service of the Church, have been undeniably successful. Unconsciously or consciously, however, these same goals have fostered personal achievement based upon competitiveness, migration from the original family or tribe, and the establishment of important voluntary groups, such as Church, political party, or national state. Such shifts are not intrinsically evil developments; but as Catholic missionary schools have become part of the national educational systems, they must be replaced by evangelization which stresses social conscience and duty to the common welfare.

When Paul VI visited Africa in 1969, he recognized the difficulties as well as the hopes of Catholic assemblies. When John Paul II celebrated a century of evangelization (1980) with Zairean Catholics, he did not anticipate that the Christian Gospel would collapse into the local culture, but that it would help "these cultures . . . bring forth from their own living tradition original expressions of Christian life, celebration and thought."[5] The Pope views Catholic inculturation into Africa as a work that will require lengthy discussion, spiritual discernment, and the liberation of those elements that announce the paschal mystery of Christ.

LATIN AMERICA—THE LOCAL CHURCH'S LIBERATION OF LOCAL SOCIETY

African Catholicism is a hopeful world where life seems omnipresent, even in its darkest depressions, as in Uganda in the mid-1970s or South Africa in the 1980s. Latin Catholicism is a world looking for hope. The waves of evangelization, first from the fifteenth to the

nineteenth century, then during the period of colonial liberation and
European immigration (1800–1914), and finally into the present,
have left the countries of Middle and South America poor, exploited,
and Catholic largely by symbolic affiliation.

Spanish colonial empires brutally enforced a uniform cultural
Christianity. Hispanic conquest rooted the authority of the religion
and state in the towns, replacing the ruling classes (whether in
Mexico or Peru). They spread in concentric circles, setting up plantations which gave the population of worker-Indians to the explorers,
organizing village settlements even further away, and giving missions
to Jesuits and Franciscan or Dominican friars who patrolled the
edges of the empire.

Religion was the mark that separated the incorporated from the
uncivilized. Christianity, built upon the rubble of ancient temples,
replaced a state-controlled priesthood. Despite the small armies
(Hernando Cortes [1485–1547] had 508 soldiers, 100 sailors;
Francisco Pizarro [1471–1544] about 177 followers; friars in
Mexico and Guatemala never exceeded one thousand), conversion
to Catholicism defined civil loyalty.[6] In this post-Reformation
world, attachment to local community (town, village, tribe) was
intense; but religion, not language or race, was the distinguishing
loyalty which founded the nation. With Spanish dominion came the
Catholic religion.

The heirs to this social situation have largely been the ruling
oligarchies, wealthy established families whose industries and political affiliations controlled the government, communications, armies,
utilities, and—religion. It is a society based upon dependence, a
paternalistic institution in which the children receive what remains.
Leonardo Boff (b. 1938), the Brazilian theologian, has enumerated
the symptoms of this dependence:

> Hunger, infant mortality, endemic diseases, cheap manual labor, de-
> teriorating pay scales, abandonment of the schools by young people
> who must help their families eke out a living, a lack of participation and
> freedom, an inability to gain recognition of the most basic human
> rights, political corruption, and control of the nation's wealth by a small
> but powerful elite.[7]

In such a situation, the Catholic Church has chosen to speak the
language of the oppressed. In the mid-1960s, Catholics recovered the

voice of the local Church and its ability to criticize, on the basis of the Gospel, governmental and ecclesiastical leaders for their neglect of the disenfranchised. In 1964, Ivan Illich (b. 1926), now of Cuernavaca, Mexico, spoke at Petròpolis, Brazil, on the revision of pastoral strategies in the Latin American Church. Gustavo Guttierez (b. 1928) described theology as critical reflection upon the institutionalized violence of the governmental regimes. Guttierez's thought was refined in the ensuing years and was published as a fountainhead of later indigenous theology (A Theology of Liberation, 1973). Basing their work on the educational methods of Paulo Friere ([b. 1921], Pedagogy of the Oppressed, 1970) and listening intently to the experience of the revolutionary Ernesto Ché Guevara (1928–67) and Camilo Torres (1929–66), a priest who joined the guerrilla movement, Illich, Guttierez, and others began to offer an ecclesial perspective that was authentically of the Gospel, society, and the Third World.

After a period of trial and error, the Catholic Church of Middle and South America met at Medellín, Colombia (1968). Vatican Council II (1962–65) had spoken of the underdeveloped countries, the relationship of the Church and the world, and renewal. Medellín offered a vision of the planet from the standpoint of the poor countries, described the role of the Church in that world as liberation and provided guidelines for the transformation by the Church of a society living in misery and injustice.

When Pope John Paul II visited Middle and South America ten years later, he did not, as was sometimes misinterpreted by the public press, denounce the qualitative leap made at Medellín concerning the Church's role in the renewal of society. On the contrary, he spoke of a human dignity based upon the Gospel and the difficulties inherent in bringing that to specific configuration. In an address at Oaxaca, Mexico, he spoke of himself as the "voice of those who cannot speak or who have been silenced. It is not Christian to continue certain situations that are clearly unjust."[8]

For Pope John Paul, the local church is an authority. He usually chooses to confirm the direction taken in local episcopal conferences (except in Holland, as we have noted), only reminding them of their international responsibilities to the Gospel and their unity with the worldwide Church, symbolized through his office. In speaking to

Brazilian bishops a year later, he remarked that there must be an "affective" dialogue which will permit constant openness to the work of the Spirit in the local communities of God's people. This collegial Spirit on the local level will encourage active discussion of the concrete problems of the peoples who make up the Church. In this way, "the church can actually contribute to the transformation of society by helping it to become more just and to be founded on objective justice."[9]

THE THIRD WORLD AND CHURCH INVOLVEMENT

Since better than 70 percent of the Church's population will exist in Third World countries by the year 2000, and since that Church is, on the whole, utterly poor and extremely young, its growing sense of who it is and what it must do is of crucial importance to Catholicism. The local Church's involvement in political and social change and the international, even papal, support for such change is part of the response. The criticism of its theology and the fears for its social absorption or annihilation are equally significant.

The Programs

Formerly, the Churches of Asia, Africa, and the Americas south of the United States were the object of political, economic, and social maneuvers by others. Now, in their multicultural complexity, they have discovered that they can create themselves. But becoming conscious of the ability to make history as well as to suffer it means achieving an independence which is sometimes hesitant, often violent, and occasionally mistaken. In their attempts to develop self-renewing cultures, Third World countries have found it difficult to move beyond the common biases and successes of democratic liberalisms, autocratic socialisms, and repressive Marxisms. But their only concrete alternatives have been the unredeemed oppressions of present authoritarian governments. The choice has not been abstract—the "best of all possible governments."

The concrete task of the Church in the Third World has become to assist peoples in their search for the most liberating options in the situation. This regularly means education from nonliteracy to the visual and aural technology of contemporary communications equipment, the replacement of numerous clerical missionaries from Europe or the United States by a few native lay ministers, and the establishment of political clout necessary to exchange poverty of land, medicine, and clothing for ownership of property, personal and familial health care, and food.

Nor can this work be seen as somehow alongside the Church's commitment to the Gospel. Though Christian faith contemplates the Kingdom of God first, the neighbor is the first citizen in the New Heaven and the New Earth. Asian Christianity's focus upon transcendence, Africans' joyful embrace of the giftedness of God's love, and Middle and South American emphasis on freedom meet in the Incarnate Word.

The human dignity of every individual, of tribal or national cultures, of international interdependence is the will of God as disclosed in Jesus who ate with the outcast, loved sinners, and lived with the poor. Jesus is not a "revolutionary in the emotional and ideological sense of violent and rebellious reaction against the sociopolitical structure. Perhaps a suitable description of Jesus would be Liberator of a consciousness oppressed by sin and all alienations and Liberator of the sad human condition in its relationships with the world, the other and God."[10]

The Plans—Theology of Liberation

The thought that has emerged from the confrontation of the Gospel with this Third World situation is often called the Theology of Liberation. It takes seriously two loyalties: to the Tradition of loving service proclaimed in Jesus of Nazareth and to the particular human situations in which theologians find themselves.

The original impetus came from the social encyclicals of popes, from Leo XIII's *Rerum Novarum* (1891) through Pius XI's *Quadragesimo Anno* (1931) to John XXIII's *Mater et Magistra* (*Mother and Teacher*, 1961), *Pacem in Terris* (*Peace on Earth*, 1963) and *Populorum Progressio* (*On the Development of Peoples*, 1967) of Paul VI. As historical documents, these papal letters acknowledged in unmistakable terms the responsibilities of Catholicism to the social order. They favored, rather than dreaded, the eventual socialization of economies. They asked, as a matter of justice, not charity, that the rich nations aid the poorer nations of the world. They denounced repressive regimes and called for the reform of social, economic, and political wrongs. They made it clear that religion could never be a merely private matter without public consequences.

This official Catholic teaching was encouraged by the beginning dialogue between Marxists and Christians. These unlikely conversation partners appeared on both sides as intrepid, conciliatory spirits, neither the Stalinist remains of an official Soviet ideology nor the Catholic dogmatic anticommunism of the Cold War period. On the one hand, the Marxists were revisionists, whose attitude toward Karl Marx (1818–83), the German revolutionary socialist and social and economic theorist, had shifted from his materialist critiques of history and his denunciations of religion as the alternative for concrete implementation of human freedoms. Catholic interest was sparked by the papal encyclicals and their personal concern for the authentic dignity of the human person.

The thinkers' common purpose—the liberation of humanity from all oppression and the removal of repressive societal structures—created a collaborative climate which has largely persisted. So Ernst Bloch (1885–1977), with his philosophy of hope leading to Utopia, the sociological critiques of Max Horkheimer (1895–1973) and Theodor Adorno (1903–69), and the social-critical philosophy of Jurgen Habermas (b. 1929) and the Frankfurt School promoted a milieu in which Christians and Marxists could study the phenomenon of society and religion together.

John Baptist Metz (b. 1928), a student and colleague of Karl Rahner (b. 1904), has offered perhaps the most coherent vision of this dialogue from the Catholic perspective. Metz is aware that concrete Marxist social legislation, whether in the Soviet Union, its satellites such as Poland or now Afghanistan, or even the more Stalinist forms of Eurocommunism, is utterly at variance with a Christian understanding of the world. Nonetheless, through conversation with these social and political thinkers, Metz wants to propose a precisely Christian theology of the *world*.

A religion privatized by the enthronement of the middle-class individual will not provide a theology that will serve the contemporary world. The whole project of the Church must be the achievement of a critical liberty of faith, not a nostalgia for the past traditions which might have embodied Catholic meaning. Metz stresses the primary role, not of concepts and doctrines, but of the liberating story, the critical character of a disturbing memory, and the concrete witness to that explosive memory of Jesus in the present. This theology is beyond mere self-reflection; it aims to change the world. It is beyond the neurotic assimilation of whatever political compulsion appears, and it is radically interdisciplinary in its search for the nonabstract solutions that will transform the world.

These notions have been expanded, repeated, and concretized for the Third World by many Latin American theologians: Gustavo Guttierez of Peru; the Brazilian Leonardo Boff ([b. 1938] *Jesus Christ Liberator*, 1972); the Uruguayan Juan Luis Segundo ([b. 1925] *A Theology for Artisans of a New Humanity*, 1971); the Argentine lay historian Enrique Dussel ([b. 1934] *Historia de la Iglesia en América Latina: Coloniale y liberación, 1492–1973*, 1974); the Chilean pastoral theologian Segundo Galilea ([b. 1928] *Espiritualidad de la liberación*, 1973); and many others equally persuasive and eloquent.

Some of these individuals are priests, some laymen and women. All are passionately convinced of the Catholic Church's role in the reversal of oppression and in its ability to found a new society. They all put a premium upon partisanship in the specific political debates of their countries; they do not believe in an abstract Christianity devoid of cultural embodiment. Grace must always be seen as on the side of one class or another. For them, involvement in what is true is a presupposition to discovering the truth of the Gospel in this world. The God of Christians is a constant Critic of society, the eschatological "No" to all limited or oppressive structures. His love will endure until the entire world is ultimately redeemed.

SPECIFIC STRATEGIES OF
WORLD TRANSFORMATION

Every thinker has his or her particular plan for the revolutionary changes required in Third World societies. Those committed to a Theology of Liberation are willing to trust to the dialogue of grassroots communities in the local Church, to the ecclesiastical debates about prudence and tolerance of difference, and to the political arguments which so easily sanction the status quo. What they are unwilling to condone and tolerate is the abusive power which totalitarian governments use to destroy the conversation. And thus they suffer.

So there are martyrs in Chile, Panama, and Argentina; the assassination of the archbishop in El Salvador. The rejection of either the colonialisms of the past or the developmental neoimperialism of the present has placed those who side with the poor in danger. Nor are foreign missionaries immune: four church women from the United States were brutally murdered in El Salvador and an Oklahoma priest was killed at his Guatemalan Indian mission.

The Third World Churches are busily redefining their decentralized relationship to the international Church. A polycentric world prohibits uniform legislation in all matters. Their ecumenical activism, their use of grass-roots religious formation in education, their concentration on family life and the redefinition of the lay-clerical relationship mark the vibrant character of this Church.

When the Third World Church provides an example, a parable for the entire Catholic community showing the intermediate procedures, rules, offices, and processes for implementing its critique of society and its renewed governance of the Church, it will have stepped beyond being only a visionary, authentically apocalyptic criticism of the present. The faithfulness of these believers to their particular situations, a fidelity unto death, discloses to them and to the worldwide community of Catholics an uncanny event—that the ignored and despised, the betrayed, forgotten, and impoverished can become the most human story of all.

NOTES

1. Crawford Young, *The Politics of Cultural Pluralism* (Madison, Wis.: University of Wisconsin Press, 1976), 182–86.
2. Cited in Frantz Fanon, *Black Skin, White Masks* (New York: Grove Press, 1967), 9.
3. Wahlbert Bühlmann, *The Coming of the Third Church,* trans. Ralph Woodhall and A. N. Other (Maryknoll, N.Y.: Orbis, 1977), 151.
4. *Vatican Council II: The Conciliar and Post-Conciliar Documents,* ed. Austin Flannery (Northport, N.Y.: Costello, 1975), 13–14.
5. *Origins,* vol. 10:1 (May 22, 1980), p. 5.
6. Young, *Politics of Cultural Pluralism,* 432–35.

7. Leonardo Boff, *Liberating Grace,* trans. John Drury (Maryknoll, N.Y.: Orbis, 1979), 84–85.

8. *Puebla and Beyond,* ed. John Eagleson and Philip Scharper, trans. John Drury (Maryknoll, N.Y.: Orbis, 1979), 294–95.

9. *Origins,* vol. 10:9 (July 31, 1980), p. 131.

10. Leonardo Boff, *Jesus Christ Liberator,* trans. Patrick Hughes (Maryknoll, N.Y.: Orbis, 1978), 240.

FURTHER RELATED MATERIAL

Overall surveys of Third World Church experience are rare. Wahlbert Bühlmann's *The Coming of the Third Church,* trans. Ralph Woodhall and A. N. Other (Maryknoll, N.Y.: Orbis, 1977) is still useful. Rosino Gibellini's *Frontiers of Theology in Latin America,* trans. John Drury (Maryknoll, N.Y.: Orbis, 1979) presents current programs or positions by contemporary Latin American theologians and social critics. Martin Jay's *The Dialectical Imagination: The History of the Frankfurt School and the Institute for Social Research, 1923–1950* (London: Heinemann, 1974) offers an overview of the recent social-political criticism which has generated the Marxist-Christian dialogue.

13

A CATHOLIC VISION

And though the world, at last, has swallowed her own solemn laughter
And has condemned herself to hell:
Suppose a whole new universe, a great clean Kingdom
Were to rise up like an Atlantis in the East,
Surprise this earth, this cinder, with new holiness!
　　Thomas Merton (1915–68), from "Senescente Mundo"

Though educated in the pre-Vatican II church, Flannery O'Connor (1925–64), the irrepressibly Southern author, was convinced that Catholic vision must change. Like many 1950s believers, she knew that a "child's faith [was] all right for the children, but eventually you have to grow religiously as every other way. . . . What people don't realize is how much religion costs. They think faith is a big electric blanket, when, of course, it is the cross. It is much harder to believe than not to believe."[1]

She recommended a French Jesuit who inspired thinking Catholics with the confidence that it was possible to be committed both to the Tradition and to contemporary human and natural sciences. "He was a paleontologist—helped to discover Peking man—and also a man of God." For many contemporary Christians, this man who had spent his life hunting among rocks for signs of primitive humanity in Asia, South Africa, the United States, and Europe, a man who was forbidden by his Roman superiors to publish his religious reflections upon science during his lifetime, became a visionary prophet of Catholicism.

Pierre Teilhard de Chardin (1881–1955) worked as a medic during World War I, gained success as a geologist through his successive tours of China, and never ceased thinking through the scientific context and its consequences for Christian faith. What his theological writings lack in rigor, they gain in vision. As O'Connor remarked: "I don't suggest you go to him for answers but for different questions, for that stretching of the imagination that you need."[2]

Teilhard was herald of an age in which science and religion might become partners in a dialogue toward the rebuilding of the earth. In two of his most popular works (*The Phenomenon of Man,* 1959; *Divine Milieu,* 1960), he saw the universe developing ever greater systems of complexity. In this increasing spiral, quantum jumps occurred in consciousness, such as the emergence of humanity and the development of its self-conscious reflection. As a consequence of the incarnation of Jesus, the material universe is moving toward an ultimate point of intensification and convergence in Christ. What we must have to appreciate creation "is much less new facts (there are enough, and even embarrassingly more than enough of these in every quarter) than a new way of looking at the facts and accepting them. A new way of seeing, combined with a new way of acting: that is what we need."[3] The Lord of creation was witnessed by both science and religion.

The scientist trusted in the christological unity of faith and reason, Church and world, and by that conviction offered to Catholics a synoptic statement amid growing social and religious pluralism. The historical revivals (patristic, liturgical, biblical) revealed how multifaceted the Tradition had been. The post-World War II cultural differences of believers threatened the unity of Catholicism. Vatican Council II legitimated indigenous diversities in worship, practice, and the expression of belief. As a result, it is not uncommon to hear both active and disaffected Catholics asking themselves what characterizes the Church's identity. How do I know I am still Catholic? What focuses the kaleidoscopic explosion of diversity?

CATHOLICISM IS ITS TRADITION

The center of Catholic identity remains the faithful affirmation that God has acted in the past in Jesus of Nazareth proclaimed as the Christ when he gathered up in his words and work the people of Israel, that he acts in the present through the Spirit, and that he will continue to act in the future, transforming the universe until it is transparent to divine love.

Catholics believe that the faithfulness of God is rendered concrete in all history. They are convinced that it is decisively represented in the structure, sacraments, and preaching of the believing community. There the unique saving action of Jesus is disclosed anew in the authentic actions of the past and present, the official authorities and ministries within the church, and the worship of believers. In these social expressions, the incarnation of divinity in humanity has been extended until the end of history.

CATHOLICISM IS SACRAMENT

If the Catholic Church is its Tradition, it is not yet the Kingdom of God. To canonize its history would be stupid as well as blasphemous. To say that Tradition is the meaning of the Church is not to say that God does not show the divine reality in created nature. On the contrary, Catholics believe that in Jesus Christ both historical traditions and natural religious yearnings have their fulfillment. Jesus is both sign of what the world is to be and the historical reality of its Presence. He is Sacrament of our meeting with God.

The Church is the effective, though partial, presence of our encounter with this Christ. When the Church gathers in worship, it proclaims what it is and hopes to become: God's people graced by his love. The Eucharist, the central act of Catholic worship, may serve as an example of what we mean. In this sacramental celebration, the ordinary signs of sharing, of giving and receiving, of resolving conflict and alienation are crystallized in a meal of bread and wine. The quite standard fare—grains of wheat kneaded into a single loaf and grapes crushed to form one cup of wine—is gathered into the memory of a single individual. Nature is reshaped by history.

Marked forever by Jesus' words "This is my body; this is my blood," the simple elements disclose one in Whom Christians trust for the meaning of their lives and for the significance of the universe. The words spoken, the gestures made, the elements used do not merely remember the community. They continue to stand over against the believing assembly as a call to unity and peace, a challenge to love one another. Believers must become what they share— the Body of Christ.

Nature is caught up into a particular biography and reveals its authentically universal meaning; personal stories are challenged by the Word to become what they most want to be—forthright love without fear. For Catholics, this "great exchange" between the

Divine and the human occurs at crucial moments in their lives: birth and growth into maturity, the assumption of new tasks and roles in the community, personal and communal failure, sickness, and death. The seven sacraments—Baptism, Confirmation, Orders, Marriage, Reconciliation, the Sacrament of the Ill or Dying, and the Eucharist —are misunderstood if they are seen as natural magic or reduced to the merely subjective memory of wishful historical thinking. On the contrary, God's action for humanity in Jesus is so real and lasting that it abides as his gift in every dimension of our existence.

For Catholics, the sacraments are signs that effect what they signify. The natural signs of cleansing water, strengthening oil, nourishing food, the promising word, and reconciling or confirming hand are graphically specified in Christ's history of death and resurrection as his own inaugural baptism, his anointing Spirit, his table fellowship with sinners, his undying faithfulness to his people, his words of forgiveness, and his call to apostolic leadership.

In the course of Catholic history, these sacramental rituals have continually reshaped themselves according to the needs of the culture and the demands of the Gospel upon that particular society. But in all situations, Catholics believe that Christ remains present as transfiguring Lord through these signs prayed by the faithful community. Their effectiveness is the gift of God; their enactment is the task given believers.

SACRAMENT IS HISTORY—
THE CUMULATIVE INCARNATION

Just as the early history of a child marks its adulthood, so certain aspects of the Church's past remain part of its meaning. Embedded within the narrative we have related is a set of cumulative achievements and requirements of which an authentic vision of Catholicism must take account (see Fig. 1, p. 183).

If Catholics are faithful to their own past, they will always meet (1) their origins in image, symbol, and story, (2) their social and institutional embodiment in doctrines, creeds, and authoritative councils, (3) their diverse interpretations inviting systematic and theoretic thought. Yet (4) these progressive cultural embodiments would be pointless, if they ignored the salvation they seek to understand. The challenge of the prophets reminds the community that the

Figure 1

	(1) 100–300	(2) 300–600	(3) 600–1300	(4) 1300–1600	(5) 1600–1800	(6) 1800–1900	(7) 1900.......C.E.
Influential Philosophers	Plato Aristotle Plotinus Proclus →			Nominalism William of Ockham →	Descartes Wolff →	Kant Schelling Hegel →	Kierkegaard Nietzsche Marx Heidegger →
History of Catholicism							
Questions Raised	Images Symbols Stories	Social Institutions	Reading Question Disputation *Summa*	Conversion History of Church Sin–Grace	Church-State Relations Religious Piety	History Method Praxis	Myth-Legend Modernity Secularity God
Major Movements	Jewish-Christianity Gnosticism Scriptures	Worship Canon Creeds Office Councils	Biblical Interpretation Scholasticism Crusades Inquisitions	Humanism *Devotio Moderna* Conciliarism Reformation	Scientific Method Enlightenment Catholic Revival	Rationalism Liberal Theologies Neo-Scholasticism	Vatican Council II Religious Freedom Theologies of Liberation
Major Prophets, Traditionists, and Visionaries	Justin Martyr Irenaeus *The Shepherd of Hermas*	Augustine Benedict	Gregory VII Thomas Aquinas Francis of Assisi	Luther, Zwingli, Calvin; Trent, Jesuits, Bellarmine	Jansen, Pascal, Galileo; Manualist Theologies	Drey Newman Kleutgen Leo XIII	John XXIII Guttierez Lonergan Rahner Schillebeeckx
Permanent Exigencies	Symbolic	Communitarian Interpretive	Systematic Theoretic	Dialectical Critical	Methodological	Transcendental	Communicative
Emergent Fields of Theology		Trinity Christology	Sacraments Ethics Soteriology	Anthropology Grace	Ecclesiology Dogmatics Moral Theology Missiology	Philosophy of Religion Revelation and Faith Eschatology	Religious Education Pastoral Studies Comparative Religion

story of Jesus must be interiorized, but also that the will to understand is always a gift.

The probing attempts (5) to face modern and contemporary pluralistic cultures over the past three hundred years have not always been successful. Some Catholics have wanted to jettison the past to travel lightly; others have wanted to package each item without wondering whether some past baggage is worth carrying. But the contemporary world of scientific method, critical self-understanding, and historical self-making (6) refuses to disappear. They continue to ask whether it is possible to respeak the images, symbols, and stories, to reinterpret the conflicting understandings, to resocialize the doctrinal structural norms, and to rethink the theological discipline as a respected voice among contemporary claimants for the construction of our world (7). More importantly, our world continues to ask whether these reinterpretations will be more than merely human words, whether they can be what they claim to be—Divine words whose consoling, reconciling force may be reexperienced, freshly disclosed, and newly understood.

This movement we have sketched over some nineteen hundred years is not due simply to external forces pushing against the Christian community. For it has sometimes been said that the doctrines of the early Church, like that of the Triune God proclaimed at Nicaea (325 C.E.), were only defined because someone denied them. But in fact the energy of the Gospel itself as it encountered new cultural horizons invited the developments.

What we think of now as specifically Catholic aspects of Christian history, such as Scholasticism, medieval Christendom, or baroque art emerged from questions, interpretations, and judgments made by believers over the centuries as a response to the Gospel. Medieval theories about salvation arose due to issues raised by the Pauline images of ransom, adoption, and sacrifice. Systems were necessary simply to coordinate the various doctrines of the community. And Christian governments of one sort or another keep emerging because the call of Christ was not simply to fishermen in Galilee, but to all men and women. As Catholic history developed, it encountered new forms of life which it constantly attempted to understand and transform.

The characteristic Catholic past remains part of the present duties of the community. Although our symbols, institutional interpretations, theories, and practice cannot repeat that past, they will echo it in new ways. The focus of unity for Catholics will remain the same: sacramental life, the official leadership of bishops and pope, and the prophets and visionaries who hover at our peripheral sightlines, forbidding compromise with evil and challenging believers toward heroic charity. The Catholic Church sees itself as an *ecclesia semper reformanda,* an assembly always (in need of) reforming itself according to the call of the Gospel and the human situation.

A NARROW VISION?

Is this a tunnel vision of the world? Is it some fixation on a pristine point of the past which seems intrinsically more perfect than our present? Hardly.

Catholicism has a fundamentally universal outreach. This evangelical program is not abstract, a merely vague intention to offer warm comfort to millions. Rather it is a universal call which is reached by sharp interest paid to its own particular Tradition and to the local situation in which it finds itself. The Catholic trust in the underlying "stuff" of its own history is a conviction that its very specificity has ultimate significance. The believer gives a cup of water to one "little one," because in that single human face the All discloses its love.

Yet even this formulation is too abstract. Catholicism's difficult work into the next millennium will require listening to, thinking through, and acting upon the common cultural experiences of our planet: the growth of secularized humanity; consumerist economics; bureaucratization of both capitalist and socialist economies; and the reactionary attitudes of fundamentalist religious, national, and racial movements.

If the spiritual meaning of humanity is to be proclaimed to these concrete problems, then intercultural, interreligious, and transnational dialogues must occur. The global humanity that is emerging from the confusions of this century will demand an authentic hearing from believers so that the true universality of the Gospel may be preached.

This task—plunging into the particularities of our own Tradition and the human situations of those to whom we speak—will also be accomplished under a new and difficult state of Diaspora. This dispersal of believers among the culturally disinterested will not be unlike the experience of the Hellenistic world at the beginning of our common era. In this, Christians will have much to learn from their Jewish brothers and sisters who have suffered the isolation of surrounding social structures and the difficulties of maintaining belief and practice under the persecution for religious values held up to an indifferent world. For with their Lord, Christians have little reason to assure themselves that earthly success will be theirs. Smaller Christian communities, less economically established, again prophetically visible, may be called upon to preach the Gospel to increasingly hostile societies.

DOES CATHOLICISM HAVE
A CONCRETE PROGRAM FOR THE FUTURE?

Some people, even Catholics themselves, think that there is a blueprint for the Christian future of the world. Some place this treasured program in a literal or allegorical reading of the Scriptures, especially the *Book of Revelation;* some put it in the Pope or in some message locked away in the Vatican library's vaults. But in fact, any such printout of the future would be a misunderstanding of the Christian message—and more importantly, of the Christian God.

The God we worship is not a God who discloses the day and hour of the divine will for our world; indeed, it is hidden in the Cross and Resurrection of Jesus Christ. Catholic Christians have no special access to a computerized version of the crystal ball. In fact, they must trust in God's presence and promises in the past, their loving interpretation of that past in the present, and their discerning hope for God's Grace in their future. Catholics react to contemporary events with the measure of intelligence, wit, and grace granted them by faith, hope, and love. The tools available to them remain the stories of the Gospel and Tradition, the interpretations of the prophets and teachers of the past, the theories and systems which collected the truth and anticipated the precarious present.

Now Catholics are most likely to be found at the edges of moral and religious issues in our societies: problems of life and death—abortion, war, health care for the handicapped or senile, security for the poor and disenfranchised; problems of the quality of life—working conditions, just wages, education, family life, marriage, and divorce; and sociocultural and economic planning—political campaigns, think tanks, nuclear disarmament, and diplomacy. These public questions have become the crucible in which Catholic (or rather global) identity will be formed.

In the disintegration of the classical certitudes of society, Catholics have become conscious with others that virtue cannot be merely a private affair. Patience, courage, prudence, justice, and temperance are not primarily intra-Christian matters, but must wend their way into the larger world. In this sense, Catholics expect their institution as it embodies the Good News to proclaim, confront, and transform social structures with the same vigor and creativity that it met Semitic, Greco-Roman, Celtic, Germanic, Slavic, and New World cultures.

For the self-making of humanity since the Enlightenment has not been an unalloyed success by anyone's measure, let alone a Divine standard. What was once a series of national warring states has become a world in search of organic unity in which power must be guided not by opportunism but by wisdom. With the possibility of destroying whole regions of the earth, even entire populations, through nuclear self-destruction, no single individual, no government can afford to be less than globally conscious—even if it is only searching for some place to preserve its own survival.

The unthinkable holocausts of this century have given rise to the equally unthinkable possibilities of "life" after nuclear war. We can resign ourselves either to the long cycle of human decline, narrowing our experience to self-interest, impoverishing our understandings of the world through heart-felt blindness, tunneling our judgments into self-protective bunkers, and fencing our values with fear; or, facing our disenchantment with the technocratic elite, we can collaborate toward a new society.

Achieving a new, federated, pluralistic, global social order will be difficult, entailing suffering for the "haves" as well as the "have-nots." And none of us likes pain. So we establish elaborate defense mechanisms to protect ourselves from deprivation, hoping that we can stave off the nihilism which threatens destruction.

In this mixed world, compromised between authentic values of development and despair, the Catholic community offers the Gospel of Jesus. It proclaims a community *within* suffering, not an escape from it. It combines individuals into a loving family of faithful, hopeful agents whose lives contribute to the liberation of the most authentic social and personal impulses. In any societal transformation, in any transculturation of Gospel values, martyrs appear— whether the bloody witnesses to liberation in Middle and South America or Asia, or the confessing dissenters in developed countries whose work, actions, and persons are isolated, muted, and sometimes lost in silence.

Catholic prophets are supported by their institution when Pope Paul VI speaks to the United Nations and cries: "No more war, war never again!" The institutional vision is instanced when small basic communities of Catholics take the Eucharistic readings, pray over them, and apply them to their personal, familial, and working lives. The society is judged by Catholic visionaries when men and women march upon governmental assemblies in support of human life. Catholics, rather than dealing some prepackaged deck of cards to a less-than-waiting world, search for the *legitimate means* of societal and personal transformation that will allow a new earth to be granted by God. The harsh work of disclosing the Gospel *within* the world and of confronting the world *with* the Gospel is at the heart of Catholic sensibilities and understanding in this century.

Thus Catholics and their pastors have begun to be a people on the margins, individuals caught between the social bodies of world policy. They hope to become a place of dialogue in which reconciliation may occur—a situation of centering in which transcendence may again appear. They recognize that the world cannot envision itself anew unless they themselves enact the transformation they expect of society. Their compassion for one another will be their suffering with the change of society itself. As they interrelate rich and poor people and nations, primitive and scientific societies, they hope to become a unified narrative voice on behalf of authentic humanity.

Every social institution at present pretends to universal dominion: political ideologies—whether socialist or capitalist—supranational businesses, racial hegemonies, even religious polities. Catholicism cannot identify with any of these powers. To face the fact that despite its own historical temptations and sins, it is not an ideology—whether political, economic, racial, *or* religious—but a faith in God's future for the world requires a slip from the old cultural moorings and a self-conscious launch on its own evangelical mobility. That process is even now taking place.

There remain controversial ecclesiastical issues (mandatory celibacy for presbyters and bishops; sexual, marital, familial, and ethical conflicts; the ordination and roles of women; the authentic collegiality of authority; etc.) to be resolved. Even more important, there are external questions (such as war and peace or genetic engineering) to be undertaken. Each goes to the heart of the Gospel, each emerges from the vital organs of a struggling culture, each requires the difficult prospect of laying down one's life for one's friends.

But Catholics have never wanted for prophets, visionaries, or the authentic proponents of Tradition in the past. The contemporary versatility of Catholic internal conversation is vigorous; and if it has sometimes shown the sinfulness of men and women, it has also disclosed the heroic charity of saints and the glory of God. Jesus' declaration that he would never leave his Church untended ("I am with you always, even to the end of time"—Matt. 28:20, NEB) through the gift of his Spirit (John 14:15–17) has verified itself in the history of this people. Catholics have no reason to lose their trust that God will bless his Church with the individuals and movements necessary to conserve its past, challenge its present, and transform its future.

The modern meaning of Catholicism rests upon the command to preach the Good News. Catholics do not have reason for nostalgia or despair—but only for excitement at the tasks which await the apostolic community of believers. As Pope Paul VI said in his *Encyclical Letter on Evangelization:*

> May the world of our time, which is searching, sometimes with anguish, sometimes with hope, be enabled to receive the Good News not from

evangelizers who are dejected, discouraged, impatient or anxious, but ministers of the Gospel whose lives glow with fervor, who have first received the joy of Christ, and who are willing to risk their lives so that the Kingdom may be proclaimed and the Church established in the midst of the world.[4]

Now, of course, there are only hints and guesses, hints followed by guesses, as T. S. Eliot has said in his *Four Quartets*. But, in this matter of God's Kingdom, ours is only the trying, the attempts at achievement. The rest is not our business.

NOTES

1. Flannery O'Connor, *Habit of Being,* ed. Sally Fitzgerald (New York: Farrar, Straus & Giroux, 1979), 354.

2. Ibid., 477.

3. Pierre Teilhard de Chardin, "The Convergence of the Universe" (23 July 1951), in *Activation of Energy,* trans. René Hague (New York: Harcourt Brace Jovanovich, 1970), 294–95.

4. *Acta Apostolicae Sedis,* LXVIII (1976), par. 80, pp. 72–75. An English text may be found in *Evangelization Today,* ed. Austin Flannery (Northport, N.Y.: Costello, 1977), 48.

INDEX OF AUTHORS

INDEX OF SUBJECTS

W9-DHG-357 M88
1972

COLORADO MOUNTAIN COLLEGE
DB27.M881972   SP
                                      Musulin, Stella.
       Austria and the Austrians.

1 03 0000005935

Austria

AUSTRIA
and the Austrians

STELLA MUSULIN

With a Foreword by
W. H. AUDEN

PRAEGER PUBLISHERS

New York · Washington

COLORADO MOUNTAIN COLLEGE
LRC---WEST CAMPUS
Glenwood Springs, Colo. 81601

BOOKS THAT MATTER

Published in the United States of America in 1972
by Praeger Publishers, Inc., 111 Fourth Avenue,
New York, N.Y. 10003

© Stella Musulin, 1971

All rights reserved

No part of this publication may be reproduced, stored
in a retrieval system or transmitted in any form or
by any means, electronic, mechanical, photocopying,
recording or otherwise, without the prior permission
of the Copyright owner.

Library of Congress Catalog Card Number: 71-173443

Printed in Great Britain

Contents

7

Illustrations

9

Illustrations

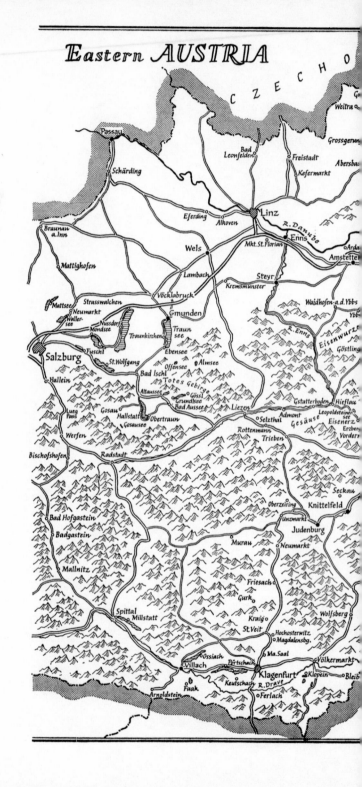

Eastern AUSTRIA

CZECHO

G

Weitra

Grossgerun

Passau

Bad
Leonfelden

Freistadt

Abersba

Schärding

Kefermarkt

Eferding

Alkoven

Linz

R. Danube

Braunau
a. Inn

Enns

Arda

Mkt. St. Florian

Amstette

Wels

Mattighofen

Lambach

Steyr

Kremsmünster

Waidhofen a.d. Ybbs

Vöcklabruck

Mattsee

Strasswalchen

Gmunden

Ybb

Neumarkt

Waller-
see

Nussdorf
Mondsee

Traun
see

R. Enns

Eisenwurz

Fuschl

Traunkirchen

Ebensee

Göstling

Salzburg

St. Wolfgang

Offensee

Almsee

Hallein

Bad Ischl

Totes Gebirge

Altaussee

Gössl
Grundsee
Bad Aussee

Liezen

Gstatterboden

Hieflau

Lueg
Pass

Gosau

Hallstatt

Obertraun

Selzthal

Admont

Leopoldsteiner
see

Gosausee

Rottenmann

Gesäuse

Eisenerz

Werfen

Trieben

Erzberg

Vorderr

Bischofshofen

Radstadt

Seckau

Oberzeiring

Knittelfeld

Bad Hofgastein

Unzmarkt

Judenburg

Badgastein

Murau

Neumarkt

Mallnitz

Friesach

Gurk

Spittal

Millstatt

Kraig

Wolfsberg

St. Veit

Hochosterwitz
Magdalensbg.

Ma. Saal

Völkermarkt

Ossiach

Pörtschach

Villach

Keutschach

Klagenfurt

Klopein

Bleib

Faak

R. Drave

Ferlach

Arnoldstein

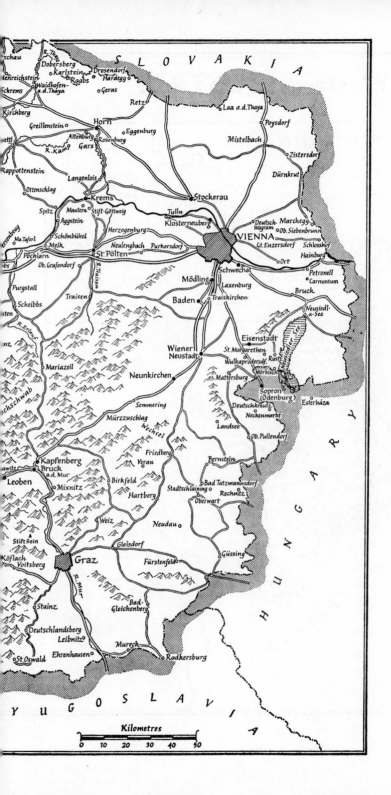

SLOVAKIA

chau
Dobersberg
Karlstein
Waidhofen
a.d.Thaya
Schrems
Kirchberg
Greillenstein
wettl
Altenburg
Rappottenstein
Ottenschlag
Spitz
bsenburg
Ma.Taferl
Pöchlarn
bs
Purgstall
Scheibbs
sten
nz
Mariazell
chschwab
Kapfenberg
awitz
Bruck
a.d.Mur
Leoben
Mixnitz
Stift Rein
Köflach
Voitsberg
Stainz
Deutschlandsberg
Leibnitz
St.Oswald
Ehrenhausen

R.Th.
Raabs
Drosendorf
Hardegg
Geras
Retz
Horn
Eggenburg
Rosenburg
Gars
R.Kamp
Langenlois
Krems
Mautern
Stift-Göttweig
Aggstein
Schönbühel
Melk
Ob.Grafendorf
St.Pölten
Neulengbach
Purkersdorf
R.Traisen
Traisen
Herzogenburg
Neunkirchen
Semmering
Mürzzuschlag
Wechsel
Friedberg
Vorau
Birkfeld
Hartberg
Weiz
Neudau
Gleisdorf
Graz
R.Mur
Bad-
Gleichenberg
Mureck
Radkersburg

Laa a.d.Thaya
Poysdorf
Mistelbach
Zistersdorf
Dürnkrut
Stockerau
Tulln
Klosterneuburg
Deutsch.
Wagram
Marchegg
Ob.Siebenbrunn
VIENNA
Gt.Enzersdorf
Schlosshof
Schwechat
Ort
Hainburg
Mödling
Petronell
Laxenburg
Carnuntum
Bruck
Baden
Traiskirchen
Eisenstadt
Wiener
Neustadt
St.Margarethen
Wulkaprodersdf.
Rust
Mattersburg
Mörbisch
Sopron
(Odenburg)
Esterháza
Deutschkreutz
Neckenmarkt
Landsee
Ob.Pullendorf
Bernstein
Bad Tatzmannsdorf
Stadtschlaining
Rechnitz
Oberwart
Güssing
Fürstenfeld

H U N G A R Y

Y U G O S L A V I A

Kilometres
0 10 20 30 40 50

Western AUSTRIA

THE PROVINCES OF AUSTRIA

UPPER AUSTRIA — Linz, Salzburg

LOWER AUSTRIA — Vienna

BURGENLAND

VORARLBERG — Bregenz

TYROL — Innsbruck

SALZBURG

EAST TYROL

STYRIA — Graz

CARINTHIA — Klagenfurt

Boden See

Mt. Pfänder
Bregenz
Dornbirn
Bezau
Hohenems
Götzis
Rankweil
Feldkirch
Fontanella
Damüls
Gr. Walsertal
Bludenz
Lech
Flexen Pass
Zürs
Brand
Schruns
Montafon
Galtür
Ratikon Mts.
Silvretta Mts.

Allgäu Alps
Bregenzer Wald
K. Walsertal
R. Lech
Lechtaler Alps
Arlberg
St. Anton
Reutte
Zugspitze
Fern Pass
Nassereith
Imst
Landeck
Ladiso
Prutz
Pfunds
Hochfinstermünz
Nauders
Wildspitze
Obergurgl
Ötztal
R. Inn

R. Rhine
LIECHTENSTEIN

SWITZERLAND

IT

Foreword

As Baroness Musulin says, with documentary proof, the average Englishman's knowledge of Austrian geography is very vague, and his knowledge of her history almost nil. Even those who have been there are apt to imagine that Salzburg is a city in the Tyrol. When, in 1925, I left England for the first time to attend the Salzburg Festival and then on to Kitzbühel—both sadly changed since then—I don't *think* I made this mistake, but I can't be sure.

As for those who have not, when, a few years ago, President Jonas paid a state visit to England, the Lord Mayor of London kept referring to Australia. It must be admitted, however, that President Jonas's knowledge of England was not very extensive either, for, in the course of a speech, he said: 'There has been a historic friendship between Austria and England ever since the time of Richard I.' (Austria, perhaps, had reason to be grateful, for the ransom paid to get him back enabled Vienna to build a new city wall.)

That the average man should have a vaguer notion of Austria than of most foreign countries may be partly due to the fact that, when one considers her geography, it seems a miracle that she should exist at all.

Austria possesses mountain ranges and deep rivers. But it is a curious fact that these natural barriers have not, on the whole, been accepted as political frontiers. The all-important Danube certainly marked the 'limes', the northern frontier of the Roman Empire, but it was never an Austrian frontier—today it is not even a provincial boundary. Geologically speaking, the highland plateau north of the Danube forms the southern tip of the great Bohemian massif; climate and vegetation of the Hungarian 'puszta' begin in the Vienna basin. The highest alpine range in Austria has never been a state frontier. And it was not until 1918, when

17

mountains already possessed very little strategical significance and would never again have any at all, that it had ever occurred to anyone to declare the Brenner to be a natural and therefore desirable national frontier.

* * *

If we suppose for a moment that England, Scotland and Wales were not an island but were surrounded by land inhabited by related peoples, we might well be surprised that those three countries had ever become one nation.

* * *

If ever a political event took place in defiance of all realistic probability it was the liberation of the eastern provinces of Austria, and part of the capital, from Soviet Russian occupation. Into the almost straight line down from the North Sea which divides Europe into two halves, Austria presses forward like a battering ram.

To this day, despite the automobile and mass communications, the inhabitants of the various provinces differ greatly from each other in temperament, dialect, dress, domestic architecture, etc. When, a few years ago, the Austrian Army was on manoeuvres and entered the Tyrol, the peasants rushed out to repel an invasion.

If they have recently developed, as I think they have, a stronger sense of all being Austrians, this is probably due, as Baroness Musulin suggests, to their common experiences, firstly under Hitler and then under the Allied Occupation.

The case of the amateur historian is this: civilization means, in part, self-awareness throughout all the stages of cause and effect, and to understand the thought and behavior of people to-day one must know their heritage. To know anything about the psychology of the South Tyrolese, for example, of the Serbs and Croats, of the Czechs and Slovaks, it is essential to dig down a long way. The same is true of the Slovene Carinthians whom we shall happen on later.

This is the task which Baroness Musulin has attempted and, in my opinion as an amateur reader of history, with triumphant success.

She begins with the Vorarlberg, then moves eastward through the Tyrol and the Salzkammergut, then southward to Carinthia and

Foreword

Styria, then northward to Upper and to Lower Austria (where we both happen to live within half an hour's drive of each other), then eastward again to Burgenland, then back to end in Vienna. To each of these areas she devotes a chapter which is more or less complete in itself. This has the advantage for a reader that he can take the chapters in any order he chooses, according to his personal interests or the place he is planning to visit next. To every kind of curiosity, to the lover of scenery, of history, of architecture, of eccentric characters and touching romances, she has something to offer. Anybody, for example, in search of perfect material for a movie, could hardly do better than to consult her accounts of the adventures of Maria Clementine Sobieski, the future bride of the Old Pretender, or of Eva Kraus, *die Hundsgräfin*, with whom Napoleon fell in love when she was a housemaid in Schönbrunn, or of Anna Plochl, the daughter of a Styrian postmaster, with whom the Archduke Johann fell in love when she was twelve and he was thirty-four and finally married after patiently waiting for thirteen years. More suitable material, perhaps, for an historical novelist than a film-director is the life-story of Anna Neumann.

Anna married six times. This comparatively rapid turnover gave rise to ugly rumour and suspicion among her numerous tenantry, though never among her peers, of poisoning or witchcraft. Her biographers consider that she was an extremely able administrator of her husbands' estates which had snowballed into her hands, and that she drove herself to work as a distraction from her grief over the death of her first four husbands whom, uncommon though this may have been, she had married (as she was beautiful as well as rich the choice was ample) for love. Having lost her only daughter, Anna found herself at the age of 76 a fourfold widow with great possessions and no heir other than a step-nephew who had married a nonentity; he was not, Anna thought, a promising founder of a dynasty. Her decision was soon made, and she now married a thirty-year-old man, Ferdinand von Salamanca, Count Ortenburg.... Anna's whole intention, it must be realised, was to find a worthy heir, on the assumption that, after her death, the young widower would at once marry a girl who could put the old lady's ambitions into effect. Simply to have given away her estates to any local nobleman was not the answer. To her horror, the plan misfired because Ferdinand was tubercular and within five or six years he was dead. Anna, living at Murau Castle in Styria, was now 82, and failing. There was little time to lose. An old friend, a statesman from the Imperial court, called on her and made a suggestion. How about the twenty-eight-year-old Count Georg Ludwig von Schwarzenberg, whose only barrier to a brilliant career in diplomacy was a lack of private means? Georg Schwarzenberg called at Murau, and she evidently liked what she saw. The odd pair were married.

Baroness Musulin has had both the curiosity and the opportunity to explore all the Austrian provinces in detail, so that she probably knows the country a good deal better than most people who were born there. Very few Austrians, for example, have visited the Mühlviertel, near the Czech border in Upper Austria, which was Adalbert Stifter's country: she has. The same is true of her historical reading. Not many Austrians, in my experience, realize that, for most of the sixteenth century, 'practically the entire nobility of Austria, most of the townsfolk, the mining and industrial workers and a section of the peasantry' became Lutherans, so that when, in the seventeenth century under pressure from the Jesuits, the Habsburgs put the screws on, many of the most intelligent and skilful persons in the country were obliged to emigrate, a fact which, in part, explains the character of the Viennese.

The relation between Art and Society is so obscure that only a fool will claim that he understands it. How, as Baroness Musulin asks in her concluding chapter on Vienna, is one to explain the extraordinary eruption of genius in that city which began during the last decades of the nineteenth century and lasted until the late 1920s, manifesting itself in every field, literature, music, painting, philosophy, medicine? When it began the empire was already dying on its feet, and it continued after its total collapse. Why? Even more extraordinary in my opinion were the artistic achievements of men like Nestroy and Adalbert Stifter living in Metternich's police state. More than that, I cannot help wondering if they could have written what they did under a more liberal regime. Talking of Stifter, Baroness Musulin says that he, like the composer Bruckner, 'has not travelled well'. Of Bruckner this may be true, but of Stifter I would say that he has not travelled, period: until a few years ago nobody had attempted to translate him.

But I must stop and leave the reader to enjoy *Austria* by himself. I know of few books of this kind that are at one and the same time so instructive and such fun to peruse.

W. H. AUDEN

Acknowledgements

I would like to express my gratitude to Hofrat Dr. Franz Steininger, Director of Publications in the Nationalbibliothek, Vienna, for granting me research facilities, to Gabrielle Altgräfin zu Salm-Reifferscheidt-Raitz and Dr. Robert Kittler of the Portrait Collection and Picture Archives of the Nationalbibliothek for their imaginative assistance over the illustrations; also to the Austrian State Department of Tourism and the Department of Tourism, Municipality of Vienna.

Among those friends who have helped me I particularly wish to thank Mrs. Richard Goddard-Wilson (Lavender Cassels) and Frau Dr. Walburga von Cornides for reading the manuscript and pointing out errors and infelicities; Frau Dr. Lilly von Sauter, Curator of Ambras Castle, for information about Philippine Welser; Herr Max von Marquet for much enlivening conversation and for giving me the run of his library; and Frau Ann Tizia Leitich and her husband Dr. Korningen for their kind interest and advice.

If it had not been for W. H. Auden's encouragement I should never have got started, and the debt of gratitude which I owe to him for writing the introduction hardly needs emphasis.

1

A Glance at the Map.
Who are the Austrians?

A group of visitors to Austria were sitting around the dinner table in a private guest house in the mountains. The American diplomat had been up since daybreak in order to reach the Grossglockner Pass before the crowds arrived, the English county couple had been shopping in Salzburg, the girls had spent the day deepening their tan beside the lake and the young man in the Old Etonian tie had joined them after tennis. Their host, a man whom, after many years' experience, the ways of paying guests could no longer surprise, still clung to the view that his foreign visitors must surely know something about the country that they had taken so much trouble to visit, or if not, that they would like to learn. He expected very little, however, and had once been heard to say that the really distinguishing factor about his Anglo-Saxon visitors—he apologized for the probable inaccuracy of this generally accepted label—was that their knowledge of Austria, its geography and history, varied in inverse ratio to the amount of money which had been laid out on their education.

This evening, during the saddle of venison and cranberry sauce, it had been quite a pleasure to learn that all members of the party supposed themselves to be in the Tyrol, because this was exactly what he had expected. People always did, and it was almost certainly a mistake to disillusion them. Salzburg was the town, they thought, and everything west of that including the province of Vorarlberg was the Tyrol. Just this once he permitted himself the luxury of counting off the nine provinces, explaining as he went

25

COLORADO MOUNTAIN COLLEGE
LRC---WEST CAMPUS
Glenwood Springs, Colo. 81601

along that Upper and Lower Austria were not a vague designation for the alpine and lowland regions respectively, but provinces; in fact the oldest of the lot.

Not everyone was listening: crisp little funnels made of a light sponge mixture, containing wild strawberries and topped with whipped cream, were being handed round. Having rapidly counted the funnels and divided the result by the number of persons present, the host asked who could tell him the names of those countries which share a common frontier with Austria. The county couple did rather well over this because they had arrived by car from Germany and were going on to Venice, and the diplomat contributed Switzerland, but after that there was silence. The host rallied the Old Etonian, who was dabbing at his tie with the corner of his napkin:

'Come along now: conjure up a map in your mind's eye. Where is the eastern frontier of Austria?'

'A little hot water,' said the young man thoughtfully, 'ought to do it. The eastern frontier, sir? I should say approximately on the shores of the Black Sea.'

How much do people really want to know? Somewhere between the bland '*étonnez-moi!*' attitude—one of vague but pleasurable expectancy combined with disinclination to burden the mind with facts, and the eager thoroughness of the guide-book addict, lies a third alternative. This is to choose a table—either in fact or in imagination—under a shady chestnut tree in a Gasthaus garden well away from the main road, and call for a well-chilled Viertel of white wine. Then, the rough edge of one's thirst slaked, and with peace beginning to descend on one's soul, to push the drink a little to one side and spread out a map of Austria upon the table. It should be a realistic map, showing the bumps: on no account should it be one of those mendacious affairs designed to show motorists how to whirl their cars from one tourist centre to another, and on which only those who know the country and therefore need no map would realize the presence of towering mountain ranges, of glaciers, ravines and vast belts of forest. In a word, it should be a physical map. Not only so that a childish pleasure in picking out the white areas of eternal snow, the purple or dark brown mountain regions and the green foothills may be indulged, but also because Austria is a country of great contrasts. And if these contrasts are blotted out, the nature of this country, its history and development, and even its situation today cannot be grasped.

Austria is an awkward shape, like a recumbent string bag with ill-assorted contents. From Bregenz on the eastern shore of Lake Constance to the Neusiedlersee on the frontier of Hungary, its full length is just under 600 kilometres, but at its narrowest it is only 34 kilometres wide, 260 kilometres at its broadest point. Whoever has patience with figures may care to know that the total frontier measures 2,637 kilometres, 784 of which are shared with the Federal Republic of Germany, 548 with Czechoslovakia, 430 with Italy, 360 with Hungary, 311 with Yugoslavia and 198 with Switzerland and Liechtenstein. These distances begin to come to life when we notice that, if we run our eye down the line running from north to south which divides western from communist eastern Europe, Austria (including its capital) protrudes into eastern Europe like a wedge, and the length of frontier which it shares with these countries amounts to nearly half of the total.

Austria is, of course, predominantly an alpine country. To be more exact, it contains the eastern alpine range which is generally defined as starting at the line linking Lake Constance and Lake Como across the Hinterrein valley and the Splügen Pass. From the frontier on the Austrian sector of the Rhine plain, the Vorarlberg foothills quickly lead on to high mountains which march in stupendous progression from west to east, reaching their climax with the Grossglockner and the Grossvenediger. Deeply scored valleys run from west to east, cross-hatched with a series of side-valleys lying almost parallel to one another. The reason behind this dignified and orderly design is that the west–east valleys mainly run along dividing lines between geological formations: the upper reaches of the Inn, the Salzach and the Enns rivers lie between the central alps and the northern limestone range. In the south of Austria there is a parallel furrow which leads through the valleys of the Pustertal and Drave between the central range and the southern limestone zone—the Dolomites. To the east of the Grossglockner massif the fugue-like procession begins to lose its regularity, and part of the charm of the area from Carinthia up to Vienna is its unpredictability. Valleys may lie at any angle, wooded foothills, rolling hill country and tablelands lead on to the Styrian alps and to the snowfields at the doorstep of Vienna: the Rax and Schneeberg.

With what attention can be spared from the wine and the peaceful surroundings, it might be worthwhile to consider for a moment the importance to Austria of its main lines of communication. Take, for instance, the Brenner Pass. Of all the alpine routes, none is more significant than the Brenner because it has always been the shortest and most direct link between Germany and Italy. The approaches to the pass on both sides are gradual and can be kept open all the year round, factors of inestimable importance for trade as well as for the movement of armies from Roman times. Since the days of the pre-Roman civilizations, a constant procession of wagons carried the mineral wealth of Austria to Italy, bringing back raw materials for Austrian industries, foodstuffs and luxury goods from overseas. The Romans somehow managed to keep the Grossglockner open all through the winter, an astonishing achievement which has never been equalled since. They used a slightly different route over the summit from the present one, but from time to time they must inevitably have suffered heavy losses from the avalanches which thunder unhindered down those slopes, lying as they do so far above the timber line. All the same, compared with the Brenner, the Salzburg and Carinthian passes are long and wearisome. Early travellers to the south who succeeded in putting the Grossglockner Pass behind them, found themselves in Lienz, still facing the Gailberg and Plöcken Passes before they could trot down to Tolmezzo. Many of them will have preferred to go round by Spittal, where they would meet the traffic which had come over the Katschberg. If you run your finger down this route from Salzburg to Villach and notice the relative altitudes compared with the Glockner road, you will begin to agree that, in the days before the Mallnitz railway tunnel was constructed, the Katschberg road over the Radstädter Tauern was the most logical central route across Austria: the best way, for example, for a traveller to take who wanted to go from Venice to Salzburg and on to Munich and Regensburg.

In modern times, the main traffic between Czechoslovakia (Bohemia) and Italy has passed due south through Vienna to Wiener-Neustadt, then south-west over the Semmering and on down to Villach, branching off earlier (via Bruck-Graz or Klagenfurt) for Yugoslavia. But this diagonal route only came into use during the late Middle Ages, as a result of a shift in the political frontier. Formerly, Vienna was only of importance as a trading post on the Danube. The focal point of this eastern area of Austria was the L-shaped junction where the River March, descending from the north, meets the Danube near Hainburg. This is the meeting point of two ancient trade routes, the River Danube, and the Amber Road from the Adriatic to the Baltic. Avoiding the Leitha mountains, outermost ripple of the Eastern Alps, the Amber route followed the road south via Sopron (Ödenburg) and Szombathely (Steinamanger), both of which towns are now just inside the Hungarian border.

Austria possesses mountain ranges and deep rivers. But it is a curious fact that these natural barriers have not, on the whole, been accepted as political frontiers. The all-important Danube certainly marked the *limes*, the northern frontier of the Roman Empire, but it was never an Austrian frontier—today it is not even a provincial boundary. Geologically speaking, the highland plateau north of the Danube forms the southern tip of the great Bohemian massif; climate and vegetation of the Hungarian *puszta* begin in the Vienna basin. The highest alpine range in Austria has never been a state frontier. And it was not until 1918, when mountains already possessed very little strategical significance and would never again have any at all, that it had ever occurred to anyone to declare the Brenner to be a natural and therefore desirable national frontier. In fact, the Tyrolese have always formed one united people, one dukedom and one diocese. The way in which the Tyrol's internal lines of communication were cut in half becomes quite clear if we locate Nauders, to the south of Landeck, and trace the road down to Meran, round the loop which connects Bozen and Brixen and then east along the Pustertal valley to the Austrian frontier a few miles

from Lienz. The old circular route round the Tyrol was snipped off
on each side, and the rough curve between Landeck and Innsbruck
and round to Lienz now begins to look as incomplete as a hat
without a face beneath it.

In these days of social mobility it may seem a waste of time to
speculate on the origins of the inhabitants in a particular province.
Surely, in a country of this size, the people are by now all so mixed
up that the amount of Germanic, Slav or Celtic blood they may
have in their veins is of little interest? The truth is that there are
profound cleavages in Austria which are partly the result of racial
heredity and local history, and partly the result of geography, and
these things add up to the truism that modern Austria is very
difficult to govern from Vienna—a capital city right up at the
extreme east end of the country, whose inhabitants have not much
in common with the population of the Tyrol and Vorarlberg except
the German language. There are forces of attraction which draw
Austrians out and away from their own centres. If your Salzburg
friend is not at home, he may be in Munich; that Vorarlberg
businessman, whom you thought you might look up in passing, is
probably in Zürich; your Styrian friends are fishing in Croatia. The
real surprise would be to run into one of them in Vienna. All this is
perfectly natural because it arises from practical considerations: the
normal flow of trade or simple personal convenience. But the
causes lie deeper. If we suppose for a moment that England,
Scotland and Wales were not an island but were surrounded by land
inhabited by related peoples, we might well be surprised that those
three countries had ever become one nation. '*L'Autriche, c'est ce qui
reste,*' said Clémenceau during the peace negotiations after the First
World War: modern Austria was to be what remained after the
member states of the Austro–Hungarian Empire had gone their
own way and after certain frontier changes had been carried out in
the interests of the victors. For centuries, the Austrians had
possessed the habits of mind which belong to a supranational
people. They had, as it were, been used to living and working in a
coaching inn at the busiest crossroads in central Europe. The
Austrian Republic, this miserable remnant, was not a viable unit,

not an entity—above all it seemed not to be a nation. This was a feeling shared by innumerable people who grew up in the twilight of the Habsburg era. It took the Nazi occupation, the disappearance of the name of Austria and the loss of all national identity to change that feeling. Even then, a general sense of nationhood only came gradually and with difficulty, and one would not care to put too much money on betting that to a Tyrolean 'Austria' means more than 'Tyrol'. Allowing for the effects of such a traumatic shock as the loss of an empire almost overnight—the British have had more opportunities to cushion the emotional impact—those who lacked enthusiasm for '*ce qui reste*' were forgetting their early history. After centuries of expansion, the Austrians were now approximately back where they started: an assembly of small but sharply differentiated provinces with their roots as a nation in the ancient Babenberg Marches. During the early centuries of this growth, the inhabitants of the western alpine regions came to differ greatly from those in the east, and with the emergence of Vienna as the magnetic pole of an empire, these differences tended to increase, better alpine road and rail communications notwithstanding. After civil war, the Nazi era, military occupation, the shifts in the political structure and in zones of affluence from east to west since the last war, there have been many occasions when this often sorely tried population has asked the very question that may pass through the mind of any visitor: WHO *ARE* THE AUSTRIANS?

The Danube valley in Austria has always formed part of one of the principal transcontinental thoroughfares. Armies, hundreds of thousands strong, the great migration of peoples, colonizers, missionaries and traders have all streamed along the shores of this river. 'I can't think,' said an American woman one day, 'why you make such a fuss about the Danube. Why, the River N. in Carolina is twice the size of the Danube, but we don't keep on about it. Who cares about all these unwashed barbarians pounding up and down?'

To this challenge a number of answers are possible, expressed in varying degrees of pomposity. Leaving the historical and romantic content of the River N. in Carolina to take care of itself, it could be said that some 'barbarians' washed more than others, and accordingly, that there are quite clear demarcation lines in Austria today between areas in which people pay much attention to these matters and those in which they pay less. In any case, whatever their personal habits, these hordes were to some extent the ancestors of the modern Austrians, so it will be as well to sort them out. The Danube is only part of the story.

The earliest inhabitants of Austria to leave any permanent traces were the Illyrians, who were attracted into the maze of valleys in the eastern half of Austria before 2000 B.C. They probably settled first in Styria and Carinthia, gradually moving across to the Tyrol and Vorarlberg. The Breuni, who gave their name to the Brenner, were said by the Roman historian, Strabo, to have been Illyrians, and they presumably came along the Pustertal from Venetia. Finally, as farmers, miners and traders, the Illyrians spread all over the area covered by Austria today. Above all, they were miners: the Illyrians were drawn to Hallstatt by the salt deposits which were to play such an important part in the development of the Salzkammergut and of Salzburg. An almost greater attraction was copper, to be found over large areas of the country. At much the same time, immigrants had come from Spain and from northern Germany and Scandinavia. These peoples, who appear to have lived side by side relatively peacefully, developed a very high degree of civilization in the period between about 1700 and 700 B.C.—a thousand years of prosperity known as the Hallstatt period, during which Austria was supplying much of the demand for copper over a large area of Europe. It would be interesting to know what the population of the country was at the summit of the late Bronze Age. To take only one small sample from a later period, it is thought that when the Romans arrived in the district the present centre of which is Zell-am-See, they found a Celtic–Illyrian population which was no less numerous than it is today. At all events, Austrian historians like to see the blending of widely disparate cultures as evidence of the unifying role of this area four thousand years ago.

Now comes the next layer. 'Clad in coats of mail, armed with huge shields and long swords of iron, fighting not only on foot but either on horseback or from their war chariots, they were irresistible

1. Innsbruck, from the water-colour in the Albertina by Albrecht Dürer

2. Lead Mining

opponents for the peaceful inhabitants of the Danube lands,' said A. W. A. Leeper in his *History of Mediaeval Austria*. These were the Celts arriving on the scene from the north and north-west of France and western Germany in about 400 B.C.; they probably came down the Danube valley and spread across central, eastern and south-eastern Austria. They became the overlords and employers of the Illyrians, and their coming marked the end of the Hallstatt culture in Upper and Lower Austria, though it survived in parts of Styria and Carinthia for another two or three centuries. Work in the salt-mines continued, however, without interruption, but new methods of refining the raw salt were introduced. The Celts brought their language and a new religion, they were the first builders of towns—consisting merely of primitive huts—and among these first towns was Vienna. They also brought their knowledge of iron-smelting and founded the vital iron-ore workings near the Styrian–Carinthian border. Somewhere in this region they built their capital, Noreia, the exact site of which has never been definitely pinpointed because of the existence of other towns with the same name; one suggestion is Neumarkt. This was the first organized state on Austrian territory. But it would be a mistake to think that the Illyrians disappeared from the scene. The fact that many mountains and rivers kept their Illyrian names, while towns or villages developed by the Celts were allowed to keep the Illyrian names for the locality, is taken to show that within a few generations after the arrival of the Celts the two peoples (or, to put it more accurately, the two groups of associated tribes) had in fact merged into one. But while all the way from Bregenz to southern Burgenland a chain of towns (Lorch, Wels, Passau, Salzburg, Linz, etc.) show their Celtic origin, the more remote districts of North and South Tyrol and of Vorarlberg remained a stronghold of the Raetian peoples who are thought to have been of mainly Ligurian–Venetian (Illyrian) stock, and there is no doubt that in those alpine valleys the old way of life persisted for centuries, and its echoes are dimly perceptible even today.

The history of the early peoples reminds one a little of the traditional educational system of the British upper classes. Eminence at preparatory school is swiftly followed by pariah status at the bottom of the public-school ladder. After many years, almost Olympian majesty and power precede social extinction at university or almost ritualistic dirt-biting in the armed forces. Thus, in their turn, the Celts were subjugated by the Romans.

The Roman era in Austria need not be discussed here in detail because what we are immediately concerned with is the identity of the Austrians, and the Romans left a meagre heritage behind them. In 15 B.C. they took the Celtic kingdom of Noricum without a struggle, and began to build the string of fortresses along the Danube which would ensure the defence of this buffer region against the ever-increasing pressure of the Germanic tribes. Romanization of the three provinces, Pannonia I, Noricum and Raetia II, corresponding roughly to the territory of modern Austria, went ahead fast. What 'Romanization' meant was much the same as in other outlying areas of the empire. It meant acceptance of Roman law and administration and acquiescence in the unifying effects of the *pax romana*. For provincial auxiliaries and locally recruited members of the public administration it meant nominal obeisance before the official deities. In return, there were vast material bene-fits: flourishing trade, personal security, first-class roads and, in the towns, good housing. But while there was no need for the new official class wholly to abandon its ancient native culture, the lower classes and—as always—the farming community, remained basically unaffected. When the Romans withdrew, leaving three once-flourishing provinces to their fate, they left behind only a thin substratum which is just worth mentioning as part of Austria's ancestry. In A.D. 433 the Romans were obliged to give up Pannonia (which included the present-day Burgenland and the Vienna basin) to Attila's Huns. By the end of the century, civic order had broken down over most of the country, the population south of the Danube was subjected to repeated plundering attacks from across the river, the routes down to Italy had been all but cut off by the Goths, and in the mountains the nobility and clergy were hurriedly building the first stone towers and fortifications for the protection of the people and their cattle. The next century and a half brought a dual develop-ment which began to set the pattern for the future: the entry of the Bavarians and the Slavs.

It might be as well to sum up the situation at the end of the sixth century.

There is now a clear racial cleavage between the east and west of Austria. In Vorarlberg, the Germanic Alamanni have conquered the country and their dialect inflections and genetic characteristics will prevail from now on; the Raetians have withdrawn to the mountains. In Tyrol and throughout the west of Austria, remnants of the Romanized population are hanging on, though they will not do so for very long; they have been much encouraged by Theodoric the Goth in his attempts to prop up the old Roman administration. The Breuni, now Latinized Raetians, have maintained their identity and will continue to preserve their autonomy into the eighth century. Latin speech will survive in the Vintschgau until the seventeenth century, and Ladin (similar to the Romansch of the Grisons) is destined to live on to this present day in the Gröden and Enneberg districts of South Tyrol. In short: Roman influence still persists in the west, but in the east it has disappeared altogether. The Bavarians are busy colonizing the Tyrol and Salzburg and are working their way slowly towards the Vienna Woods. Meanwhile, the Slavs are being pushed and led into the east of Austria by their Avar overlords and are fanning out to form an arc through the east of Lower Austria, the Burgenland, Styria, Carinthia and East Tyrol, gradually absorbing what is left of the Celtic population. Further advance west is checked by Bavarian resistance. Later, the 'alpine Slavs' in the last three of these provinces will be partially dislodged and absorbed by peaceful German settlers.

The two main divisions of Austria have now been laid down once and for all: a Germanic layer on a firmly established Raeto–Roman foundation in the Alps, and Germanic mixed with Slav plus Celt in the eastern territories.

In the year 899 the Magyars burst into western Europe. Again the eastern districts below the River Enns had to be abandoned by the Bavarian farmers and their administrative bodies, and left to the mercy of those most ruthless invaders. The general destruction was such that there are no records to show to what extent the colonists survived. It can be assumed that the majority fled, were massacred or expelled. After the Battle of the Lechfeld in 955, when the

Magyars were driven out of western Europe for ever, the Bavarians gradually returned from behind that historic dividing line, the River Enns, and spread eastwards. But now a new and important factor in the Austrian family tree came on to the scene: the Franks, brought in by the Margrave Burchard. The Bavarians re-colonized the rectangle bordered by the Enns in the west, running south of Melk and St. Pölten and closing at a line between Rekawinkel and the Schneeberg. The Frankish settlers set to work to clear the forests beyond the Danube, and ended by claiming the whole area between Raabs on the River Thaya down to Krems and St. Pölten, and the River March. The result has been a very considerable difference in dialect, planning of farms and outbuildings, and in local customs within one province—Lower Austria. Before the end of the eleventh century Franconian farmers had peopled the Burgenland as well, encircling the Neusiedlersee and spreading into parts of modern Hungary. These Franks and Bavarians (both groups, of course, spoke German though their dialects differed) were unconsciously adopting a position of great historical significance—they had now thrust a wedge between the Northern and the Southern Slavs.

There were to be no other fundamental changes in the population of Austria except in Vienna. During the centuries of Habsburg expansion, Vienna no longer stood at the extreme end of the country, but had become the centre of an empire. A glance down the lists of names in the Vienna telephone book will explain the consequences better than pages of description. The empire has dissolved, but the names remain. After German, they are predominantly Czech, followed by Hungarian, Polish and Croatian.

The question 'Who are the Austrians?' has been answered on purely factual lines. But facts are not everything. To discover more, we shall have to start on our journey.

2

Vorarlberg

A giant is reclining in a deep chair with the Arlberg at his back. His left arm lies on the Silvretta and the Rätikon alps, and his feet are dangling in the Rhine. This caricature overlooks the undulations in the upholstery and the giant's extreme discomfort, and it can be cast aside almost at once. The point of the sketch is that the giant, embodiment of the inhabitants of the Vorarlberg throughout history, is facing west. He is little concerned with what is going on in the rest of Austria, and when he gets to his feet he will be standing on the broad highway of the Rhine valley.

Local government offices display the text of the *Land* constitution which firmly reminds all comers that the Vorarlberg is an independent state and that it joined the Austrian Federal Republic of its own free will. Only a few years ago a passenger ship was launched at Fussach on Lake Constance. The Minister of Transport in Vienna wished her to be called after a former Austrian President, Theodor Körner; local opinion preferred the name *Vorarlberg*. The minister insisted, the patriots were adamant. The result was a near-riot involving about thirty thousand adult citizens, the minister's person was only protected with difficulty and the name *Fussach* has entered the language as a synonym for a political graveyard.

The Vorarlberger are often accused—sometimes by themselves —of *Kantönligeist*: narrow-minded provincial patriotism. Almost entirely cut off from the rest of Austria for most of their history, they have learnt to manage their own affairs with a minimum of interference from either princes or central governments. They produce some of the sharpest business brains in the country, their industries in the great 'textile belt' between Bregenz and Bludenz are as up to date as any of their kind in Europe, but this has been done without the creation of hideous conurbations, and the individuality of old family concerns has been preserved. There are villages in the Vorarlberg such as Zürs and Lech which are familiar to skiers everywhere, but on the whole the province is little known to British and American travellers. It has much in common with neighbouring Switzerland and Liechtenstein, but the differences run deep. It has the highest birthrate in Austria. The first turbine in the Austro-Hungarian empire was switched on in Thüringen and the first electric light bulb in Kennelbach, the first telephone in the monarchy was spoken into in Dornbirn where, in 1893, a chemist called Kofler was the first of the Emperor Franz Josef's subjects to set off for a drive in his own car. There were primary schools in the Vorarlberg a hundred years before Maria Theresa introduced them throughout her domains. An enterprising people, but as we shall see later, often rigidly bound to tradition and profoundly self-sufficient.

When St. Columban arrived in Bregenz soon after A.D. 600 he found a township, the old Roman Brigantium, now decayed and abandoned, from which the Raeto–Roman population had largely withdrawn. He discovered a small Christian church in which the Alamannic inhabitants had hung heathen objects of worship, an experience shared by his companion and more enduringly successful pupil, Gallus, on his trips inland. There is a story that St. Columban 'cast the heathen idols into the lake'—a melodramatic gesture which may have been caused by the saint's frustration at being unable to speak the local language. His Latin sermons would have been appreciated by the Romanized Raetians, but to the germanic Alamanni his words meant nothing. Armed, however, with the relics of St. Aurelia which he had brought with him from Strassburg, St. Columban not only rededicated the church under her protection, he founded beside it the first monastery in German-speaking lands; the parish church of St. Gallus in Bregenz is thought to stand on the site of the Columban foundation. Columban's sanctus bell remained in use in the church for centuries: apart from tradition, its authenticity is supported by the composition of the metal, the technique and straight lines of which are all evidence of its Irish origin. Since 1955 the bell has been preserved in the cathedral of St. Gall in Switzerland.

Bregenz recovered its former prosperity comparatively quickly. Lake Constance forms a barrier between the Swabian alpine fore-lands and the Swiss mountains, and the only way round the lake on the eastern shore is the narrow strip of land at the base of Mt. Pfänders. It was a vital strategic spot on the route from western Germany down to the Swiss Grisons and to Italy: medieval Bregenz, perched on its terrace sixty feet above the lake, could have checked the movement of armed men in either direction. Where trade was concerned, matters were a little different. As time went on the merchants of Bregenz handled the export of timber from the Bregenzer Wald and there was a local trade in corn and salt, but in the days of Charlemagne the main weight of long-distance trade bypassed the town altogether by crossing the lake from Lindau to Fussach, then either continuing the journey by boat along the Rhine to Chur, or by road to Feldkirch. The stature and the wealth of Bregenz grew parallel with its political importance as a centre of government.

The name Montfort still means a great deal in the Vorarlberg: it is under the banner of the Montforts that the province rides into battle against any measures of the federal government in Vienna in which a threat to its constitutional rights is suspected. In feudal times, families were apt to call themselves after their place of residence or their principal fief. This was some improvement on mere epithets such as 'the Fat', but it has frequently obstructed historical research. The first Montfort of whom we can be certain was Hugo of Tübingen, who inherited the fief of Bregenz from his father-in-law and called himself Graf von Bregenz. But in about 1206 he caused a significant and long-term shift in the power structure of the Vorarlberg by moving for safety's sake to Feld-kirch, where he rebuilt a 'mountain stronghold' above the town. The Montfort family, now his vassals, were of Romansch origin and related to the lords of Tarasp. As *ministerialen*, or imperial bonded knights, they had lived in the area for nearly two hundred years. Hugo now pushed them out, took over their castle and adopted the name. By the close of the thirteenth century the Montforts had gained possession of the whole area from the Allgäu to the Silvretta, and from the Arlberg to the Rhine. On the whole, they were not a bad lot. They opened up the country by introducing settlers to the almost deserted alpine areas, although this did involve the gradual withdrawal of the old Raeto–Romansch inhabitants before the German-speaking Alamanni. They built roads, including a rough track over the Arlberg Pass, to the great advantage of the growing towns Bludenz and Feldkirch, and they encouraged trade and the industrial crafts. Perhaps their main and most permanent achievement was to bring in the Swiss 'Walliser' and settle them in the Grosses Walsertal.

The presence of the Montforts and their cousins the Werdenbergs persisted for four hundred years, but towards the end their influence rapidly declined. Instead of consolidating their position they made the fatal mistake of dividing up their properties by inheritance. Inevitably, they also quarrelled among themselves, and at one time there was bitter dissension between the Montforts and the Werdenbergs; as a result of all this they sank to the level of a more or less improverished squirarchy. The Habsburgs, meanwhile, were very anxious to gain a hold on the Vorarlberg so as to link up the Austrian territories with their ancestral estates in the Swiss Aargau and in Alsace, and they proceeded to mop up the Montfort estates one by one. To the Habsburgs a matter of common sense, the Swiss saw in this policy the looming spectre of Habsburg aggrandisement, and they decided to stem the tide. At the fateful Battle of Sempach in 1386 the heavily armoured Habsburg cavalry was defeated by the more agile Swiss. In 1405, during another outburst of hostilities, the men of Appenzell swarmed up the valleys of the Vorarlberg until they were brought to a halt by the eastern alpine barrier.

Apart from the most important fortresses defending the Rhine valley, the countryside was also peppered with small castles in which the local knighthood lived in primitive discomfort. Hundreds of these knights had died on the field of Sempach, and in the storm which now swept through the country their innumerable forts were reduced to ash and rubble, never to recover. Only the citadels Hohenbregenz and Neuburg held out; the Schattenburg at Feldkirch and Neu-Montfort were captured but not destroyed.

The Appenzell invasion had no political consequences because the leading families had entered the service of the Habsburgs and would always remain loyal to its interests. But it was the end of an era, the beginning of a new way of life for the citizens of the Vorarlberg. New men had already come to the fore: 'Those of Embs', the Hohenems family, who founded their fortunes in war and in public service as imperial bailiffs. The rise of the Ems family went hand in hand with a rapid increase in freedom for the general population. By the end of the fourteenth century the people of Feldkirch and, to a great extent, those of Bludenz, had been able to achieve their release from serfdom and had become independent *Landesbürger*. In future, only citizens and peasants could be members of the *Landtag* or provincial parliament, no members of the nobility and no priests might serve on it. The power of the *Landtag* was considerable because it held the right to confirm or reject the edicts of the imperial bailiff including those on taxation. This had a lasting effect on the democratic sense of responsibility of the Vorarlberger; it was one of the factors which led to their likeness, in civic life, to the Swiss. It coloured their whole attitude towards 'authority', royal or republican, which is free and relaxed, at the opposite pole from the tendency to sullen but almost instinctive servility which has been a characteristic of the Viennese.

A tour round the Vorarlberg can be done either clockwise or anti-clockwise. We propose to take the second alternative and make straight for Hohenems, four miles from Dornbirn on the road to Feldkirch.

Jakob Hannibal I, Count Hohenems, was one of the most celebrated mercenaries of his time. Like his ancestors who had fallen at Sempach and in 1405 at Stoss, he was a servant of the Habsburgs. He administered the imperial domains in the Vorarlberg, had a hereditary seat on the Imperial Diet and ran his own estates. At the conclusion of a campaign against the Venetians Jakob applied for extended leave. He complained that almost uninterrupted absence from home was causing him to neglect pressing business and the care of his family. He might have added that in the light of the appalling mortality among the newly born, he was scarcely able to visit his wife, to whom he was devoted, often enough to secure the continuity of his line. She, Hortensia née Borromeo, was the sister of Charles Borromeo, Cardinal Prince-Archbishop of Milan, the great Catholic reformer and saint to whom the Karlskirche in Vienna is dedicated. Medici blood ran in her veins. She did not, so far as we know, complain in writing of her loneliness in the old castle at Alt-Ems; perhaps she could not. The biographer of the Hohenems family, Ludwig Welti, says in an aside that even as late as the sixteenth century there is an almost complete lack of information on the way that the wives of soldiering nobles lived on their country seats, probably because they could neither read nor write. The desk work which awaited Jakob Hannibal when he came home must have been daunting. During the past two hundred years his ancestors had become lords of the manors of Neuburg, Feldkirch, Bludenz, Bregenz, Tannberg and Sonnenberg, and as head of the family he had to deal with the affairs of unmarried female relations.

Of Jakob Hannibal's two sons, Marx Sittich, a flamboyant prince of the Church better known to posterity as Marcus Sitticus, and Kaspar the great landowner and administrator, far the more genuinely religious of the two was Kaspar. As a boy he had been present at the deathbed of his saintly uncle, whom he deeply revered. His mother's piety and the anxious advice of old uncle Cardinal Altemps in Rome after the death of his father, both had their effect in forming his character. A tireless worker, his mind full of international politics, local administration and the continued advancement of his clan, his later years were clouded by distress at the wild extravagance of his useless son and disagreement with the Archbishop of Salzburg, Marcus Sitticus. He was constantly plagued by gout, piles, and probably by arthritis. As he stumped painfully round his late Renaissance *palazzo* which might well have been lifted straight from the plains of Lombardy, along corridors packed to the ceiling with trophies of the chase, he was burdened with worry over the future. Evil times were coming. And in any case, all the work of his lifetime and all the accumulated effort of past generations could, and almost certainly would, be dispersed by his effete son Jakob Hannibal II.

Writing at the close of the nineteenth century, the art historian Samuel Jenny complained that by skimping expenditure on the buildings and grounds of Hohenems, Kaspar spoiled the effect; he failed to carry out the original magnificent design which would have been so worthy of his family. 'A great deal which should be carved in relief is only painted, and the provision of statues to adorn the recesses in the courtyard wall, in the arcades, corridors and stairways, was entrusted to superior stonemasons rather than to sculptors.' From the perspective of the early seventeenth century, the problem was not quite so simple. Kaspar was not short of money, but as the years passed he fell more and more out of sympathy with the extravagant splendour with which Marcus Sitticus loved to surround his person and office. The archbishop's attendance at the Diet of Regensburg in 1613 was royal in the number and stupefying irrelevance of his suite, both military and domestic. Kaspar went to Regensburg too, but was irritated by the empty pomp, unimpressed by the business done, and he left early. Up to his death in 1619 Marx Sittich was for ever urging Kaspar—they corresponded frequently and at great length—to press on with building work at Hohenems, but met with stubborn resistance. Europe was on the brink of the Thirty Years War. Kaspar was embroiled in all the problems brought by the religious and social unrest in western Austria and the neighbouring Grisons, and he felt that unnecessary expenditure was out of tune with the times. Later, he would have to watch helplessly while the Duke of Friedland's army moved down through Feldkirch and Lustenau to Mantua, burning, looting and terrorizing the population on its way. These were the totally undisciplined troops whose terrible advance was so vividly described by Alessandro Manzoni in *I Promessi Sposi* (*The Betrothed*). Marcus Sitticus and Kaspar von Hohenems lived in different epochs: except in a few sheltered places the archbishop's ideas were no longer in demand.

Hohenems bred famous warriors, administrators and prelates. It also bred one of the leading writers of court epic poetry in the thirteenth century, Rudolf of Ems. He is described as a fluent and

43

melodious writer of verse, and also as a keen student of human nature, of philosophy and religion. A merchant of Cologne is the subject of *Der gute Gerhard*, whose pious mode of life and edifying conversation is recorded, as well as the good advice he gave to the Emperor Otto I. Rudolf's *Willehalm* tells the story of a young prince of Brabant who went to England, fell in love with and married Princess Amelie, daughter of King Reinher. Like other poets in the age of chivalry, Rudolf of Ems drew a clear line between physical love, *liebe*, and *minne*, spiritual affinity. Graf Kaspar knew of the existence of Rudolf. Did he know that he had in his possession one of the greatest treasures of world literature? Manuscripts A and C of the *Nibelungenlied* came to light in 1755 in the library at Hohenems. How did they get there? After more than two hundred years this is still the Mystery of Hohenems.

There are ruins of Montfort castles at Fraxern, on the mountain above Klaus, and at Götzis on the road to Feldkirch. But their principal stronghold was the Schattenburg which dominates Feldkirch and is the largest and best-preserved citadel in the Vorarlberg. This is the castle which was taken over by Hugo von Montfort in 1206; it came to be called Schattenburg later in its history. Feldkirch has taken a series of batterings in its time. It was devastated during three wars, the last occasion being the Napoleonic campaigns in 1799 and 1800, and it was all but destroyed by fire in 1697. The town walls were demolished in the nineteenth century. In view of all this, it is surprising that so much of the original character of the old town has survived, in the form, for instance, of the delightful arcades in two of the squares. The view of the town and castle from among the vineyards on the Ardetzenberg is one to rejoice the hearts of amateur photographers; the scene is enclosed by the Gürtisspitze, an offshoot of the Rätikon range.

Only a few minutes' drive from Feldkirch, the church spire of Our Lady of Rankweil forms the apex of a great triangle growing from within the massive rock and the towers and bastions of yet another Montfort castle; the whole structure is a landmark for miles around. Rankweil is a market town and a health resort and has its textile and metal industries, but at weekends, particularly at those times of the year which Catholics associate with the Virgin Mary, the centre of the town is a beehive. Rankweil is the chief place of pilgrimage in the Vorarlberg and still attracts thousands of pilgrims every year. It is easy to overlook another, even more venerable church, standing in a humbler position at the base of the vast cliff. This is St. Peter's, founded in the seventh century by two Merovingian kings, Dagobert I and Siegebert I, for whose souls mass is still said to this day. While investigating the history of St. Peter's, a question was cleared up that had vaguely puzzled me for some time. Many churches in the uplands of Vorarlberg date from the ninth and tenth centuries—St. Vinerius in Nüziders for example, and St. Sulpitius in Frastanz. Then why has hardly any Romanesque church architecture survived and comparatively little early Gothic? It is blindingly simple: the builders used timber. They formed a shallow apse of stone with extended sides to enclose a small chapel or choir. The body of the church was of timber and so was the bell tower or steeple. It was not until much later that they added a vaulted roof to the choir section, and stone walls replaced the old wood. The high altar would then be brought forward and the space behind used as a sacristy. The Raetians used stone in domestic architecture whenever they could, and the earliest churches in other parts of Austria were built of stone, so why timber was considered good enough for the laity in the Vorarlberg must remain a matter for conjecture. All the highland areas in the province were originally missionized from Chur, and the centre of the mission was Vinomna, the old name for Rankweil. But it also became the seat of the *Gaugericht*, or country tribunal, for the whole country from Lake Constance to the Septimer Pass and from the Wallensee across to the Arlberg. According to ancient German tribal custom the court was held in the open air and close to the main road: at one time it used to assemble in front of St. Peter's church, but later it moved to the meadows in Müsinen between Rankweil and Sulz. The court is first mentioned in 774, and documentary evidence of its early existence dates from the time of Charlemagne. In 1408 it abandoned its *alfresco* sittings and withdrew for greater security to the castle on the hill. The reason why a second church was built so close to the first is a very human one. It has been mentioned before that, where the population of the Vorarlberg is concerned, the main point about its history is the gradual disappearance of the old Raeto–Roman peoples as they were pushed out or absorbed by the Alamanni, one of the great tribes of the German-speaking peoples. Both sectors of the population were Christian or, in the case of the Alamanni, becoming so. They were not at war with one another, but the idea of joining together in prayer held no appeal for either, and the Alamanni built their own church, rather pointedly perhaps, inside the old Roman fortress on the hill.

Bludenz is an excellent starting point from which to branch out into the alpine regions of the Vorarlberg because it lies at the junction of five valleys: the Brandnertal, leading to the Rätikon alps and the Lüner See, Montafon, Klostertal, Grosses Walsertal, and Illtal in the Walgau—the valley which leads up from Feldkirch. Montafon is the most densely populated of them all, but it still keeps its distinctive character and is remarkably unlike the other valleys in the way of farm building, customs, dialect and national dress. The reason is that for four hundred years the Montafon valley belonged to that curious clerical state Chur-Raetia. Long after the rest of the country had been colonized from the north, Montafon hung on to the old ways, to Roman law and to the Romansch language of which remnants survive in the dialect at the present time. The place names are often particularly interesting: there is the mountain Traumenier, which may mean a 'true menhir', or druid's stone. The folk museum in a Raetian farmhouse at Schruns gives a vivid picture of the old way of life.

Members of the early Celtic church used to go to enormous trouble to transport their dead over long distances so as to bury them on ground which they held sacred. In south-west Wales they used to take them across by boat to Bardsey Island. This fact came to mind while reading a short collection of pious verses and thoughts on local lore written by a Montafon schoolmaster a generation ago. At one time, he tells us, the people of Galtür (over the next ridge in Tyrol) would carry a corpse a full day's march up the Jambach valley, over the nearly 9,000-foot-high Futschöl Pass and down into the Swiss Engadine, where they laid it thankfully to

46

rest in the cemetery at Steinsberg-Ardetz. But what, asks the school-master rhetorically, did the people of Galtür do when all the furies of winter raged on the mountain pass and the whole narrow valley was nothing but a trackless waste? They buried the deceased deep in the snow, and there they left him until harbingers of spring and unmistakable signals from the dear departed told them that the time had come to remove him to a holier place.

The threat of isolation in the Montafon was dispelled in two ways: discovery of the silver deposits in the Silbertal attracted the attention of Europe's first millionaires, the Fuggers of Augsburg, who took over the workings but had to abandon them in 1570 when the seams were all but exhausted. Meanwhile local craftsmen had become used to working for part of the year in the Rhine valley. This movement to and fro brought a whiff of the outside world into their part of the highlands which influenced the general attitude towards 'foreigners'. When the age of tourism dawned in the nineteenth century, the people of Montafon took the lead.

At one time the Montafoner would no doubt have looked on the inhabitants of the Grosses Walsertal, with their Swiss origins, as foreign interlopers, and perhaps they still do. The euphonious name Fontanella is an echo of the first settlers who lived on in the superstitions of later generations as the 'wild people', men and women covered with hair who would swoop down from the heights to terrify the shepherds and milkmaids. These hairy ones were certainly too few in number to make much impact on the countryside. In the thirteenth century the Counts of Montfort encouraged alpine farmers from the Canton Wallis to migrate to the interior of the Vorarlberg. During the next century the flow increased and most of the new colonists settled in the valley which was now called after them—the Grosses Walsertal. (The Kleines Walsertal is a political curiosity, because although it belongs to Austria it has no direct communication with the Vorarlberg, uses German currency and rates as 'abroad' to the Austrian customs authorities.) It is not surprising that the Walser showed no desire to leave their new country. In places they were badly threatened by avalanches which have never ceased to thunder down the great open pastures, in successive winters, where there were too few trees to prevent their formation. But this is wonderfully fertile land. On the slopes of the Damülser Horn in early summer before the first crop of hay is cut, the grass seems taller and richer, the humming of insects more insistently audible than anywhere else at this altitude. It is easy, however, to think romantic thoughts in the mountains; a very different matter to exist there all the year round and scrape enough of a living to bring up a family. No one would willingly live on the higher levels if a farm were to be had lower down. About a third of all Austrian farms are at alpine or sub-alpine altitudes. An average mountain farmer may own twenty-five acres of productive land together with fifty acres of standing timber. If he owns no forest land he will usually possess annually accruing timber rights, and have an alpine pasture or grazing rights on a communal pasture. But the word 'average' is misleading. There are farmers who own eighty or more head of cattle, while below-subsistence holdings provide grazing for no more than six cows, a few heifers and enough potatoes can be grown to maintain one or two pigs. A great deal has been done in recent years by bringing electricity to most of the highest farms and by building roads, to make life easier. Even so, they remain at a long distance from their markets, and on steep slopes mechanization of work is not always possible. To add to the difficulties, hired labour has become almost unobtainable. This fertile valley, the Walsertal, is better off than many, but depopulation of the higher slopes and plateaux began during the eighteenth century. The nearby timber had been felled and there was too little left to see people through the long winter; forestry was not the exact science that it has become since then. The cumulative effects of intense isolation and inbreeding began to be felt, and if one smallholding had to be given up because there was no one left able or willing to carry on, the effect was felt by all the rest. Scattered communities such as Bürstegg, Zug and Hoch-krumbach—at over 5,300 feet the highest of the three—were, for the time being, slowly abandoned. Damüls very nearly suffered the same fate. Less than an hour's walk from the Faschina Alm above the Walsertal, it is the highest village in the Bregenzer Wald, but it was saved just in time by the late nineteenth-century discovery of the beneficial properties of alpine air combined with brisk exercise.

3. Old Inn at Ladis

4. The Stubai Alps near Innsbruck

Damüls became a success as a skiing resort, and as voluntary walking has now all but died out, a road is being built which will not only make the village accessible from the Grosses Walsertal but also create a magnificent new circular tour in the interior of the Vorarlberg.

Bored with history, only mildly interested in the way of life of the people of a small district in a small European country, the reader may be flipping over the pages to discover when an attempt will be made to describe the beauties of the alpine peaks and the eternal snows. One difficulty is that our generation has become too self-conscious. The attitude of educated people to high mountain scenery has undergone a number of changes. Among eighteenth-century travellers a common emotion was consternation. They were thunderstruck by the towering immensity of the alpine chain with, to quote one writer, its 'horrible ravines' and its savage peaks, the height of which could only be guessed at. In the Age of Reason awe was an embarrassing emotion, best mastered by scrupulous attention to the study of nature. Only discover what a mountain was made of, draw up lists of the plants which grow on its slopes, and it would be reduced to intellectually and spiritually manageable proportions. Soon, no gentleman and scarcely a lady would walk in the Alps—and how they walked—without a little hammer and a bag for samples. The new interest was amply catered for in *A Handbook for Travellers in Southern Germany* (i.e. Austria) published by Murray in 1837. The Age of Romance which—to anticipate for a moment—was to take the Tyrol captive for ever had begun, and with it the start of an unending stream of descriptive literature. After all this how can anyone, now, dare to describe a mountain? To a traveller of any sensitivity, his first sight of a mountain range, so much higher than he had supposed that he has to adjust his normal angle of vision, is so overwhelming that to insert chatter between him and this experience is almost an impertinence. This is a personal matter: should he not be left to absorb it alone?

The word 'alone' must be withdrawn at once. The mountains are overpopulated by tourists, over-tamed and covered by a cat's

49

cradle system of cable railways and chair lifts. The view can be admired from behind plate-glass windows, on the glacier's edge gulasch soup can be bought and eaten. The demons have departed.

Perhaps this also is untrue. Every year a few people walk off into the mountains, never to return alive: not only the skilled alpine climbers, but groups of young tourists whose enthusiasm outruns their knowledge, who set out, often regardless of warnings, in threatening weather and badly equipped to face the sudden fury of blizzards or the unexpected descent of dense cloud. The challenge is still there, the majesty, the mystery and even the terror.

Certainly no one could be ungrateful for that triumphant piece of mountain road building, the Flexenstrasse. Between Bludenz and Imst lies the long skeleton of the Lechtal Alps with an almost vertical cliff on the southern flank. The only place where a north to south link could be achieved was at the Flexen Pass, where the saddle descends to 5,400 feet. Long stretches of the road are hewn and tunnelled out of the rock face and roofed-in passages protect the cars and their passengers from avalanches which shoot harmlessly into the ravine. After Zürs and Lech the road into the Bregenzer Wald leads through one of the most magnificent stretches of country in the Vorarlberg, over the Hochtannberg Pass. This is all high plateau, great expanses of rolling alpine meadows out of which erupt stark limestone peaks. There is even a calm sheet of water to complete the landscape: the Körber See, more a tarn than a lake. Downhill now, along the Bregenzer Ache, past the northern cliff of the Knisfluh at Mellau, through the district capital, Bezau, to Andelsbuch which is one of the oldest villages in the Bregenzer Wald, and on down to the Rhine valley.

3

Tyrol

Rather in the same way that the English discovered Switzerland, they also discovered the Tyrol. One might go further and say that, to some extent, they invented it.

For centuries, the Tyrol was a place where people stopped on the way to somewhere else. The early travellers were quite right in thinking of the country as a crossroads: that has always been its strategic significance and, where trade is concerned, the source of its wealth. (The name Tyrol is of Illyrian origin and means a crossing or thoroughfare; it is quite incorrect to spell it with a y, but this is not entirely a gimmick of the age of tourism, as there is a sixteenth-century precedent in the spelling Tyrall.) Fynes Morison and Joseph Addison were birds of passage who kept to the beaten track and would scarcely have dreamt of exploring the side valleys. The exceptions—traders for the most part—were in the Tyrol for a serious purpose, not for pleasure. Albanus Beaumont in 1792 marks the onset of the little-hammer-and-bag-of-specimens era which lasted for approximately a hundred years. But he carefully observed the people and saw no sign of acute poverty in the valleys. The country people were tall, strong and robust, 'as mountaineers in general are'. He found them remarkably cheerful, and was struck by their mildness of manner and honesty. They were excessively devout and addicted to the veneration of 'a number of images, according to the forms of their religion', and yet not bigoted. He praised their urbanity, hospitality and good humour.

Clarissa Stuart Costello is almost unique in that she loathed the

Tyrol and everything in it. Recording her impressions as she hurried through from Venice to Switzerland in 1846, she complained of the 'guttral spluttering' of the local inhabitants. She disliked their garish taste in colours and mentioned particularly the red church towers and the 'tawdry daubing' on the houses in Steinach am Brenner. Her sensibilities were offended by overmuch wealth, leading to vulgarity and ostentation. Innsbruck was an oven (as well it can be) surrounded by a girdle of burning hills, whose snows mocked the traveller. No cooling breeze brought relief at sundown which heralded instead the arrival of a devilish sirocco. The 'coarsely hollowed out arcades' of the old town were low and dirty, the national dress 'strange and hideous', the Arlberg 'a frightful mountain'. She was quite clearly in a filthy mood, and it says much for the people she met (who were no more immune to *Föhn* headaches than she was) that she recognized their qualities: travellers, she admitted, were treated with great courtesy, sincerity and good will taking the place of beauty and grace. In England, Mrs. Stuart Costello's older contemporaries associated the Tyrol with the victories of Andreas Hofer over the Napoleonic invaders and the Tyrolese' lone stand after Vienna had capitulated. It aroused their sympathy to the tune of thirty thousand pounds which were transferred by Baring in London to Steiner & Co. in Vienna.

A note of admiration for the Tyrolese, individually or as a nation, can be heard through all the writings of visitors during the eighteenth and nineteenth centuries. They included Goethe and Bettina von Arnim, but the Anglo-Tyrolean literary love affair began, perhaps, with Sir Walter Scott's *Tales of a Grandfather* and reached a climax with D. H. Lawrence.

A certain effortless sense of identity and mutual appreciation may always have been felt by natives of Britain's Celtic and Gaelic fringe. In 1448, Archduke Siegmund of Tyrol sent three of his courtiers to fetch his bride, Elinor Stuart, daughter of James II of Scotland, whom he married in the following year. Elinor seems already to have spoken French and German: she certainly became so proficient that she was able to translate a novel from French into German. As she lived in Tyrol until her death in 1480, dividing her time between the Habsburg residences at Meran, Ambras, Thaur, Fragenstein, Hörtenberg and Imst as well as the estates in the Breisgau, it would be interesting to know whether any of her letters to her family in Scotland have survived. She enjoyed the chase, nowhere more than in the countryside round Pertisau on Lake Achensee; she wrote to her namesake, the Empress Eleonore in Vienna, and told her all about it.

There was a small band of Englishmen who really came close to the Tyrolese. These were the early alpine climbers, men of the calibre of F. S. Smythe who, pronounced individualists themselves, found a common language with a people whose ready friendliness overlays a deep reserve. But while the romantic cult of nature's gentleman with erotic and even daemonic overtones was in full swing, and before the country had been almost swamped by tourism, a native historian described his own people as he saw them.

He divides the inhabitants of Tyrol into two main categories: those of mainly Alemannic origin, related to the Vorarlberg highlanders, and those whose ancestors were the Bajuvarii, the ancient Bavarians. The first group live in the area of the Upper Inn Valley and are described as serious and rugged. In a country which has produced a great number of prominent men in the fields of art and the sciences, the Oberinntal people are superior to all others in intelligence. The Pustertaler in East Tyrol he considers no less intelligent but a trifle calculating. The Lower Inn Valley, the area east of and including Innsbruck, he finds inhabited by people who happily combine amiability and altruism, in which they exceed all others. To this disinterested generosity he links a rather noisy *joie-de-vivre* and pronounced sensuality which account for the Unterinntal being the home of Tyrolean folksong. He mentions the well-known religious devotion of the poorer highlanders—'this comes from the heart'—their daily attendance at Mass where possible and devotions at home. Sexual morality is much the same as in most highland areas, but 'this is not the land of virgins', and he points out that sons take over the farm comparatively late, and consequently marry late. Frankness, honesty and reliability are the characteristics of the Tyrolese, together with a strongly developed sense of justice and the rule of law. 'Money matters and contracts are sealed by a mere handshake, accompanied by the indispensable bottle of wine.' But the historian must be taken up on the word 'mere': throughout the west of Austria the handshake before witnesses has always had the binding force of contract, and it still has today. He ends by saying that the highland Tyrolese are extremely conservative, distrustful of all innovations in agriculture and have little interest in increasing the productivity of their farmland. Careful, even mean with money, they tend to drink too much home-distilled schnaps.

In what sense did the English 'invent' the Tyrol?

Anglo-Saxon visitors have always been uncertain where the province begins and ends. As the Tyrol's fashionable image grew, so did the tourist's desire to be inside the magical ring even if he happened to be staying in the province of Salzburg. From this wish it was a short step to mental usurpation of quite extensive stretches of country. The record is thought to be held by a visitor to 'Gmunden, in Tyrol': Gmunden lies in Upper Austria at the eastern end of the Salzkammergut, about one hundred miles from the Tyrolese border. This kink has its wholly beneficial aspects. As one Salzburg hotelier said: 'I beg you not to correct them—I've lived on their delusions for years.' The Tyrolese, of course, look upon their frontiers in a different light. A few years ago small-scale army manoeuvres were held near the Hochfilzen Pass, on the old road between Saalfelden and St. Johann in Tyrol. Detachments faced one another across the border, and gradually those on the Salzburg side began to press back their opponents to the west of them. Suddenly becoming aware of what was happening, the neighbouring Tyrolese farmers rushed into their houses and barns, seized sticks and staves and even guns, and advanced in angry groups to repel the astonished invaders. A retired Prussian general was watching the scene through field-glasses, and he said later that in all his career he had never seen the like.

The Tyrol, then, is a state of mind. In practical terms it is an alpine area in which the great fissure of the Inn Valley severs the northern limestone alps with the Lechtaler and Karwendel ranges from the broad mass of the crystallite Central Alps; the eastern boundary lies in the slate zone of the Kitzbühel Alps. Apart from the Grossglockner, the highest peak in Austria which is shared with Salzburg and Carinthia, the highest mountain in the Tyrol is the Wildspitze. In this icy wilderness between the Reschen Pass and Obergurgl lies the vast expanse of glacier known as the Gepatschferner.

The road between the two passes, Fern Pass and Reschenscheideck which is the watershed of the rivers Etsch and Inn, is the north-south route from Augsburg and Munich to the Engadine. Seen from the western end of the country at Landeck where the Arlberg route joins in from the west, this is also the shortest way to Meran and Bozen.

While one is driving through mountainous country it can be fun to play the castle game. If you had to defend this valley, that junction, where would you build your stronghold? After a time the game palls because the castle is almost always where it ought to be: it may be concealed from view, lost among trees and undergrowth, but a closer look will reveal it. The castle at Nauders, the Naudersberg, began as one of many unassuming centres of administration for the Upper Inn Valley. During the Swiss wars of independence it gained in strategic importance and became the seat of a court of justice which had penal jurisdiction over the whole of the Lower Engadine. It was extended before and particularly during the reign of Archduke Siegmund and—like so many other fortifications—the invention of gunpowder compelled a further strengthening of the structure. But the really crucial spot is at Finstermünz where the Inn flows through a deep gorge and the old road crosses the river at the Innbrücke. Welf, Duke of Bavaria, left a small garrison there to guard the spot when he was on his way back from a campaign against Chur. Both Siegmund and the Empeorr Maximilian I developed this small fort, and nothing that now remains dates from before the end of the fifteenth century. It consisted of an inhabited tower bestriding the road, linked to a second tower on a jutting out rock which used natural caves to add to the available space. Looking down at the main tower it is easy to see that the wooden bridge was originally built much lower down, on the ground level of the broad passage through the tower.

The Oberinntal is quite unlike the lower reaches of the Inn.

After each dark, narrow ravine it is a relief to emerge into the wide terraced valley between them with its chain of towns and villages with odd names such as Pfunds, Prutz, Fliess and, after the chief town Landeck, Imst. In Pfunds there are a number of very fine old houses and inns to show that this was one of the post stations on the express coach route to Switzerland and Meran. Passengers, four to a coach, and mail were carried on to the next coaching inn at an average speed of seven and a half kilometres per hour, and a village of this size would always have twenty-five to fifty horses standing in readiness.

The name Landeck goes back no further than the thirteenth century when the castle was built by the founder of the province of Tyrol, Meinhard II. But there were settlements in the neighbourhood in the La Tène period: a considerable number of small male figures, forged out of metal, have been excavated and it is thought that they were made for export. Landeck was an ideal site for a town, and when at last a proper road was built over the Arlberg in 1824, followed in 1880 by the railway with its nearly seven-mile-long tunnel, Landeck forged ahead. It is now the main centre and shopping town of one of Austria's principal winter sports areas. The drive up to Ladis, the spa near Prutz, is well worth making to see the characteristic farm houses with their decorative *sgrafitti*, outside staircases and separate baking ovens; there is no telling how long these traditional forms—some of those at Ladis are fifteenth century—will be allowed to survive. Grins was the favourite spa of the celebrated Margravin of Tyrol, Margarete 'Maultasch', who, widowed and having lost her son, bequeathed her country on 26th January 1363 to the House of Habsburg. A few months later she abdicated and the rest of her life was spent in Vienna.

Imst lies at the western corner of a small triangle of roads, the apex at Nassereith leads over the Fern Pass and under the shadow of the Zugzpitze into Germany. This is the lowest pass leading from the Inn Valley to Bavaria between the limestone alps, and is often said to be the most beautiful. In ancient times it was known as the Via Claudia Augusta after the Emperor Claudius who rebuilt the road in A.D. 46. Alternatively, the road branches off at

Nassereith to Reutte, the centre of the Ausserfern district. Nassereith is well known for a carnival procession, held every five years, the 'Schellerlaufen'. Imst has its 'Schemenlaufen' in which a splendid variety of traditional masked and costumed figures take part: witches, wild men, bear-leaders and bird sellers.

Were these birds originally canaries? During the seventeenth century the canary breeders of Imst were trading their wares as far afield as St. Petersburg, Constantinople and Madrid, and they even had their own depot at Moorefield Square in London. At the beginning of the last century they began to lose ground to competition from the popular Harz singing birds—though it appears that men from Imst were also engaged in this enterprise—and when in 1822 a great fire destroyed many houses in Imst including those of the canary breeders, the trade came to an end.

After Imst there would be two good reasons for keeping to the base of the triangle along the course of the Inn. One would be to explore the Ötztal, at the top of which lies Obergurgl, the highest village in the Austrian alps. Skiers or summer visitors who take the chair lift up to the Hohe Mut may be too preoccupied or too dazzled to count the glaciers that lie spread before them, and may like to know that there are no less than twenty-one.

At an altitude of well over 6,000 feet—the Rofenhöfe (Hof = farm or court) lie even higher than Obergurgl—how do the farmers manage to scrape a living? The upper end of the Ötztal has its own peculiarity in that a current of warm southern air finds a channel between the peaks into the valley, and this means that barley, for example, can be grown up to nearly 5,300 feet. Generally speaking, these side valleys are all comparatively warm and dry. In the Tyrol, very strict laws regulate the ownership and inheritance of farms: no sales or divisions of property may be made which would reduce the total area below a size calculated to provide a minimum subsistence for five people. Ownership cannot be shared. Even so, on slopes so steep that the shallow humus may be washed away and have to be carried back in baskets, or where the hay-makers—and as the saying is, even the chickens—must wear crampons to keep from slipping, life is hard indeed. The best land, farmed by the earliest settlers, is always on the terraces of

what are known as the middle highlands. The swampy river
meadows, always threatened by floods, were unpopular; we
noticed this in the Rhine Valley of the Vorarlberg, and it was no
different in the Inntal. The higher areas, above the fog belt, were
considerably warmer: this is why all the old routes go over the
mountains. Those settlements which did lie on the valley bed were
on fertile alluvial ground, where streams from the side valleys
flowed into the main river, or else on the low terraces of the main
valley, on the sunny side. Wherever he was, even stone age man
always settled in a sunny place.

The second reason for keeping to the main road on the way
to Telfs and Innsbruck? To see Stams monastery, which should be
marked with several stars. When the young Konradin, last of the
Hohenstaufen, was beheaded in Naples in 1268, his mother founded
this monastery in his memory. After the death of her first husband
King Konrad IV, Elizabeth married Meinhard II, Count of Görz
and Tyrol. At that time she was living in the old Merovingian
fortress of Petersberg, not far from Stams. She did not live to see
the consecration which was celebrated with great pomp in the
presence of Meinhard, Elizabeth the consort of King Albrecht I,
and seven bishops. The monastery rapidly gained a position of
influence. In 1362 the Emperor Karl IV deposited the imperial
insignia at Stams for safe keeping, and on one brilliant occasion
Maximilian I entertained the ambassador of the Sublime Porte at
Stams, together with the emissaries of the Holy See, Spain and the
Doge of Venice. Until 1600 all the sovereign princes of Tyrol
were buried in the vaults of Stams.

Innsbruck is young compared with Wilten, the oldest monastic
foundation in North Tyrol: its history began in the middle of the
sixth century. It was apparently founded by the giant Raymon,
who, having killed his rival Thyrsus near Seefeld, was stricken
by remorse. He had admired the Benedictines at Tegernsee, and
he now decided to follow their example and build a monastery.
This he did, using the blocks of limestone which he found lying
on the site of the Roman town Veldidena (Wilten). This story
must not lack its dragon, nor does it. Raymon and his labourers
found their work gravely hampered by a monster whose pestilen-

tial breath they found displeasing; it was also playfully inclined to wrap its tail round the newly built walls and pull them down. 'Sorely afrighted', the workmen begged Raymon to do something, whereupon the giant commended his labours to Almighty God and chased the dragon into a cave, where he killed it in a manner 'most masterly'. The only detail which may cast doubt on the chronicler's veracity is the date of Raymon's death which is given as 878.

Innsbruck's beginnings were more prosaic. In 1180 Count Berthold of Andechs made a barter agreement with Wilten Abbey by which he acquired the land on which stands the old centre of Innsbruck. Here he developed the existing village into a market town. It may have been as part of the price to be paid that Berthold presented two of Wilten's greatest treasures to the abbey: the chalice and paten which are both in the Kunsthistorisches Museum in Vienna. The chalice, made by an unknown master craftsman in about 1170, bears designs which were shown at the Council of Trent in 1562 as evidence that the laity had formerly received Holy Communion in the two forms of bread and wine.

Innsbruck's great days as the residence of a sovereign prince began with the reign of the first Habsburg to establish a permanent court in the Tyrol: Archduke Friedrich IV 'of the Empty Purse'. He had two reasons for this decision. He was now in closer contact with the original home of the Habsburgs, the Habichtsburg and the estates belonging to it in the Breisgau. Equally important, the Tyrol was a convenient base from which to pursue his incessant conflicts with the men of Appenzell, the Bishop of Chur and later with the Confederates as a whole. To gain a firm foothold in the region was not easy because the nobility and clergy had become used to running the country as it suited themselves. But Frederick wooed the citizens with privileges and the peasants with liberty, and set up a just and well-organized administration. The major humiliation of his life (and the reason for his nickname) was brought about by his misjudgement in backing the cause of the would-be Pope John XXIII and facilitating his flight—under cover of a tournament—from the Council of Constance. The antipope's disappointment was not assuaged by a crossing of the

Arlberg Pass during which the roughness of the road caused him to be thrown out of his cart, and the duke's situation was no better. Declared an outlaw by the Emperor and his domains forfeited to the crown, he was imprisoned and his brother was installed in his stead. But the citizens and peasantry refused to accept the new prince, who was obliged to withdraw. With the consent of the Emperor, Frederick of the Empty Purse reassumed sovereignty, removed his capital from Meran to Innsbruck, and built himself a courtly residence. 'Friedl' decided not to adapt the old Ottoburg which had belonged to the now extinct family of the counts of Andechs. Instead, he bought two houses and a large area of ground nearby, pulled down the houses and built his New Court; the name Neuhof was to distinguish it from the Ottoburg. Nothing is left of this palace: the whole structure as it was in the time of Maximilian I was destroyed by fire in 1534. The Emperor Ferdinand I rebuilt it in Renaissance style, but his palace was so shaken up by an earthquake that there was nothing for it but to start again. The Hofburg in its present form was built to the orders of the Empress Maria Theresa, complete with imperial suites, and the Great Hall. Magnificent though it is, it cannot entirely console one for the loss of Frederick's building, of which however a record survives. In the late autumn of 1494 the young Albrecht Dürer left his home in Nürnberg—there was an outbreak of plague in the town at that time—and embarked on a journey which took him through the Tyrol to Italy. On arrival in Innsbruck he settled down on the left bank of the Inn and painted his water-colour picture of the river with the boats drawn up at a wharf, and the houses and towers behind them. He also painted an inner courtyard of the Neuhof. These pictures are said to be the first carefully observed architectural drawings in the history of art and Dürer never did anything of the same kind again. Both are preserved in the Albertina in Vienna. The Neuhof picture finally gave the answer to a problem connected with the Goldenes Dachl. This unique balcony with its golden canopy was built on the instructions of Maximilian I as a comfortable place of vantage from which he and his family could watch the dancing on the square below. Miraculously, it survived fire, earthquake and the building frenzy of the Baroque era. There should never have been any doubt that the structure dated from the reign of Maximilian—the evidence is carved all over it—nevertheless an opinion that the balcony was built by Archduke Frederick was evidently current for centuries. The truth underlying the myth is that Frederick did build a golden roof, probably to defy the mockers who gave him his nickname. If the subject of Dürer's water-colour really is the Neuhof in Innsbruck, and experts are certain that it is, then here is the visual evidence: a little turret window juts out from the corner of a building. The projection is roofed in with slates, and they are unmistakably golden. The roof is much smaller than Maximilian's, but even so it cost Frederick 200,000 ducats; by comparison the entire building site only cost 526 ducats. The technique of gilding copper was well known throughout the Middle Ages and many church spires in the Tyrol probably sported a golden cross or weathercock.

Of all the entertainers watched by Maximilian and his consort under the shelter of the golden roof he may have preferred the 'Morisken' whose acrobatic movements are recorded in stone relief below the balustrade. Their remarkable dance, known variously as the Moresca, Moriske or Maruschka, once represented the battle of Christianity against the non-believers: in Spain where the dance is recorded as early as 1137, these were the Moors; hence the name. The English Morris dances had a quite different significance connected with the coming of spring, but the Moorish connection is the same. The sixteen dancers vied with one another to see who could carry out the most difficult contortions, and it was traditional for a woman to present a token prize of an apple or a flower to the winner. The celebrated carving of Maximilian with his two successive wives shows Maria of Burgundy holding an apple. She is the queen of the dance: she was also the great love of Maximilian's youth, whose early death he bitterly mourned.

The designs for the carvings on the frontage of the Goldenes Dachl were made by Gilg Sesselschreiber, a painter from Munich. Eight years later Maximilian called in Sesselschreiber again and entrusted him with a task which was almost to be the death of him: the planning and construction of the Emperor's tomb with the bronze figures around it which, today, is seen as one of the most important works of the Renaissance.

Sesselschreiber was faced with an appalling task. No one had ever before cast such large statues in bronze. The artist had to open up a workshop where the sculptor could model the figures in wax, and the founders had to be taught how to cast them in bronze. Sesselschreiber was a sensitive man, subject to fluctuating moods and extremely irritable. He was also quite indifferent to expense. Maximilian bore with Sesselschreiber's temperament for sixteen years, but in the end he sacked him, an action which of course interrupted the artistic continuity of the memorial. In 1519 Maximilian died in Wels and was buried in Wiener Neustadt, but work on the tomb continued for another forty years. Among the scenes from the life of Maximilian shown on the sides of the sarcophagus are his two meetings with Henry VIII at the siege of Téroulanne in 1513. Interests of state made allies of the King of England and the Holy Roman Emperor, and Henry and Elizabeth I both imported arms and gunsmiths from the Innsbruck 'Armorey'. But the friendly relationship between the two houses at that time was due to the fact that Maximilian's Burgundian wife Maria was a daughter of Princess Margaret of York, the sister of Henry VIII, who was married to Charles the Bold of Burgundy.

In the minds of the Tyrolese the memory of Maximilian lives, far more than in any empty tomb, on the cliff of the Martinswand, a chain of almost perpendicular rocks a mile long and two hundred feet high, west of Innsbruck. The Emperor was out hunting chamois, got into difficulties on the cliff face and could neither advance nor withdraw. The legend said that the populace prayed and lamented on the road below while the local priest held up the monstrance, hastily fetched from the nearest church to bless and comfort the imperilled sovereign. Angels now appeared and guided him back to safety. About ninety years after the event the scholar Masson, who travelled through the Tyrol to Italy believed that the rescue had been carried out 'with the help of engines'. Albanus Beaumont scrutinized the Martinswand with his usual care, identified the rock with its nearly parallel strata as a kind of calcareous *scintillans stratosus grisens*, repeated the angel story ('the inhabitants are rather superstitious') and commented that Hertius in his *History of Germany* believed that Maximilian was first seen to be in difficulties by a shepherdess, who told her brothers, and that he fetched ropes with which he drew the Emperor to safety. Whatever the truth of it, the Emperor himself probably found the whole incident rather embarrassing.

Maximilian was the greatest sportsman of all the Habsburgs and he was the first to pay careful attention to game preservation as this is understood today. At a time when people were still terrified of the remote alpine peaks he introduced chamois-hunting as a sport of princes. Even with the help of beaters, and whether he shot with a crossbow at about a hundred yards or closed in for the kill with a spear, the sport called for considerable skill and endurance. One of his spears can be seen in the collection at Tratzberg Castle near Jenbach. They were often as much as eight yards in length, with a short blade at one end.

In the summer of 1518 Maximilian held an imperial diet at Augsburg, but he was already failing and longed for the mountains of Tyrol. Like all the Habsburgs constantly beset by lack of money, he had left a sea of unpaid bills behind in Innsbruck. When he came home, the innkeepers refused to provide lodging for his suite. Deeply wounded, Maximilian left Tyrol, never to return.

In the memories of people who have known Ambras Castle one thing invariably stands out: Philippine Welser's bathroom. It is unique, and it was built for a remarkable woman. The bath itself is really a small swimming pool about six feet by nine, lined with copper. It took 180 gallons of water to fill it, more, perhaps, than the Empress Maria Theresa, living a hundred years later, would have used in a year. It must have been much talked of at the time as was its owner. But while most of the panelling, the floor and the frescoes in the changing room are all as she knew them, the rumours attached to her person became legend, the legends turned into accepted fact and it took much determined work on the part of recent historians to dispel them.

Philippine Welser was no *poule de luxe*. She was a member of the great Augsburg merchant dynasty of that name and she became the morganatic wife of Archduke Ferdinand II. Ferdinand may first have set eyes on Philippine at the Diet of Augsburg in 1548, but this is only assumption. Whenever it was, this was no stormy love affair in early youth: at the time of their marriage in 1557 Ferdinand was twenty-eight, Philippine thirty. They married secretly with only one witness—her aunt Katharina von Loxan—and the news had to be kept from Ferdinand's father, the Emperor Ferdinand I. In due course he had to be told. The Emperor's fury on learning that his son, a reigning Habsburg prince, had married a member of the bourgeoisie, was only softened when Philippine—'a picture of beauty and the comforting angel of the poor'—implored his forgiveness; the story goes that she prostrated herself before him in the guise of a pilgrim, and presented him with a petition. The Emperor forgave his son and daughter-in-law, but he insisted on the marriage remaining a secret. The children of the marriage (there were two sons, Karl who became Margrave of Burgan, and Andreas who received the Cardinal's hat under Pope Gregory XIII) were of course barred from the succession. The extraordinary secrecy with which all this was carried on meant that in the eyes of the world, even including the ambassadors at the court of Ferdinand, II Philippine was no more than a concubine. This was literally true, because under imperial law a marriage contracted without the permission of the parents was invalid, whatever the Church and even the Pope himself might have to say about it. In spite of the cloud under which she had to live, Philippine was evidently a happy woman. In Italy, it was now the fashion among princes to live outside their capital city. Ferdinand decided to do the same, and he found in Burg Ambras, which had been crown property for some time, a suitable place for development. Having built a castle in Prague, he already had some experience, and he now set to work on Ambras. Tyrolese, Dutch and Italian artists were brought in, a vast park dotted with lakes was laid out complete with temples of pleasure, grottoes and statues. The family moved into the castle in 1567, but work continued for twenty years. Ferdinand assembled one of the greatest art collec-

5. Vulture Country

6. Ambras Castle

tions in Europe. The library included the celebrated Ambras Book of Heroes, there was Montezuma's feather crown and the Cellini salt cellar (now both in Vienna), an armoury, and a large number of mechanical contrivances. Philippine, to whom Ferdinand made over the castle as a gift only three months after he received it from the emperor, led a busy life. She was a most capable housekeeper, wrote two cookery books in her own hand and took great care—he had a weak digestion—of Ferdinand's health. She also assembled an apothecary and dispensed free medicines to all who needed them. The marriage was made public, and one can imagine the sensation this caused, in 1576. Four years later Philippine, 'lover of all troubled hearts', died. 'Our gracious lady', said Ferdinand's subjects, 'is a most woeful loss to us.'

It is impossible to say when the idea that Philippine had been murdered first gained currency. The common people knew that among the nobility were many who wished her out of the way so that Ferdinand might marry again and provide direct heirs to the succession. They may have suspected the worst. But nothing was ever put in writing. The seventeenth century was silent, but between 1705 and 1711 stories appeared in print alleging that Philippine has been murdered in her bath. The floodgates of legend were now opened wide, and there was no end to conjecture. In 1889 the historian Josef Hirn sifted the facts and addressed the Austrian Historical Society on the subject. He complained that the custodian of Ambras, while showing Philippine's bath to visitors (for a substantial consideration) was telling them that her attendants had first administered opium and then severed her main artery and allowed her to bleed to death. The truth was that Philippine died in her bed, probably of a liver and gallbladder complaint, in the presence of her husband. At all events the local people have never forgotten her. Nearly four hundred years later, if changes are made in the castle or its grounds, people of the district write indignant letters asking 'What would Philippine Welser have said to that?'

On 27th April 1719 a Polish princess attended the evening service in the Capuchin Church in Innsbruck. On the way back she ordered her coachman to stop at the court church of St. Francis, and here she alighted and went straight to the Silver Chapel where she remained for some time sunk in thought beside the tombs of Ferdinand II and Philippine Welser. She then rejoined her mother for the evening meal.

In 1718 the Stuart cause seemed not to be altogether hopeless. James Edward, the Old Pretender, had the tacit support of Spain, Russia, Sweden, Modena, Parma and the Vatican. He was now thirty, and it was time to marry. His choice fell on Maria Clementine, the youngest daughter of Prince Jakob Sobiesky, son of the Sobiesky who raised the siege of Vienna in 1683. 'A man', we are told, 'of amiable disposition and tender feeling', his income derived mainly from the privy purse of the Emperor Charles VI in Vienna. Jakob Sobiesky, pleased that a daughter of his—the others were provided for—should marry 'King James III', agreed to the betrothal and prepared to send his wife and Maria Clementine to meet James Edward in Italy. These preparations were immediately noticed by an agent of the Hanoverian court of St. James, and on the very night that the party left Breslau, he rushed to London with the news. King George I who had no wish for his rival to marry and father a string of Stuart pretenders, at once packed the Breslau agent off to Vienna with an urgent request that the marriage be prevented at all costs. He implored Charles VI to arrest the party when they entered the Tyrol. Meanwhile, the ladies and their suite which included a senior mistress of the robes, a woman of the bedchamber, a Herr von Chateaudoux with manservant and a Monsieur La Haye (John Hay, titular Earl of Inverness, an emissary of the Pretender's), lurched along the road to Augsburg on their way to Innsbruck. On 3rd October they arrived in the Tyrolean capital and settled thankfully into their rooms in the most comfortable inn in the town. This was the Widow Rosina Kammerlander's 'Zur Goldenen Rose', where, incidentally, Montaigne had stayed in the time of Ferdinand and Philippine. He was very comfortable there in spite of his disappointment at not being invited to stay at court; Ferdinand was feeling anti-French at the time and did not invite him. The

Polish ladies had hardly composed themselves after their tiring journey when they were waited upon by spokesmen for the government of Tyrol whose kind speeches of welcome made it perfectly clear that the whole party was under arrest. There they remained for six months. Not, however, in the inn: Baron Reiffen, a privy councillor, placed his town house in the Maria Theresien Strasse at their disposal, they were provided with every comfort and were treated—these were the Emperor's orders—with the respect due to their station. Nevertheless, they were surrounded by spies, and strict security precautions were taken. On the day that they arrived in Innsbruck, every licensed coachman and cab driver in the town was sent for by the Town Hall and forbidden under pain of dire punishment to drive a member of the Polish party anywhere at all without express permission. Charles VI now put heavy pressure on Clementine's father to cancel the engagement, but the frantic Sobiesky refused to give in. He wrote longwinded and emotional letters to the foreign minister Count Sinzendorf and to Charles VI. He pointed out that the King of England would remain an ally of the House of Habsburg just so long as he remained afraid of the Stuart pretender, and not a day longer. If James Edward were prevented from marrying Clementine he would undoubtedly marry someone else. Unfortunately, Sobiesky made a fool of himself by first letting it get about that the young couple had already been married by proxy, and then having to admit that this was untrue. All the same, in view of his financial dependence his courage was surprising.

All through the long winter in Innsbruck the party played patience and plotted escape. By February all was settled but to carry it out would take time. First, application was made to Vienna for permission to return home to Breslau, and this was granted. Late in April, a rescue party filtered into Innsbruck in disguise. They were Charles Wogan, a passionately loyal Jacobite, a Major Misset and wife, Captain Toole and two other men, and Mrs. Misset's maidservant who was to swap places, in true operatic tradition, with the young princess. They arrived in two groups, allegedly from Flanders. On 27th April Clementine went, as we know, to church, and her reason for choosing the most

distant church possible for her devotions was to ensure that she
would be seen and her presence noted. She now retired to her
room, pleading a chill, and the authorities and their spies never,
consciously, saw her again. At 11 p.m. the servants went to bed,
but the kitchenmaid noticed at about 11.30 that Chateaudoux
went and stood at the entrance to the house. An almost minute
by minute reconstruction of what followed was drawn up later
by the Innsbruck authorities. After Clementine had left the house
disguised as a man there was one moment of agonized suspense
when two watchmen heard a woman's voice and went to investi-
gate, but the escaping party was able to continue on its way to the
inn where the Jacobites were staying. By two o'clock in the
morning Clementine was well away, at break of day she was
already over the Brenner, and by ten she was on Venetian territory. She had a start of thirty-six hours and there was no hope of
catching her, but Chateaudoux, who had left after the main party
and was carrying all Clementine's jewellery, was seized and
imprisoned for nearly three months in Rovereto. The jewels
were returned to the Princess Sobiesky who soon afterwards
went home to her husband in triumph. At the time of the flight
James Edward, oddly enough, was in Spain, but a proxy marriage
was arranged in Bologna through his intermediary the Earl of
Dunbar. In Rome, Clementine was received with enthusiasm by
the whole of society, and at that time she was evidently capable
of winning genuine affection. As for the Old Pretender, a man of
indeterminate character in whom dissipation and melancholy
mingled, the mother of Bonnie Prince Charlie stood him for five
years and then entered a convent. She and Philippine Welser
both married in defiance of the will of the Habsburg Emperor.
But if, as Clementine stood beside the tomb in the Silver Chapel
that night, kind Philippine could have looked into the future,
her bones might well have rattled with horror and commisera-
tion.

A cavorting monster plies between Innsbruck and Hall. It has
done so for many years; may it live for ever. In coaching days the
distance was no greater than it is by tram—half an hour at most.

So the question arises: what is this rabbit-warren of a medieval town doing so close to Innsbruck? To seize on the guide book information that this is the point at which the River Inn becomes navigable is to rejoice too soon; the river carries just as much water at Innsbruck, where the first bridge was built. The fact is that no one quite knows. Hall became the stopping place for the big river boats and barges: these were nearly 120 feet long and drew small craft behind them, the whole convoy was drawn by teams of up to twenty horses. The upstream distance from Kufstein to Hall took five days, downstream only six hours. Upstream went cereals, cattle for slaughter and edible fats; the downstream traffic was mineral ore, timber, wine, cloth and luxury goods which had come over the Brenner from Italy en route for Bavaria, Bohemia and Vienna. Bulky goods also went by raft, and on arrival the trunks of timber were dismantled and used for firewood. Only small boats plied upstream, past Innsbruck as far as Telfs, where there used to be corn and salt depots, and here everything was unloaded and carried on by land over the Fern Pass, the Arlberg or south-west to the Engadine. The merchants of Hall hardly needed Innsbruck, particularly once they had managed to secure trading privileges such as the right to maintain bonded warehouses and to compel all through traffic to reload in Hall. And this through traffic was able to bypass Innsbruck altogether by using the Ellbögner road through Ampass and Lans into the Wipptal, the valley leading to the Brenner. The curiously elongated lower square of Hall was a later development. It had become a pressing necessity because the crowds of carts had engulfed the centre of the town and were choking the approaches to the top square. The people were able to avoid the streets filled with cursing, polyglot drivers and their laden carts by taking refuge in a whole network of narrow passageways, staircases and intercommunicating back yards, in which strangers can still enjoy losing themselves.

When, in 1280, a citizen noticed deer licking rock on the mountain, the Hall salt industry was born, and in time Hall had a larger population than Innsbruck. But the old rivalry was settled by the inevitable choice of Innsbruck as the centre of government—it lay on the vital 'imperial highway'—and the residence of the reigning archduke.

The old Mint in Hall was founded in 1477. For the past two hundred years the needs of the country had been supplied from Meran. Archduke Siegmund needed more money, and for trading purposes as well the volume of currency in circulation had to be increased without debasing the coinage. Rich finds of silver in the mines at Schwaz, more extensive than the seams in 'Old' Tyrol, made it seem reasonable to shut down the Mint in Meran and move to Hall. To the inconvenience and expense of transporting the silver over the Brenner and back, particularly in winter, another factor arose. There was a serious danger of Turkish incursions along the Pustertal into South Tyrol, in which case the Mint, complete with its set of coinage stamps (presses had not yet been introduced), would have been cut off from the capital. Nor were the Swiss Confederates wholly to be trusted; they might well be tempted to break through the Vintschgau to Meran. After endless procrastination, the move of master coiners, skilled workmen and their equipment was at last effected, and on the Feast of the Assumption, 1477, the first coins were struck in Sparberegg Castle, where the Mint remained until in 1567 Archduke Ferdinand II moved it into the ducal palace of which the Münzturm is the tower. Siegmund was delighted. There was a childish element in his nature: he loved being fêted by his miners, he enjoyed throwing handfuls of money to the poor. But although he insisted on having a hand in every aspect of public administration, neither he nor his nobles had any real understanding of government, and they were helpless to control events. Disillusioned, Siegmund lost all pleasure in ruling and began to brood over abdication. When the members of the Landtag discovered that their sovereign was busy making arrangements to mortgage the whole of the Tyrol to the King of Bavaria they took immediate steps to restrict his constitutional powers and to tie the succession to legitimate Habsburg heirs. This action by the burghers and peasants of the Tyrol is worth noticing: it was the second time that, only recently emerged from the feudal age, the people decisively influenced the destiny of their country without reference to nobility or clergy—and at the same time proved their loyalty to the Habsburg dynasty. It would not be the last: this thread was to run right through the history of the Tyrol. In 1490, probably thankfully, Siegmund abdicated in favour of his nephew, the later Emperor Maximilian I. He was now 63. A humanist all his life, a great patron of the arts and of architecture but always a sensualist and not a little debauched, Siegmund now lapsed into childish ways. He became obsessed by coins and loved to thrust his hands into dishes full of gold and silver which his retainers brought to him. Six years after his abdication he died and was buried in the Cistercian Abbey at Stams.

What were these coins which—partly of course because they bore his image—gave such joy to Siegmund? In his time the artisans in Hall were stamping out groschen, gulden (the 'golden' pfennig, introduced to replace the debased Viennese silver pfennig at the rate of 240:1) and taler. Austrian patriots are careful to point out that the taler, ancestor of the dollar, took its name from the Inntal. The Joachimstaler, from which the dollar is widely thought to have derived, was introduced thirty years after the Inntaler coin.

'It was the pleasantest voyage in the world', recorded Joseph Addison in 1702, 'to follow the windings of this River Inn through such a variety of pleasing scenes as the course naturally led us. The time of the year, that had given the leaves of the trees so many different colours, completed the beauty of the prospect.' By his time, quiet (though not always peace) had begun to fall on the Inn Valley. The days when, within the short distance between Hall and Kundl, a string of fifty foundries blazed day and night, had gone for ever. The triumphant years of Schwaz and Rattenberg were comparatively short, but merely between 1500 and 1560 two million kilos of silver and forty thousand tons of copper had been raised from shafts extending for hundreds of miles. Miners are always exclusive people, which is why the parish church of Schwaz has two west doors, one for the miners to enter by, the other for ordinary mortals. The end came fairly suddenly: the mines, which—largely mortgaged to the ubiquitous

Fuggers—had financed an empire, were ruthlessly exploited and the two hundred-year-long harvest came to an end. Schwaz was taken by the Bavarians in 1809 and a terrible fire destroyed much of its old beauty. But Rattenberg's sudden decline into poverty and obscurity, the fact that it mercifully slept right through the Baroque era, preserved its late medieval character almost intact. In the height of the summer season fifty thousand cars pass through the narrow main street of Rattenberg each day. How many of their occupants have time to enjoy what it would be worth coming across Europe to see? Ideally, Rattenberg should be approached from the west, after dark, and a full moon should be suspended just above the twisted chimneys. In these circumstances a skein of witches on broomsticks, in full flight across the roofs, can be added optionally by the beholder.

The Achensee, on the other hand, ought properly to be approached by rail. These small-gauge local railway lines, which are dying out fast, are a joy, particularly where, as on the Achensee line, it is possible to stand outside on the end platform. This whole district was a hunting ground greatly beloved of all the Tyrolean archdukes and their families from Elinor Stuart onwards. Ferdinand II and Philippine had their own Venetian galley on the lake, and they built a large shooting box near Pertisau in order not to have to impose on the hospitality of the landowners, the monks of twelfth century St. Georgenberg.

The Tyrolese have acting in their blood. The masked dances and processions of Imst, Nassereith and Telfs are prehistoric in origin and will surely continue with undiminished vigour for all time. It is only natural that these performances—or ancient rites—should be kept alive with one eye on the competitive tourist industry. All the same, it is hard to believe that they would die out if there were no foreign visitors. The ritual content has evaporated. What remains is love of tradition, of play-acting, of dressing up. Solemn religious processions such as the Antlass Ride at Brixen im Tal, which is a thanksgiving for preservation during the Thirty Years War, are in a different category. The Tyrolean love of the theatre seems to be scarcely affected by the cinema and television: there are still one hundred and ten amateur theatre companies in the province. The passion plays at Thiersee (since 1799) and Erl (1613) which developed from the medieval liturgical drama in the monasteries are perhaps all the more authentic in that, being less internationally known than Oberammergau, their audiences consist largely of Austrians and Southern Bavarians. A recent season in Erl brought ninety six thousand people to the box office.

The gayest, the 'most typically Tyrolean', valley of all is the Zillertal. The Zillertal musicians, with their harps and zithers and their yodelling, were well known at the courts of Europe. They sang for the Czar, for Goethe in Weimar and for the King of England. The Josef Rainer company created a sensation in London at their first visit in 1827. Recommended by the Austrian ambassador Prince Esterhazy, they were quickly passed on from one town house to another, and were commanded to appear before King George IV. The future Queen Victoria was so enchanted by them that the group was engaged to perform during the coronation celebrations in 1838. The singers captured London society to such a degree that for many an English soprano it became obligatory to learn 'these wild, inimitable songs' and to wrench from her delicate throat a more or less authentic yodel. London hostesses might rave about the Tyrolean national dress, but Queen Victoria, feeling that a little added refinement would be beneficial, ordered the Rainers to be fitted out with new costumes. The Zillertal singers now underwent a remarkable transformation. The men were given neat little collars and skin-tight cutaway jerkins vaguely resembling a livery, while the women's skirts which formerly stopped at the lower calf now almost touched the ground. And was it the addition of hoops, wadding or simply a number of petticoats that makes them look like modified crinolines? For the 1851 Exhibition the successor company under Ludwig Rainer performed in London and, in 1855, in Paris where the famous song '*Auf der Alm, da gibts koa Sünd*' ('on the alpine pastures there is no such thing as sin') is said to have made a deep impression on Napoleon III.

Oddly enough, the Zillertal only became part of the Tyrol in 1805; it was formerly under the jurisdiction of the archbishops of Salzburg. To show it, here is the boundary between the red and the green 'onions' on the church steeples. In the seventh century Zell am Ziller was a monk's cell, Mayrhofen the later monastery's home farm. Being ecclesiastical territory, the valley kept, for the most part, clear of war. But it is almost a freak of religious intolerance that at such a late date as 1837 (just before the Rainers were taking part in the coronation celebrations in London) four hundred and fifty men and women of the Zillertal, being Protestants, were forced to emigrate to Silesia.

Religious piety and love of fantasy: the two elements seem to come together in the popular cult of St. Romedius, who is said to have been born in the castle above Thaur, a village as rich in folklore as any in the Tyrol. Romedius rid himself of his worldly goods and, with two other holy men, led the life of a hermit at Nonsberg in South Tyrol. Having decided one day to visit his bishop in Trent, he found that unhappily his mule had been eaten by a bear. Because or perhaps in spite of its satiated condition St. Romedius was able to tame the bear and persuade it to bring him without delay to his destination.

Few people have ever heard of Peter Prosch of Ried in the Zillertal, who wrote one of the most enchanting autobiographies in the German language: *The Life and Adventures of Peter Prosch, or, the Wonderful Destiny, Written in the Days of the Enlightenment.* As a penniless boy Peter walked to Vienna and was received in audience by the Empress Maria Theresa; later in life he was able to write a vivid account of the death of her husband Franz von Lothringen in Innsbruck. On his travels he was welcomed at the high tables of the powerful Bavarian noblemen, rough practical jokes were played on him by young aristocrats and he was the confidant of elderly ladies. He knew all the gossip between Regensburg and Innsbruck, he was witty, observant, kind, appallingly accident-prone and a shocking coward; he was the last of the court jesters. The most striking elements in his character were very typical of his country: independence of mind and a capacity for seeing people as individuals, regardless of their station in life.

After Wörgl the Inn flows north past Kufstein, marks the frontier for a time and then vanishes from our sight. Kufstein is a real blood-and-thunder fortress of great historical interest and it owns an enormous remote-control organ. The eastward journey now leads into the world of the Kaiser-Gebirge and of the gentler Kitzbühel Alps to the south. The spirits which haunt the Kaiser range, in particular the Wilde Kaiser, must easily outnumber the alpine climbers. Ghosts of lost treasure hunters infest every ridge, col and cranny; in some subterranean cave sleeps a prince, watched over by seven giants; there is a female giant in the Totenkirchl; and the souls of all the most disliked inhabitants of the surrounding hamlets await the Day of Judgement. It is easy to believe all this, but not that Charlemagne lies, as yet another myth insists, beneath the Fierce Kaiser. He is elsewhere: asleep, while his beard grows longer and longer, under the Untersberg near Salzburg.

Whoever visits Kitzbühel at the height of the winter or summer season knows, no doubt, what to expect. From the west, the quieter approach is through the Brixental, past the Hohe Salve, a photogenic mountain which, it is recorded, the Empress Marie Louise, wife of Napoleon Buonaparte, was 'graciously pleased to ascend'. The idea of visiting the local museum while in Kitzbühel may seem mildly eccentric, but it is worth it if only for two reasons. There is a cross-section of the silver mines which in their day were the deepest in the world. The rich citizens of Kitzbühel built their substantial houses out of their profits, but they scamped the town walls which, although between twelve and fifteen feet thick, were hollow. In the room in which the relics of the first days of skiing are displayed there is a slightly faded photograph of Countess Lamberg performing, though from no great height, one of the first ski jumps in history; this should not be missed.

We are now back very close to where, only a few years ago, the Tyrolese farmers rushed out to repel the Austrian army on manoeuvres: near the Hochfilzen Pass, above Fieberbrunn where Margarete Maultasch came to drink the waters and was cured of a fever. The fact that all the high farms are gradually being made accessible by road is of primary importance to the owners. To the general public it is also an inestimable advantage. Here, it means that the car can be turned off this comparatively lonely pass road and within five minutes we are once again up in the hills, looking back to the Wilde Kaiser, letting our thoughts range back over the Tyrol.

It is a platitude to compare the Tyrolese with the Highland Scots. Is there any truth in it? What made the Tyrolese into a closely knit, staunchly independent nation?

The oldest democratic constitution on the European continent was voluntarily bestowed on the Tyrol by Meinhard II in the Freedom Charter of 1342 which expressly confirmed 'ancient usage'. It guaranteed the rights of all classes of the population and established the principal elements of genuine popular representation: the right to ratify or reject taxes and legislation, and to act as a check on the processes of government. The *Landibell* of 1511 granted to all Tyrolese the right to bear arms—this could only have been attempted in a country where serfdom was unknown. Such was the strategic importance of the country that in future no one, whatever his station, could be called up for military service elsewhere, but he had to be ready at all times to defend his country. This Tyrolean *Waffenfreiheit* was to have startling effects. In 1703, during the War of the Spanish Succession, the Bavarians and the French attacked the Tyrol simultaneously from the north and south. The imperial authorities and the chiefs of staff in Innsbruck were so taken by surprise that they capitulated without a shot being fired. But the inhabitants of South Tyrol and of the Upper and Lower Inn Valley took up arms and forced the invaders to withdraw with heavy losses on the Brenner, at the Pontlatz Bridge near Landeck, and at Rattenberg. That done, they marched into Innsbruck with flags flying and drums beating and relieved their crestfallen rulers. The whole series of defeats suffered by the Napoleonic troops at the hands of Andreas Hofer and his men happened after the defeat of the Austrian armies and the resulting peace treaty of Znaim.

These are the people who were compelled to cede to a foreign power which had not defeated them in war, the original core of their country: South Tyrol.

Tyrol

One result of this loss is the isolation of East Tyrol which, separated from North Tyrol by the Tauern range, has always looked along the Pustertal towards Brixen. The Glockner pass which leads due south to Lienz, is impassable in winter. It was inevitable, therefore, that East Tyrol should become a backwater and that the thinly scattered upland inhabitants should have to contend with serious economic problems. The Felber-Tauern tunnel road linking Mittersill below Pass Thurn and Matrei in East Tyrol, will do much to help these lonely valleys. Meanwhile, this remains one of the few really unspoiled areas of alpine Austria.

Considering its ripe age, Lienz has a disappointingly modern appearance. No less than six great fires (in 1444, 1598, 1609, 1723, 1798 and 1825) progressively obliterated the character of East Tyrol's capital town which grew from a cluster of houses where the Isel flows into the Drave. But Lienz makes up for any possible architectural shortcomings by its situation at the gateway to the Dolomites. And—after the rapid descent from nearly 8,000 feet the sight of palm trees makes the point with dramatic effect—one has the distinct impression that this is where the south of Europe begins.

The Counts of Görz chose Lienz as their residence and built Bruck castle, probably on the site of a Roman citadel which would have guarded the entrance to the Isel Valley. Count Leonhard and his wife Paula née Gonzaga commissioned Simon von Taisten, an artist who worked in a number of churches in the Pustertal and South Tyrol, to paint a series of frescoes in the castle chapel. The scene of the death of the Virgin Mary shows Leonhard and Paula, both delicately graceful and exquisitely dressed, in the left foreground. Leonhard was the last of the house of Görz. When he died in 1500 the province passed by inheritance to the Emperor Maximilian I and became part of the Tyrol. They are both buried, with others of their line, in the Gothic parish church of Lienz which mercifully survived the fires.

Diggings carried out during recent years on a site three miles south-east of Lienz have brought to light much new evidence concerning the old see of Aguntum. The early fifth-century episcopal basilica built in place of a smaller existing church is

on a hill jutting out into the valley. The remains of a gateway
and a ring wall make it appear that the whole site must have served
as a place of refuge for the inhabitants of the town of Aguntum.
By the end of the sixth century the Slavs under their masters the
Avars had penetrated the valley of the Drave and the Bishopric
of Aguntum, last heard of in 604, was swept away. The Slav
name meaning 'desolate' is such an unsuitable description of the
cheerful Pustertal that it must have referred to the devastation
caused by the invaders, or to the battles in which, somewhere
within this area, Duke Tassilo I of Bavaria brought the Slav
incursions to a halt.

The present day East Tyrolean would like an invasion—of
tourists and of industrial investment, but the difficult situation
is not helped by the fact that all the main roads into and from the
Austrian provinces are weighted by toll charges. We, however,
are making a tour which is both factual and imaginary, and we can
pretend that we are following the old northward path over the
Tauern range, driving our cattle before us, perhaps, to the richer
grazing on the slopes of the Pinzgau.

We are now in Land Salzburg.

4

Salzburg

Bishop Rupert of Worms came to Regensburg, was amiably received by the Bavarian Duke Theodo and was allowed to baptize him and the members of his family. This event, which took place in A.D. 696 in the second year of the reign of Childebert, King of the Franks, by no means marked the summit of Rupert's ambitions; he left the consolidation of Christian life in this area to others. What he had in mind was to bring back into the fold such scattered pockets of Christianity as might have survived the withdrawal of Roman occupation from the frontier provinces of Noricum and the devastation brought about by the barbarian invasions. The bishop rode on towards the south until he came to a lake, the Wallersee, which seemed to him to offer a suitable locality for a diocesan headquarters. Here, in a small village now called See-kirchen, he settled for the time being. Scouts were dispatched to explore the surrounding country and they soon reported that only two hours' ride to the southwest, they had come upon the ruins of a large town. Some of the houses they had seen were of great size and wonderfully wrought, but trees were growing in and among them, and the streets and squares were almost stifled by undergrowth. Once he had seen the place for himself the bishop must have realized that this was Iuvavum—or Claudium Iuvavum to give it its full name—and he gave up the idea of building at Seekirchen. The legal position was soon clarified. Duke Theodo allowed Rupert to take over the ruined town, granting him full possession of the urban area including the castle on the hill and the temple at its foot, and the surrounding land three miles in circumference. A church was soon built and dedicated to the apostle Peter, and a monastery in which from that day onwards the Benedictine discipline has been followed. On the nearby hill, the Nonnberg, he built a convent and installed as abbess his cousin Erentrudis; today this is the oldest surviving religious community for women in the world. Salzburg was born again.

In choosing this site in an abandoned, impoverished and sparsely populated frontier district of a fallen empire as a base from which to missionize most of present-day Austria, Bishop Rupert is assumed to have had various considerations in mind. He could have chosen Regensburg, which at that time was already a prosperous town. But in Roman times Salzburg (the name first appears in 816) had stood at the point of intersection of vital lines of communication. He was now in direct touch with the surviving Christian communities, descendants of a romanized population who still spoke, as they would for another century and more, the Romance language. Finally, canon law requires that the seat of a bishopric shall be a town, and as Iuvavum was still in legal existence Rupert would save himself much valuable time and trouble by putting this proposal forward rather than by starting from scratch at Seekirchen. To suggest that he admired either the town or the view from the hill would be to commit a solecism, but he will have noticed the advantages from the defensive point of view; they are too obvious to be overlooked.

When visiting a strange town it is often well worth trying to see why it came into existence just where it did. In Salzburg, the best idea is to take the lift up to the Café Winkler on the Mönchsberg. The obligation to *konsumieren* can be evaded: simply lean on the wall and look towards the fortress, and over the roofs and spires to the river below. In imagination, allow all signs of human activity to vanish, leaving only the natural features: this is the scene as the Celtic tribes knew it before the coming of the Romans. The plain at the base of the alpine foothills is partly moor, partly swamp. The River Salzach meanders across it narrowing as it flows between the two limestone cliffs which stand out like islands in the alluvial basin. On the right bank as the river

7b. Anna Neumann von Wasserleonburg, founder of the Schwarzenberg fortune, in about 1600

7a. Philippine Welser, morganatic wife of Ferdinand II of Tyrol

REVERENDISS. ET ILLVSTRISS. PRINCEPS D.D.WOLFGANGVS
THEODERICVS ARCHIEPISCOPVS SALISBVRGENSIS. SS.SEDIS
APOSTOLICÆ LEGATVS NATVS.

8b. Wolf Dietrich von Raitenau, Prince-Archbishop

8a. Salome Alt

passes between the cliffs there is a bow-shaped piece of land. If
there are to be human dwellings anywhere in this vicinity they
must be here, their backs to the cliff and facing the river. If there
is to be a road it must be on this side as well, because here the ground
is dry. (The last patches of this primeval swamp were not drained
until early in the nineteenth century.) As a natural building site
the place has a satisfyingly obvious inevitability, and its permanency
was established for all time when command of the salt trade, the
river traffic and the alpine road brought a bustle of mercantile
activity which, swept away during the dark ages, was to be resumed
and expanded from the eighth century onwards.

There is not much left of Roman Iuvavum. Most of it lies
buried beneath medieval Salzburg. But the cliffside catacombs are
unique in Europe north of the Alps: where else do we get such a
vivid idea of the ordeal of the early Christians? We catch a glimpse,
from contemporary records, of St. Severin hurrying from Enns to
Salzburg to warn the population that nothing can hold back the
advance of the invading peoples. In A.D. 471 St. Maximus tried to
hide about four hundred of his parishioners in his chapel, deep
within the catacombs, but they were discovered by the invaders,
murdered and their bodies thrown down into the cemetery. Those
others who were able to, fled to the south, or withdrew into the
limitless forest, to the terrifying, myth-laden mountains.

St. Rupert broke a silence that had lasted for more than two
hundred years. He sent priests to seek out the scattered population,
and a chronicle written two or three generations after his time
tells of 'two men of God' (one bearing a Roman name) who went
into the 'wilderness' of the mountains about the Lueg Pass to pan
for gold and to hunt. One night they had a vision in which they
were told to build a church and a monastic cell; a sharp and timely
reminder in view of the evident lapse in their sense of priorities.
The ultimate consequence of this vision was Bischofshofen, a
railway junction at which many a visitor to Austria has been
stranded. Meanwhile, Rupert himself was constantly on the move
and his personal reputation grew. He found the heathen tribes
a more straightforward problem than the so-called Christians,
whose faith has been described as hopelessly *'verwildert'*. And it must

be admitted that, infuriated by his attempts at reform, the people
of Salzburg at last threw out their patron saint, and it was only
when the Englishman St. Boniface finally established the Church
throughout Bavaria that the body of the first Bishop of Salzburg
was returned to his ungrateful diocese. The guide books need so
much space to describe the rococo glories of St. Peter's Church as
it is today that they usually offer little more than the flat statement that St. Rupert's tomb is there too. But it is worth pausing
beside it. The plain stone tomb is illuminated by a dim light and
lies slightly below floor level surrounded and protected by a
barrier and grating. This is the very heart of Salzburg.

What extraordinary men they were, the successors of St.
Rupert, soon to become archbishops, then prince-archbishops of
Salzburg. To what extent were they different from their contemporaries in other countries? There were princes of the Church
elsewhere who, some of them, were just as magnificent, just as
worldly, no less crafty and perhaps far more influential. And yet
there does seem to have been a quality possessed by the archbishops
of Salzburg at certain moments in history which tends to set them
apart. There is a portrait of Wolf Dietrich von Raitenau (1587–1611)
which is extraordinarily evocative. The figure is firm and compact,
the pointed beard closely trimmed, the mouth is that of a man who
will brook no nonsense. It is the face of an intelligent, highly alert
man, and his short-cropped hair is slightly reminiscent of a wire-
haired terrier. It comes as a surprise to realize that the cap, perched
at a carefree angle on the back of his head is a priest's talar. Wolf
Dietrich came of the old Swabian nobility. His father, a warrior
of some reputation, married a Countess von Hohenems from the
Vorarlberg and in due course sent his son to be educated in
Rome. There Wolf Dietrich absorbed all the luxuriant love of the
arts, of colour and form of the *cinquecento* and he came to see the
furtherance of the arts as the first duty of princes. A nineteenth-
century historian has described him as unscrupulous, contemp-
tuous of the rights of others, a cunning man who identified himself totally with the Catholicism of the Counter-Reformation in
general, and with the Jesuits' teaching in particular. He was a
man of strong emotions, by nature perhaps more a soldier than a

priest, more an administrator than a scholar, who abolished the citizens' *Landtag* and expelled all the Protestants from his territory. Having dealt with those two not unrelated problems he began to build.

Wolf Dietrich von Raitenau is the man who built the town as we know it today, but to do it he had to destroy most of medieval Salzburg. If we look down, preferably from the castle, on to the Chapter and Cathedral squares, we have to realize that all this area was once a network of narrow streets, and of houses closely huddled together round the enormous Romanesque cathedral. Before he could build his Renaissance town, Wolf Dietrich had to clear all this away. He had been longing to tear down the cathedral but was probably uncertain whether even he could get away with it. He was helped by a fire which broke out in the oratory, though it only consumed the roof. The Archbishop is said to have looked so pleased at the news that a rumour immediately circulated that he himself knew a good deal about the origin of the fire. There was little wrong with the fabric and the whole vast structure had to be destroyed by explosives. Curiously enough, the new cathedral was smaller than the old one. So contrary was this to general practice elsewhere that in subsequent generations few people seem to have realized the fact. In recent years it has been proved that the apse of the old basilica, standing at a slight angle across the present site, began as it were close to the entrance to the main post office, while the west door stood some yards within the walls of the palace, the *Residenz*. Wolf Dietrich also had to rehouse the victims of his wholesale slum clearance activities, and even his resources were limited. Tempted by the wealth of the monastery at Berchtesgaden he tried to seize and incorporate it in his own archdiocese, but this inevitably brought about a quarrel with the Duke of Bavaria. Instead of withdrawing, pacifying the duke or brazening it out, Wolf Dietrich now lost his nerve and fled to the mountains where he was ignominiously recaptured and imprisoned, first in Werfen castle and then in his own fortress of Salzburg where after five dreary years rendered even more wretched by attacks of epilepsy, his life ended.

Salzburg had come a long way since the days of the early

medieval bishops. There had been Virgil, 'a thing of dread to Boniface because he lectures on the antipodes, which is to deny Christ and His Church', who was formerly Abbot of Aghaboe. Bishop Arno, first Archbishop and like Rupert also a Frank, was on terms of friendship with Charlemagne's counsellor Alcuin and in constant touch with the Frankish court. This was essential, because the defeat of the Avars and the extension of Frankish rule beyond the borders of western Hungary enormously extended the sphere of power and responsibility of the bishops of Salzburg. The monasteries at Mondsee, Chiemsee and Mattsee were already in existence and the Carantanians were under the pastoral care of priests from Salzburg. Contemporary documents show that the administration of Carantania and Pannonia was the predominant task of the archdiocesan authorities. To put it differently: they had to colonize, 'germanize' and bring Christianity to the inhabitants of Carinthia, Styria and Lower Austria. (The claims of Salzburg to jurisdiction within western Hungary only came to an end when King Stephen of Hungary founded the Archbishopric of Esztergom with ten, subsequently twelve suffragan sees. St. Stephen's daughter married Prince Edward, son of Edmund Ironside, and was the mother both of Edgar the Aetheling and of St. Margaret of Scotland, becoming the ancestress of English and Scottish sovereigns.) Suddenly the Magyars invaded Austria, and all the lands 'won by sword, cross and ploughshare' seemed to have been lost once again. In the year 907, somewhere in Lower Austria where rolling hill country merges into plain, they utterly defeated the Frankish armies. All the western leaders were slain and the country overrun, and while the fate of Salzburg is not exactly known, many of the churches and monasteries of the new era were burned to the ground. The sufferings of the population lasted for forty-eight years. In 955, one of the resounding dates in European history, the Magyars were crushed at the Battle of the Lechfeld and were pressed back into their domains, never to return.

Among those who died fighting in the front ranks of the western army in 907 were three priests. They were the Bishops of Salzburg, of Passau and of Brixen. This was what it meant to be a prince of the Church in this part of the medieval world. He had to

combine the qualities of a condottiere, of an explorer in little
known and often hostile country, and an administrator of vast
estates. The archdiocese of Salzburg had already acquired a great
deal of property. Spiritual jurisdiction ran from the Inn to the
Drave, from the Zillertal valley to Styria and along the borders of
Lower Austria and the Burgenland, and it contained the four
suffragan sees of Chiemsee, Lavant (known as the 'prune see' on
account of its poor revenues), Gurk and Seckau. For generations,
large gifts of land and persons had been accumulating and now
included many thousands of farms, great expanses of forest and
alpine pasture, as well as extensive hunting rights. The salt mines
had always been the cornerstone of Salzburg's natural resources,
and there were deposits of gold, silver and iron ore in which the
archdiocese possessed a monopoly of mining and trading rights.
But for centuries the property consisted of a confusing mass of
individual estates. The final transformation of Salzburg into a
principality came about in the time of Eberhard II in the first half
of the thirteenth century, and the consummate artistry with which
he and his successors played on law and circumstance to further
their interests worthily compares with the tactics of any contemporary ruling prince. As for prayer and mortification, that was the
business of the Abbot of St. Peter's. Briefly, this is how it was done.
Rivalry and friction between Salzburg and neighbouring Bavaria
there would always be, right through to the middle of the nineteenth
century. But the archbishops always sided with centralism against
fragmentation, with the Babenbergs and the Habsburgs against
the feudal nobility. This brought about a continuous rain of gifts
to the Church, market and customs privileges and the right to
mint coinage. Many of the old noble families, moreover, held their
properties in fief from the Emperor and the Dukes of Bavaria, but
the German *Lehnrecht* only recognized direct descent from father
to son. The mortality among the aristocratic families as a result of
the crusades gave the archbishops the chance to intervene, declare
an inheritance invalid and the estate as forfeit to the archdiocese.
This explains the fact that in course of time the old nobility
of Salzburg all but ceased to exist. The castles that you see as
you drive through Land Salzburg have not been abandoned by

impoverished aristocrats unwilling to go into the half-crown business. The later fifteenth- or sixteenth-century buildings were estate offices from which the church lands' finances were run by bailiffs.

Warlike qualities were shown by the archbishops well into the seventeenth century. Pilgrim von Puchheim (1365–96) decidedly preferred armour to clerical vestments, and although there was no doubt about the frontier between Salzburg and Bavaria—this had been fixed by two separate treaties more than a hundred years before—he scrapped tirelessly with the Dukes of Bavaria. He was fortunately spared any twinges of Christian conscience because the Pope had been kind enough to bestow on him the 'personal right to engage in war'. Pilgrim was the first in the long succession to surround himself with all the pomp and glitter of Italian court life: pages, cavaliers, beautiful women, the drama, poetry and music. The most significant and at the same time mysterious figure at his court was the 'Monk of Salzburg' of unknown identity. Professor Bernhard Paumgartner, Austrian musicologist and director of the Salzburg Festival, has written of him: 'At a time of linguistic confusion when Middle High German was merging into New High German, the courtly art of the minnesang now in its last throes brought forth a great artist. ... The beauty and power of his simplest melodies are wonderful. His art stands at the threshold of a new age when the new German language and a profound development in polyphonic music coincide. This highly talented man was probably the last great composer of plainsong.' And it was Pilgrim, the warrior and lover of courtly splendour, who in 1393 created a fund to support a choir which would study and perform the art of polyphonic song in the old Minster.

If a native of Salzburg were to be asked: 'Which, in your opinion, was the downright nastiest archbishop of them all?' he would very likely say 'der Keutschacher'. If the predecessors of Leonhard von Keutschach (1495–1519) had little patience with the growing demands and pretensions of their citizens, he himself had none whatever. And when the Emperor Frederick III granted to the burghers of Salzburg the right to elect their own mayor and corporation without consulting their overlord the archbishop, adding to this all the privileges of *Reichsunmittelbarkeit*, 'der

Keutschacher' acted. He invited the town worthies to a banquet. Along they came in their robes of silk and velvet, no doubt in the comfortable state of mind in which a glowing sense of their new dignity mingled with pleasant anticipation of the fine meats and wines, the music and poesy which lay ahead. Their disappointment fully equalled that of the oysters with the invitation of the walrus and the carpenter. Hardly had they arrived than they were roughly seized, bound and dumped upon sledges on which they were swept fifty miles away to Radstadt. It was a winter's night, there was snow on the ground, and they had neither coats nor blankets. The teeth of the town fathers chattered, and not only from the bitter cold: the presence of the chief executioner, riding quietly among the guards, had not escaped them. It all ended as one might expect. The unfortunate dignitaries were allowed to return to their families, but not before, under oath, they had laid all their rights and privileges back into the lands of their lord, now and—ostensibly—for all time to come.

While Archbishop Keutschach, whose rather inappropriate emblem, the common turnip, can be seen today at many places on the fortress of Salzburg, was an unmitigatedly nasty man, a competing case could also be made out for his successor Cardinal Matthäus Lang von Wellenburg. His case is, however, a little more complicated and depends on the point of view. Matthäus Lang was a statesman, a minister and confidant of one of the greatest Habsburg emperors, Maximilian I. The problems of his reign would have made high demands on the wisest of statesmen, and while they were nowhere dealt with without suffering and bloodshed, the province of Salzburg was at least spared the worst aspects of the Reformation. The great Paris Lodron would even succeed in keeping the province out of the Thirty Years' War. But Matthäus Lang had the widespread peasant rebellion to contend with. The citizens opened the gates to the 'evil, obnoxious rabble' and Lang fled to the castle. Here, with the spectacle of His Eminence under heavy artillery fire from his own subjects and parishioners, we can leave the prince-archbishops of Salzburg: saints sometimes, often colonizers, warriors and skilled administrators, but never less than absolute rulers over their land and people.

Two British musicians were in Salzburg for the Festival. Together, we had seen a performance of the immortal mystery play on the Cathedral square. The cry '*Jedermann!*' had sounded from the tower of the Franziskanerkirche and its echo had been taken up by voices on the castle ramparts. Through the open doors of the Cathedral the swelling roar of the great organ had announced the salvation, in death, of the soul of Everyman. In the evening, Herbert von Karajan had conducted *Don Giovanni*. As we left the Felsenreitschule we felt drained of emotion but in no mood for dinner in a noisy restaurant. Sausages and beer under the trees at Tomaselli's suited our mood better, and after a stroll round the town we would drive home to Zell-am-See. The walls of the old houses, where the heat of the sun had rested on them, were still warm to the touch, but a breath of cool air from the hills gave us a little new energy for our walk.

The floodlights were picking out first one church façade, dome and pinnacle, then another, causing the two men to stop in their tracks. Inevitably, we talked of Mozart: of the kick in the pants —one of the most significant gestures in the history of music— administered by Count Arco. 'I have read a little Austrian history', said the cellist, 'and it is odd the way the same aristocratic names recur over and over again from the late middle ages down to the present day. It has a curiously theatrical effect, as though a repertory company were to perform an unending series of historical plays but always using their own names. War and pestilence, child mortality, Reformation and Counter-Reformation—nothing, not even ancestor shrinkage through incessant intermarriage—could stem the determined progress of these families. How did they do it?'

'Well', said the violinist, 'largely it was the inflationary effect, wasn't it, of the continental as opposed to the British system: all the sons of a count are counts. A nobleman can put as many peers into the world as his wife can bear. And while in England, younger sons and their descendants could very rapidly sink out of sight, their Austrian equivalent, bearing the same name and, usually, the same style as the head of the family, had to be provided with a position and an income in keeping with the dignity of the clan.'

'As a result', I agreed, 'practically all the higher official appointments throughout the empire were held by noblemen, to almost claustrophobic effect. Just look at the members of the Salzburg Cathedral Chapter in the time of Mozart. Originally, these twenty-four celibate clergy had to give heraldic evidence of knightly ancestry covering the three preceding generations. But in fact, by the eighteenth century there were hardly any canons of Salzburg of such lowly rank. When Mozart's arch-enemy Archbishop Count Colloredo assumed office there were only two barons among them, but three princes: Hohenlohe, Lobkowitz and Schwarzenberg, and the remainder sounded like a roll-call of the Austrian nobility.'

We came to a halt in the middle of the Chapter Square. The fortress above us seemed to be floating on a dark sea. 'This morning', said the cellist, 'I called on Michael Haydn, Nannerl Mozart and Sigmund Haffner in the world's most enchanting cemetery.'

'Don't forget the grocer Hagenauer', said his friend, 'or perhaps I should say: the importer of luxury foods, in whose house Mozart was born. I also poked around and discovered the graves of Abbot Johannes Staupitz, who I now learn was Luther's superior in his religious order and also his confessor in Wittenberg. There is the excellent baroque composer Paul Hofheimer. And General Collins, commander of the Rainbow Division, who marched into Salzburg in 1945 and determined to be buried here: which, twenty-one years later, he was. Salzburg gave him a grave of honour. Why?'

'This is not as odd as it seems,' I said. 'Once it had shaken down, the American occupation of Salzburg became a most amicable and co-operative affair. Someone with a light touch should write a comparative social history of the Austrian zones of allied occupation from 1945 to 1955.'

'Didn't we bomb Salzburg?' asked the violinist doubtfully.

'The western allies did drop a number of singularly pointless bombs which were meant for the railway station. One or two hit the Cathedral. Nowadays'—we were walking back to the car which we had parked outside the Goldener Hirsch—'there is a quite different problem. Many of the old houses are crumbling under their own weight, and the town council faces an almost desperate challenge. A number of houses are in a dangerous state, and the owners and tenants have little interest in investing large sums in internal restoration and conversion; they would often prefer to live in a sunnier place, away from these narrow lanes.'

As we got into the car the cellist hung back. 'Let me say goodbye to my beloved horses. I adore this wonderful background. Did ever a horse drink at a more beautiful fountain?'

'It solved a practical difficulty,' I said. 'Fischer von Erlach was faced by an ugly warehouse behind the fountain which spoiled the look of the whole square. He built the high screen to conceal it, and the equestrian scenes were painted to relieve the plain white marble.'

As we drove out of the sleeping town the stars were beginning to pale.

If on a clear, sunny day, a visitor were to declare that he had only five minutes to spend in Salzburg but insisted on admiring one matchless view and taking one photograph, there could be only one answer. He should be led, ignoble creature though he must be, to the Mirabell Garden, told to stand with his back to the home of Salome Alt, and look. He would see, framed by two baroque flower vases on pillars, the formal eighteenth-century garden with its glowing planes of colour, a tall, swaying column of water in the central fountain, the whole enclosed by stone figures and a high formal hedge. Beyond, the twin towers of the cathedral, and, dominating the whole view, the fortress of Salzburg. The effect is theatrical, calculated and hardly leaves room for improvement.

What would the women's magazines make of Salome Alt if she were alive today? Consider the situation. She was said to be the most beautiful woman of her time. She was virtuous, loyal and discreet, and she bore her husband many children of whom ten survived infancy. An alluring touch of mystery owing to her unapproachability would compensate in news value for her mono-tonous domesticity and allow speculative innuendo to alternate with praise of such single-minded devotion to husband and family in the midst of a permissive society. But Salome's very existence was an excruciating source of scandal, tabu then and tabu today: she was the wife of that Archbishop of Salzburg whom we met earlier, Wolf Dietrich von Raitenau.

Salome Alt was born in 1568, the seventh child of Wilhelm Alt, Salzburg merchant and town councillor. The story may be true that Wolf Dietrich seduced and to all intents and purposes abducted her one day while she was in the palace on business for her father. At all events she was settled in a wing of the palace, and the archbishop's passionate dependence on her became such that they went through a form of marriage. Later, as all the world knows, he built Mirabell (it was called Altenau) so that she should have a house of her own and the children a garden to play in. But what form of marriage was this? The semi-official version is that, at the time, he had only taken minor vows. But there is another, according to which von Raitenau, already in office as archbishop, ordered a Cathedral canon to marry them secretly, under the pretext that a dispensation from the Pope had been applied for and received. Salome probably half believed him because she wanted to, but the canon, according to this story, never did. He suffered agonies of remorse and finally committed suicide. Salome certainly played the part of a lawful spouse until the day of her husband's downfall: twenty years during which she sat on his right at table even in the presence of foreign statesmen. If she was the strictly brought up, pious middle-class girl that tradition alleges, her profoundly anomalous position—it cut her off completely from her own kind—must have troubled her, but the legitimization of the children by the Emperor Rudolf II will have consoled her greatly. To imagine Salome standing on the terrace of Mirabell and gazing miserably up at the fortress in which her Wolf Dietrich was held prisoner, is fortunately quite unhistorical. When the crisis came Wolf Dietrich sent her and the youngest children out of the province into Carinthia. He tried to follow them but was betrayed and captured. Marcus Sitticus left her in peace and she spent her remaining years in Wels.

The parks and gardens of Salzburg: it is difficult now to imagine the time when, mile after mile, one led on to another. To list the country houses of the nobility and gentry in the purlieus of the town would be wearisome, but there were at least fifty: seven along the avenue towards the choicest pearl of all, Hellbrunn, eight on the Mönchsberg, eight round the Kapuzinerberg, five in Gnigl, five in Parsch and Aigen, and many others in a wider radius. Some of these chateaux, built usually for the use of relations or retainers of the archbishops, by Cathedral canons or wealthy town burghers, went through long periods of decline, and some never recovered their original dignity while others have been lovingly restored by their recent or present owners; one example is Anif. Leopoldskron was commissioned by Archbishop Count Firmian in 1736 as a home for his nephew, but only a century later it had come into the hands of the owner of a series of shooting booths, who sold off everything of value including the collection of paintings. Later, we hear of a head waiter as *bourgeois gentilhomme* in residence, of ex-King Ludwig I of Bavaria, a writer, a notary public and a banker; at intervals the great rococo mansion was used as a public bath and for prayer meetings. At last—and there are very few men to whom Salzburg owes as much as it does to this genius of the theatre—Max Reinhardt brought Leopoldskron back to life. A rather sadly futile ghost haunts Klessheim Castle. In 1866 the Emperor Franz Josef, unable to tolerate the presence of his youngest brother Ludwig Viktor ('Lootsy Wootsy') in Vienna, banished him to Klessheim. Apart from occasional visits to his town house on the Schwarzenbergplatz, here he lived, a recluse surrounded by servants and a vast art collection, until his death in January 1919. That these treasures, in the same way as the original contents of Leopoldskron, were sold off for a fraction of their value, is of no great consequence now, but it is sad that a number of the personal possessions of Salome Alt were among them. They went to a Spanish destination: where are they now?

To have to sweep on without another word about the exotic characters who lived in these castles and mansions in the neighbourhood of Salzburg is almost intolerable, but space must be found for the 'Hundsgräfin'. To anyone who can claim, at the least, a Welsh grandparent, the Austrian custom of bundling together appellation and association to form an epigrammatic whole is as natural as it is convenient. When Eva Kraus was born in 1785 at Idria in Croatia she may soon have come to love dogs but she was far from being a countess; her father was a miner. By 1805 Eva had succeeded in finding a niche in Schönbrunn, and so, in a sense, had Napoleon Buonaparte, whose entry into the capital of the Habsburg Empire took place in that year. Napoleon was evidently dazzled by her. He ordered a portrait of the miner's daughter as 'Venus in Repose' by the court artist von Lampi, and there is even a story that he married her—yet another in the series of thoroughly tiresome weddings which have cropped up in these pages; it will not be the last. Married or not, when Napoleon left Vienna he took Eva with him dressed as an imperial adjutant, and as such she accompanied him on all his campaigns. Safely, for the moment, at Versailles, she gave birth to a child, and Napoleon bestowed on her 480,000 florins and the title of Baroness von Wolfsberg. When in 1812 separation became inevitable, Eva lived successively in Vienna, Bregenz and Salzburg, but in 1828 she bought the 'Rauchenbichlerhof' in Gnigl near the town. It seems to have taken three years for the house and grounds to be brought up to her standards. At first, she maintained an almost regal though thoroughly eccentric style of living. House and garden were alive with cats and dogs, all eating off silver dishes and sleeping on silken cushions until, at last, they were laid to rest in a specially constructed mausoleum in the park. Meanwhile, however, Eva's former guardian, Philipp von Mainoni, had been playing fast and loose with her capital, and having gambled it all away he committed suicide. The great days were over. There was now nothing to be done but to sell off the pictures and furnishings. A small pension granted by Franz I would have been enough to live on, but she sank into a state of extreme eccentricity, culminating in mental derangement and squalor. Poor Eva the Dog Countess was now living in a cottage in the grounds, where, on 15th April 1845, in bitter poverty, she died.

The Rupertiwinkel—literally 'St Rupert's Nook'—is the patch of Bavarian land containing Bad Reichenhall and Berchtesgaden which must be traversed to reach Lofer and the road over Pass Strub to the Tyrol, or beyond Lofer to Zell-am-See. There is an alternative, inland route to the Grossglockner over Pass Lueg

and along the valley of the Salzach. This intrusive tongue of
alien ground dividing Salzburg from a large sector of its own
province was always a nuisance and it still is. Each of the low
hill passes, each narrow defile into the Pinzgau has been bitterly
contested, in the days of the present revolts, in the Napoleonic
wars and even in 1945. It was in that year of the collapse of the
Third Reich that the mayor of a certain village in the vicinity
proposed to abolish the nuisance by seizing the Rupertiwinkel for
Austria. Leaving aside the fact that Austria has no historical
claim to any part of Bavaria, it was the kind of mad idea which
might conceivably have been successful. If Austrian resistance
fighters could have taken possession of Reichenhall, staking even a
token claim to the alpine redoubt while the front between the
armies was in flux and before the entry of the Americans, the
history of Salzburg might have taken a different turn. But the local
men were at the war fronts. The passes, every road, every forest
path on these approaches to Berchtesgaden were held by SS units.
The whole area was crammed with troops in retreat from the
western front. By May 1945 all means of civil communication by
rail, post, telephone and radio had ceased to function and movement
by civilians was almost impossible. Otto Skorzeny was at Weissbach, Fieldmarshal Kesselring and his staff were at Alm near
Saalfelden. What could a band of local patriots, fired by the deeds
of their ancestors against Napoleon's allies, do under such conditions? And what would the American staff officers say to a
concerted rush by the Men of the Pinzgau to occupy St. Rupert's
Nook? The mayor was, and doubtless still is, a romantic, but
also an Austrian patriot of the old school; may his like never die
out.

Even now there are some remarkably lonely stretches along
this Lofer road. Whoever doubts this should try driving along it
late in the evening, in bad weather, in a car which is giving audible
warning of incipient breakdown. The emptiness is most striking
between Weissbach and Saalfelden where, on the flat valley floor,
road and river are on almost the same level. In autumn, the steeply
rising forest contains a most fortunate mixture of conifer and
deciduous trees, their shades ranging through pale lemon, deep

crimson and rust. Even on a rainy day, it is as though one were driving through a sea of flame. On a summer night, after an evening at the Salzburg Festival, Unken, Lofer and Weissbach are asleep. We had lingered overlong in Salzburg, it is now after three o'clock, and as the valley broadens a point of light shows in the back bedroom of a farm. A mile or two further on, the back bedroom of another farm is in darkness but light in the kitchen shows that someone is preparing the first breakfast. Further on still, the windows of a front bedroom shine out. The farmer and his wife are up: for them, the day has begun.

Until now there have seemed to be few ways out of this narrow valley. At Unken, it would be easy to overlook the entry to the Heutal, a broad basin leading off into a number of side valleys and ravines. An old Baedeker describes the Schwarzbergklamm as the most magnificent gorge in the 'German' alps—a strong claim in this particular district. It was made accessible by Ludwig of Bavaria, but later on the approaches fell into disuse and the place was left to the eagles, the harriers and the eagle owls. And to Something Else. It was 'behind the Fuchslehen in Unken' in the year 1779 that a certain Hans Fuchs was chased by *Tatzelwürmer* (semi-mythical creatures which appear frequently in alpine folk-lore) and died of fright. The horrid event is recorded on a memorial tablet, and a local chronicler remarks that *Tatzelwürmer* are as swift as their bite is poisonous and the best way to escape them is to run in a zig-zag course. A still better plan would be to make straight for the old coaching inn and have a drink. The owners still cherish a red cut-glass goblet with a silver lid, presented by the Empress Maria Anna when she was in flight from the revolution of 1848. The gift was a token of gratitude to the innkeeper's wife for having lent her a raincoat.

But no country inn in this part of Austria can easily compete with the 'Bräu' at Lofer. The name is all that remains of a flourishing brewing industry in the village which used to supply the whole of the Pinzgau with from eleven to twelve thousand casks (each containing 56 litres) of beer every year. Brewing ceased, unfortunately, in 1926. The 'Bräu' has only one conceivable disadvantage, that it is usually crammed with customers, but the souvenirs of the

Napoleonic wars in the Tirolerstube should be inspected even if it means treading on the feet of fellow guests to get at them. If there is no room at all, there are rival establishments such as the Steiner-wirt which displays the following motto: 'God bless thy coming in if thou art thirsty, God bless thy going out if thou hast paid the bill.'

The mildly alarming drive up to the Loferer Alm—the biggest common pasture in the Pinzgau which has been in full use since the fifteenth century—is well worth while for a close view of the gleaming grey flanks of the three-pronged Loferer Steinberg. The whole floor of the Lofer valley was once a lake. A large piece of the Grubhörndl mountain broke off and thundered down to the valley bed where it blocked the course of the Salzach river, a cataclysm which explains the noisy turbulence of the Salzach at Lofer as well as the rocks of all sizes that lie scattered about the Bairau, the nature park beyond the Devil's Bridge. Reference to the Devil reminds one that in 1943 the head of the valley was made a closed area in which research was carried out into acoustic death rays. Using a reflector over three yards across, super-sonic waves were to be used to paralyse the nerve centres of ground troops over a distance of several miles while aircraft pilots could be attacked in the same way. The experiments were unsuccessful.

Under the modern pressures of life the old ways are disappearing at a startling rate. The most striking loss is the traditional Salzburg farmhouse with the stone and mortar base and timber first floor. One particular valley contained eight farms of this type only ten or fifteen years ago. Now they have all gone, to be replaced by modern houses which, while not necessarily unpleasing, have lost the original proportions of breadth to height. The first houses had no chimneys. A shallow depression in the stone surface of the open cooking range contained the fire, and the smoke escaped as best it could among the rafters, pickling them as it went. A few of these stoves are still to be found in huts on the high pastures, but soon, entirely unregretted, they will have gone for ever. The huts too—models of the normal housing built by the early colonizers—are on the way out: how many young people, today, are willing

9a. Archduke Johann, his wife Anna *née* Plochl and their son Franz, Graf Meran

9b. The Empress Maria Theresa with her eldest daughter, the Archduchess Maria Anna, in about 1768

10. The Danube in Lower Austria

to live for months in the loneliness of the mountains, with no comforts other than they can carry up on their backs? But where this way of life is disappearing, so is one of the most moving sights of the farming year: the *Almabtrieb* in early autumn, when the cattle are brought back to the farm, the leaders sounding their bells and wearing gaily beribboned wreaths of alpine flowers round their horns.

The whole countryside between Saalfelden and Zell-am-See is unusually rich in folklore because this was one of the first districts in the mountains of Land Salzburg, and the first in the Pinzgau, to be colonized in the Middle Ages. Until recently *Brettlrutschen* could still be heard as a euphemism for death. The *Brettl* was the plank on which the corpse was carried to its place of burial and slid (*rutschen*) into the grave. The plank, with the name and dates of birth and death of the deceased, was then nailed to the outside wall of his barn to serve as a memorial. The 1,300-year-old custom was confined to a small strip of country stretching roughly from Maishofen to Alm near Saalfelden, across to Leogang and over to the Hirschbühel above Weissbach, but now the last of them are rotting in the sun and wind and soon the last of them will have been thrown away. I have found a variant of this custom near Faistenau (above Fuschl) where the planks, all with serrated edges, were nailed lengthwise to a tree standing where two lanes forked. The pre-Christian *Perchten*, the most weird of all the masked figures in Austrian folklore—the irregular staccato rhythm of their unaccompanied dance was used by Bruckner in the scherzo of his fourth symphony—will be kept alive by tourism. But one local survival owes nothing to the interest of foreigners: the *Frautragen*. In the week before Christmas a painting of the pregnant Virgin Mary is brought from one farm to another to commemorate the Holy Family's search for lodging. The new hosts greet it with ceremony, set it up in a prepared place of honour and recite prayers before it. On the following evening the picture is handed on to the next house, perhaps at a considerable distance. I once took a rather unseemly part in the *Frautragen*. In the Schmitten valley at Zell-am-See the picture is contained in a case with a glass front and is held to the carrier's back by leather straps. An evening visit to the village by toboggan happened to coincide with the emergence of the farmer with the holy picture (invisible in the pitch dark) on his back. An invitation to join in the ride was accepted and, the farmer being extremely heavy and the descent steep, a most unnerving trip *à trois* followed during which the composure of the small party fell short of that which the occasion demanded.

The annual wrestling contests held on 25th July on the summit of the Hundstein are also a purely native occasion and will remain so until the rest of us either regain the use of our legs or a cable car can carry us to the top.

The legend about the lake of Zell-am-See tells that there was once a castle, with a chapel beside it, standing among green fields and surrounded by a wall. The count who owned it had two daughters, one of whom was blind. When the count died his daughters quarrelled over their inheritance, and the one who could see took deceitful advantage of her sister. At last the blind girl called upon the heavens to revenge the injustice. There came violent hailstorms, the mountain streams turned into torrents, the rising waters began to fill the valley, and when at last the storms ceased and the skies cleared, the castle had vanished beneath the waters. Fishermen say that sometimes, when the surface is quite still, they have seen the castle and the spire of the chapel. Perhaps they have. But the lake is a uniform 200 feet deep and during most of the warm months of the year plankton obscures the view into the depths. It is safer to picture the original creator of this valley and of the lake's cavity: a tremendous glacier, three thousand feet deep, above which only the tips of the Hundstein and the Schmittenhöhe protrude.

This lake's setting is surely the most superb in the entire Austrian alpine region. Allowing for a certain personal bias, there are perfectly good reasons why this should be so. Zell lies at the junction between the crystalline central range and the limestone alps, and there could hardly be a more striking contrast in any landscape than the Kitzsteinhorn with its glacier, and the grey, precipitous cliff of the Steinernes Meer. The Kitzsteinhorn has personality: it must have been even more awe-inspiring in an earlier age when the alps were far higher than they are now. In late summer it becomes a little tatty, but the reward for rain in the valley will be the sight of a new sprinkling of snow on the glacier. In summer or winter, but most of all in the clear light of early autumn, the reflection of the setting sun on the Steinernes Meer and the Leogang limestone range is no less impressive than the more celebrated alpine glow in the Dolomites. When the first blush of pink begins to creep across these sheer cliff faces the sun has already left the valleys. As the dusk falls and a breath of mist rises in the meadows, the glow deepens until the lower slopes and the crevices turn a deep purple. Gradually, the intensity fades and only the highest peaks are still touched with pink, then the last of the sunset has gone, and the watcher can turn for home.

The lake of Zell seldom freezes over until the middle of January, and it may happen slowly so that it is impossible to row across but the ice is not yet firm, or the ice may set in a matter of hours. After a time it will thicken to a depth of about fifteen inches, but even ten inches are enough to stand the strain of the annual car races, ski-jöring and other events. Where warm gases rise from the lake bed a number of holes remain in the ice, the most celebrated being the *Pfaffenloch*, the Parson's Hole into which a priest fell together with his sledge. He was drawn under the ice but managed to work his way back to the open water.

The last war left a remarkable human deposit in Thumersbach. There was a Lithuanian professor of art history with his Australian wife; there was a group of nuclear scientists who were wooed by both the Americans and the Russians and finally divided equitably into two almost equal portions; one or two former mistresses of Nazi leaders who were executed at Nüremberg lived there; anti-Nazis emerged from concealment and planned a new life. Unknown to the rest, a young man was working in the district as a farm labourer. He would later enter a monastery, be ordained at the 'Pinzgau Cathedral', Maria Kirchental, in 1958, and would devote his life to making amends for the deeds of his father, *Reichsleiter* Martin Bormann. There was a German general who lived in a hut, kept a goat and a Latvian peasant wife whom he did not allow to sit down while he and his bridge partners ate. He had a habit of letting off his rifle across the road, but was compelled to stop his target practice when residents complained of having to fling themselves down into muddy puddles. A tubby individual of Balkan origin began to organize his life on parallel lines: fruit machines in the fashionable resorts, and female all-in wrestling contests for which he hoped to find a public in Vienna. During his frequent absences on business his wife ran a nice line in porno-graphic pictures and his unspeakable little boy terrorized the household with a carving knife. Returning home one day across the frozen lake, the Balkan gentleman was unlucky enough to fall into one of the holes. There he remained for some minutes; his body, however, was kept at a surprising height above water level owing to the presence of air enclosed between his person and the inside of his fur coat. His cries for help—he was very close to the shore—were soon heard by some boys who rushed to his assist-ance bearing oars. Whether the poor man now gave way to panic or whether he was merely struggling to extricate himself, is uncertain. A neighbour distinctly heard the boys shouting 'Hit him hard—hit him over the head!' They explained later that they had been told always to bang a drowning man on the head so as to render him unconscious. The story ends happily. The corpulent entrepreneur in his sodden furs was laid upon an undersized toboggan, carefully propelled along the lakeside road and handed over to his wife and child whose greeting, as it was spoken in an alien tongue, was not recorded.

To live on the edge of that lake, as we did for five years, is to understand why the early inhabitants sensed the presence of demons all around them. Sometimes on a winter night there would be a reverberating bang, followed by a groaning howl which seemed to float across the lake on two sound levels: a deep, grinding 'arrrh' rising to a high, whining 'hoo-hoo-hoo-oo'. It is a sound to make the small hairs rise on the nape of ones neck, but the cause is quite simple: shrinkage of the ice away from the surface of the water, resulting in tremendous stress and friction.

All over Austria, on all the lakes, the old boats are disappearing. The few remaining flat-bottomed boats on the lake at Zell are seldom to be seen with the rower standing in the stern, manipulating

the single oar with its broad, curved blade; they are usually rowed
in the normal way. Even this calls for some skill because in
unpractised hands there is a tendency to go round in circles.

The view from the top of the Schmittenhöhe is unrivalled in
Land Salzburg—perhaps there is no finer panorama in Europe.
The Grossvenediger, Kitzsteinhorn, Hohe Tenn, Wiesbachhorn,
the Grossglockner—all the great names in the Tauern range—link
up with the limestone alps. The Honigkogel behind Thumersbach
is a humble thing compared with these giants, but it has two curious
claims to distinction. It is the highest wooded mountain in Europe,
and it marks the geographical centre of the continent.

One of the well-known sights of Zell-am-See, being mortal,
cannot survive much longer to be photographed by tourists, if
indeed he is still alive at this moment: 'Wurzel-Sepp', a craggy
ancient with matted hair, wearing greasy buckskin shorts and a
mountaineer's hat with chamois brush and a cluster of brooches
and badges. He carries in his hand and offers for sale a bundle of
tuberous roots, the medicinal properties of which are fairly
comprehensive but concentrate mainly on the digestive tract. But
the contents of his knapsack is more interesting. Here he has a
few pieces of rock crystal, one or two fragments of gold ore, and
possibly a small emerald, still embedded in the parent rock.

In the folklore of the Tauern range there are many stories of
mountain caves lined with crystal. In essence, they are true. The
local historian Josef Lahnsteiner has described his amazement
as he shone a torch into a crevice of the Knappenwand near
Neukirchen in the Krimml valley, and saw 'a profusion of sticks
and staves, of needles, cones and hairs, shining, sparkling, glitter-
ing and glowing with unimaginable grandeur'. Much of the
sparkle came from rock crystal, from opaque white or water clear
calcite; the colours, from apatite crystal which can be green, blue,
violet or brown. The 'sticks and staves' were green, black or, more
typically, pistaccio-coloured epidote. By the time epidote crystals
have reached the geological museums of the world they have
usually lost the long, fine byssolite hairs which hang from them in
their natural surroundings. Aquamarines used to be found in the

neighbourhood, and garnets, though the great place for garnets was always the Zillertal in Tyrol—they used to be of higher quality, even, than the garnets of Bohemia, and were regularly exported to Bohemia where they were sold as the local product.

The district of Rauris, famous for its gold mines since the days of the Romans, must have delivered up thousands of samples of rock crystal, sometimes weighing as much as fifty pounds. Among more than seventy types of mineral there is bright green and yellow titanite, pyramid-shaped, honey-yellow anatase, pale green euclase, which in its rarer forms may be wine-yellow. There is the smoky and the clear topaz—and, most precious of all, rock crystal laced with threads of pure gold.

Compared with the great collections formed in the past, the bits and pieces owned by the Ancient of Zell are modest indeed, and they reflect the unfortunate truth that the seams have run out and the glory is over. One precious stone remains. According to legend it was the source of the fabulous wealth of the Pharaohs and of Cleopatra: the emerald. There are emerald mines in Columbia and beyond the Urals, but in Europe there is one place only where they can be found—in the Habachtal, a side valley which we pass on the way to the Krimml waterfalls. Twenty-four Habachtal emeralds are set in the seventeenth-century monstrance in Salzburg Cathedral, there are others among the British as well as the Habsburg crown jewels, in Mattsee Abbey and in the Natural History Museum in Salzburg. Attempts have been made in recent years to start up new, systematic workings in the valley, but without success. The difficulty is that poor quality stones, including unsightly grey beryls, are easy to come by, while emeralds of even comparative purity were always rare and have not been found for many years.

There was no gold rush in Rauris. The constant erosion of the mountain crags brought grains of gold into many mountain streams, particularly into the stream known as the Rauriser Ache, and thence into the Salzach. Panning for gold was known in earliest times and in the Middle Ages (again according to J. Lahnsteiner) some farms in the Lungau district had to pay a proportion of their rent in gold. 'Norican gold' was certainly known is the time of the Greek historian Polybius (140 B.C.), and when in 1955 a cache of 164 Roman gold coins were discovered in Villach they were considered as evidence of Roman workings in Noricum. The heyday of gold-mining in the Rauris and Gastein area lasted for a little under a hundred years, from 1460 to 1558, and by the end of the sixteenth century a rapid decline set in which had a considerable effect on the whole social history of Land Salzburg. The quantity of ore extracted before the invention of gunpowder was extraordinary, and over the centuries the technique seems to have changed very little. The late bronze age copper miners at Viehofen near Saalbach, for instance, used the same methods as the workers in the Rauris area. A section of rock was heated by building a fire at its base, then the ashes were removed and water thrown over the rock face, causing it to crack, when wooden blocks would be hammered into the crevices and lumps made to break off. It is estimated that, in this way, a million tons of ore were removed from shafts totalling one hundred kilometres in length. The privations suffered by the two thousand or so miners can be imagined, considering the high altitude at which they were working and the long trudge to and from the mine, and the fact that every scrap of ore had to be brought down to the valley in leather skins which, tied sixteen in a row, were dragged down the slopes to the smelting works.

The thought of eagles wheeling across the ridges of the Tauern range makes the heart lift. Vultures are quite another matter, and that these unlovable birds should go about their business in Austria is surprising. One associates them with Africa, or, at the nearest, with the more remote areas of the Balkans. But each spring, when the sheep and cattle are brought to the high pastures, the vultures arrive as from nowhere, and there they stay, watching intently for carrion, until late-September. They were first sighted in the Stubach valley in 1878 when heavy snowfalls caused the death of hundreds of sheep. Suddenly, between thirty and forty white-headed vultures—they must have sensed the catastrophe from hundreds of miles off—turned up for the feast. Similar storms in 1899 and in 1903 brought them again in strength, and for many years they confined their attentions to this one small area.

The construction of the dams and the hydro-electric power stations after the war disturbed them, and now they circle over the wider area between the Gross-Venediger and the Grossglockner.

It is no use waiting to see what the weather is like on a July or August morning and then deciding for or against a trip to the Grossglockner. It is better to go to bed early, leaving the decision to the hotel porter, and, if woken, to be off early: at seven, or better, at six. Snap decisions are for May and June, or September. If tackled calmly, and with even moderate skill, this miracle of road engineering with its builder's characteristic device of a level run out after every bend, will carry one past boiling radiators, hissing sadly on the verge, up to the scarred, mossy region far above the timber belt. This is a sombre, soul-chilling world where the vegetation is thin and poor, it is not a zone which can support much life of any kind. Once the flowers and the juniper bushes have been left behind, the road is sometimes lined by boulders and scree. It is tempting to stop by a small mountain tarn and to look into its black waters, but on leaving the car the cold lays hold of one's ankles with an icy grasp. There is something consoling about the man-made solidity of the Hochtor tunnel which leads 'Onward, where the rude Carinthian boor / Against the houseless stranger shuts the door.'

National frontiers have sometimes been laid down by wicked men, more often they are the result of cupidity and ignorance; the inhabitants have seldom been asked. Provincial boundaries are usually less dramatic, perhaps quite unnoticeable, though they may mark a deep cleavage between peoples. No one could fail to notice this one. We are looking into another Austrian province, which, again, is so unlike the others.

But we can leave all that for the moment. The important thing is to push on and turn towards the Franz Josefs Höhe, the Pasterze glacier and the Grossglockner.

Black dots near the far shore—many groups of climbers follow one another up the Glockner until early afternoon—give an idea of the extent of this great sea of ice, all thirty square kilometres of it. Could anything be more motionless, rigid and devoid of all life? But the glacier is constantly in motion, not noticeably of course, but measurements prove it: slowly at the edges, a little faster at the centre as one would expect of what this is—a river of ice—and shrinking all the time. It is not totally lifeless, either, being host to a creature known as the glacier flea, whose means of support, visible or otherwise, need not detain us. Human life, on these promenades and terraces, is however abundant, but it can be evaded by walking through a doorway the existence of which is known to surprisingly few, into the nature reserve. Gone are the excursion buses, the kiosks, the sausages and beer, the flags fluttering in the breeze. A piercing whistle comes from the grassy slope between the path and the glacier, but it is only a marmot, warning his family of our presence. Until now there were few birds to be seen, but now they reappear: alpine jackdaws tumble in the air, and where there is outcropping rock, brightly coloured stone-creepers edge their way along the crevices. The flowers may not be picked, still less dug up by the roots and concealed in the picnic basket. Edelweiss will not be found here; they can be bought in pots at the souvenir stands. Gentians—type, situation and altitude depending on the time of year—are mere *hoi polloi* compared to the delicate and much less ubiquitous soldanella. But the observant walker on this six-mile-long road beside the glacier will notice unfamiliar plants among the more inconspicuous varieties of flower and grass. This is because the shrinkage of the Pasterze has produced conditions such as they were over great stretches of Europe at the end of the last ice age.

The pull of the South is strong. To swirl down now, straight-away, to Heiligenblut and beyond, would be one solution. But the plan may be different: though the Mallnitz tunnel, or past Radstadt and Obertauern, past the milestones which marked the way for Septimus Severus and his armies, and over the Katsch-berg. We have had our fill of great altitudes, the cold breath of glaciers and black mountain pools. We could do with a more relaxing climate, with warm lakes whose waters have not been drawn from the fringe of the eternal snows or from the depths of the alps.

5

Carinthia

Carinthia is a land of Romanesque and overdue Gothic architecture in which the question, who built what and why, is more confusing than anywhere else in Austria. This is partly because Carinthia was not re-Christianized by one spiritual overlord but by several. Maria-Saal was founded in the latter half of the eighth century by St. Modestus who was sent there from Salzburg; Friesach was a favourite residence of the bishops of Salzburg throughout the Middle Ages, and Gurk owed, but also violently repudiated, the same allegiance; Villach with large areas of land belonged to the distant see of Bamberg. One way and another there were Bavarians, Swabians, eastern and western Franks, men from Lorraine and Saxony, clerical and lay, all vying with one another to skim off the richer fiefs, and building churches and monasteries: Millstatt, Arnoldstein, Viktring, St. Paul in the Lavant valley, Griffen, Ossiach, Gurk, and castles of all dimensions. Powerful families such as the Eppensteins and the Sponheims enjoy a brief term of glory and abruptly leave the stage.

Among all this bustling cast one unforgettable figure stands out, for all its antiquity perhaps the most celebrated in the history of Carinthia: the Holy Hemma. The only daughter of an earl of Friesach and Zeltschach, Hemma lived as a child in Friesach castle. She lost both parents at an early age and the Emperor Henry II and his wife Kunigunde took over responsibility for her upbringing and education. She was now heiress to large freehold estates containing rich workings of iron ore, silver and lead, and these were soon united with the properties of the man she married,

Count Wilhelm von Sanngau. Her son was murdered (according to the legend, both sons) and when soon afterwards her husband died also, Hemma was left with vast possessions in Carinthia, in upper and lower Styria, in Carniola and Friaul, but with no heir. More than six hundred years later, another Carinthian woman would find herself in the same position, but she chose another way to dispose of her wealth. Stricken with grief, Hemma embarked on a truly staggering programme. Eight parish churches, one unfinished, were built with her money, but her real love was the convent in a quiet valley at Gurk, which she peopled with nuns from the Nonnberg in Salzburg. Nothing is left of these first buildings and her intentions were soon set aside by the Church, but the stone survives on which Hemma sat and watched the work as it progressed, and it is known that she paid out the wages personally once a week. She entered her convent as a Benedictine nun and died there, one of the most revered holy women of the Middle Ages, in 1045. Her beatification was pronounced in the thirteenth century, but her canonization had to wait until 1938, by a strange coincidence the same year in which her great posthumous foundation, Admont, which grew up on the site of her castle Purgstall in Styria, was confiscated by the Gestapo.

Ursus spectabilis might be the words on a notice posted up by a bear of riper years outside his winter residence in the Karawanken mountains. But His Respectability was not a title to be lightly usurped (nor is it today; it is the prerogative of the pro-rector of an Austrian university). It proves that Ursus, who commissioned the mosaic floor at Teurnia, was governor of Upper Carinthia, the western section of the province which we have approached by the road from Heiligenblut and the Grossglockner.

St. Peter im Holz is a small village on a hill beside the River Drau (Drave) near Spittal, on the site of a town which was fortified at a time when Carinthia, with the increasing pressure of the Germanic tribes on the Roman line of defence along the Danube, suddenly took on the aspect of a northern outpost of southern culture. Teurnia became a bishopric under Aquileia in A.D. 400, and in 480 we hear of church collections being made for the benefit of the distressed Christian communities on the Danube beyond the sheltering Tauern range. Practically nothing is known of the original cathedral, the foundations of which probably lie under the village church of St. Peter, but the cemetery church, excavated and in part reconstructed, makes it possible to visualize the original scene. Here Ursus and his wife Ursulina laid down the most enchanting mosaic floor ever to have been uncovered in a German-speaking country.

Spittal, with its Italianate palace, Schloss Porcia, is on the way to our most likely destination, the lake of Millstatt. Here the Romanesque cloisters should not be skimped but visited in peace and preferably often, so that the disturbing faces on the carved pillars can sink into one's mind. Originally a Benedictine abbey founded between 1070 and 1090 by two Bavarian counts, Millstatt became the principal cultural centre in upper Carinthia and is known to scholars as the home of the Millstatt Manuscript which has been in the possession of the Historical Society of Carinthia since 1845. It consists of a Genesis, a rhymed Physiologus, an Exodus, two long poems, a Paternoster and another poetic fragment, in all 167 parchment leaves. The Genesis, a free rendering of the first book of Moses, is the oldest example of German poetry in Austria, and some of the texts—sermons preached by the missionaries—give a vivid impression of the daily life of the listeners in the congregation.

A fresco on one of the pillars in the church at Millstatt shows St. Domitian, Duke of Carantania. He is wearing a halo round the cap of his rank and he towers above the abbey church of Millstatt which, so the story goes, he built on the site of a heathen temple boasting a thousand statues. The fresco is genuine late Gothic, but the story is as false as it is indestructible; a public relations gambit which outgrew the intentions of its initiator, a matter of keeping up with the Sponheims who founded Viktring and St. Paul. A monk wrote it down, and it may have grown in the mind of the abbot Henry II Count Andechs who built part of the cloisters and the west door, and who can be seen on the tympanum above the doorway, presenting the monastery to the figure of Christ in Majesty. Ill-feeling towards the real founders may also have had something to do with the development of the legend, because the miracles ascribed to the tomb of Domitian show a distinctly anti-Bavarian trend. At all events, the cult of Domitian snowballed, by the fifteenth century he was being invoked in prayer even before the Mother of God, his feast day was observed with special litanies, sermons and songs, and he had practically become the patron saint of Carinthia. The fact that he had never been canonized was unfortunate but not unprecedented; the cult spread to Vienna and High Mass was said there in his honour throughout the greater part of the eighteenth century. The Jesuits took up his cause in Rome, but too late because by now they themselves were viewed with disfavour, and finally this rousing tale was relegated to the fiction shelves of the Vatican Library.

Millstatt is associated with a small and obscure community called the Knights of St. George, an order of chivalry which in spite of imperial and papal patronage failed to prosper and petered out at last for lack of recruits to its ranks. In an attempt to shore up the prestige of the knights of Millstatt, Maximilian I bestowed on them the castle at Landskron near Villach. But they lacked the money for its upkeep, and it was not long before they were obliged to relinquish it to the crown and it was bought in 1542 by the governor of Carinthia, Christoph von Khevenhüller. The men of this historic family, owners of Hochosterwitz, were to become deeply involved in the great drama of the age, the Reformation. Landskron had been neglected for some time. The constant threat of invasion by the armies of Islam made it essential to arrest the decay of such a strategically placed citadel, and Christoph rebuilt it to the extent that, in a few years' time, he was able to be host to the Emperor Charles V. To entertain the most powerful man in the western world was a triumph in itself. But after the death of Christoph Khevenhüller in 1557 his son Bartholomew went on building, and the four-storied castle with its high tower as it appears on seventeenth-century prints, is his work. Landskron became the meeting place not only of the aristocracy, but of men prominent in the Church, the sciences and politics. 'Barthlmä' was a leading exponent of Lutheranism in Carinthia at a time when it was possible to hold these views in peace. As time went on, practically the entire nobility of Austria, most of the townsfolk, the mining and industrial workers and a section of the peasantry went over to Lutheranism. Klagenfurt Cathedral was built as a Protestant church. The Emperor was inclined to tolerance, and the Archdukes Ferdinand and Maximilian stayed at Landskron as late as March 1613. In this province the great shock came with the Carinthian Mandate of 1st August 1628 which required every nobleman to return to the Catholic fold or sell his possessions and emigrate. Barthlmä had died in time, but his heir joined King Gustavus Adolphus and fought against the imperial armies. He was killed in action in 1632 before he could hear of the sentence for high treason pronounced against him in Vienna. The confiscation of Landskron was a family tragedy which was being repeated up and down the country as landowners left, leaving their estates to relations, selling them for what they could get or letting their houses stand empty. Landskron was taken over by a Count Dietrichstein, and there seemed no reason to suppose that this 'crown of the land' was doomed. But so it was. Since 1598 Millstatt had been owned by the Society of Jesus, which now staked a claim to Landskron, arguing that the Jesuits were the legal heirs to the Knights of St. George. This they were, but they had no claim whatever on Landskron and the Khevenhüllers' title deeds were perfectly in order. The Thirty Years War came to an end, and the general amnesty which was contained in the Treaty of Westphalia specifically mentioned the Khevenhüller estates. A legal battle began which was to drag on for forty years while the Khevenhüllers fought against the passive resistance of the Hofkammer, the Chamber of Finance in Vienna. Finally, they gave up, but the long insecurity of tenure placed the Dietrichsteins in an impossible position and naturally disinclined them to spend much on upkeep. In 1812 the castle was hit by lightning, the main roof was burned out and the enormous structure was allowed to disintegrate. A Carinthian writer, visiting Landskron some time before 1863, gave a careful description of the gaping ruins, noticing particularly the unusual, arcade-like arches in the surrounding wall. 'All this', he wrote, 'endows the entire edifice with a note of luxury, speaking eloquently of the wealth of its creator.'

On a clear day the view from the ruins of Landskron stretches across the green Treffner Feld, the plain which is divided by the Drau and Gail rivers, to the Karawanken mountains. There lies Villach in its amphitheatre, junction of the roads from Vienna and across the Tauern to Venice, hub of half a dozen valleys and indirectly of many more, a centre of trade therefore, a spa, and to the local nobility right up to the eighteenth century—for seven hundred years it was Bamberg property—a thorn in the flesh. It was a meeting place for foreign traders of many nations: Germans, Venetians, Friaulese, Lombardians; only the Jews were not allowed to sleep in the town. There are quite a number of villages in Austria, lying fairly close to larger settlements, which bear the prefix *Juden*, showing that this was a place where the presence of Jews was tolerated long enough for a permanent village to develop. (Judenburg, a town of some importance in Styria, may be an exception as a family with the name Jud existed in the locality.) The Jews of Judendorf near Villach buried their dead on a hill above the village, and one of the earliest medieval Jewish gravestones has been found there. In two of the excavated graves, two skulls still wore the remains of their golden hairnets.

Fire was the perpetual threat to close-packed towns, the one enemy before which people were all but helpless. It has been rightly said that if it had not been for the great fire of 1524, to say nothing of the bombs of the last war, Villach would have been a miniature Augsburg. The great mercantile dynasty of the Fuggers, without whose loans the Habsburgs could often have put up the shutters, were, as we have already seen, closely involved in the mines of Tyrol and Vorarlberg, they had an important trading office or *factorei* in Innsbruck, and they opened up other premises in Villach and near Arnoldstein at the alpine gateway to the road to Venice, where the ruined Arnoldstein monastery, also a Bamberg property, stands on the site of a fort built by a Count Eppenstein in 1106. The celebrated treasure of Arnoldstein is the mitre which used to be worn by the abbots on the high feasts of the Church. It was made at a time, during the first half of the fourteenth century, when embroidery reached a very high level. The whole surface of the mitre is covered in embroidery in brightly coloured silks on a gold thread groundwork, framed by closely set flat beads simulating pearls, and panelled with portraits of saints. (It is now in the Museum of Applied Arts in Vienna.) But it cannot be claimed as of local origin and is now thought to be Venetian. Perhaps the Venetian craftsmen wove the golden hairnets of Judendorf?

The great fire of 1524 was only a temporary setback to Villach which had entirely overtaken the old capital, St. Veit, in size and importance. On the crest of the wave of early capitalism, the town was resurrected in the spirit of the Italian renaissance, and wealth was created which, in its ultimate effect, had come down to the present day. Four influential families were involved in the boom. The founder of the Dietrichstein fortune (they began as *ministeriales* in the service of Bamberg) was Sigismund, a councillor and confidant of Maximilian I, who became governor of Styria. His wife's name was Barbara von Rottal, but it now seems to be proved beyond question that she was a natural daughter of Maximilian. The Khevenhüllers came from the upper Frankish lands, probably during the fourteenth century; trade and mining led on to purchase of extensive estates and appointment to high office. The magnificent tombs and monuments of these and other prominent families in St. Jacob's Church owe their survival to the courage of the elders of Villach. An Austrian scholar, Grete Mecenseffy, has proved that the texts on the monuments show pronounced Protestant leanings, and that for this reason orders were given during the Counter-Reformation for them to be destroyed. But the local authorities of both persuasions, clerical and lay, refused to desecrate the tombs, and once the crisis had passed, the issue was forgotten.

Other wealthy families in Villach during its boom years were the Widmanns, now Counts Foscari-Widmann of Venice and Paternion, whose ancestor Ulrich ran the Fugger business at Arnoldstein; and, by no means least, the Neumanns. And this is where the opposite number to Hemma of Gurk takes the stage: Anna Neumann.

During the early fifteenth century the Neumanns were still peasants, scraping a living on the Neumarkt Saddle above Friesach. By 1450 one or two members of the family had gone to Villach to seek their fortunes in trade. Gradually they worked their way up to patrician status, and like other wealthy business men of Villach

11. Heidenreichstein, the northern bastion

12. Melk Abbey after it had been completely rebuilt by Jakob Prandtauer

they intermarried with the leading families of Augsburg. Wilhelm Neumann accumulated a considerable fortune which was inherited by the daughter of his second marriage. Anna married six times. This comparatively rapid turnover gave rise to ugly rumour and suspicion among her numerous tenantry, though never among her peers, of poisoning or witchcraft. Her biographers consider that she was an extremely able administrator of her husbands' estates which had snowballed into her hands, and that she drove herself to work as a distraction from her grief over the death of her first four husbands whom, uncommon though this may have been, she had married (as she was beautiful as well as rich the choice was ample) for love. Having lost her only daughter, Anna found herself at the age of seventy-six a fourfold widow with great possessions and no heir other than a step-nephew who had married a nonentity; he was not, Anna thought, a promising founder of a dynasty. Her decision was soon made, and she now married a thirty-year-old man, Ferdinand von Salamanca, Count Ortenburg. Ferdinand's Spanish forebear Gabriel of Salamanca was a fabulously wealthy man in the imperial service; it was he who built the Renaissance Porcia palace at Spittal. Anna's whole intention, it must be realized, was to find a worthy heir, on the assumption that, after her death, the young widower would at once marry a girl who could put the old lady's ambitions into effect. Simply to have given away her estates to any local nobleman was not the answer. To her horror, the plan misfired because Ferdinand was tubercular and within five or six years he was dead. Anna, living at Murau Castle in Styria, was now eighty-two, and failing. There was little time to lose. An old friend, a statesman from the Imperial court, called on her and made a suggestion. How about the twenty-eight-year-old Count Georg Ludwig von Schwarzenberg, whose only barrier to a brilliant career in diplomacy was a lack of private means? Georg Schwarzenberg called at Murau, and she evidently liked what she saw. The odd pair were married. And on a day in October 1617 Anna made a will in which, with the exception of the estates at Wasserleonburg and Treffen which went to her step-nephew, she left to her young husband all her lands in Carinthia and Styria, the Bleiberg mines, her collection of *objets d'art*,

---

her invested capital, and letters of credit worth a fortune in themselves. The saintly Hemma founded churches and monasteries; Anna Neumann launched the most powerful family in the Austro-Hungarian empire. It is pleasant to think of them both arguing it all over in another world.

Carinthia is strewn with lakes, so much so that few people could list them without hesitation. Those with an international reputation come to mind at once: the Wörther See, Ossiacher See, Millstätter See; after a pause one might remember the Weissen See. There are the better-known smaller lakes: Faak and Klopein, the warmest of them all. Large hotels, plenty of night life, a casino perhaps? But for people who could not honestly direct the recording angel to 'write of me as one who loved his fellow men' there are still lakes in Carinthia round which the entire shores have not yet been bought up, built upon, encased in concrete, railed off—in a word, developed, and a little intelligent map-reading will show where they are. They will be rather far from the principal resorts on a third-class road. Perhaps this involves too much effort. Several attractive small lakes, ponds by comparison with the Wörther See, lie among the hills to the south, in a line with Keutschach, home of 'Turnip' Keutschach, sometime Archbishop of Salzburg. Viktring, a few miles on, the former Cistercian monastery, is now a factory. There was a celebrated abbot of Viktring, Johann II, who put his talents for diplomacy at the disposal of Margarete Maultasch during the struggle for the succession to the duchy of Tyrol, and he acted as her delegate to the Habsburg court. During the fourteenth century there was no German-speaking historian to compare with Johann of Viktring: he was to that era what Otto of Freising was to the earlier Middle Ages; his aim, as the scholar Nadler put it, was 'to discover what took place and how one event gave birth to another, to see through the designs of men and to watch the face of power as distinct from its actions'.

The road past Hollenburg castle leads down to the 'Valley of Roses', across the River Drau and on to the Ferlach village which in its time has contributed not a little to the provision of instruments of power. The famous gunsmiths of Ferlach have six hundred years of experience behind them. In all the crafts of men, generations of high excellence have tended to be followed by a decline, a coarsening of design, material and execution, but the villagers of Ferlach are still making shotguns and sporting rifles of superlative quality, and their master craftsmen teach their techniques to foreign apprentices as well as to their own. No records have survived to tell of the origins of this industry, but it is thought that Flemish or Wallonian gunsmiths were brought in during the fourteenth century from Liège. In the reign of Maria Theresa the guild numbered three hundred master craftsmen, and Ferlach reached its apogee during the Napoleonic wars when they were producing on an average twenty thousand rifles a year, a figure which obviously cannot be judged in terms of a mass production armament industry.

The fact that Carinthian architecture is principally of the Romanesque and late Gothic periods has a good deal to tell us about the life of the people. Lying at some distance from the main centres of clerical and lay government, a certain cultural time-lag was inevitable, and this combined with a general tendency to carry on and to develop further styles which, in other countries, were already being superseded. The Bamberg foundation Griffen, consecrated in 1272, was the last Romanesque structure to be built in Carinthia, and traditional Gothic curches were still being built as late as the beginning of the sixteenth century. From Heiligenblut in the west, its slender spire pointing up to the summit of the Grossglockner, containing one of the most awe-inspiring triptych altar screens in Austria, to St. Paul im Lavanttal where the windows in the tower, one above the other, give a precise illustration of the development from Romanesque to high Gothic, Carinthia is studded with masterpieces of these periods. There was a particular emphasis on stained glass and murals. The earliest surviving pane of stained glass in Austria (1170) is the St. Mary Magdalen from Weitensfeld near Gurk abbey, which is now in the diocesan museum at Klagenfurt. The west window of Gurk showing the Crucifixion was made about a hundred years later at Judenburg in Styria where a great deal of the stained glass in Carinthia originated; the 'Viktring cycle' came from the court workshops in Vienna and was made in 1400.

There are towns in Austria—one is reminded of Rattenberg in Tyrol—where a sudden economic depression brought public and private building to a standstill so that the following architectural style is almost entirely lacking. In Carinthia, the decline was general with a similar effect. By the end of the sixteenth century the mines were failing (gold-mining ceased in 1587) and during the early seventeenth century stagnation set in which was made worse be religious strife. It was not only that a considerable proportion of the educated classes emigrated. This happened all over the country. It was perhaps more that so many dissidents remained. In 1604, for example, every Protestant inhabitant of Klagenfurt had to decide whether he would abjure his beliefs and stay, or sell up and go. All but forty heads of families submitted, but no mass reconciliation followed, and the people remained in two sullenly divided camps. The absence which we noticed earlier of a single, powerful centre of government, was yet another factor: who, by the eighteenth century, had much interest in spending enormous sums of money in Carinthia on 'displaying the face of power'? Not the archbishops of Salzburg; not the see of Bamberg, which, for one million guilders, thankfully relinquished its Carinthian properties to Maria Theresa in 1759. And certainly not the Habsburgs. So long as the Turkish threat continued, the defence system of castles and fortified towns had to be maintained, but that, architecturally speaking, is another story.

There are Renaissance buildings of high quality in the province but most of them were built within the era of prosperity and they were near contemporaries of the latest high Gothic. Baroque buildings exist, and of course a great number of churches were redecorated and furnished in the Baroque style, but vast edifices on the scale of Melk or Göttweig in Lower Austria are nowhere to be found. Attempts were made, as it were to put a bold face on the situation by adding Baroque façades to Gothic town houses. The impressive appearance of the Viktringer Hof in Klagenfurt was achieved by uniting individual houses to form a single frontage; the joins can distinctly be seen.

The city of Klagenfurt has a record without equal in the Habsburg dominions. The Emperor Maximilian I knew his Carinthians well: as a boy he lived for some years at Finkenstein castle near the Faaker See. In 1518, four years after medieval Klagenfurt had been destroyed by fire, he presented it by deed of gift to the burghers of the town on condition that they fortify it. To our ears this sounds more like a liability than a present, but the Estates of Klagenfurt were elated. They had freedom to rule themselves and their citizens, to appoint judges and councillors and to fill all posts in the public service. And they could build as they liked. They decided to incorporate the old winding streets in a grid system with plenty of open spaces, the total area to be many times the size of the old town. In 1527 excavation of the Lend canal joining the town to the Wörther See was begun; one reason for this was to obtain a flow of water for the moat. The Landhaus with its tall towers on either side of a horseshoe court lined with collonades gives an idea of the sense of power and dignity of the aldermen of Klagenfurt. They saw another symbol in the great dragon, the *Lindwurm*, which took forty years to carve out of slate and was drawn to the Neuer Platz by three hundred youths dressed in white. Humiliation came to the dragon after the last war, when the tip of its tail failed to bear the weight of a British soldier; it snapped off and both fell to the ground.

In 1809 the town walls of Klagenfurt were demolished on the orders of Napoleon, and for the whole province a time of poverty and even of hunger and destitution lay ahead. But during the reign of Maria Theresa and until the latter part of the eighteenth century there was a brief economic revival, and Klagenfurt, remote backwater though it was, felt the shock waves of the Age of Enlightenment. Some remarkable people were living in or near the provincial capital at the time. Perhaps no one ever did more for Carinthia than Reichsgraf Franz Josef von Enzenberg, a great public servant, a determined, energetic and cultured man. There was Baron Franz von Herbert who has been called one of the most distinguished figures of the Enlightenment, a close friend of Pestalozzi, Wieland, Schiller and Novalis, who joined the 'Jena Circle' to study philosophy. The Herberts were descended from the English family of that name but had lived in Carinthia since the end of the seventeenth century. Enzenberg and Herbert were both

members of the lodge 'Zur wohltätigen Marianna' (philanthropic
Marianna) in Klagenfurt which was founded in about 1783. Owing
to the extreme unpopularity of Freemasonry in Roman Catholic
countries during the nineteenth century and even until recent
years, the whole subject has been glossed over in the history books.
Educated Austrians today might be astonished to learn that, in
the words of Rudolf Cefarin, 'practically all the leading men in
Vienna and also in the Länder were Freemasons at that time, or at
any rate supported the aims of masonry. This applied not only to the
intellectual and hereditary aristocracy but equally to the higher
ranks of the Catholic hierarchy ... for example the Bishop of
Gurk.'[1] Cefarin maintains that the Emperor Joseph II (he was not
himself a mason) could never have carried through his comprehensive clerical reforms without the acquiescence of such men of
high influence throughout the realm. The rapid headway made by
Freemasonry in the Habsburg empire in the teeth of bitter opposition by the Jesuits was due to the enthusiasm of Maria Theresa's
consort, Franz von Lothringen, who was a mason, and to the
approval of her heir and in her later years co-regent, Joseph II.
She banned masonry in 1764, but after her death in 1780 Joseph
restored their rights. Another factor was probably the revived
interest in the writings of Paracelsus (Theophrastus von Hohen-
heim) who grew up in Villach where his father practised as a
doctor for thirty years. The long name and title of the contemporary
Bishop of Gurk, Franz Xavier Altgraf von Salm-Reifferscheidt-
Krautheim, conceals one of the most interesting men who ever
wore the mitre in Carinthia. His father, on record as a Freemason,
was principal tutor to the future Joseph II and later his Lord
Chamberlain, with the result that a friendship between the heir to
the throne and Franz Salm developed which was to last all their
lives. The breadth of Salm's intellectual interests enriched the
exceptionally brilliant circle of friends who met at the lodge
'Zur wohltätigen Marianna', and his sense of adventure and his
passionate love of the mountains focused his attention on the still
unconquered Grossglockner. On 25th August 1799, after several

[1] Rudolf Cefarin, *Kärnten und die Freimaurerei*, Vienna, 1932.

setbacks owing to bad weather and watched by the bishop from an alpine hut, a party of climbers from Heiligenblut reached, as they thought, the summit of the Grossglockner. Their disappointment when they realized that they had only ascended the slightly lower Kleinglockner was fully shared by the bishop who had invested a great deal of money in the enterprise. Somehow, he raised enough to try again, and on 28th July 1800, in the presence of the parish priest of Döllach, a cross was set up on the highest peak in Austria. Salm was now fifty-one. He died in Klagenfurt in 1822, a cardinal, but now as poor as the least among his fellow Carinthians.

Who was the philanthropic Marianna?

During the seventies a small community of nuns were living very frugally in Klagenfurt and wondering how they could keep going, maintain the convent in good order and care as usual for the needy. The arrival on the scene of the eldest daughter of the Empress altered their circumstances dramatically, but it also brought a new quality into their lives. As a child, Maria Anna was always delicate, and after a severe illness she began to develop a stoop; as an instrument of state the Archduchess was a non-starter. In middle age she would say that she had enjoyed the life at court with all the music, theatre and carnivals, and she was fond of the chase, but she had become impatient with its more frivolous aspects and the tedious routine. Her relationship with her father was a very happy one. That tubby gentleman Franz von Lothringen, the sight of whom in his coronation robes as Holy Roman Emperor caused the Empress to burst out laughing, was deeply loved by her and by all their children, but particularly by Maria Anna who mourned him dreadfully when he died. She fell in love: with whom, she never revealed, but it was no passing fancy; she said that she would not attempt to put it out of her mind but would preserve it always. This may well have been the case, because in spite of her piety she never took the veil; her status as Abbess of a convent in Prague was purely secular and she ruled in absentia. The Mother Superior in Klagenfurt was known to her, and when the Empress died Maria Anna retired to live close to the nuns and to share their humdrum existence. But only up to a point. During those last few years before the French

Revolution while her sister Marie Antoinette was queen consort of France, the new philosophies which were tearing Europe apart were thrashed out by Enzenberg, Herbert, Salm and their friends in Maria Anna's remote Carinthian drawingroom. Contemporaries knew her as a woman of spirit with a strong personality, open-minded and lacking in all affectation, who possessed the same sense of the absurd and the irrepressible gaiety which, in spite of the almost intolerable burdens of her reign, would occasionally burst forth from the Empress Maria Theresa. She died wearing the man's dressing-gown worn by her mother at her death. Joseph II met the nuns and found them, after exposure to Maria Anna, 'quite unlike others elsewhere'. The question is bound to come to mind: what difference would it have made if she, rather than Marie Antoinette, had married Louis XVI?

As we near the end of the twentieth century and the universe opens up before us, the odd bits and pieces of history may appear petty and irrelevant, and above all known, endlessly mulled over, the subject of a thousand doctoral theses. The case of the amateur historian is this: civilization means, in part, self-awareness through-out all the stages of cause and effect, and to understand the thought and behaviour of people today one must know their heritage. To know anything about the psychology of the South Tyrolese, for example, of the Serbs and Croats, of the Czechs and Slovaks, it is essential to dig down a long way. The same is true of the Slovene Carinthians whom we shall happen on later. Meanwhile, it is by no means true to say that the picnic litter of historical enquiry lies thickly upon every potential field of research. To the north of Klagenfurt lies an area which is still one of the most mysterious in Europe: the Zollfeld.

The concentration of ancient monuments on and in the vicinity of the Zollfeld is extraordinary. At a rough estimate there are twenty-eight prehistoric sites, thirty-six Roman and early medieval ruins and, apart from the towns, at least sixty castles and fortified places. The Zollfeld consists of the Klagenfurt basin together with its four 'holy mountains', the Ulrichsberg, Magdalensberg, Göseberg and Lorenziberg, and it is only of recent years that archaeological research on the Magdalensberg has been carried on intensively and systematically; Karnburg, the Carolingian *sedes regalis*, remains almost untouched.

This exceptional concentration proves straight away that the Zollfeld was a centre of power throughout antiquity, and cere-monies connected with sovereign investiture and with religious practices were carried on in unbroken succession into the modern era. Was the town on the Magdalensberg, whose name in spite of the large area it covered and the advanced stage of the diggings has still not been ascertained, the old capital of Noricum, Noreia? (The Styrian village which changed its name to 'Noreia' in recent times when important finds were made there, is now thought to have been done overmuch honour too hastily.) Final proof may never be found. Carantana was originally the name of the north-western part of the Zollfeld, and the Carantani were a Celtic tribe (*Kar* or *Car*, of Illyrian origin, means rock or precipice, hence Karwendel, Karawanken, Carpathians etc.) whose name came to stand for the whole region of the Carantanian Marches: Carinthia, Styria and Carniola. Philologists maintain that in their different roots and linguistic forms the names Carantana, Noreia and Virunum, the Roman capital near Maria-Saal, all mean the same thing: 'the place of friendship; of friends'; or 'men united under the gods'. To Virunum fell the common fate of being used as a stone quarry for construction on other sites. Many churches and farmhouses were built with its stones and a considerable quantity must have been used in the defences surrounding Maria-Saal church and in the church itself: the font was a public fountain in the Roman provincial capital and so was the large stone fountain in the main square at St. Veit. There is something startlingly evoca-tive about a particular stone plaque set into the south wall of the church at Maria-Saal. Here—we can study every detail—is a horse-drawn barrel-roofed wagon, not a very large one, it may have carried the mails or other comparatively light loads over long distances. The driver is a Celt, and he is wearing a cape and hood of identically the same cut as has been worn in the alpine districts of Austria ever since. It was called a cuculla after the Celtic god Cucullatus, whose homely image wrapped in just such a hooded cloak lived on in folk memory for a very long time. He was thought, like the saints Cosmas and Damian, to bring healing sleep, and is the ancestor of our sandman and the Austrian child's 'dream man', the *Traummännlein*.

If there is any time and place at which the pagan gods throw off their masks of Christian piety it is on the Zollfeld on the second Friday after Easter, during the *Vierbergelauf*, the 'run' round the circumference of the heart of Carinthia.

At midnight, the runners assemble on the summit of the Magdalensberg, and after receiving the priest's blessing, light their torches at an open fire and set off. Leaping down rough paths, through bushes and bracken, they reach the valley of the River Glan and cross over to the foot of the Ulrichsberg where they halt for their first rest. In former times, this part of the course must have been difficult: as recently as 1948, during a very wet summer, large areas of the Zollfeld became a swamp, and in fact primitive man could only cross it by boat. The run, which must be completed within twenty-four hours, follows a steep path on to the southern slope of the Göseberg and on to the Lorenziberg. Here, a priest again gives Benediction, which is signalled to the surrounding countryside by the shattering roar of those small cannon for firing salutes which are such a favourite ingredient in Austrian open air ceremonial.

This is merely a brief summary of a breathless and highly taxing run round a fixed course. But what of those mysterious bits and pieces which rouse the anthropologists to such ecstasy? It has been established that the *wilde Jagd*, the wild chase in line with the sun's course, has parallels in Celtic religion, while the carrying of torches across fields is typical of a fertility cult. The same applies to the custom of collecting leaves from trees on all four 'holy' mountains, putting them together in bunches and placing them in the fields. But in conflict with the fertility idea was the way in which the runners used to trample the young crops underfoot as they went. This destructive abandon is an element in the worship of Dionysus, whose portrait—still Grecian in the aristocratic delicacy of his features and the gentleness of his expression, the Bacchanalian decadence still undreamed of—has been uncovered on the Magdalensberg. A cult of the dead has been noticed in the carrying of handfuls of grain up to the mountains, the abode of the dead. And more evocative even than the silence imposed on the runners is the fact that, on certain parts of the journey, they may not look behind them. The sombre shades of Hades have crept very close.

Clearly, the Church had to do something about all this. To forbid the *Vierbergelauf* outright would not do. Pope Urban IV ordered that the 'wild chase' be transformed into a sedate pilgrimage, and appropriate saints were dotted about the Zollfeld to lend tone to the vulgar brawl. St. Ulrich, Bishop of Augsburg, and St. Lawrence were both called in because, between them, they had power over demons and the fires of purgatory, and also St. Helen, finder of the True Cross, because the nails of the Cross were thought to have power over evil spirits. These efforts were only partially successful because the local parishioners, instead of forgetting all else but the sanctity and the teaching of the Christian saints, simply endowed them with the attributes of the heathen gods and expected from them the identical services. That dauntless Englishwoman St. Helena, for instance, took on the semblance of a nature goddess, giving succour against drought, hail and fire. In his valuable work on the Zollfeld, Siegfried Hartwagner says that at the end of the nineteenth century there still existed a community of 'thousands of men and women' who had sworn to perpetuate the ritual of the *Vierbergelauf*, and that some still believe that Frederick Barbarossa emerges from concealment every seven years and carefully counts the participants.

The ducal throne, the Herzogstuhl, still stands on the Zollfeld. Its megalithic dignity would surely dissuade anyone not entirely insensible to *lèse-majesté* from sitting on it, though it is protected from the casual visitor by an iron fence. The last investiture of a duke of Carinthia was held here in 1615, but how it all began, no one knows, nor why and when it became a double throne, back to back. Equally mysterious is the Fürstenstein which was removed from its place near the Carolingian church at Karnburg about a hundred years ago and is now in the Land Museum at Klagenfurt.

As much as anything else, it is the relationship between these two thrones which has puzzled historians. We know a good deal

Carinthia

about the Fürstenstein, which is no more than the broken off base of a corinthian column. Approaching this essentially impromptu throne and wearing peasant dress, the duke was confronted by the seated Herzogbauer, judge of the people, the elected representative of the Carinthian freemen. The ceremony which followed included question and answer; the Herzogbauer would strike the duke lightly on the cheek, offer him a drink of fresh spring water brought in a peasant's hat, and accept the gifts of an ox and a horse. The exact order of events is not known, but a crucial element in 'taking possession' consisted in the duke riding three times round the throne. The judge relinquished the throne to his overlord, who spoke the words of the investiture oath, swinging his sword as he did so in the direction of the four winds. In the long controversy in which Germanic and Slav nationalist sentiments have played their part, the scales have come down on the side of a preponderantly Germanic origin, which is not to say that the custom was introduced by the Bavarian and Frankish colonizers. It was mentioned in the *History of the Conversion of the Bavarians and Carantanians*, which was written in Salzburg in 871, more than a century before the creation of the duchy of Carinthia as a political unity, so that it was already a well-established tradition at that time. The one factor of real significance is that the right to rule and to make laws was bestowed by the people. At times, perhaps, a rather hollow mockery, but there it was, a guiding principle which lasted well into the seventeenth century.

How does the Fürstenstein link up with the Herzogstuhl?

The Karnburg ceremony was last held in 1414, the last investiture on the Zollfeld in 1615. But that lonely throne was not a mere successor to the Fürstenstein; its obvious antiquity alone would rule out that theory, and we can assume that as long as the dual investiture was practised, they were complementary, and that latterly the Herzogstuhl ceremony took over the essentials while adding others, such as the episcopal blessing at Maria-Saal and the homage of the nobility. The peasant judge still played a crucial role, and the duke took over the judicial function, as he not only listened to petitions and bestowed fiefs, but pronounced judgement in disputes.

In 1823 a man died whose name was Josef Edlinger. He was a farmer, and the last man to claim the title of Herzogbauer, ducal peasant. His name leads straight into yet another of the mysteries peculiar to Carinthia which may never be wholly explained, a mystery which is all the more tantalizing because the available evidence points in to many directions. Who were 'die Edlinger?' Not a family, not even a clan, an élite certainly, claiming a special relationship with the overlord. Where did they come from; whence their status; why, unlike all other holders of land, were they presented with the actual title deeds to their farms with the right of inheritance?

At a rough estimate, four hundred farms were still in the hands of Edlinger families during the late Middle Ages, the great majority being in central Carinthia between Villach and Bleiburg. Before that, their numbers were probably much greater; some of their descendants may still be living on these farms, enjoying a brisk side-line in *Zimmer mit Frühstück* for tourists. One philologist believes that the name Edling is identical with the Slav *Kazaki* which survives in Russian as *Kosak*. Cossacks? Were they the lost army of Samo, whose Slav kingdom in the heart of Bohemia disintegrated after his death? This is an enticing picture, but it won't quite do, not only because *Kazaki* and the Turanian *Kazaze* are names which only appear in the seventh century, whereas *Edling* goes back to the time of Theodoric the Great. In their laws and customs they have much in common with the Armani, the free Lombardian armed peasantry. They introduced architectural forms which are north German in character, and Scandinavian-type bee-hives.

This is no place for the amateur to linger any longer. We will move on to Friesach and enjoy a rousing spectacle: the greatest tournament of all time.

Bernhard of Sponheim was a striking figure, well known at the courts of Europe, and the first duke of Carinthia to live in sovereign state in his capital, which at that time was St. Veit. For years past, there had been severe tension between himself and Margrave Henry IV of Istria, and at last the Babenberg Duke Leopold VI ('the glorious') decided to intervene. The two men should meet for talks at Friesach. This was a time when Friesach was the equal of Salzburg in size and beauty. The archbishops of Salzburg loved, as we said earlier, to stay there (perhaps it was safer); it was host to emperors, the Dominicans built their first monastery in German lands at Friesach and the Teutonic Knights one of their first hospitals. Its fame had reached the Persian cartographer Idrisi: when he drew up his map of Europe he was able to place very few towns, but he put in Friesach.

Bernhard was no lover of pomp, but he agreed to the tournament. 'A great company', says the minnesänger Ulrich von Liechtenstein, assembled. The guests were very distinguished. They included Archbishop Eberhard II of Salzburg, Patriarch Berthold of Aquileia and Bishop Eckbert of Bamberg; all three may have been brothers of Henry of Istria. There were the bishops of Brixen, Passau and Freising, the Margrave Diepold of Vohburg, the sovereign earls Albert II of Tyrol and Meinhard III of Görz, Bernhard, last of the line of Lebenau, William II of Heunburg and Bernhard of Ortenburg. 'The Sponheimer' was attended by his nobles, among them the men of Kraig, hereditary High Stewards, whose three castles stand in a close group north of St. Veit; the hereditary cup-bearer, lord of the manor of Osterwitz, and Wulfing of Stubenberg. On 6th May 1224, Mass was said early in the morning. And then, to the sound of pipes, horns, flutes and drums, six hundred knights (the number he gives is probably much exaggerated) rode on to the arena and the tremendous mock battle began. Wulfing of Stubenberg opened the contest, and soon the cup-bearer of Osterwitz was bashing in the helmets of his opponents 'like rotten pears'. The contest went on until dusk, by which time a hundred knights had lost their mounts. At last, says the minnesänger, 'some nearly unconscious with exhaustion, dropping with sleep, aching in every bone and muscle, they straggled into the town, calling for warm baths, for soothing ointments and bandages'. If the daughters of Friesach had to defend their virtue during the nights to come, on 6th May they slept on unrumpled linen.

Like others among the early aristocracy of Carinthia, the men of Osterwitz rose rapidly to great prominence, but their fall was swift and final. In 1473, one of the recurrent waves of Turkish invasion brought them to the walls of the castle which would one day serve Walt Disney as the inspiration for *Snow White and the Seven Dwarfs*. The castle held out, but George of Osterwitz was captured and held to ransom. The four thousand guilders demanded for his release were raised by his nephew and handed over, but in vain as the warrior uncle was already dead. The financial effort brought about the ruin of the family, and the fief was handed back to the Emperor. In 1510 it came into the hands of the Bishop of Gurk: none other than Matthäus Lang, who was to become Imperial Chancellor and a Cardinal, and whom we encountered in Salzburg, cornered by an 'evil, obnoxious rabble'. He built a residence on Osterwitz and improved the defences, but in 1541 the fief was accepted by the Khevenhüller family in the person of Christoph, who, in the following year, would take on the task of restoring the ruins of Leopoldskron. Thirty years later, Georg Khevenhüller bought the property, and in a very few years time he had turned Hochosterwitz, as it was now called, into a fortress of the first rank. The text of a commemorative tablet in the main courtyard, dated 1576, includes the well-known injunction to his descendents never to allow Hochosterwitz, which he had 'built up and fortified out of his own means and for the good of the State', to leave the possession of the family. Nor has it; but the visitor, looking happily up at this realization of all his dreams of what a fairytale castle should be, can be thankful that he is spared the worry of its maintenance.

The journey is quite likely to continue across the Pack Saddle into Styria, but a last backward glance ought to take in one more factor in the life of Carinthia: the Slovenes.

The Carinthian Slovenes are mainly concentrated in the Jauntal, the Rosental and in the lower part of the Gailtal. Between them and modern Yugoslavia lies the mountain chain of the Karawanken, and their way of life and even their language have been influenced by this separation and by their close contact during more than a thousand years with the German-speaking Carinthians. The early German and Slovene farmers settled in neighbouring districts and their farms sometimes adjoined one another. The German dialect took on Slav elements and vice versa; men of both nations took part in public affairs on equal terms and their names appear together as witnesses to contracts of sale. During the investiture of the dukes of Carinthia the onlookers sang songs in the Slavonic tongue. In 1612 the German medievalist Megiser commented: 'Since those (earlier) days the Wendish Carinthians and the German Carinthians have so powerfully joined one with another and intermingled, that out of two, there has emerged one people. We can still see this process in our own time.'

'This process' was confirmed on 10th October 1920 when, in a plebiscite, the Slovenes voted by an overwhelming majority to remain part of Austria. In 1945 they took up arms with their fellow Carinthians to prevent a large part of the country—it might have included Klagenfurt—from being incorporated into Yugoslavia.

6
Styria

There was one striking omission in the chapter on Carinthia: the fact that it was part of the British zone of occupation after the last war. The other half of this zone contained Styria. Supposing for one irrational moment that the old principality of Carniola—it was an integral part of inner Austria for six hundred years—had been scooped in by the forces of occupation, they would then have been ruling over the whole of the original dukedom of Carantania. Nothing, of course, could have been further from the allied mind; if anything, the idea was to hand over a chunk of Austria to Yugoslavia. As for the 'other ranks', they wisely confined their attentions to recuperation after the long slog up through Italy, and to their frats. This shame-faced term referred to forbidden fraternization with local girls, and its life was happily too short to warrant inclusion in the supplement to the *O.E.D.*

On a pouring wet day in June 1946 a small group of people assembled in Mariazell. There was a British officer who had driven down from the Rhineland in a jeep, three girls in khaki wearing the tabs of the Allied Commission, and several Austrians of both sexes. The village was thinly populated; the basilica which harbours the Magna Mater Austriae, chief religious shrine of the Habsburg empire, stood almost deserted, waiting for the tide of pilgrims to resume its ebb and flow. The hotels and inns were empty, so that the Anglo–Austrian party had their hotel to themselves. They had come for a wedding, and although innumerable bridal couples and their relations have gladly travelled long distances for this privilege, the motives which drove our bride and bridegroom to choose this church were mixed. Mariazell lies just inside Styria, and Styria, as we said before, was in the British zone of occupation. The bride, who would lose her status as fraternizer the moment she married without, however, gaining anything very tangible in exchange, as the bridegroom's nationality was temporarily obscure, could at least be given away by her brother and cheered on by her women friends. The home of the bridegroom's family was in the Russian zone, but they contrived, by devious means, to get out.

The main diet of the British in Austria at that time was tinned 'm & v', finely chopped meat stew with peas, cubed carrots and turnips. Only in the officers' hotels and clubs were these items served separately, a concession which enhanced the appearance of the dish without improving its flavour. For safety's sake the uniformed members of the wedding brought, as well as drink and the absolutely genuine cake from Wales, a few tins of 'm & v' and some essential supplementary Naafi issues. But the Austrians had done better. They had brought not only fresh vegetables but venison, shot in imminent risk to life and liberty in the Russian zone. And it shall not be forgotten that the hotelier, revolted by the sight of the British army's idea of a passable sparkling wine, brought up the last of his champagne and put it on the bill at the listed, not the black market, price.

Some people can find inspiration, grace or healing at the shrines of Europe: Lourdes, Fatima, Alt-Ötting, Mariazell; others cannot. All they see is superstition, commercialization, loudspeakers and buses. There are crowds, buses and loudspeakers in Mariazell today, but little else to offend agnostic susceptibilities. And the question is worth pondering: what is it that, over so long a span of years, has compelled a stream of Hungarian and Slav peasants to tramp across hot plains into the mountains of Austria to kneel before a small, rather primitive Gothic Madonna? And why did princes, kings and emperors come? Ferdinand II; Leopold I who made the pilgrimage eleven times; Charles VI? For a considerable part of the way they too went on foot. So do some of their Habsburg descendants today. No cars or buses for them: they walk, carrying in turn a heavy cross. The simple answers—from the religious, agnostic or historical point of view—are quickly to hand, but if one cohesive element is left out, no clear shape emerges. This is the distinctive Habsburg piety, the *pietas austriaca*; theatrical and profound, aggressive, dynamic and yet obsessed with death, eternity and the transcience of all temporal power, embracing a wholly mystical supranational concept of empire. In spite of all that can be said against them, the Habsburg concept of rule was far more sensitive to the individuality of subject peoples than can be credited to most other imperial systems past or present. When the forces of nationalism exploded the containing glass bell of the Habsburg mystique, the whole structure crumbled.

The pilgrims' southern route to Mariazell leads past the Brandhof, the country house which the hero of Styria, Archduke Johann, built as a model farm and in which he lived with his wife, the postmaster's daughter Anna Plochl. In 1946 there was no public road transport, but we heard of a lorry which would be leaving two days later at four in the morning. Much determination and a little bribery reserved us precarious perches on a rickety plank in the stifling, overcrowded interior. As we bounced down the winding mountain road I remembered the Brandhof as it was before the war, plain and unpretentious in all things, very little changed probably since the days of Archduke Johann a century before. And I remembered walking up the long slope near the house, and the shock of the unexpected view that broke away from the wooded hills close by: the majestic, snow-covered slopes of the Hochschwab. It was in this region, so we had just heard, that a British sergeant, miserable man, had shot one of the last remaining male ibex in the country.

The steep ascent and descent from Mariazell lay behind us and we were grinding along a level road. Through the one very small opening in the side flap of the lorry early morning light had begun to show up the unshaven faces of the men with their rucksacks, and the gaunt outlines of the women. Longing for fresh air I squeezed my way closer to the opening and saw, across the thin blanket of mist on the fields, a jagged line of dark grey peaks. A spot of pink settled on the tip of a crag, and slowly the whole screen was washed over by a rosy flush, moving across and downwards until every crevice was filled with light.

We thankfully turned our backs on the lorry in Bruck an der Mur. Bruck's greatest treasure is the house built by a wealthy ironmaster, Pankraz Kornmesser, at the end of the fifteenth century; it is the finest Gothic *Bürgerhaus* in Austria if one excepts the enchanting Bummerlhaus in Steyr. And now we must take our bearings. We are on Route 17 which runs from Vienna to Klagenfurt, at the junction of the road to Graz. Nearly all the high alpine regions: the Styrian Salzkammergut, Dachstein, Gesäuse, Hochschwab and the eastern outriders of the Tauern range lie to the north and north-west of this line which slices Styria in half, leaving only the Seetal Alps and the Stubalpe near Judenburg and Knittelfeld to the south of it. The rest is all green land: enormous areas of forest, switchback country, steep inclines, sudden drops, but also wine country and the apple orchard of Austria. Quite illogically and apart from the fact that it does include the capital, it often seems as though this green land were the real Styria. The alpine areas could belong to other provinces; this part could not. It is a cul-de-sac, rather isolated from the tourist stream, quiet, unaltered and welcoming.

The history of the eastern Steiermark and its whole development can be summed up in one sentence. It lay open to incessant invasions by marauding bands and whole armies from the east, it was marchland, the fence along the Austrian crownlands on the east. This accounts for the string of fortified towns facing Hungary, from Radkersburg, whose fortress on the south bank of the Mur is now in Yugoslavia, up to Friedberg on the Wechsel. Here lie Gleichenberg, Fürstenfeld, Hartberg and all the other fortified towns, castles and citadels, the greatest of which is the Riegersburg.

Looking up at the Riegersburg as it lies along the full extent of a basalt cliff fifteen hundred feet high, we can well imagine that this is the largest citadel in Styria, perhaps the largest in Austria, although the Turks were exaggerating when they called it the greatest in all Christendom. But the Riegersburg as we see it now is only a shadow of its former self. The descending lines of walls, battlements, towers and gateways, winding down to the cliff base, have vanished. A natural site of this kind was often built on and developed in logical sequence by the earliest inhabitants of the country and on through the Middle Ages, and the Riegersburg was no exception. It reached its fullest extent in the middle of the seventeenth century when an ambitious building programme was carried out by a lady whom her subjects and their descendants called 'Naughty Lizzie'.

Katharina Elisabeth, Countess Galler, *née* Wechsler, brought up at Radkersburg Castle, was the last of her line and she inherited the castle in 1648. Her predecessors had been a quarrelsome and bucolic lot: one drinking bout went on for three weeks, if the author of the words on the north window of the Knights' Hall was not merely boasting: 'anno 1635 ye 6 April ye debauch did begin and each day was drunkenness until ye 26 dtto.'

It was a patriotic duty to have spent sixteen years and a great deal of personal effort and money on the fortifications, but *die Gallerin* was one of those people with a passion for building; she would have built in any case, anywhere. There is a note of defiance in the words inscribed in her summer dining-room: 'Building is my joy and cheer / What it costs I am aware.' She had other joys, being a celebrated rider and sportswoman; her nickname would have referred to indoor forms of hospitality. On 1st September 1664 it seemed imminently probable that the Riegersburg's defences would be put to the test. Enemy forces were lined up along the frontier of Hungary at St. Gotthard and Mogersdorf, and for days the local population had been streaming inland. The fortress itself was crammed with refugees. But this time, the enemy came no further, Count Montecucculi drove them back across the River Raab at Mogersdorf, a victory which was of great significance for the outcome of the siege of Vienna in 1683 as it provided an essential breathing space and served (in places where complacency reigned) as a warning of worse to come.

While the defeat of the Turks in 1683 brought an end to this age-old peril, the Styrian and Lower Austrian marchlands still lay open to invasions which were no less devastating in their effects for all that their range was more restricted. The sufferings of the Hungarian peasantry, unemployed soldiers and vagrants combined with the injured pride of the Hungarian nobility to create a nationalist uprising against the hated Habsburgs the virulence of which, for a long time, the government in Vienna persistently underestimated. In 1704 small-scale warfare broke out against the almost defenceless and for the most part demoralized population of eastern Styria. The *Kuruzzen* were a fierce and ruthless riffraff under skilled command of men such as Karolyi and Anton Esterhazy; the central government replied to appeals for arms and money with astonishing indifference; the Styrian command was hopelessly overtaxed. By the time the power of the rebel forces in Western Hungary ended for the time being after the counter-invasion under Field-Marshal Heisters, the surviving Styrians were in a mood of revolt against their own landlords, in hundreds of villages hardly one house was habitable, thistles grew in the fields, there was no seed, scarcely any cattle or horses or a piece of intact agricultural equipment. At Neudau, new settlers were brought in from Swabia but few remained for long, and recovery was slow because the terms under which the landlords induced their tenants to reclaim the land were in most cases harsh, and they themselves were hard pressed by Graz and by Vienna. But at least, the old cry of terror, 'The Kuruzzen are coming!' was heard no more.

A little further inland from the Riegersburg and to the north, the most worthwhile places to see are grouped fairly closely together around an oval. In the valley of the Feistritz on a plateau surrounded by the river on three sides, Herberstein Castle combines most delightfully a variety of architectural styles from the beginning of the fourteenth century to the end of the seventeenth century. It has been called, all too frequently, the most romantic castle in Styria, but it is certainly a remarkable fact that—in spite of all hazards, including the Counter-Reformation, which hit Styria quite as violently as it did Carinthia, with similar social consequences—the castle has been the home of the Herberstein family since 1290, a record which must be hard to equal. One parallel comes to mind in the case of Blonay Castle in Switzerland, but there are runners up closer to hand. The Counts of Saurau, who died out in the male line in 1870, owned Premstetten near Graz from 1448, and Pux near Murau has been lived in by the Prankh family since 1443 with an interlude from 1856 to 1872. The

Renaissance castle at Stubenberg is quite close to Herberstein:
this is another of the great feudal names of medieval Styria which
have survived down to the present day. Frondsberg looms above
the road to Birkfeld: it was a Herberstein fief in the thirteenth
century and also belonged for a time to the Montforts of the
Vorarlberg, who, at the time of their greatest expansion, had a
considerable interest in Styria.

There is a rather odd connection between these two families.
The first fortified place called Stubenberg was built on a steep
promontory not far from the present castle which began as the
home farm of the original castle. The lords of Stubenberg lived
there for only forty years, but by that time the name had stuck
to it. One of the residents was a burggrave of the powerful Stubenbergs who may or may not have been a relation; at any rate he took
the name of the castle. He, Herwig von Stubenberg, built his
knightly residence on a hidden shelf above the Feistritz, and in due
course this place in turn was called after him: 'Herwig's Stone',
which merged into the name Herberstein.

'Very old families', we say, nodding happily like Trollopean
old ladies, who would not be interested to know that family trees
of equal length can be found among the 'lower classes': near
Leogang in Land Salzburg for instance, where one farm has been
owned by the same family since the twelfth century; and in Styria.
In 1163 a parish church was consecrated in the village of Mönichs-
wald. The event was a milestone in the campaign to open up the
dense forests in the north-east of Styria, and many important
personages including the Archbishop of Salzburg took the trouble
to attend. A man called Wecil was there also, representing the
peasantry, and the hill on which he worked, hacking down timber
and clearing the land, came to be called after him: Wetzelberg.
His descendants still live there today. The Adam family, innkeepers
at Pürgg, are said to have lived there for over a thousand years.
If so, they were well established in this village opposite Mount
Grimming in the Enns valley, long before the Johanneskapelle was
built on the nearby hill. They must have attended the opening
ceremony towards the end of the twelfth century and marvelled
at the frescoes—a complete *biblia pauperum*—which entirely cover

the inside walls, and will have pointed out to their children, as people have done ever since, the scene showing a battle between cats and mice.

Turning almost due east at Birkfeld, the snake-like tour continues to Vorau. The first monks came to Vorau from Seckau, the great Benedictine foundation which has been the spiritual centre of Styria at all times. Here is a mild, more open landscape, but perilously near to the frontier, and the generous lines of the close were a necessity in times of danger as the monastery would have had to shelter not only the villagers and farmers but their horses and cattle as well.

To the south, the hills are higher again, the roads lie at a steeper gradient and at Pöllau the parish church is larger than one might expect; it used to belong to a monastery which was dissolved in 1785. A tablet set in the wall to the left of the altar says:

'In 1532 wellnigh the whole of this market town was burned down by the Turks, the parish sacked, many youths and maidens led away to slavery. In 1585 within three months 1,800 persons died of the plague which in 1599 also carried away 1,200 members of the parish...'

'The Turks', pestilence, and even locusts: these were the three plagues of Styria. How did people survive it all? Out in the countryside, they hid. How this was done has remained a secret, forgotten and never investigated. The two main problems facing the scattered peasant population were: to hide their womenfolk and children during an attack, and to give the enemy an impression of far greater numbers than were actually available. In the course of years they dug a rabbit warren of tunnels, leading from one homestead to another and sometimes from an exposed position on a hill all the way down to the valley. The entrances were sometimes in the cellar of the farmhouse, but frequently under cover of a nearby tree. The older Styrian farms sometimes have a lime tree (which the Slav peoples held sacred) close by, and as lime trees often become hollow in the course of their long life it was possible to make the entry to the tunnel accessible through the hollow trunk. How the long tunnels were ventilated is not clear, but gaps for air under cover of bushes were probably placed at frequent intervals, and it is thought that wet brushwood was drawn in to increase the oxygen supply. There are certainly tunnels of remarkable length in other parts of Austria outside the Alps: one joins two castles near Amstetten and must be at least two miles in length. The entrances were bricked up some years ago to prevent accidents to amateur explorers.

From the village street in Pöllau one looks straight across to the mountain of the same name. Having come as far as this there must be no murmuring: Pöllauberg must be visited for the sake of the view. And of course for the church. Yet another baroque pilgrimage church on a hilltop, and a rather obscure one at that—must we bother? If possible, we should. Gothic Pöllauberg was rebuilt by Joachim Carlone. He belonged to the remarkable dynasties of Italian builders and architects from Lake Como, from where many master builders were brought in after the first Turkish war to reconstruct and modernize the eastern fortifications. The 'Comasken', as they were nicknamed, grew in numbers and influence, helped by the effects of the Counter-Reformation, and a branch of the Carlone family lived in Graz. They made a niche for themselves to such effect that for three generations a Carlone was the municipal master builder in the provincial capital, and they held similar posts in other parts of the country. As time went on they adapted themselves increasingly to the different demands of an alien milieu, but their architectural conceptions were conservative, and this accounts for the time lag between the major architectural projects in Styria and those in Upper and Lower Austria. While Joachim was working on Pöllau (he may only have been carrying out the plans of Carlo Antonio Carlone, the architect of St. Florian) Fischer von Erlach, a native of Graz, was building four churches in Salzburg. Not until the first third of the eighteenth century did the specifically Austrian form of baroque architecture achieve its synthesis between Italian and German elements, and with it such triumphant individuality that no one could any longer say—as in seventeenth-century buildings in Styria one often does: 'Really, we might be in Italy.'

If one were approaching from Carinthia a rewarding idea would be to drive all along the southern frontier of Styria, ending at

Radkersburg (where Naughty Lizzie acquired her experience of fortifications). Two of the possible entries from Carinthia lead through villages called after St. Oswald, the fortified church at Eisenerz is also dedicated to him and there are others, including one in Upper Austria. It is rather strange that the cult of Oswald of Northumbria, king and martyr, came to be revered throughout southern Germany, Austria and Northern Italy. On the banks of the River Mur, at Ehrenhausen, the defences were built by the celebrated victor over the Turks in the fifteenth century, Ruprecht von Eggenberg. His mausoleum on the west side of the castle is often considered to be superior to the mausoleum of Ferdinand II in Graz which, apart from the interior decoration, was completed shortly before the Emperor's death in 1637. Later, J. B. Fischer von Erlach used the idea of architecturally detached forms (in this case the statutes of two overpowering warriors) in the columns which flank the frontage of the Karlskirche in Vienna.

Mureck, on the north bank of the Mur about halfway to Radkersburg, is fairly typical of so many small towns which have kept much of their medieval appearance including the long, rectangular market place. A bridge now leads across into Yugoslavia. One of those builders from Como, Andreas Bertoletto, rebuilt the castle and its defences for the Stubenbergs who owned the place for the trifling space of half a millennium, from 1401 to 1931.

To explore Graz thoroughly would take fully as long as to explore Salzburg. People sometimes compare the two, usually to the disadvantage of Graz, but there is little point in it: Salzburg is, perhaps, more beautiful, more light-hearted; Graz lacks the frivolity of the cloth.

Graz spent centuries of its existence in comparative obscurity. There were settlements here in prehistoric times but the Romans preferred other routes: across the mountains to the west, or the amber road to the east. In course of time the site became convenient, as the castle hill was eminently defensible and the Mur fordable. The decisive change in the town's fortunes came in 1564 when the three sons of the Emperor Ferdinand I divided Austria between them and Charles II chose the 'inner-Austrian' lands, Carinthia,

Carniola and Styria, whereupon Graz became a capital city and the seat of a royal residence. Inevitably, the town houses of the Styrian nobility mushroomed, and here they all are: Attems, Dietrichstein, Effans d'Avernas, Galler, Herberstein, Khuenburg, Saurau, Stubenberg, Trauttmansdorff and the rest. Eggenberg, in the suburbs of modern Graz, is the finest baroque castle in Styria.

If there were time for only one thing it would have to be the Zeughaus, which is not a museum but a full-scale armoury. Originally, the arms were kept in the attics of the Landhaus and in vaults in the town walls, but this inconvenience was overcome in 1642 when a depot was created which made the arms and equipment instantly accessible. With the development of the weapons of war, the stocks naturally altered and increased, but the armoury was always in a position to equip thirty thousand men. Today, this splendid collection still includes two thousand complete sets of armour and 7,300 hand combat weapons of all kinds, and about 8,000 firearms dating from the beginning of the sixteenth to the first half of the eighteenth century.

Whether the intended route is to or from Carinthia over the Pack saddle, or from Graz to Knittelfeld and Judenburg, it must not be forgotten that between Voitsberg and Köflach lies Piber, the stud of the Lipizzaner horses. In Vienna, the Spanish Riding School is included in every package tour and it is the holy of holies to lovers of horses whether or not they can tell a levade from a courvette. Piber on the pastureland below the Gleinal-penspeik is the nursery of the Lipizzaner and their home.

The Mur valley also has much to offer: not only Strassengel and Stift Rein, the oldest Cistercian monastery in Austria (it beats Heiligenkreuz by a short head); there is also an obscure village called Mixnitz where there are dragons. The temptation to indulge in dragon lore has been resisted fairly well so far, and in fact, although legends of this description are particularly thick on the ground in this area, the Mixnitz dragons can be pinned down and identified as prehistoric cave bears. (A mounted skeleton is displayed in the Lower Austrian Museum in Vienna.) These bears lived in caves in the devon chalk mountains above Mixnitz, and the length of their tenure was remarkable. After the 1914-18 war when fertilizers were in short supply, 23,000 metric tons of deposit—the decayed remains of the bears and their kill—containing 3,000 tons of phosphates, were taken from the caves. The bones and teeth which alone weighed 250 tons made it possible to study these animals throughout the course of their development and decline.

The rather smug legend about the Erzberg runs as follows. The spirit of the mountain asked the early settlers to choose between a seam of gold ore to last for one year, silver for twenty years or iron ore for ever. They chose iron. There is a geological connection between the once so rich seams of silver and gold in the Tyrol and the Tauern alps (where, presumably, the inhabitants were not consulted) and the gigantic Erzberg near Eisenerz. The *Grauwacken* zone is a seam of sandstone-like rock, resulting from the decomposition of basaltic rocks *in situ*, and it contains precious metals at one end, while the Styrian area is rich in iron ores. The rust-brown terraced cliffs of the 2,400 feet high Erzberg, which have been worked since Roman times, would have appealed to Rider Haggard: a whole, almost inexhaustible mountain of iron ore. And the quality is very high, with an average iron content of 45 per cent.

After the dusty glories of the iron mountain, the Leopoldsteinersee, a very small but quite enchanting lake just beyond Eisenerz on the road to Hieflau and Admont, is a refreshing contrast.

In the Styrian highlands all routes are good provided that they lead at last to the Gesäuse, and it scarcely matters whether the River Enns is followed upstream or down. But if it had been more convenient to turn north near Judenburg or at Unzmarkt (both castles are variously given as the original home of the Liechtenstein family and of the celebrated minnesinger Ulrich von Liechtenstein) the Tauern road, the most important Roman route in Styria, takes one through to Trieben and Rottenmann and to the banks of the Enns at Liezen. There were silver mines at Oberzeiring and gold at Pusterwald, and the whole valley is dotted with the rather eerie relics of an earlier industrial age.

The Gesäuse is a wild gorge cut between limestone cliffs by the churning waters of the River Enns. The narrower stretches can sometimes seem dark and threatening, but soon the cliffs withdraw a little, and near Gstatterboden the alignment of the ravine is such that the view is clear all the way up the northern flanks of the Hochtor and the Planspitz. There must be no rushing through the Gesäuse, and, if feasible, one should stop for lunch: baked grayling—a splendid fish and a change from trout—with a dry white wine. It was during just such a meal, with a companion who has climbed every peak in the area and can describe, between mouthfuls and with stabs of the fork, the various stages on the ascent of the Hochtor, that the subject came up of the wild game in the surrounding mountains.

'When did the last wild ibex die out?' I asked him.

'I read somewhere', he said, 'that an ibex was shot in the Tyrol in 1708, but there were so few left that they rounded up the rest and put them in a zoo. At one time there must have been considerable colonies about because the Romans used to have them brought down for use in entertainments in the arenas.'

'Then what killed them off? Disease, or poaching?'

'Both. Only it wasn't their own diseases that they died of, but those of credulous humanity. Literally every portion of their bodies was held to have medicinal properties of some sort to cure complaints ranging from cancer to colic, and from jaundice to worms. Even the dung was used, and Ferdinand II used to take extract of ibex dung for his gout. There was an apothecary's shop in Salzburg where they sold nothing else but morsels of dried and powdered capricorn.'

'An archiepiscopal monopoly?'

'Oh of course, but only in theory. The value of the ibex was such that poaching flourished all through the alps, and as the gamekeepers were most strictly disciplined in the Salzburg domains, conflict between them and the poachers, in other words the peasantry, was bitter and violent. It almost amounted to a form of guerrilla warfare, particularly in the Zillertal. But you can't kill a good, sturdy superstition even if you exterminate its object. Popular fancy simply transferred its gaze to the chamois, which might well have shuddered to learn that to perils from

avalanches, falling rocks, landslides, foot and mouth and sportsmen, it must now add this medical notoriety.'

'And do you think that the ibex will hold their own now ?'

'Re-introducing them has been a very slow business, but their
numbers are large enough now to make their survival a fair certainty. You can thank Archduke Johann, by the way, that the
chamois weren't exterminated too, at any rate in this part of
Austria. During the eighteenth century stalking was not in favour
among royalty. At a drive for Charles VI in Upper Styria there
were three thousand beaters and he shot one hundred and three
chamois himself.'

Inevitably, the next stop is Admont. The monastery buildings
were gutted by fire in 1865 and rebuilt in neo-gothic style; a loss
which can be borne with composure compared with the thought
that the library all but went up in flames as well. This library was
always known as the most important collection in Austria and
southern Germany, constantly added to by purchase, bequest,
exchange and the work of Admont's own copyists and illuminators.
In 1380 it possessed 640 Latin manuscripts, and it is an interesting
comparison that over a century later the Vatican Library itself
owned no more than 794. Great emphasis was placed on the natural
sciences and in the sixteenth century the abbots could still boast that
they possessed a copy of every extant work on these subjects. The
botanical illustrations, in particular, are superb. The present
library contains about 120,000 volumes including 1,060 manuscripts of which the oldest fragments date back to the eighth
century, and 900 incunabula. The nuns of Admont were as diligent
with the pen and brush as anyone else, and they were also celebrated for their holiness, their learning and their talent for teaching
which earned them the name *sorores literatae*. There is no doubt that
Admont enjoyed an exceptional succession of abbots. They were
men of high intellectual stature, formidable theologians but also
humanists whose learning ranged over all the fields of knowledge
in their day. In September 1939 the Nazi régime sequestered the
monastery and all its possessions, and in 1941 two thousand works,
mainly on botanical and medical subjects, were taken to the notorious laboratories at Dachau. During the confused weeks which

followed the collapse of Nazi resistance and the end of the war, the head librarian made his way with great difficulty to Dachau, retrieved the whole collection and brought it back to Admont. It is to be hoped that his account of this personal triumph has been placed on record: what will the rubber stamp of Dachau concentration camp in each volume mean to posterity?

Frauenberg, a pilgrimage church on the small mountain which seals off the valley to the west of Admont, received considerable impetus from the wave of piety which swept the country after the release from the Turkish menace, as well as from the shift in population from the eastern areas of Austria. An inventory made in 1717 lists quantities of those frightful votive offerings, so popular a form of religious expression at the time: hearts, eyes, heads, legs, breasts and babies in swaddling clothes. They were made of silver—no one would have bothered to list offerings formed, as they more commonly were, out of wax—and were usefully employed during the Napoleonic wars. At that time the monasteries were all forced to hand in a proportion of their treasures to be melted down for coinage, and Admont was probably thankful to be able to gain time by relinquishing these horrors first.

Votive objects, a wholly pagan survival, are one thing; *Votivbilder* are another. These simple, artless paintings used to be hung in the west end of churches and chapels throughout the alps as a thanksgiving for an answer to prayer or for deliverance from some danger or affliction. Sometimes they show the town in flames, with a procession of penitent citizens praying for divine intervention. These charming pictures are of great interest because they provide exact evidence of the dress worn by the townspeople and peasantry over a period of some two or three hundred years.

About halfway between Rottenmann and Selztal, a tree-covered mountain flank throws out an arm along which, sheer precipice below it, lies Strechau Castle. Here, on 21st July 1823, Johann of Habsburg-Lothringen, Archduke of Austria–Hungary, met Anna Plochl to discuss plans for their married life. His diary records: 'The weather had turned bad, and it poured with rain all night. The Brandhofer's companions' (he always wrote of himself in the third person) 'were Huber, Zahlbruckner and the painter

Loder. Early on the 21st the mountains were seen to be covered with fresh snow. Mist lay on the heights. Nonetheless, the party set off on foot, a light open one-horse cart following, up to the Reiteregg as being the better crossing to the Strechau ravine. All went well at first, but they soon came upon snow as deep as their boots, and cold wind; determined not to be diverted from their purpose they traversed the saddle, treading out a path in the snow for the horse, pushing and supporting the little cart, because here is no carriageway but only a track for cattle; down they went into the ravine of Strechau where for a time they halted. Meanwhile the clouds had parted and the sun shone upon fair meadows and mountains. The party pursued its way through the vale, and soon were joined by the bailiff. After two hours they arrived at the narrow defile where the path from the vale of Oppenberg unites with it—here they were met by the girl and her father, and now all continued joyfully towards the castle.' The diarist goes on to describe the courts and buildings of Strechau (the property belonged to the monks of Admont), and the interior of the rooms and furnishings which had clearly not been altered in any essentials since the castle was built. The men, and Anna Plochl, stayed there for two days, mulling over the situation as it affected Anna, her father and the archduke. They must have touched on the pre-dominant problem, the attitude of Johann's brother Franz and his advisers; but this major anxiety seemed to have been dispelled. Franz had given his written consent, and 'as the weather was fine much time was spent out of doors. The Brandhofer and the girl sat in the small garden beneath the trellised arbour, conversing on all things, he informing her of every aspect pertaining to his circumstances, and his property, in short of all that she would be called upon, as *Hausfrau*, to manage; she from time to time questioning him, commenting, and making suggestions where appropriate. These discussions and the exchange of letters had the consequence that *das Mädchen*, now fully informed, was in a position to assume her new responsibilities at an hour's notice.'

The two actors in Styria's immortal romance did not realize it at that moment, but they had in fact reached a crisis in their affairs which would not be resolved for six years.

13a. A farmhouse at Drosendorf in Lower Austria

13b. On the edge of the great plain of Hungary

14. Vienna in 1609: the medieval core is clearly visible. Notice the old Hofburg, and the substantial burghers' houses beyond the Danube canal (below)

Johann was born on 20th January 1782 in Florence to Marie-Louise of Bourbon, wife of the Grand Duke of Tuscany who came to the throne as Leopold II in 1790. He reigned for only two years, and Johann's eldest brother Franz succeeded him. The archduke's conventional education was broadened by contact with some of the prominent intellects of his day, in particular with the Swiss historian Johannes von Müller. His experiences during the Napoleonic wars, his *pro forma* responsibility for the defeat at Hohenlinden when he was only eighteen, and the very questionable blame attached to him for the late arrival of his army, after a forced march, on the scene of the Battle of Wagram in 1809, both discouraged him profoundly. It was then that he made contact with Andreas Hofer, the Passeier innkeeper and leader of the Tyrolese resistance against the French and Bavarians. Before this final crisis, in 1804, he carried out the Emperor's instructions to reorganize the whole defence system of Inner Austria, Tyrol, Carinthia and Styria, and in so doing he acquired a detailed knowledge of the topography of Austria which no other Habsburg, not even Maximilian I, can ever have possessed. And in that same year the wife of Jakob Plochl, postmaster in Aussee, gave birth to the first of her thirteen children. She was christened Anna. Johann, at that time, was twenty-two.

Thoroughly out of tune with the political trends in Vienna after 1809 and forbidden to enter Tyrol, Johann went through a period of accidie which he overcame by immersing himself in the lives and fortunes of the Styrians. In the east, the country had recovered from the destitution of the early eighteenth century. There had been a few really progressive landowners: Count Johann Wenzel Purgstall of Riegersburg, for example, had drained marshes, helped the farmers to improve their crops and had brought in modern agricultural machinery from England. But generally speaking the farmers' life was much as it had always been, while the upper reaches of the Enns valley and neighbouring industrial areas were in the grip of a depression which, with occasional improvements here and there, had lasted ever since the seams of precious metals had petered out three hundred years earlier. The auxiliary crafts and trades were affected. The Erzberg was still worked by primitive methods, and individualist and mutually hostile entrepreneurs reduced the profits still further. The archduke went everywhere. He spent his whole time with artisans, innkeepers, farmers and local officials, studying their problems, observing the techniques of every craft and considering how they might be improved. He climbed mountains and made the first ascent of the Gross-Venediger. Graz University, the Joanneum, the College of Technology, and the College of Mines at Leoben were all, directly or indirectly, the result of his constant efforts to raise the standard of education. In 1815, the year of the Congress of Vienna, he accepted an invitation by King George IV and went to England to study the latest industrial and technological developments in mining and the manufacture of iron and steel. He appears to have noticed more than he was intended to: the British owners who took him round their factories would not have credited a Habsburg or any other royal prince with the ability to absorb what he was seeing. But on his return home Archduke Johann immediately went to work at Vordernberg, the old ironworkers' town which has now been superseded by Donawitz, and there he bought a house and a foundry, persuaded the other owners to form a co-operative society and converted the firing system in all the foundries of Vordernberg and Eisenerz to coke.

This remarkable prince with one foot in the age of enlightenment and the other in the industrial revolution, was a romantic in his love of the simple life and in his belief in the essential nobility and guilelessness of country people. But he was far from being either gullible or indiscriminate, and merely chose his friends on identical principles, whether—like Count Saurau, governor of Styria—they were aristocrats, or whether they belonged to the minor bourgeoisie with their roots in the peasantry: men such as the foundry owner Vinzenz Huber, or his secretary, bailiff and confidant Johann Zahlbruckner. He rejected all suggestions of a dynastic marriage, having, he said, seen too much unhappiness in these circles. It may be true that the romantic side of his character saw in Anna Plochl the personification of a mystical union with Styria: simplicity, virginity, piety and diligence warmed by gaiety and affection. Anna, 'Nani', possessed all this. But their story cannot be understood in terms of a *mésalliance* between a prince in flight from court life and a comely country girl. He remained at the Emperor's disposal at all times and took office as Imperial Administrator, *Reichsverweser*, in 1848-9; the people of Frankfurt hailed Anna as 'Anna von Deutschland'. The wide-ranging mind of the man who was arguably the most intelligent of all the Habsburgs, in a different category altogether from his brother the Emperor, found in 'Nani' Plochl the only woman with whom, in modern jargon, he could communicate. 'After many bitter years', he wrote to her after the meeting at Strechau, 'can I be blamed if, having found at last one by whom I may hope to be understood, I should wish to have this person constantly beside me, to be told all that I think and feel? To me it is not enough that I should be understood, that I be considered a good and affectionate man and judged accordingly, but rather should there be, at last, one who shall perceive the source of all my doing and striving . . . to whom without reserve I may disclose all things, because the motives and the impulses which drive me forward are known.'

In 1816 Archduke Johann saw Anna for the first time at a village dance. She was twelve, he was thirty-four. Three years later she and three of her friends, all well chaperoned, went on an outing to the Toplitz-See (where Nazi treasure is believed today to have been sunk in the waters of the lake) and Johann began to take notice. Other meetings followed, always in company, at Gössl, at Gmunden, the Schwarzensee and, in October 1822, in Salzburg. Zahlbruckner tells how he, the Archduke and Anna wandered out through the Cajetan gate to Nonntal, and it was here that the decisive talk took place between the two lovers. Zahlbruckner, hovering at a discreet distance, would not have dared to interrupt the *tête à tête*, which in fact lasted only half-an-hour, and on their return to the city gate at 11 p.m. they found it closed. Nothing would induce the corporal on duty to admit them: he was only, he insisted, carrying out the orders of the supreme military command (Archduke Johann himself) to shut the gate, keep it shut and let no one in after eleven. Zahlbruckner fumed, Anna trembled and the Archduke laughed, but they walked round and gained entry at another gate. Anna was handed back to the anxious innkeeper's wife at whose hostelry she was staying, and ended up her happy evening with a meal of baked carp and red wine. On the following day Johann spoke to Anna's father and the long struggle began.

Kaiser Franz, whom his brother was unable to approach until the following February, consented to the marriage and two months later confirmed it in writing. It was on the strength of this that the party met at Strechau. But in the meantime the Emperor had mentioned the matter to his advisers, the story leaked out and the drawing-rooms were in a turmoil. A few of the archduke's friends sympathized, but their views counted for nothing against the hostility of Metternich and other men to whom his liberal mind and progressive policies were unpalatable and his supposed political views deeply suspect. (Only the year before, the Styrian hunting dress designed and worn by Archduke Johann had been forbidden in Vienna.) The Emperor changed his mind. Johann, after a further audience, agreed to hold back from marriage, but he kept the original document (it is still in the possession of his descendants) and said that he meant to take Anna into his household. He returned to Styria depressed and embittered, feeling that the Emperor was destroying the happiness of two people by listening to the advice of men whose own private lives would by no means bear close scrutiny.

This is the point at which the story becomes an unusual social document. The careful, discreet description in Johann's memoirs of the household arrangements in his houses show that he intended it to be understood by everyone that he had not made Anna his mistress. Why not? Why such self-sacrifice and control by a man who was deeply in love and was not getting any younger? Who would have thought any the worse of him for taking a mistress?

But to think on these lines misses the point. From the outset, his declared intention had been marriage, and noblemen did not sleep with their future wives. To have lived with her openly would, in any case, have defeated his object: to wear down the Emperor's resistance; in the long run, concealment would have been impossible. In his own eyes, to marry Anna against the wishes of his sovereign would be tantamount to blasphemy; he must surely relent in the end, and any personal breach was unthinkable. From all that we know of the Archduke Johann, 'living in sin' and defiance of the sovereign will, would have been equally out of character, and there is no avoiding the impression that he was genuinely devoted to his brother, a man for whose character and régime it is almost impossible to feel much enthusiasm. And what of Anna's position in the public eye? She, the postmaster's daughter, must be accepted on her own terms by one of the most caste-ridden societies in Europe. Everyone, from the Emperor and Metternich downwards, must be shamed into doing so.

At last, in February 1829, Kaiser Franz took pity on the patient couple ('I can see', he had said to the Archduke not long before, 'that you are about at the end of your tether.'). They were married secretly, with only two witnesses, shortly before midnight in the chapel at Brandhof. Johann was forty-seven, Anna was twenty-five. The thought that they might remain childless can hardly have occurred to either of them, but it was not until ten years later, when all hope of a child had been given up, that Anna gave birth to a son—Franz. By that time she had come a long way, but not only in the sense that she had come up in the world. She had had Metter-nich's spies to contend with, bent on digging up and reporting even the mildest indiscretion. With infinite tact, patience and warmth of character she had had to disarm jealousy and suspicion not merely among the aristocracy but among her own contem-poraries and the middle-class wives of Vordernberg and Graz. She had been made a Baroness (Freifrau von Brandhofen) in 1834 and in 1850 Franz Josef raised the family to the rank of Grafen von Meran. In 1859 Archduke Johann died in his town house in Graz; Anna, Countess Meran, lived on till 1885 and died where her life began, in Aussee.

During the 1880s the Empress Elisabeth was often in the neigh-bourhood of Aussee. That horror of all official and even personal recognition which had developed over the years had become a severe neurosis, but the physical resilience which so exhausted her ladies in waiting showed no signs of flagging. Many years before, three months after their wedding in 1854, she and the Emperor Franz Joseph stayed in Aussee and were received with all the customary speeches and flag-waving; in the following year they came again and ten years later they brought the Crown Prince Rudolf and their daughter Gisela. In the eighties there were no flags. She came, as inconspicuously as possible, and she walked and walked: up the Loserberg from Altaussee, up to the high pastures on the Pfeiferalm and Brandalm, down to the Grundlsee. A marble slab in the shooting box at Elmgrund records: 'After a ten hour walk from Offensee, Her Majesty the unforgettable Empress Elisabeth spent the night here from 21 to 22 June 1888.' After that one would suppose that she might have been a little tired. But no: on the 22nd she took an extensive stroll before making the descent to Grundlsee. On the following day she walked to Altaussee, ascended the Tressenstein and rested at a farmhouse on the shoulder of the mountain. A lady in waiting, hurrying ahead, warned the women of the house not to appear to recognize the Empress, who, when she arrived, was evidently far from exhausted. After a drink of milk and a friendly chat with the women, she examined the house from attic to cellar and was full of praise for its cleanliness and the clear evidence of good husbandry. That night was again spent at Grundlsee, and the next day was a Sunday. The Empress went to Mass at Aussee (on foot, but to save time she drove back). In the afternoon she walked, as she so often had before, through the 'Koppen', along and above the course of the River Traun to Obertraun on Lake Hallstatt. It was her last visit, because after the suicide of her son Rudolf at Mayerling she could no longer face these familiar scenes.

7

Upper Austria

More people can link arms and roar, 'Oh Salzkammergut, Salzkammergut, la-la-la', than could say what the name stands for. The Salzkammergut lies in three provinces. Styria has the Aussee, Grundl and Toplitz lakes, Salzburg has the small but spectacularly beautiful Fuschlsee and all but half the northern shore of the Wolfgangsee (but not St. Wolfgang). Upper Austria has the two largest lakes, Attersee and Traunsee, as well as the Mondsee. But it is not considerations of size only that make it logical to discuss the whole lake district in one chapter rather than piecemeal in three: Upper Austria contains the heart of the Salzkammergut and it holds, as it were, the copyright.

The word *Kammergut* means literally Chamber Estate, that is to say, crown lands the revenues from which flowed directly into the sovereign's exchequer—the *Kammer*. The archbishops of Salzburg might be supposed to have had enough salt at Hallein, but nevertheless there was constant friction with the Habsburgs over the workings between Lake Hallstatt and Gosau. Gradually, the crown gained possession of Aussee, Hallstatt and Ischl, and the Emperor Maximilian I bought out the private shareholders and brought the salt industry in these areas entirely into the hands of the state. To complicate the story, Aussee remained as a separate unit governed by the *Hofkammer* in Graz until it was transferred to the central authority in 1741. The pocket of land at the southern tip of Upper Austria enclosing the lake of Hallstatt, the Gosau district and the whole of the upper Traun valley up to Ebensee was the original, authentic Salzkammergut. It was only when the *Kammergut* as such no longer existed that the name came to be applied, loosely and with no boundaries to mark its beginning and end, to the whole of this unrivalled series of lakes which lie among the Osterhorn group and the Tennengebirge, the Totesgebirge, the Höllengebirge and, mightiest of them all, the Dachstein.

So vital were the salt mines to the Habsburg exchequer that this original Salzkammergut became a phenomenon for which it is difficult to find a parallel: a sombre, introverted land which no one might enter without a visa, into and out of which no one might marry. The life of the entire population was caught up and organized into a system which can be looked upon as paternal or as mildly diabolical in its totalitarianism, but it was certainly consistent and efficient. To have been born within sight of the Salzberg where men have mined salt for three thousand years, in the Gosau district or in the valley of the Traun, was to find oneself in a welfare state. There were hospitals, free medical attention and pensions. If people were to marry young, and thus raise the birthrate, then there must be housing, and so the building of cottages was encouraged. There was exemption from military service and no taxation. But this planner's dream by no means confined itself to the men who were directly engaged in production or even to the allied trades and—the solecism cannot be resisted—the infrastructure. Management of the woods and forests was exemplary because timber was an essential factor in industry and in daily life, but it was forbidden to grow corn, and there was no question of the population being self-supporting. Its needs were supplied from elsewhere, and this too was carefully organized. In 1569 the order went out that the farmers in the districts around and to the south of Kremsmünster were to deliver all their corn to the market at Gmunden. Failure to do so would result in confiscation of property or even in a sentence of death. Meat was brought in from the land on the western side of Lake Traun, and if this was not enough further supplies were imported from Styria.

This strange monopolistic situation was not, of course, cemented overnight, but the combination of privilege and isolation together with a highly rational use of labour gradually set its stamp on the whole district. The entire social structure was different from anywhere else. 'The rich man in his castle, the poor man at his gate': this traditional picture does not apply. There were not only no nobility around the shores of Lake Hallstatt and along the road to Ebensee, there were no farmers either in the usual sense but only smallholders, an army of state employees and a minor bourgeoisie; two of the 'estates of the realm' were missing from the scene. The spiritual centre was Traunkirchen, but the Church had little direct authority over the lives of the people. Were they happy? Compared with the slowly deteriorating situation of the farming communities in Upper and Lower Austria which led to the peasant revolts in the sixteenth and seventeenth centuries, they led a sheltered existence. And yet there was almost perpetual discontent, basically because the system was too rigid. Those shifts and balances which, even in a clearly stratified society, could sometimes relieve intolerable pressure, were unable to operate because they were absent. There was the sovereign, and there were his minions, but very little in between.

Between Lake Hallstatt and the other lakes of the Salzkammergut there is a complete contrast in mood. At Hallstatt it is as though a colony of swifts had built their nests at the base of the Salzberg, clinging, because it is their nature, to a protected but apparently inconvenient place. The Illyrians whose two thousand graves gave the name of Hallstatt to an epoch in prehistory must have found the site as cramped as we do today; presumably no one ever built lake dwellings on timber piles just for the fun of it. The water is still, sombre, almost black. It is a fjord-like lake, the village in its setting one of the most resplendent jewels that Austria has to offer. The threat of a murderous road development has hung over Hallstatt for years but has now, one hopes, been averted for all time.

The Attersee is a great sheet of water, lined with hotels and pensions, covered with sailing boats: it should either be made use of or seen from a distance. There is a tantalizing view of the Attersee from the autobahn, but I also remember an early morning after a night spent in a very small farmhouse in the hills above the lake on the southern side. Breakfast had been a slice of black bread off the immense family loaf, washed down with cocoa, with the children to keep me company at the scrubbed board table. In the early morning light, the view on the drive down was all that one could ask for. All the same, I prefer the Mondsee because it is more manageable, and Lake Wolfgang because, in contrast to the Traun valley, this is a more light-hearted, open landscape with large prosperous farms and impressive architecture.

As soon as Mondsee comes in sight one is bound to wonder what such a large parish church is doing in this small town. Behind the bold Italianate façade, the origins of the most venerable abbey in Upper Austria go back to A.D. 748 when it was founded by Utilo II, Duke of Bavaria and father of the celebrated Tassilo who made a pact with the Huns in defiance of Charlemagne. Benedictine monks lived and worked in Mondsee Abbey for a thousand years, and it cannot be an illusion to feel that the profoundly civilizing influence of the rule of St. Benedict had a permanent effect on the people among whom they lived.

The figure of St. Wolfgang, too, is wholly benevolent: he was no pomp-loving prince of the Church, although as Bishop of Regensburg his power and influence were considerable. The famous altar screen at St. Wolfgang inevitably reminds one of the triptych at Heiligenblut, which, carved in the direct tradition of Michael Pacher, was brought from the workshops at Bruneck in South Tyrol nearly thirty years after the screen at St. Wolfgang was lifted into place.

Michael Pacher was born between 1435 and 1440, the son of a vintner at Neustift north of Brixen, where the 'Pacherhof' is still standing. His travels in Italy and his study of the work of Mantegna taught him a great deal, in particular how to use the effects of light to deepen perspective, but his style remained within the sphere of German Gothic. In 1471, when the Abbot of Mondsee commissioned Pacher's masterpiece for St. Wolfgang, the artist's reputation was largely confined to the Tyrol, but he must have been highly recommended by the superiors of monasteries in Salzburg or southern Bavaria. The immense screen was made almost entirely in the workshop at Bruneck, and it took nine years to complete. Pacher was then faced with the problem of transport. The initial stages took the precious load over the Brenner to Hall, then down the River Inn by boat to Braunau. Up to this point Pacher had to bear the expense, from Braunau onwards the cost was borne by the abbey, but responsibility for damage was Pacher's throughout. The weighty but fragile carving was brought on in further stages by cart to Mattighofen, Strasswalchen, Irrsdorf and Mondsee, and finally, perhaps in mingled triumph and terror, by raft to St. Wolfgang, where the by no means negligible work of erection, minor repairs and touching up remained to be done. What this journey from South Tyrol must have cost Pacher in sheer nerve strain can be imagined when we realize that the shrine is thirty-four feet high and when the screens are opened to their fullest extent (which used to be allowed only on high feasts of the Church) nearly twenty feet wide. Upper and Lower Austria are rich in carved altar screens. The Kefermarkt screen is only a few years younger than the one at St. Wolfgang (1490–1498) but its religious mood is harsher, more tortured. It is also dedicated to St. Wolfgang, but even now, after endless research, its creator is unknown. By the middle of the last century it was rapidly deteriorating and was saved by the united efforts of the parish priest and by Upper Austria's leading novelist Adalbert Stifter who devoted several years to supervizing the work of restoration. The same fate—decay from the attacks of woodworm and dry rot—nearly overtook the later (1520) but exceptionally fine screen at Mauer near Melk, mainly because until quite recent years its existence was hardly known. It is carved out of lime wood and, like the Kefermarkt screen, is unpainted. As with all these altar screens its principal charm lies in the vivid, lifelike reproduction of the contemporary men, women and children who served as models. There is another most beautiful example (1500) in the little village of Gampern near Vöcklabruck.

Ideally, one should not only make a tour of the whole Salzkammergut but also try to see as many as possible of the smaller but highly dramatic lakes: the Gosausee (south-west of Hallstatt) and the Irrsee (north of Mondsee) which, at the time of writing, is still the kind which hardly bothers to change for dinner. There are little lakes and tarns in remote places: the Langbathsee (from Ebensee), Offensee, Almsee and so on. The main routes for a tour are easy to see on any map. Between Salzburg and Bad Ischl the road looks down on to the exquisite Fuschlsee. This is a wonderful drive at any time, but even more so in autumn when the deciduous trees among the pines are changing colour. The Salzkammergut federal route links the Styrian lakes and Hallstatt to the rest of the group, and from Bad Ischl, the axle of the whole area, the old salt road beside the river takes one to Lake Traun which the Romans called 'felix', on to Gmunden and joins Route 1 at Lambach. It is hard to believe that the road along the Traunsee was only built in 1872, so that during all those centuries when Gmunden was the administrative capital of the old Salzkammergut and its only gateway to the outer world, the entire transport of salt, supplies and personnel had to be done by boat and raft. The celebrated 'Raffelstetten Customs Regulations' of A.D. 906 mentions 'salt boats' on Lake Traun, and some of them must have looked very like the big craft with their impressive carved bows which can be seen during the Corpus Christi celebrations today.

It was the tall, frail old gentleman known as Onkel Jules, permanently seated in his upright *Biedermeier* armchair, wearing a black velvet skull cap and smoking his two-foot-long carved pipe with its painted china bowl, who told me, years ago, something of the history of Gmunden and who spoke of the mysterious owner of the Schloss Ort.

Ort consists of two castles, the Landschloss and the Seeschloss, joined by a four hundred foot-long wooden bridge which, in itself, has a long history as it is first mentioned in 1110. Originally, the castle on the lake was a Gothic structure built round a triangular courtyard with arcades on two sides. Parts of the old castle remain, such as the massive gate tower, though the onion cupola is a seventeenth century addition dating from the restoration of the castle after a fire during the peasant war in 1626. The Landschloss mainly goes back to the first half of the seventeenth century, but it was very considerably modernized during the nineteenth century and later. It has been crown property since 1689, but in 1869 it was bought by Grand Duke Leopold II of Tuscany. He died not long afterwards, and in 1876 his widow, Maria Antonia, gave the property to their son Archduke Johann Salvator of Tuscany;

many of the interior alterations were carried out by him. Like his namesake, Archduke Johann also found the burden of royalty hard to endure, so much so that in 1889 he renounced his title and privileges, married a girl called Milly Stubel and adopted the name Johann Ort. But his newly-won freedom was short. In the following year he boarded his ship, the *St. Margaretha,* at Chatham and set sail for Buenos Aires. The ship was last sighted on 12th July 1890, and then it disappeared without trace. So far as we know, that was the end of the *St. Margaretha,* its crew and its owner, the reluctant Habsburg Johann Ort.

The whole aura of the latter-day Habsburg court lies so heavily over Bad Ischl that you either revel in it or you do not. To ignore it is difficult. If Nikolaus Lenau was complaining of *Erzherzogerei* around Aussee during the first half of the nineteenth century, his darkening mind could hardly have borne the rustic court life of Ischl in later years when it basked in the rays of imperial patronage. Ischl's royal epoch began in the 1820s when it was discovered by Franz Joseph's parents, and as time went on the royal family's regular summer visits inevitably attracted an increasing number of distinguished personages who built or rented villas in the vicinity. To be in close proximity to the 'All-Highest' while he was in holiday mood might well present opportunities which came less easily in the capital. Members of the court, high society, government and diplomacy donned the once frowned upon, now *de rigueur* grey suits with green facings, took up their walking sticks and went for long, bracing constitutionals (though they would not have called them that; the word 'constitution' still had a dubious ring.) But it is more interesting to think of Bad Ischl as an irresistible magnet for the empire's artists, writers, poets, actors and composers. In their day all the painters of nineteenth-century Austria set up their easels around Ischl: Waldmüller and Gauermann, Jakob and Rudolf von Alt, Moritz von Schwind who painted the frescoes in the foyer of the Vienna Opera, and the man who gave his name to an era: Hans Makart. Bruckner often played the organ in church, Brahms spent several summers in Ischl and many of his works were composed there; sometimes he would spend an evening with Johann Strauss. How many operettes, how many waltzes were composed in Ischl? Certainly *The Merry Widow*, born in Lehar's villa 'Rosenstöckl' (he died there in 1948); and Emmerich Kalman, Carl Michael Ziehrer, Oscar Straus and Edmund Eysler were all there at various times, composing and performing. Competition to perform on the stage at Ischl was intense, and from the programmes and casts it is clear that the leading actors and actresses of the German-speaking world played there, so that the Kurtheater became something even more than a projection of Viennese theatre life. Everyone had some motive apart from the salubrious air and the wholesome waters: even King Edward VII, who hoped to woo Franz Joseph away from the German alliance. He came three times, in 1905, 1907 and 1908. The works of many among that great assembly live on, but in those days only one figure mattered: the old gentleman, moving slowly in the early morning light, along the path, through the wicket gate which led to the Villa Felicitas where the one person lived in whose company he found friendship and consolation: *die gnädige Frau*, Katharina Schratt.

The people of the Salzkammergut have often teetered on the verge of revolution, and the last time was in 1957 when the 'Ischler-Bahn' was closed down: to give it its official title, the Salzkammergut Local Railway. They are still convinced that it was a major blunder. What splendid things small-gauge railways are, what a unique opportunity they give to enjoy the view undisturbed by traffic, what fun it is to stand on their end platforms, holding on to the rails; how glorious are their steam engines where these still exist—and exist they do.

Austria used to be rich in small-gauge railways and quite a number have survived. The first railway on the European continent was the line from Linz to Budweis, which was opened in sections between 1827 and 1832. The reason why this type was chosen in many parts of the country was simply that it was that or nothing. A narrow-gauge track is infinitely cheaper to construct because far less earth-shifting is needed. The tracks took up even less space than an old-style country road, and as they were able to take in their stride curves more than twice as sharp as those which even the slow, normal gauge trains of the time could tolerate, they could bumble along winding valleys causing a minimum of disturbance. Many of these railways came to remote villages just in time to save the economic situation of the people by linking up with the new industrial life of the country; now they are a burden and socially superfluous. But there is a case to be made for retaining the lines in some tourist areas and in places which are not yet fully developed beauty spots. Those steam engines are admittedly a mixed blessing. A shower of sparks and red-hot particles of coal streams from the engine which plies between Weiz and Birkfeld: a rousing sight from a safe distance, but to stick ones head out of the window is inadvisable. Flame-spewing models of this type with their pan-shaped funnels date from the end of the last century, and although one locomotive bearing the date 1889 which I noticed only a few years ago no longer appears on the official list of rolling stock, I believe it to be still working. Some of these engines began their years of service far beyond the frontiers of modern Austria, in Galicia, the Bukovina, Transylvania and Bosnia-Herzegovina. Rather younger models are still used in the coal-mining areas and also at Pertisau in the Tyrol where the line is almost solely used by tourists. But most small-gauge lines were electrified early in their career: the Pinzgau Local Railway (Zell-am-See to Krimml) for example, and the Mariazeller-Bahn. This line was a great success from the outset, as it carried the main western flow of pilgrims to Mariazell, and its character as a true alpine railway after Laubenbachmühle made it imperative to go over to electricity. The view from the train on the long ascent should cure anyone who supposes Lower Austria to be a monotonous province. And there is the Ybbstal Railway, which runs along the emerald green, trout-filled waters of the River Ybbs beneath sheer cliffs between Gstadt and Göstling, to the Lunzersee.

The fact that the western autobahn links the northern lakes of the Salzkammergut is a great advantage even to fast-moving migrants, but many Austrians, even, may well wonder whether they will ever again drive along the old Federal Route 1, which for so many years drove them nearly mad but which, after all, did and does have so much to offer.

Lambach, on the Roman road between Salzburg and Linz, was even in those earliest times the branching off point for the route to the Salzkammergut, and the favourable situation where a stream flows into the Traun persuaded the Frankish Counts of Wels-Lambach to build their castle at this spot. But in 1040 the last of the family turned the castle into a monastery for twelve canons, and in due course it became a Benedictine abbey. An important discovery was made only a few years ago when Romanesque frescoes were uncovered in the choir of the original church which was consecrated in 1089. After the restoration work which has taken some years to complete, these late Ottonian frescoes showing pronounced Byzantine influence are generally recognized to be among the best of their kind. Lambach Abbey has its own theatre, where the fare offered would usually have been of an edifying nature. But for the opening night on 23rd April 1770 something a little lighter was appropriate, as the theatre was to be officially opened by Marie Antoinette en route to her wedding in Paris. The play chosen was *Der kurzweilige Hochzeitsvertrag* (*The Diverting Marriage Contract*) by Fr. Maurus Lindemayr. (If only she could have been not merely diverted, but stopped in her tracks, sent to take the waters in Ischl—anything, rather than on to Paris.)

On no account must anyone think that they may now drive slowly down the hill below the monastery walls and on towards Wels. First, there is Stadl-Paura.

This is by any reckoning the most extraordinary church in the country. 'Mysticism in stone' is a trite but not wholly inappropriate definition of Baroque church architecture, and the designer of Stadl-Paura set himself the ambitious task of expressing in stone the theological concept of the Trinity. Basically, it is contained within an equilateral triangle, with square towers at each corner. The proportions of the towers in relation to the walls are perfect and the whole structure is unified by the round dome with its three-cornered, pyramid-shaped lantern surmounted by the eye of God. Any possible dogmatic objections to a triangular structure are dispelled in the interior. Something of the architect's intention has been lost in the course of time, but it still remains clear: a

15a. St. Stephen's Cathedral, from a painting by Rudolf von Alt

15b. The Karlskirche looking towards the walled city in about 1840

16a. Am Hof in about 1823, from a contemporary print

16b. Vienna from the Belvedere, from the painting by Canaletto

circular church, to be entered at will from three directions, with absolute equality between the three altars dedicated respectively to the Father, Son and Holy Ghost, and unity as the dominating principle throughout the whole execution. The reason why, in practical use, the parishioners have departed a little from strict theological principles becomes evident as soon as the visitor notices that he is continually rotating on his heel, a movement which may assist concentration in Dervishes, but not in Christians. The building opposite the main entrance (and there we have it: the church has no business with a main door) used to be an orphanage for the children of fishermen who were drowned in the River Traun.

In ceremonial mood the Romans used to call Wels Colonia Aurelia Antoniana Ovilava, for everyday purposes it was Ovilava. Medieval 'Weles' covered only a quarter of the former area, but the sequence of architectural styles shows that it grew steadily, and the merchants' houses on the long, curved square and throughout the old town are mainly Gothic and Renaissance. Maximilian I, who made Wels his capital, died in the castle in 1519. Six years before the death of Maximilian, the young Hans Sachs came to work in Wels, where according to his own account he was visited by the muses and called to be a poet.

We must now draw in the Innviertel, a wedge of rich farming country between the Inn and the Danube which was not incorporated in Austria until 1779.

There is no need to be put off Braunau on the Inn because it was Hitler's birthplace, nor even because a number of people are still attracted to it for the same reason; Braunau remains noncommittal and does not care for this notoriety, one way or the other. The medieval character of the town is still very much present and it is worth while to drive round to the western side and notice the way the houses were built up against the town walls, and holes pierced in the walls to make windows. Here and there wooden balconies cling to the old fortifications in a way that one cannot remember seeing elsewhere in Austria.

The Inn is broad and runs for most of its course between Braunau and Schärding. It used to be alive with waterborne traffic. Even in 1872 a register of shipping recorded 2,108 ships, barges and boats plying on the river. And at Schärding, where nothing but a footpath separates the colossal watergate from the river, it is just possible to imagine the hubbub in the days when transport by water was infinitely preferable to transport by land. Schärding is a health resort where the particular form of hydro-therapy is practised which was invented by the Catholic priest Sebastian Kneipp, and the inns are filled with refugees from the régime which demands abstention from coffee, alcohol and spicy foods. The one really essential factor in any such course of therapy is to avoid association with one's fellow men as far as possible, and during a month spent at Schärding I divided my outdoor hours between pacing the banks of the Inn, exploring the town and picking ticks off a tame deer in the park. It would be truer to say: exploring the two towns, because there are two halves, an upper and a lower. The lower town is predictably old and picturesque, but the real interest so often lies in the detail, and here one caught my eye: a high water mark to the right of and *above* the arch of the watergate, showing the almost incredible level once reached by the Inn in its most ferocious mood. The upper town square is breath-taking if only for its sheer size, and it is lined by an unbroken series of gabled houses, painted in carefully graduated shaded of yellow, blue, red, pink and green. Very few still have their original Baroque or Rococo stucco decoration as the houses were repeatedly damaged in hostilities between Austria and Bavaria; if we except post-war damage in 1945 the last time of stress was 1809. In April of that year Kaiser Franz received Andreas Hofer and his brother-in-arms Josef Speckbacher at the inn 'Zum goldenen Kreuz' and heard their report on the campaign in the Tyrol, but only a few months later Schärding, which was strongly defended and offered bitter resistance, was heavily shelled, stormed and captured.

Before a start was made with regulating its course by dynamiting the rocks which lay in the bed of the river, the Danube was a dangerous river and for centuries the whirlpools were notorious, particularly the boiling rapids below Linz. After Passau, swollen by the waters of the Inn, the Danube often has to force its way along narrow channels between the dark Sauwald forest and boulder-strewn cliffs. Dr. Charles Burney was unwise enough to travel down to Vienna during his tour in 1772 in the cabin of a float, 'a huge and unwieldy machine a quarter of a mile long and loaded with deals, hogsheads and lumber of all kinds'. It was late August but the weather was inclement and the doctor was short of blankets and provisions. The cabin was draughty, and he did his best to stop up the chinks with hay and splinters of wood, but he 'wanted internal comfort', and ravenous though he was, had to throw his bits of fly-blown meat and mildewy bread (why, only twenty-four hours out of Passau?) into the Danube. Dr. Burney liked to make homely comparisons: 'The shore on each side, for a considerable way below Passau, has hills and rocks as high as those at Bristol'; the river's course to Engelhartszell was 'so compressed and shut up as to be narrower than the Thames at Mortlake', but going through the Struden rapids was really no worse than shooting London Bridge. The people were rude and uncultivated, as wild and barbarous as their country, but he noticed a natural talent for part-singing among the soldiers and peasants on the river banks.

Mrs. Frances Trollope and her daughter who made the trip down to Vienna by river in 1835 did not enjoy themselves either. It poured with rain. The ladies had to 'crowd into a little deal box with three or four incessant smokers ... with no more power to help ourselves than a parcel of poultry packed alive in a basket'. Oh why, she exclaimed in her letters, had she decided to travel by *ordinari*? Why had she allowed herself to be deceived by the capricious kindness of an initial sunny day? 'This abominable river has now the dull leaden hue of despair; every object on its dim and misty shore frowns gloomily upon us as we pass along; our hands are cold, our feet are wet, and each looks at the other with lack-lustre eyes that speak but of discomfort and ennui.' The villages at which they stopped for the night offered scandalous accommodation, little food and no heating. (Dr. Burney nearly starved.) The village by the abbey of Engelhartszell, for example, now a very pleasant market town, 'offers us almost the worst accommodation we have yet met with. I can give you no idea of the chill misery of the room in which we are going to dine, to sup, and then to sleep. The rain patters against the windows, and the wind howls; and yet the *frau,* unpitying, declares that her stoves have not yet been prepared for fire, and therefore fire we cannot have . . . [And] if, as my maid had contrived to make her understand, I insisted upon having clean sheets put upon the beds, I must pay extra for them, for it was not the custom of the house to change the linen for every change of company. Now, in this matter of the sheets, I am happily independent; but does not this give rather an awful idea of the establishment in general?'

Frances Trollope was a much-travelled woman and by no means an inveterate grumbler. When it was possible to enjoy herself, she did so, and she was an indefatigable walker, thinking nothing of a three-hour stroll before breakfast. (What a lady-in-waiting she would have made to the Empress Elisabeth.) She tells us nothing about the magnificent loop in the Danube at Schlögen, but describes the beauties of Aschach. By now she was avid to get to Linz, 'now in sight, with its multitude of military outposts, and its noble entourage of magnificent hills. This approach is glorious, it deserves all that has been said of it.' And then: 'the comforts of our hotel, of our civilized well-tamed "Black Eagle"! What a fine thing is an easy sofa! and a large handsome room, and good coffee . . . and all the other so often overlooked and neglected comforts that bless our daily existence! If you wish to know how much they are really worth, come down the Danube in an *ordinari.*'

It would certainly be wiser to drive from Passau to Linz (until at last this stretch of autobahn is built) along the evocatively named Nibelungenstrasse, which, at Schlögen, gives up all attempts to follow the twisting course of the Danube. The whole country-side rapidly loses its rather grim character, it opens up, becomes warmer and more friendly: we are coming to the 'orchard of Austria', the district which for centuries was known as the 'Schaunberger Ländchen' after the counts who ruled over it from their castle which lies just to the west of the road to Eferding, and later from Eferding Castle itself. The story goes that in the days of the feud between the Babenbergs and the Counts Schaunberg who were trying to set up shop on their own in the *Ländchen,* Duke Albrecht III laid siege to Schaumburg Castle (its later name) and erected three bastions from which the siege guns could be operated. The defenders got in first by catapulting barrels filled with human excrement at the tent of Duke Albrecht, who, after a pause to assemble the appropriate ammunition, retaliated in kind. For how long these barrels flew backwards and forwards the contemporary chronicler does not say, but finally the insurgents withdrew.

A little further back near Hartkirchen there is a road junction leading to Aschach, a spot which brought cries of rapture from Mrs. Trollope. She must have noticed the building that had always served as the toll-house and is known as the Faust-Schlößl, but will not have heard the legend attached to it.

It is not certain when the famous magician and alchemist Dr. Johannes Faust was in Linz, but it must have been between 1489 and 1493 when the Emperor Frederick III held court there while the Hungarian Matthias Corvinus occupied Lower Austria and was reigning in Vienna. According to the local legend, Faust took a fancy to Aschach and came to live in the house which is now called after him. Predictably, the devil now turns up disguised as a vagrant, and makes his pact with Faust: he will fulfil all the alchemist's wishes, but at the price of his soul. Faust sets the devil a number of tasks, each more difficult than the last, and demands at length that the devil shall build a tower on the house, taking no longer over it than the hours between the morning and evening angelus. Evening approaches, and Faust rows quietly across the river intending to ring the bells before the right hour has come, but the devil sends ravens to peck through the ropes which hold the bells. It is not entirely clear from the story who won the bet, but it must have been Faust because the devil lost his temper and banged a hole in the tower which no mortar has ever been able to close. The Faust-Schlößl went through many hard times and after occupation by Russian and American forces after the last war it was almost a ruin, but was patiently restored by its present owner and is now a hotel.

A mile or so south of Eferding lies one of the bloodiest battle-fields in the history of the peasant wars, at a place called Emlinger Holz. In 1626 the peasantry captured and held Eferding, and had managed to seal off the river traffic by throwing ropes and chains

across the Danube at the sharp bend near Neuhaus. The ships of
the Bavarian army under General von Pappenheim broke through
the boom during the night of 18th July, and brought reinforcements down to Linz which was besieged by the rebels. In the
ensuing battle more than three thousand rebels were killed.

From here it is no distance to the Renaissance castle at Alkoven,
Schloss Hartheim, which has horrific associations of a very different
kind to live down. It was used during the Nazi régime as a place
where the mentally handicapped including children were gassed.

After another six miles or so we have come to the greatest
church in the Rococo style in Austria: Wilhering. Like all Cistercian
abbeys, Wilhering was built in a remote valley, and the rapid
industrial expansion of Linz is hardly felt there even now. Of the
original building of 1146, part of the cloisters and the Romanesque
west door have survived. Just inside, the fourteenth-century tombs
of the Counts of Schaunberg (Schaumburg) seem to be guarding
Wilhering from the rival attentions of the sovereign dukes. When
the old abbey burned down in 1733, a grandiose set of buildings,
including state apartments and a library was planned, but shortage
of funds forced the abbot to cut his designs to more modest
proportions. Standing in the centre aisle one afternoon, listening
to the chant of the monks, I was struck by the contrast between the
stern Cistercian rule and the irrepressible gaiety of the surroundings, between their white and black robes, and the turquoise and
pink, the white and the gold: in a word—the sheer elegance of the
whole abbey. Was a prevailing fashion imposed on the abbot?
There might be some truth in this, but the real answer can be found
in the dedication of the church to the Virgin Mary and in the
designer's intention to represent her ascension into Heaven. The
success of the whole scheme turns on the use of Rococo, not as
mere decoration, but as the essence and purpose of a design which
is structurally plain and uncluttered. After these soaring lines and
soft, clear colours, the flower beds in the forecourt seem almost
crude, but there is also a quiet and, at any rate on weekdays,
seldom-visited garden, with trees, flowering shrubs and pools,
where anyone may wander about and rest without being
disturbed.

The Mühlviertel is the country north of the Danube which has fallen on hard times because, as it lies along the frontier of Czechoslovakia, it has become something of a cul-de-sac. It always offered rough living conditions for its farming community as the climate tends to be harsh; the summers are dry and cold winds blow in winter. Now it is threatened by depopulation. The forelands of the Bohemian mountain chain lie across the Mühlviertel and lap over into Lower Austria. As far as the River Feld-Aist, it is rolling hill country; east of Freistadt and Kefermarkt high plateau is deeply grooved by fast streams. It was not, by the way, the mills driven by water power which gave their name to the Mühlviertel, but the River Mühl. There is a 'greater' and a 'lesser' Mühl, and beside the former stands Schlägl Abbey. Hardly one in a hundred thousand visitors to Austria is likely to go to this utterly remote place, but the abbey possesses a surprising collection of pictures, including works by Altdorfer, the Master of Frankfurt, David Tenier, Loini Bernadini, Correggio, Veronese, Luco Giordano, and Martin and Bartholomäus Altomonte. Abalbert Stifter, a major Austrian novelist of the nineteenth century, wrote about the Salzkammergut, but the real 'Stifter country' is the Mühlviertel. There is perhaps a slight favour of *Cold Comfort Farm* about his characters, but his landscapes are sharp and clear, and these scenes have altered very little; if anything, they may be more lonely than they were in his time. He was particularly fond of the Haselgraben, a narrow valley between Linz and Bad Leonfelden. Both Schaunberg and Wildberg castle in the Haselgraben are associated with King Wenceslas IV of Bohemia who was notorious for his cruelty, was deposed in Prague and brought to Vienna but managed to escape across the Danube, where after a few weeks in hiding he was recaptured. Wenceslas is mainly remembered as the reputed murderer of St. John Nepomuk, one of the most popular saints of the baroque age whose statue can be seen in innumerable towns and villages throughout eastern Austria and Bohemia. The story, believed by generations of Catholics but now thought to be a fairy tale, is that he was confessor to the king's consort, Queen Johanna, and was thrown into the Moldau for refusing to satisfy King Wenceslas's curiosity in respect of his wife's sins.

Wooden farmhouse in
Bregenzer-Wald,
Vorarlberg

A trio of single-unit
farmhouses in East Tyrol

Single-unit type in
Pinzgau, Land Salzburg

'Pair' farms in Upper
Carinthia

'Cluster' type in Upper
Styria

Four-sided farmhouse in
the Hausruck district,
Upper Austria

The Upper Austrian block form, or 'Vierkanthof'

Lower Austria, three-sided farm

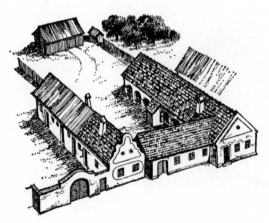

Extended and 'hook' farms, Burgenland

Stifter's novels describe the four-square farmhouses which are so characteristic of Upper Austria. They are spread over a fairly wide area, but the two-storeyed variety are mainly found in the Mühlviertel and in the district between the Rivers Enns and Traun. Much scholarship has gone into the study of Austrian farmhouses, their historical development and the different ways in which men planned the relationship between living and working space. Everyone who drives through Austria must be struck by the fundamental difference between the farms in, say, the Tyrol and those in Upper Austria, or between Carinthia and Burgenland. It is almost as though the early farmers had never heard of each other's existence and knew nothing of each other's way of life; more truly, of course, they were faced with different situations. The alpine farmer had, generally speaking, only one enemy, the elements, while the enclosed world of the eastern farmsteads is obviously defensive in character. But one would like to know much more. The illiterate peasant who first realized that it would be a most rational and convenient thing to be able to get up in the morning and—since it was pitch-dark and cold—walk from the upstairs landing straight into the barn and throw hay through a trap door into the feeding trough below, was a man who would make a name in industrial management today. However, others thought differently, and unfortunately it has always been comparatively easy to discover what men did, but more difficult to deduce why they did it. Subsidiary forms to be found in adjacent or even in the same districts need not detain us. The principal types which the traveller will see in Austria are the wooden farmhouses of the Bregenzer Wald, the broad, stately stone houses of the upper Inn and Lech valleys, the single-unit farms of the central and lower Inn valley and its Salzburg variants, which contrast with the 'pair' farms in Land Salzburg where the dwelling house and cowhouse stand side by side. There is a variant of the Salzburg *Paarhof* in East Tyrol and the west of Carinthia (and here an eye must be kept open for the big wooden frames for drying the hay in wet weather, they are to be seen nowhere else but in this part of southern Austria). These are the four main alpine farm types. The eastern alpine *Haufenhof* is only distantly related to them: the literal meaning of the name is that the buildings lie in a heap or huddle, and they certainly stand in a very loosely co-ordinated cluster. The roofs are steep and, particularly in Styria, probably gabled. This type begins in the Lungau district of Land Salzburg, is spread across upper Styria and Carinthia, and ends in the forests of the Wechsel. Now comes a totally different concept: the four-sided farmsteads mainly found in the Innviertel district of Upper Austria, and then Stifter's magnificent *Vierkanthöfe*. The rather more humble but equally pleasing version with only one storey is scattered across all Upper and Lower Austria. The three-sided farms of Lower Austria (with their fellows in the east and west of Styria) cannot compete with the *Vierkanter* in dignity. But the frontage is extraordinarily attractive, the wall joining the parallel lines of the buildings, the arched gateway and the warm colours—Baroque yellow, ochre or pink—are more homely than the forbidding blocks of the *Vierkanter*, and they give an atmosphere of their own to the quiet villages to the north and west of Vienna.

In all that part of Upper Austria which lies north of the Danube there was only one through passage where towns were likely to develop: the 'Feldaist hollow', the old trade route from Enns and Mauthausen up to Bohemia, once so important, now irrelevant. Freistadt has its back to the wall. But anyone who may make the effort to see Kefermarkt (which we noticed earlier in connection with the altar screen there and at St. Wolfgang) should carry on to Freistadt. The main square and the whole layout are remarkable because this is an unusually clear, unspoiled example of early town planning. The pioneers worked out the ground plan on geometrical principles and constructed their town as a unit. In most towns which developed gradually, the main square may tail off at the ends, or there will be side lanes leading into it. But here the square is sealed off by a row of houses at each end in such a way that the exits at the four corners are not immediately apparent. This produces an effect which can sometimes be noticed in Italy: almost like an immense hall with the roof open to the sky.

Linz is a brash, still rapidly growing industrial town into which a holiday visitor is unlikely to stray, though this is a different matter from saying that Linz is unpleasant to live in. It has its

mainly Baroque centre and its stately merchants' houses; it has the
Danube and makes good use of it; there is the celebrated local
hill, the Postlingberg, and the forest of Wilhering Abbey. It was
sheer absentmindedness that brought me, about ten years ago, face
to face with the Martinskirche. After recording a talk in the local
broadcasting studios and having an hour to kill before the train
left, a tendency to seek higher ground which mankind shares with
the sheep brought me on to the small hill within the town called
the Römerberg. Here there was a clearing, and a row of cottages.
Children were playing and ducks were waddling. And in the middle
of a patch of grass stood St. Martin's, the oldest church in continuous use in the whole of Austria. How small they were, these
Carolingian churches: on the day when Charlemagne himself
heard Mass here, there can only have been room for a few of his
companions.

We now have to go back a bit, because there is a route to be
explored which lies further to the south. St. Florian can very
easily be reached from the autobahn, but Kremsmünster and
Steyr are in a direct line between Lambach and Amstetten. First,
there is a recent discovery: the frescoes at Pucking, a small village
on a side road about halfway between Wels and Linz. They were
first noticed in 1946 and it has taken many years of patient work
to free them from the layers of plaster and whitewash which had
concealed them for so long that their existence was unknown. The
marvel of Pucking is that the frescoes cover the whole interior
of the church. The entire walls, the vault and ribs, an area of more
than nine hundred square feet are decorated with three thousand
stars and with the sun and moon, all in the brilliant original
colours which integrate the various groups and individual forms
into a perfect symbolic unity. Austrian art historians consider
this to be the most important find for many years, and point out
that this mid-fifteenth-century work in its high Gothic style stands
in complete contrast to the late-twelfth-century frescoes which fill
the interior of the chapel at Pürgg in the valley of the Enns.

The dissolution of Mondsee Abbey left Kremsmünster as the
oldest surviving monastery in Upper Austria. Duke Udilo of
Bavaria is all but forgotten, while his son and heir Tassilo who

founded Kremsmünster in 777 is still remembered for one reason that he would recognize, and for another which might surprise him. He rose in revolt against Charlemagne's creation, the Carolingian German Empire, and in 788 he was divested of his dukedom and banished to a monastery. The chalice which he presented to the Benedictines at Kremsmünster is still there, and it is one of the oldest in the Christian world. Perhaps it is reasonable to say that the Tassilo chalice owes its twelve-hundred-year span of life to the fact that it is made of a relatively base metal; had it been gold or silver its chances of survival would have been slight. But it is mainly copper, partly gilded, and inlaid with silver. The figures engraved on the cup and the whole design show the powerful influence of the art of the Celtic Church brought to Central Europe by the Irish monks. (The chalice normally shown to visitors is a replica, but the original can be seen on written application.) The curious 'Tassilo candlesticks' at Kremsmünster are almost equally venerable and a distant relationship to the chalice is apparent, but as they were made some time after 788 the name is misleading.

All monastic communities needed a plentiful supply of fish, but seldom has this situation been placed in such a formal setting. The monumental basins at Kremsmünster are eighteenth century, but there were fish pools here before. One was removed to make way for a home farm, the other was said to have stood on the spot where Tassilo's son Günther was killed by a wild boar.

A royal or learned visitor staying at Kremsmünster would have been very comfortable indeed. The guest rooms are neither too large nor poky, and the exceptionally fine Baroque stoves (built in unusually large sections) would have worked up a wonderful fug. And the library is a place in which to work in comfort, more than can be said of the vast, lofty halls containing the collections at Admont, Melk or Vorau. Kremsmünster library consists of four rooms divided by wide arched doorways, and its form is so finely proportioned, the decoration so light, that the splendour is never oppressive. The most valuable works are two Gospels (the Codex Millenarius) which are over a thousand years old.

For the record: the eighteenth-century observatory in the abbey garden is more than one hundred and fifty feet high and is popularly known as the 'Mathematical Tower'. There is a long tradition of astronomy at the abbey which is still maintained today.

To call Steyr the 'Austrian Birmingham', as more than one guidebook has done, is enough to put anyone off. Old Steyr used to be a centre of the industry which brought iron ore down the River Enns to make weapons, swords and knives which were sold as far afield as Venice and Constantinople, and the metal industries are the mainstay of the town today. But mercifully, all this has been kept well at bay, and as a result Steyr is still one of the best-preserved old towns in Austria and its main square one of the finest in the country. For its size, Steyr contains a daunting amount of sightseeing, but no one must miss standing on the bridge below the castle, the old 'Stirapurch' of the Counts Lamberg, and watch the waters of the Enns and Steyr as they meet, flow side by side and hesitantly mingle. And the visitor should look into one or two of the hidden courtyards behind the Gothic houses of the main square or its side streets. They are lined with arcades, and the stone pillars on the upper balconies are so finely sculptured that they might be carved woodwork brought in from the alps. Of all these secretive little courtyards, one of the best is at 16 Kirchengasse, the 'Dunkelhof'. Most precious of all is the 'Bummerlhaus' which conceals no less than three courtyards with colonnades, as well as a Gothic spiral staircase.

A few miles to the west of St. Florian in the village of Ansfelden, Anton Bruckner was born. While he was still only a boy his father, the schoolmaster, died and he was taken in as a chorister by the monastery school. He taught for a time at Windhaag near Freistadt, and in 1848, then aged twenty-four, he was appointed organist at St. Florian and stayed there for ten years. Later on this abjectly humble, hesitant, unworldly little man—an obsessive snuff-taker; the ivories of his piano are stained an unappetizing brown—became organist at Linz Cathedral. The years of his triumph and depression in Vienna ended with his death on 1st October 1896.

It would be highly invidious to attempt to tie down a composer of his stature to a landscape or to anything whatever outside the language of music. All the same, this province of Upper Austria is contained within it. The country dances are there; he even uses the strange, irregular tapping of the Pinzgau *Perchten*. There is none of the blazing colour of the Salzkammergut, the cold of the glaciers or the majesty of the Dachstein. But the rolling hill country is in his music, the northern plateau, the dense forests and the Danube. The spiritual force within the symphonies as well as the Masses is Bruckner's intense, almost Baroque piety to which most Austrians, if they have any music in them, respond almost by instinct: it is familiar to them because it speaks the same language as the architecture and decoration of their churches. After the bitter hostility of Brahms and the critics had been lived through and overcome, Bruckner was accepted by the public as one of the greatest composers of his epoch, but he has not found a place in the everyday repertoire of the world. Like Adalbert Stifter, he has not travelled well.

Anyone can walk on the memorial slab which marks his burial place in the crypt beneath the organ loft at St. Florian, but on the first of many visits to the monastery church I never noticed it. The Vienna Philharmonic Orchestra filled the whole space up to the back pews, and they played a Bruckner Mass to a packed congregation among whom were the President of Austria, Wilhelm Miklas, and the Chancellor, Kurt von Schuschnigg. It was in the late summer of 1937, and half a year later Austria ceased to exist.

There is a gallery of paintings by Altdorfer at St. Florian: a valuable collection and well worth a visit. A slight element of hazard may be involved in inspecting them during the off-season and alone: it is possible to be locked in, as I was, and left for an hour or so to study that artist's remorseless attention to realistic detail in his representations of the crucifixion and other scenes of martyrdom.

In these earlier periods of art it is sometimes the background of a picture that interests one more than the whole. The minor figures may pulse with life, or the landscape may be of such documentary importance as the Vienna Kärntnerstrasse in the Visitation by the 'Schottenmeister', or the view of Vienna Castle between the figures of Ferdinand III and his consort Isabel of Portugal. Baroque art, with its totally different intentions and pretentions, is another matter. Either we respond to it, selectively of course but on the whole with enthusiasm, or we flee from it; to pick at it is usually a mistake. Myopia is a disadvantage: cupids are often maddening, saints theatrical, pulpits bloated, but the whole effect is glorious. The great wave of Baroque adaptation and new building in Austria inevitably destroyed much of the work of past ages, although we have to admit that, when they could, architects often incorporated the most valuable elements, such as Romanesque portals, in their designs. But when Thomas Schwanthaler built the high altar at St. Wolfgang he showed a humility which was rare at any time in refusing to consign Pacher's masterpiece to oblivion. He set it up further down the chancel where it was bound to impair the effectiveness of his own work. In some cases the works of seventeenth- or early eighteenth-century builders were adapted soon after their time in a way that they would have found excruciating. Schlierbach, originally a medieval Cistercian foundation in Krems valley, may have been a trifle overladen with stucco in the first instance, but by the time late eighteenth-century decorators had superimposed their carved and gilded convolutions, flowers and all kinds of knick-knacks, Carlone would hardly have known the basilica as his own.

The reputation of the Carlones from Lake Como who, as we said earlier, held office for three generations as municipal builders in Graz, naturally spread far beyond the frontiers of Styria. Carlo Antonio Carlone built Baroque Schlierbach and Garsten near Steyr, he made one of the ornamental basins at Kremsmünster and carried out the adaption of the church, but his work there was completed by a successor whose genius equalled and perhaps exceeded his own: Jakob Prandtauer. C. A. Carlone's masterpiece was the church of St. Florian, where his colossal pillars lend stability to the new *trompe-l'oeil* technique, introduced in Rome only ten years earlier and used here for the first time in Austria, to produce an effect of enormous, ethereal height. This almost cathedral-like church was begun in 1686, and by the time Carlone died in 1708 he had brought about an infinitely ambitious synthesis of mathematical and musical principles contained within an all-embracing spiritual concept.

The perfect proportions of the double staircase at St. Florian were also designed by Carlone, but just as Prandtauer extended the Carlone tract of ornamental basins and completed his work on the church at Kremsmünster, so he adapted and carried out Carlone's ideas for the staircase which, alone, is worth driving a long way to see. To Prandtauer, these were assignments among many others which he carried out with his usual personal attention to every detail, but they were of subsidiary importance compared to his supreme creation, Melk Abbey.

We have nearly reached the edge of Upper Austria, the historic divide on the River Enns. Along the Danube on both sides, the roads have to make a wide circuit to avoid marshland and water meadows. The northern road crosses the fertile Machland plain, passes the former Cistercian monastery of Baumgartenberg on its way to Grein, an attractive small township on the river at the entrance to the Strudengau enclave. Grein's minute theatre, built in 1790, is in its unaltered form the oldest in Austria, and still has the original lock-up seats—and a box from which prisoners in the jail next door could watch the performances.

Mauthausen, across the Danube from Enns, is a pretty village which still suffers from the notoriety of its name. To spend a night there would be an ordeal: the desolation of spirit blowing down from the former concentration camp on the hill is too oppressive. Seen from the car park, the towering walls are a surprise. This was the outer assembly yard. On the higher ground, a light breeze blows across the field where the national memorials have been set up. The trickle of visitors passes a talkative Lazarus at the gate. Inside, groups, couples, tend to split up, to move about singly. The notices on the huts are terse and euphemistic, the tablets on the containing walls are unassertive and an increasing effort is needed to go close up and read what happened at that spot. Here, the individual fate is still faintly discernible, not quite lost in the unknowable vapours of Auschwitz and Treblinka. It is a few minutes' walk to the cliff's edge: at their base are the deserted quarries which once supplied the streets of Vienna with granite cubes for paving stones. There is hardly a sound to be heard in the whole camp. But this is not the silence of a cemetery or even of an old battlefield. It is the silence of a generation that has no words to describe what it has seen.

After the last war the Enns river formed the boundary between the Russian and the American zones of occupation. No one might cross the Enns bridge without showing his pass at the Russian control point, and the usual human dramas which this familiar situation produces followed one another daily. Here the West ended, the East began. If ever a political event took place in defiance of all realistic probability it was the liberation of the eastern provinces of Austria, and part of the capital, from Soviet Russian occupation. Into the almost straight line down from the North Sea which divides Europe into two halves, Austria presses forward like a battering ram. Tactical give and take on the international scene, a small element of miscalculation over Austrian oil reserves, the endless patience of western negotiators but also the moral courage of Austrian statesmen and workers in industry, restored Austria's national identity.

The River Enns had been in a similar situation before. To the peaceful Slav settlers, the Enns marked the approximate western limit of their pioneering efforts, while to their masters the Avars, the Enns line was the limit of their sphere of power. To the Bavarians, therefore, the Eastern March was the land west of the Enns. They got along perfectly with the Slavs, but officially, so to speak, barbarism began here. In 791, down came Charlemagne with his armies; Theodoric and Wagenfried took the left bank of the Danube, Charlemagne followed the right bank and the imperial fleet brought the provisions down by water. The vast assembly camped for three days near Enns. The Avars were driven back, but in 907 the Mongols swept forward from the Hungarian plains and for fifty years, until the Battle of Lechfeld, the Enns river again found itself the seam joining two worlds. In the thirteenth century the historic 'Lands Above and Below the Enns' became an administrative reality but it was not until 1918 that the 'Crownland above the Enns' took the name of Upper Austria.

The words 'near Enns' are a deliberate anachronism. At the time when Charlemagne was holding his three days of prayer and supplication before he attacked the Huns, Enns did not exist.

He was in Lorch, the old Lauriacum, which is worth visiting now that extensive excavations have been made. At the centre of the Roman line of defences from Carnuntum on the Amber Route and Regina Castra (Regensburg), Lauriacum developed at the spot where the 'iron road' from Eisenerz bisected the line of defences along the Danube, the *limes,* and it became the headquarters of the II Legion. When hostile pressure no longer came from the north, but from the east, the town and camp on the Enns swivelled round, as it were, by ninety degrees to face the new situation. Roman Lauriacum, rebuilt after repeated devastation, lived on during the Carolingian era, but Lorch, as it was now called, lay on the plain, and Enns Castle was built in about 900 on the hill to provide a defence against the Mongol invasion. But it was only in the twelfth century, the great age of citadel building, that the surrounding fortifications went up, and the town within them. If we stand on the main square now, we can see how typical it is of its kind: large and regular, a planned town of generous proportions. The proud sixteenth-century watchtower, symbol of the new power of the middle classes, is six times the height of the surrounding houses and tends to dwarf them. The early fourteenth-century Wallsee chapel which was incorporated in the parish church has a connection with the first Austrian Habsburg in that the Wallsee brothers from the manor of Walchsee in the Habsburg Forelands, accompanied Rudolf to Austria and rose to great, though not long-lived, prosperity and influence.

8

Lower Austria

Whenever I have been away from Austria for some weeks or months and am scudding along the Westautobahn heading for home, there comes a moment when, if it is afternoon and the sun is shining, I am suddenly seized by a sense of urgency. A glance at my watch, at the angle of the shadow cast by a tree: I must get to Melk before sundown. The attraction of Melk Abbey, the incarnation of the Baroque spirit, is so insistent that it seems to be something more than a purely isolated architectural miracle. Surely it has some broader meaning in the life of this eastern province?

The landscape of Lower Austria changes slowly, there are no abrupt contrasts. The last mountains of the eastern alpine chain stand within the province, but now they gradually soften to a mere ripple which dies on the plain of the Vienna basin. This fragmented province with various focal points but no natural centre apart from Vienna, does possess unifying characteristics formed by history and situation. Perhaps it is not too fanciful to see two facets: grave and gay; two predominating qualities: attraction and repulsion.

The tensions produced by a frontier situation have been a permanent factor from earliest times and are still as relevant as ever. Lower Austria has always exercised a powerful attraction on its eastern, southern and northern neighbours. There came a time when this magnetism took on a different aspect, the other bastion of western Europe became the pivot of an empire. Even then, the inner paradox, the dual forces of attraction and repulsion, were still active, and when the tension became too great and the slender thread snapped which held the Austro–Hungarian empire together, Lower Austria found itself just where it was before: on the demarcation line between East and West. Essentially, it was still the marchland of the Dukes of Babenberg, the original Ostarrichi, the Eastern Realm.

More than 400 fortified castles still stand in Lower Austria, 130 ruins are dotted about the landscape, 88 fortified churches played their defensive role in times of emergency, and the sites are known of nearly 500 other castles and fortified places which have disappeared leaving no trace behind them. If the course of history were unknown these figures would still speak for themselves: this was a massive, intercommunicating (though in fact not closely co-ordinated) defence system in depth. The five-sided towers at Freienstein and Schauenstein point a wedge like the keel of an upturned boat in the assumed direction of attack. The smooth surfaces and minute, high-up windows of Heidenreichstein, the moated fortress on the frontier of Bohemia, are deliberately cold and forbidding, breathing stony immobility and defiance. Psychological warfare is no invention of modern times. Just as animals raise their hackles and snarl, and men wear frightening masks, chant spells or shout rude words (design and phrasing have altered with the years, the basic content hardly at all), so it was by no means the least of a castle's functions to intimidate, and induce, if possible, discouragement and voluntary withdrawal.

Here are the two sides of the coin: repulsion and attraction, the sword and the cross. In total contrast to the citadels, the Baroque abbeys beckon, shine out like beacons into the land, warm, beautiful, compelling. In the open countryside (town architecture is based on different principles) the effects which the sacred and profane buildings of that epoch were intended to produce are not often comparable. The nobleman has left his uncomfortable castle on the hill and has built his new, palatial residence in the valley below. Concealed by trees, it is quite likely to be undetectable at a distance. The servants, even the gardeners, are not permitted to walk within sight of the windows, or only in the early morning before the owner and his family have risen from their beds. Fellow peers are meant to be impressed and, above all, the sovereign; the 'public', in any modern sense, does not exist.

The view of Melk Abbey which we see from the autobahn is imposing and eminently satisfying, but this aspect is false in that it distorts the architect's intentions, giving an impression of an abbey lying in a valley. For this reason it really is not enough merely to curl down the exit from the motorway into the town and to approach the monastery by the main entrance at the rear. Melk was, of course, intended to be seen from the valley floor, from the road or from the river itself. The climax of this natural approach comes with the view from the Danube car ferry. Now the abbey rears forward on its cliff site, the whole frontage is bathed in gold while the enclosed terrace, broken by a structure which is a proscenium arch in all but name, draws the eye forward. This is Baroque *Welttheater*—all the world's a stage.

If Abbot Berthold Dietmayr had not had the courage and judgement to bestow the building contract where he did, Melk might never have become one of the major triumphs of Baroque architecture in Europe and Jakob Prandtauer's name might now be ranked with those of lesser men. When Prandtauer went to live in St. Pölten in 1689 he registered as a sculptor, and when he started work at Melk his achievements to date amounted to no more than a series of minor building operations including a chapel, a garden pavilion and extensive renovations to Ochsenburg Castle near St. Pölten. The task before him was one with which his contemporaries were familiar: to take a hotchpotch of buildings which had grown up over a period of seven hundred years, and to create a unified structure; but the problem at Melk was greatly complicated by the limits of the site on an extended slab of rock. To raze the whole conglomeration in one go was out of the question; the work of Melk Abbey could not be held up for a generation. The foundation stone was laid on 29th June 1702. Prandtauer went ahead on well-tried lines with Vignola's Il Gesù in Rome as a model, constantly dashing off to St. Florian, Krems-münster, Sonntagberg, Garsten or St. Pölten but supervising every detail of the work. He was lucky in his patron. The reign of Abbot Dietmayr (1700 to 1739) was an unenviable one, as he must have spent his entire term of office surrounded by dust and scaffolding. Dietmayr was a man of culture and taste who was Chancellor of Vienna University in 1706, and if Melk was Prandtauer's life work, it was Dietmayr's no less. Money for the enormous project had to be found, and when a fire broke out in 1738, destroying much of the work of nearly forty years, the shock was too much for the abbot and he died in the following year. Neither man was able to see the end of it—Melk was completed in 1747 by Prandtauer's pupil Josef Munggenast—but it remains the work of an architect and master-builder who, apart from the Carmelite Church in St. Pölten, was otherwise fated to complete what others had begun or to collaborate with that titan of his age, Johann Bernhard Fischer von Erlach. In 1945, the Russian command which had allowed its men to plunder their way through Lower Austria in truly time-honoured fashion, placed a guard on Melk Abbey and allowed nothing to be touched.

In the rush to get to Melk before the sun dropped into the Danube several small worlds have been left by the wayside, and they must be gathered in. South of the Danube there is Amstetten, Ardagger, Waidhofen on the Ybbs and all that stretch of country known as the Eisenwurzen.

Just below Amstetten, on the river Ybbs, lies an undistinguished village called Neuhofen with a unique claim to fame. The parchment dated 1.11.996 in which the name of Austria was mentioned for the first time, referred to property at Neuhofen, *'in regione vulgari vocabulo Ostarrichi'*. Through an accident of history this deed of enfeoffment, only one of so many which charted the reclamation of the 'eastern realm', survived, and with this naming *Österreich* was born. But *Ostarrichi* also envokes the name of a goddess: Ostara, daughter of the storm god Thiasse, who was the spirit of spring, of youth, morning and sunrise; of Easter. These are not two meanings, but one. The German language has always called the East *das Morgenland*, land of the morning.

The Eisenwurzen district lies between the rivers Ybbs and Erlauf. It is the Lower Austrian part of a larger area in the alpine forelands which extends from the Krems valley to the Traisen, whose inhabitants used to make a good living by the manufacture

of all kinds of goods made of Styrian iron. The scythes, swords
and razors from the workshops of the wealthy ironmasters were
celebrated for their high quality throughout Europe and the
Middle East, and although the countless small family firms up and
down the valleys began to die out as the result of concentration and
rationalization as far back as the sixteenth century, there are still a
few left. Waidhofen on the Ybbs has that distinctive character—
quite different from the feel of a primarily agricultural centre
like Amstetten—which develops when particular skills have been
practised for hundreds of years. Craftsmanship, specialized and
kept constantly in tune with demand in distant places, develops
self-awareness and a high level of culture. The burghers and
artisans of Waidhofen possessed a feeling for quality which
included the furnishing and equipment of their houses. And not
only in Waidhofen itself, but in the other towns and villages
in the neighbourhood: Ybbsitz, Gresten, Scheibbs and Purgstall.
A typical example of a prosperous ironmaster's house in the
Eisenwurzen is Amon House at Lunz which exudes middle-class
self-confidence, comfort and well-being. It is worth mentioning
because it may catch the eye of a traveller, who, deprived for too
long of lakes, is making for the Lunzer See, where great fields of
narcissi are in flower in May and June.

There is another Waidhofen in Lower Austria: right up on the
northern frontier on the River Thaya.

All along the banks of the Thaya stand a chain of citadels,
scowling relics which once formed the outer defence line against
Bohemia. In the time of the early Babenberg dukes the line lay
along the River Kamp, but when colonization of the dense forests
of northern Austria had reached its fullest extent, it lay along
the Thaya, and the Kamp became the secondary line of defence.
On the eastern edge of the Vienna Woods there was an outer
defence sector in which the castles stood for the most part where the
valleys run out on to the plain: Perchtoldsdorf, Mödling, Baden
and Weikersdorf. One of the responsibilities of these forts was
to protect the old north-to-south road. The links on the inner
chain were Kammerstein, Johannstein, Rauhenstein, Rauheneck,
Merkenstein. Fortified churches stood at the ready in Perchtolds-

dorf, Mödling and Traiskirchen and there were many more. In
Babenberg times the southern frontier of the *Ostmark* was the
River Piesting, and the twelfth-century castles were all intended to
defend the northern frontier of Carantania; consequently they lie
on the south bank of the river. All this country is now, of course,
well within the province of Lower Austria. But the Carantanians
were not only mindful of attack from the east. As they were
almost equally disinclined to allow encroachment from the west
they had to have a dual strategy. Invaders from the east were
confronted by Starhemberg, Fischau, Brunn, Frohnberg and
Scheuchenstein, from the west by Emmerberg, Dachenstein,
Stein-Meiersdorf, Wulfingstein, Puchberg, Schrattenstein and
Stixenstein.

The idea of fortified churches may seem mildly shocking but
they had their logical place in the protection of the population
against an invader who was hostile to Christianity, and their role
was wholly defensive. In an emergency, women and children took
refuge in the body of the church, while the men prepared to repel
attack. In some churches, all the necessary equipment was kept
in an upper story, including pitch and sulphur. The parish church
at Hochneukirchen has twenty-four embrasures, and there are
two channels, technically known as moucharabies, above the
doors through which boiling pitch could be poured on to the
heads of the invaders. Not far from Amstetten there is a particularly
fine example at St. Peter in der Au. The church, which is joined to
the moated castle by a covered gangway, has an inner and an outer
shell. A circumvallation or walled passage lies against the inner wall
and is carried like a viaduct on a colonnade with pointed arches.
Pitch and sulphur could be poured through the gap between the
outer and inner walls.

It is probably an illusion to suppose that of the hundreds of
thousands of foreign visitors who fill the popular resorts, more
than a handful can be persuaded to explore the northern districts
of Lower Austria, Waldviertel and Weinviertel. The Waldviertel
('forest quarter') is still comparatively undiscovered; the broiler
society has not yet caught up with it; the international bus tours
go elsewhere. A wonderful peace lies over the highlands of the

Waldviertel, the air is good because the average altitude is between 2,000 and 3,000 feet, the Frankish villages are attractive and friendly, and there are far more Romanesque and Gothic churches and monuments, Renaissance and Baroque town and country houses, paintings and frescoes by the finest masters of the Baroque era, medieval citadels and picturesque ruins, than we can possibly cope with. Geologically speaking this is very ancient country, a granite and gneiss plateau which was already worn down when the Alps were beginning to be pressed into shape. The whole area slopes down gradually from west to east. Massive granite boulders lie scattered in the forests and meadows, sometimes in such a way that their origin as an accident of nature almost seems suspect. The best known 'foundling' as they are called locally is the Wackelstein (wobbling stone) near Schrems. Although it weighs several tons it is so delicately poised on the broad slab of granite beneath, that it moves at a touch.

The conventional way to tour Lower Austria north of the Danube is to begin at Krems on the Danube, drive up the valley of the Kamp to Gars and Horn and then due west to Zwettl or, alternatively, north-west and north to the River Thaya. But as, mental digressions apart, we are moving across the country roughly from west to east, we will keep to the two lines of defence of the Babenbergs, and strike due north from the Danube.

The drive from Grein would reach its first climax in the view from the castle ruin at Arbesbach, 'fang of the Waldviertel'. A few miles to the north-east on the road to Zwettl, Rappottenstein castle is a well-preserved, originally twelfth-century citadel, a very extensive structure with five courtyards, but compact and extremely photogenic. During the rebuilding operations in 1548 corner towers were added, which at that time were a novelty in Austria.

The parish churches in these villages, at Gross-Gerungs and in fact throughout most of the Waldviertel, are visibly Romanesque in origin, going over into Gothic but, of course, usually adapted in Baroque style. Weitra is a most attractive walled town and the Renaissance castle (1600) possesses its own theatre. After Gmünd, forest and arable country merges into moorland where storks sway awkwardly over small lakes and ponds. The exquisite proportions of the country seat at Kirchberg am Walde (a contemporary of Weitra castle but with an early Baroque frontage) reward the effort of plunging down the third-class road from Gmünd. King Charles X of France took refuge with his friend Duke Blacas at Kirchberg, and his entourage is believed to have included his brother the Duc d'Angouleme with his wife, daughter of Marie Antoinette, as well as Hermopolis, Archbishop of Paris, and several French noblemen. In later years—in the meantime Charles X had died of cholera at Goricia—a frequent visitor to Kirchberg was the Comte de Chambord, later Henri V.

All these notabilities passed through Schrems, a town favoured by history in that, while other roads to Bohemia fell into disuse during the Thirty Years War, particularly the competing road through Heidenreichstein, this one was maintained. The convenience of this road from Horn brought the Empress Maria Theresa and Franz von Lothringen to the inn 'Zum Weissen Rössl' and in their time the Emperors Franz and Ferdinand. Both slept at this inn. But it was in the castle that Mozart spent the night on his way to the première of *Don Giovanni* in Prague; possibly the White Horse was the more comfortable of the two.

Flowering heather, wild lupins and forest line the eight miles to Heidenreichstein. With its 125 feet high, 15 feet thick walls, this impregnable cornerstone of the north-west has never been restored, and the original furnishing is still there: beds, immense cavernous cupboards, and oak tables which are guaranteed a thousand years old. Properly speaking, the Thaya defences begin at Dobersberg; the river flows past Karlstein Castle, and at Raabs, where the lower branch of the river which flows through Waidhofen joins the Moravian Thaya, the reflections of the keep and bastions and of silver birch trees meet in the slow-moving waters. The way in which all these castle and ruins lie above or on the banks of the river adds enormously to their charm. After Raabs, the Thaya squirms and twirls through the woods, performing a series of convolutions which the main road entirely ignores until a chance encounter at Eibenstein sends both flying off into a joint pirouette which only subsides at Drosendorf. But we should certainly go, at whatever inconvenience, in pursuit of the river, because near the village of Kollmitzgraben one of the most extensive fortified places in Austria lies enclosed in a loop of the Thaya. The castle stands on a hill which is three parts surrounded by water, and the gap in the loop is closed by a castellated wall, more than 160 yards in length, popularly known as the 'Bohemian Wall'.

The upper town of Drosendorf is also surrounded on three sides by the Thaya, which now sweeps off into Czechoslovakia, but after wiggling through the forests in thinly populated country returns to Austria near the tremendous fortress at Hardegg. Incidentally, there is a curious object in the village church at Hardegg: a cross carved from the mast of the frigate *Novara* on which the unfortunate Emperor Maximilian, brother of the Emperor Franz Joseph, sailed to his doom in Mexico.

The history and changing appearance of all the historic buildings in the Waldviertel are on record in the museum in the newly restored castle at Riegersburg, the finest among all the Baroque country residences in Lower Austria north of the Danube.

The Premonstratensian monastery of Geras is on the old main road between Drosendorf and Pulkau, but Riegersburg and Hardegg are on the new Thaya valley road which leads down to Retz. A change comes over the landscape as the Waldviertel district ends and the Weinviertel begins. These lowlands once lay under the sea, but Retz, a planned town laid out by Count Berchtold von Hardegg in 1300, lies on a terrace above the shore of this primeval sea among a patchwork quilt of fields and vineyards. Its dominant feature is the broad onion dome popped on to the Gothic tower of the town hall, and like many towns in Austria, particularly Horn, Krems and Eggenburg, some of the houses are decorated with Renaissance *sgraffiti* which are not necessarily to everyone's taste. Now and again an old windmill presents an unusual sight in Austria: there was always plenty of wind here but too little water-power.

The Weinviertel, all that part of Lower Austria between the Manhartsberg and the old Amber Route on the River March, is very little known—even to the Viennese. Some of the villages are celebrated for their wine, and connoisseurs rush off on Sundays

with their empty two-litre bottles and bring back replacements
in the evening. But even in this, the Weinviertel has to compete
with the Burgenland and with the Wachau and the wine districts
round Vienna. The country itself seems not to be much admired
by the Viennese, and many people admit that it gives them the
willies. And in a way it is true that there is something eerie about
this open, unprotected landscape, the bare or sparsely afforested
hills. 'We have never recovered from the Swedes,' said one
inhabitant, meaning the last phase of the Thirty Years War. As we
drive through one scruffy village after another we search in vain
for stately, prosperous-looking farmhouses. Few have been done
up in recent years. But to my mind this is glorious country—wide
open, free and uncluttered. No speculator has so far coveted the
Weinviertel, no expensive cars are drawn up in front of pseudo-
rustic weekend cottages. A few writers and artists have dug
themselves in, and the suggestion that they might prefer a house
on the Semmering would be greeted with shouts of laughter.

It was while I was brooding over a map of the familiar ground
in and around the valley of the Kamp and humming a tiresome
folksong about Langenlois that my eye fell on the name Gneixen-
dorf. Not a place to which travellers should be dispatched hotfoot,
but there was some association. Later, the memory snapped into
place. Beethoven used to stay in the castle which was owned by
his brother Jan. In 1826 he wrote his last works there, including
the Quartet in B minor, opus 130. Beethoven was now a very sick
man. The rooms were badly heated, the food unsuitable, and these
physical discomforts aggravated the turbulence in his mind. Poor
Beethoven had reached the stage where he stormed about the house
and garden, quarrelled with the servants, and rushed, shouting
and waving his arms, across the fields to Stratzing. Or he would
walk to Langenlois, about four miles each way. He was in urgent
need of medical attention, but perhaps even more, of careful
nursing, and in December he returned to Vienna sitting on an
uncovered milk cart. The journey, which was his last, took two
days. The summers of that obsessive walker were usually spent
at Baden—the spa was then basking in imperial favour, hence
its distinctly *Biedermeier* flavour even now—where he sometimes

disappeared from his lodgings for days and nights at a stretch. At the end of one particular stroll down to Wiener Neustadt (about fifteen miles) he was taken for a tramp and put under lock and key, but late at night his identity was vouched for by the frantic director of music, a man called Herzog. The mayor apologized in person and a carriage was provided in which Beethoven was brought back to Baden in the morning.

The best jumping-off point for a tour of the Kamp country is Gars. It is an attractive place in itself, and from here Rosenburg, Altenburg and Greillenstein can easily be visited in one day.

There is plenty of literature on Rosenburg Castle, and the history of this bastion at the point where the river makes a right-angled turn to the west must be summarized in a few words. The origin of the name is unknown, but it is believed to be the castle referred to in one of the oldest Austrian ballads, uncertainly attributed to Walther von der Vogelweide: 'Es steht ein Schloss in Österreich'. The small, irregular medieval structure was taken by the Hussites when they burned and sacked Altenburg Abbey; in 1620, three hundred people including women and children were murdered on the premises; it was the chief centre of Lutheranism in northern Austria, place of assembly for members of the influential 'Horner Bund', the Protestant Federation of Horn. With all this violence and intellectual strife in mind, the immediate approach to Rosenburg is startling in its spaciousness and gaiety. The tilting yard is a film set where velvet and damask draperies seem to lie along the arcaded galleries, from which ladies cast favours to their cavaliers on the sward below. This is not entirely romantic nonsense. Large though it is, the courtyard is too small for a medieval tournament, and in any case it was not built until the seventeenth century, while a print dated 1673, which shows an aerial 'prospect' of Rosenburg, simply calls the Turnierhof the 'outer court'. The explanation is that at that time a popular spectator sport was the carroussel, in which competitors on horseback, wearing the old-time dress of the days of chivalry, showed their skill in lancing targets or favours. This was all part of the mood of the time. Another aspect of it is the loggia high up on the castle wall. From the architectural point of view it is just an appendage, a spacious balcony stuck on at a dizzy height, but it was an admirable answer to a need to get out into space, to feel the freedom of a vast, unconfined landscape.

There are some grounds for believing that instruments of torture were used to frighten more often than they were actually applied, and most people who examine the collection at Greillenstein will feel that if any one of these means of persuasion were placed in a threatening manner before them, they would reveal all. Be that as it may, Greillenstein is a superb Renaissance castle which must not be left out, any more than the Benedictine Altenburg which, 'a heap of stones' after persistent ravages by Hungarians, Hussites, Lutheran townsfolk and Swedes, was rebuilt in high Baroque style by Josef Munggenast. Here it is worth while to go round and look at the east end of the church, to see the architect's solution for turning a Gothic choir into a Baroque frontage, with niches and statues of saints.

One of the joys of Lower Austria now lies ahead, where part of the irregular course of the Kamp with its flood areas and swamps has been turned into a series of splendid artificial lakes. Even at the height of summer the traffic is light and the shores of the lakes are not yet overcrowded.

Zwettl lies ahead at the junction of the roads from Weitra and Krems. The abbey's chapter house is one of the oldest in existence. The cloisters are late Romanesque, strongly influenced by Burgundian Gothic because the abbots used to travel to Burgundy for conferences and brought stonemasons back with them to Zwettl. The original abbey church was rebuilt by Munggenast, but the indefatigable Prandtauer came along once or twice to lend moral support to his pupil.

The oddest stories often turn up in the most unpromising surroundings. Take Kühbach. In 'Badger's Ditch' near the hamlet of Kühbach near Zwettl, stands a ruined chapel. The legend tells of a blind beggar whose dog led him to an elderberry tree and began to bark. The begger poked around with his stick at the foot of the tree, a spring gushed forth, the beggar washed his eyes and regained his sight. The tale is fairly typical of its kind in that it contains two common ingredients: a tree, and water, but now the legend produces its baffling curtain line: the beggar was St. Thomas of Canterbury.

This is a clear case of history falling upstairs. The connection of Thomas à Becket with Austria begins in a wholly logical manner, clearly and amply documented, and ends in a thicket. When the Archbishop of Canterbury was murdered, the shock waves rolled across Europe with the force of a major eruption. The general consternation was particularly acute among his fellow archbishops who were constantly involved in the conflict between Church and crown which broke Thomas à Becket, but their feelings were shared by the senior members of the reigning house of Babenberg who had to steer a tricky course between Rome and Frederick Barbarossa. Conrad III of Salzburg was both: an archbishop and a Babenberg, a son of Duke Leopold III and Agnes von Hohenstaufen, a man who, politically and by ties of blood, was closely connected with the Emperor, but who took the part of the Pope on several issues. Thomas à Becket was canonized—with exceptional celerity—in 1173, only three years after his death, and five years later Archbishop Conrad dedicated the old chapel of St. Gertrude in the cliff of Salzburg's Mönchsberg to the new martyr. Becket must have been personally known to many people who met him during his exile at Mouzon Abbey in the Ardennes. But the Babenberg's veneration for the martyr was unique in Europe; he became almost the patron saint of the family and it was largely owing to their fervour that the cult of Thomas of Canterbury spread so quickly across their domains. The influential Cistercians at Rein in Styria adopted him (the parish church at Althofen is still dedicated to his name today) and there must have been many private chapels, since destroyed and forgotten, in which his name was invoked. Kühbach was something rather different. In due course it became the chief place of pilgrimage in the Austrian lands connected with Thomas à Becket, and it remained so until the Reformation. In other words: to expiate really frightful sins you had to go to Canterbury, but for more ordinary transgressions Kühbach would do. Long after the Babenburg dynasty had died out, popular enthusiasm for 'Thomas von Kandelberg' persisted, and when the cult was officially revived in the fifteenth century,

his memory had become thoroughly entangled with local folklore.

Maria Taferl, called by the men of the Enlightenment 'one
of the three robbers' nests in the monarchy' (the others being
Mariazell and Sonntagberg), takes its name from the stone table
around which in pagan times a ceremonial tribal meal was held.
This shrine, which still attracts a stream of pilgrims, can be seen
for miles, standing out in high relief against the long green slope
behind it. Below, and westwards, the Danube forms a loop,
flows through the sluice gates of Ybbs-Persenbeug (the last
Habsburg Emperor, Charles I, was born in the castle) and the
scene of the Nibelungenlied begins. In this tenth-century epic,
the only poetic work in the German language which can be placed
beside the Iliad and the Odyssey, the Danube is the backcloth
from Persenbeug to Tulln, where King Etzel (Attila) of Hungary
came to meet his horrid bride Kriemhilde.

The Wachau is the most beautiful section of the Danube in
its whole course from its source at Donau-Eschingen to the Black
Sea, and the right time of year to see it is when the trees are in
blossom or when the apricots are ripe. The Wachau proper begins
at Melk and ends at Krems, and it should be savoured slowly.
So should its wines, of which a monk of Göttweig, looking down at
the terraces across the river, told me that at one time he could
identify every vintage from each vineyard.

Schönbühel, the castle guarding the entry to the Wachau
shortly after Melk, is best seen from the river itself, but we shall
have to be content with the view from the Wachau federal road
which was built to by-pass the narrow village streets. Now the
first major sensation is Aggstein, a home for eagles rather than
men, the quintessence of a robber baron's castle. The general
the idea of a 'robber baron' is of course quite unhistorical and the
term was unknown before the nineteenth century. To picture
the owners of these castles perpetually rushing down to pillage the
freight transports on the Danube overlooks the structure of the
feudal world with its strict codes and its interdependence. There are
sure to have been excesses without number, but it is logical to
assume that a vassal who plundered transports and thus diminished

their value before they arrived at the next toll station (which might be held by the Church or by the sovereign duke) would not retain his fief for long. The 'Kuenringer', who were so powerful in Lower Austria that their name is still used as a synonym for political empire-building on the provincial level, are a case in point. They called themselves the Hounds of Kuenring, and Duke Frederick Babenberg, nicknamed for his part 'the quarrelsome', found much nastier epithets to describe them, but this was largely so as to justify his action in besieging and destroying Aggstein, one of the many citadels of a dangerously overgrown subject. Aggstein certainly had a very unpleasant owner in the fifteenth century, Jörg Scheck von Wald, who did rob the Danube traders, laying chains across the river for the purpose. He laid out the castle in its present form including the notorious 'Rosengärtlein'. This 'rose garden' is a kind of gallery on the edge of the ravine on which prisoners were left to choose between dying of hunger and thirst or jumping over the precipice. The story may be true, although there is no actual written reference to it before the seventeenth century. But the 'Rosengärtlein' lies just beneath the residential part of the castle, and surely the ladies would have found the whole business a little unappetizing?

All the villages on the left bank—Schwallenbach, Spitz, Joching, St. Michael with its fortified church—deserve a close look. But now there is another broad bend in the Danube, and Dürnstein lies ahead, dreaming still of Richard Coeur de Lion, as well it might considering the hard currency that he attracts. But then for the Austrians, King Richard was a money-spinner from the outset. He mortally offended Leopold Babenberg during the Third Crusade (1190–2) by tearing down his colours from the walls of Acre, maintaining that as a King he himself took precedence over Leopold, who was a vassal. He was rash enough to travel back to England, even though in disguise, through Leopold's domains, and he was arrested in the village of Erdberg outside the walls of Vienna. He is said to have been recognized while working in the kitchens of an inn on the site of Erdbergstrasse 17 (later the 'Birkenstock-Haus' where Clemens and Bettina von Brentano used to stay), tried to flee but got only as far as Nr. 41 in the same street, probably the home of the local gamekeeper. He spent his comparatively brief captivity at Dürnstein; the story of his minstrel Blondel singing beneath the tower and discovering his whereabouts is a fabrication, Mrs. Trollope's rapturous 'Alas! poor Blondel' notwithstanding. The ransome which the English had to pay up for his release was a windfall for the Austrians (even though the Emperor kept half for himself) at the very moment when they were planning gigantic expenditure on defence. It financed the construction of the moat round Vienna (Richard's companions were made to take part in the work), much of the cost of the new town at Wiener Neustadt, and even helped with the walls round Enns and Hainburg. Public opinion in England, however, viewed a severe outbreak of fire in Vienna in 1193 as a clear sign of divine disapproval, and when Leopold died in Graz in the following year they could not have been less surprised.

According to an Austrian historian, the legend of King Arthur and the Holy Grail may have been brought to Austria by Richard Coeur de Lion. Arthur himself makes a surprising appearance in an obscure village south of Vienna where an almost incredible wealth of historical event and legend comes together, carefully recorded in picture and text on the walls of a chapel in the church at Maria Lanzendorf. First on the scene is St. Luke who, 'when he travelled from Dalmatia through Germany and then returned to Macedonia, preached the Gospel at this place to the Marcomanni and to the first few Christians A.D. 70 or 77.' Next: 'Marcus Aurelius defeated the Marcomanni here', which is fairly accurate, but now comes: 'Arthurus crown prince from Britain erected for the Christian soldiers . . . on this heath a chapel in honour of St. Luke, having found here a stone upon which was inscribed: "Upon this spot St. Luke preached the Gospel to the Christians." The year could no longer be deciphered, but the stone was found in the year of our Lord 508.' Finally: 'Carolus Magnus defeated the Huns on this heath and caused this chapel to be rebuilt A.D. 791.'

An odd place. And as it is not for an amateur to comment, it will be better to hurry back to the Wachau, to Schallaburg which has got left behind as it lies south of the Danube near Melk. This is one of the most important castles in Lower Austria because of a unique feature: the central courtyard with its forty-eight colonnades, decorated all over with terracotta figures symbolizing the pagan, classical-mythological and Christian worlds; all the intellectual luggage of the Renaissance.

Travellers on the Danube seem often to have exclaimed as they first caught sight of Göttweig that it looked more like a palace than a monastery, and this was essentially the advice offered by the Imperial Vice-Chancellor Count Karl Schönborn when the original building conveniently burned down in 1718: let Lukas von Hildebrandt be entrusted with the work, and let him build a new monastery 'which would not savour all too much of monks'.

Seen from the river bank at Stein, the distant white building floating on the hill top not only savours little of monks, it might almost be the temple of Apollo which once stood near the site of the first monastery. Nothing could be more palatial than the Imperial Staircase, or more regal than the state apartments, although it is not certain what right the *Napoleonzimmer* has to the name; Napoleon lunched at Göttweig on 8th September 1809 but he did not spend the night. Perhaps he had a short nap.

Krems *und* Stein now lead into one another without a break. In the days when a Roman garrison manned the river service at Mautern, when Odoaker crossed the Danube just here on his march to Rome, and when St. Severin was hurrying up and down the Wachau rallying his anxious flock, there was a village between Krems and Stein called Und. This is no feeble medieval joke; the name was a corruption of *ad undas*, on the river.

South of Krems, we can follow the *Barockstrasse*, and carry on over the Riederberg in the direction of Vienna, or perhaps join the autobahn at St. Pölten. This section of the autobahn offers a very fine view of W. H. Auden's garage, and, from the next hill, of Neulengbach Castle where the artist Egon Schiele was jailed for pornography in 1912.

It is not easy to write about Lower Austria. There is no shape to it. Here and there a common factor can be found, in the arts, in history. But what has the Waldviertel to do with the draughty plain between Vienna and Neunkirchen? And what has the gentle world of Baden and the Helenental to do with the Marchfeld?

There is one possible answer: man's eternal passion for shooting wild animals and birds. Paradoxically, it is thanks to this passion (a very different matter from the relentless pursuit of the ibex generations ago) that the woods and fields are so filled with bustle and movement today. During an hour's stroll in the Pielach country it will be unusual not to see roedeer bounding across the stubble. There will be a hare or two, ears rashly held erect, among tufts of rough grass. In the woods, a stealthy rustling fans out ahead as a small army of pheasants retreats through the dry leaves and bracken. Here, in open arable country, there are no red deer, but there are plenty throughout Austria wherever there are thick forests; altogether about 75,000, not counting the *Auhirsche*, the heavier breed thought to be related to the Carpathian red deer, which live in the water meadows of the Danube in the Tulln Basin, in the Lobau and along the banks of the March.

In the days when hunting was still basically a royal prerogative, ceded where appropriate to the monasteries and to the nobility, venison was the main form of meat supply for those who could afford it because in the absence of potatoes and maize (which remained a scarcity long after they were known) it was difficult to feed pigs and cattle through the winter. During the first half of the eighteenth century the court in Vienna was consuming venison at an average rate of about 3,500 head of big game a year, which, plus butcher's meat, poultry and fish, was not bad going. The whole surrounding districts of Vienna were swarming with game, and wolves were a plague. In 1604 the inhabitants of Neustift am Walde, now in the 18th Vienna district, asked for a church of their own as they could not get across to Sievering because of the wolves. When the various courses of the Danube were frozen over in winter, they would sneak in from the Marchfeld and terrify the people in their cottages outside the city walls. And until the Heiltumstuhl, the arch at the top of the Rotenturmstrasse close to St. Stephen's, was demolished in 1700, priests used to pronounce the 'wolf blessing' from its upper gallery, 'so that each and all might go safely about their business before the city walls, and none who, in pursuit of the chase or occupied in the felling of timber, should suffer evil from wolves'.

Even at the end of the eighteenth century the villagers of Simmering and Meidling, now the 11th and 12th districts, could lie in bed and hear the roaring of stags in the rutting season, and in 1855 a 20-point stag was shot in Brigittenau.

Most of the reigning Habsburgs were lovers of the chase, but as sportsmen—a question of character and temperament—they varied. Charles VI was certainly a man who expected large bags: at a shoot in upper Styria in 1728 where three thousand beaters were used, 103 head of chamois fell to his gun alone. He used to shoot bears in Lower Austria, particularly at Gainfarn not far from Baden. But he was also a skilled falconer, and so in their time were Maria Theresa and Joseph II. For generations, the scene of this supreme sport of kings lay in the grounds of Laxenburg, where it was pursued with passion, skill and attention to the minutiae of heraldry and all the ritual prescribed by the office of the Lord High Master of Falconry. Maria Theresa disliked indiscriminate slaughter and was disgusted at a 'Spectacle' organized in her honour in which seven hundred stags and hinds were driven past her by packs of hounds, many of them to be savaged and drowned in the River March. It was also wholly in character when Archduke Johann wrote in later life that he was proud to say he had always shot with a single-barrelled rifle, loading it himself. 'You learn to shoot cleanly with a single barrel, to shoot sparingly and at the right moment. To blaze away but kill little is butchery and is not permitted among my entourage. I have the number of shots counted, to see how often and to what effect they are fired.' Joseph I, brother of Charles VI, was a very fine shot at a time (in the late seventeenth century) when to shoot a bird in flight was a fumbling and uncertain affair.

The lack of sympathy between the Emperor Franz Joseph and Archduke Franz Ferdinand had a political background, but the old gentleman disapproved intensely of his heir's tastes in shooting, which can only be described as coarse. The shooting rights at the southern end of the Marchfeld belonged by tradition to the heir to the throne, and the marked deterioration in quality of the superb Lobau stags which set in after the turn of this century was entirely caused by the insatiable demands of the Archduke. The gamekeepers' main function was to ensure sheer numbers rather than quality, and no culling was possible. At a typical *battue*, hordes of beaters would drive the deer in their hundreds to the royal hide, and Franz Ferdinand would shoot the stags and hinds just as they came, regardless of age, quality and prospects, often as many as a hundred in an afternoon. To a lifelong sportsman like the Emperor Franz Joseph, such goings on were most unpleasing.

I have always been fascinated by the Marchfeld. When I first knew it, very few strangers ever raised the dust between the cornfields, Vienna's traditional granary, or peered through the slits in the boarded up windows of abandoned Baroque country houses. A great deal has been done in recent years to save the fabric and to restore the dignity if not the inner life of houses of prime architectural importance: Niederweiden was one of the earliest works of J. B. Fischer von Erlach, and Schlosshof was built by Lukas von Hildebrandt for Prince Eugene of Savoy in 1729. An uninterrupted avenue leads from Niederweiden to Schlosshof, and it is easy to picture the diminutive figure of that much-beloved soldier trotting along on horseback between the trees and supervising the layout of the large park which slopes down so gently towards the March. He seems to be more at home here than in the Belvedere, though this may be a mistaken view; Schlosshof is grand enough in all conscience. The bachelor prince left Schlosshof to his unpopular niece, *'la villaine Victoire'*, née Princess de Savoie, Comtesse de Soissons et Carignan, who broke up his historic collections before giving the property to her husband—he was eighteen years younger than herself—Prince Joseph von Sachsen-Hildburghausen. The Empress bought Schlosshof in 1755, and as she enjoyed the quiet, the view and the play of the ornamental fountains, she spent a great deal of time there in her old age. Her son thought the place too grand. Joseph II was a man who judged all things on a basis of profit and loss. Sleepy religious communities whose members spent their lives embroidering vestments, tending their gardens and praying for the souls of the wicked, monasteries which displayed anything short of hectic bustle, were shut down by the hundred. Pilgrimages were forbidden, minor feasts of the church (the only holidays of the working population) abolished. He is also associated with the 'economy coffin', which worked like this: the deceased was lowered into the grave and a lever was depressed which released a trap-door contrivance beneath. The planks now parted, the corpse was left to return to the earth from whence it came and the coffin was taken away to be used again. Joseph II was in many ways an admirable ruler, but unlike his mother he knew nothing about human nature and he was remarkably un-Austrian. After she died he went out to Schlosshof and turned off the fountains.

It was after the power of Islam had been banished that the nobility at the court of Vienna built their *chateaux de chasse* on the Marchfeld: Eckartsau, Niederweiden, Schlosshof and Marchegg. But this perpetual battlefield had not seen the last of war. Napoleon was waiting in the wings.

Lay your left hand on a map of eastern Austria so that your thumb rests on Petronell, your index finger on Hainburg and your little finger on Dürnkrut, and think where else in the world, within such a comparatively small area of land, so many historical figures have made an appearance.

When the Emperor Tiberius led his Illyrian legions up the valley of the March through the land of the Quadi, a man was waiting in a fort at Stillfried, who possessed a disciplined army of 70,000 infantry and 4,000 cavalry, who ruled over central and southern Germany and the whole of Bohemia: Marbod, King of the Marcomanni, once the favourite of Augustus, now a ruler independent of Rome. Ten thousand years before Marbod arrived in what is now only a small village, Austria's first known inhabitants lived at Stillfried, but they vanished from sight during the last Ice Age. Between 3500 and 1800 B.C. the entire plateau between Dürnkrut, Marchegg and Obersiebenbrunn was thickly populated, and cave dwellings can be seen at Stillfried. Carnuntum, the vital garrison town at the junction of the Danube and the amber road (at Petronell) was the residence of Marcus Aurelius for many years; he wrote volume two of his Meditations there and is believed to have died of the plague in Vienna (Vindobona) in 180. Septimus Severus was proclaimed Emperor at Carnuntum in 193, and the year 308 saw the meeting of three Roman Emperors: Galerius, his co-ruler Maximian, and the ageing Diocletian who had retired but came to Carnuntum at the request of Galerius to discuss matters of state. It was at this meeting that Licinius was proclaimed Caesar. By the time Valerian visited Carnuntum in 375, decline had already set in.

One hesitates to drag in Charlemagne yet again, but here he is: at Sachsengang Castle, near the road from Vienna which, taking in Orth Castle, links all the places which have been mentioned so far on the Marchfeld. 'Gang', meaning a passage, is the old word for the side channels of the Danube, and 'Sachsen' refers to the Saxon colony left there by Charlemagne to till the land and act as frontier guards. It is the oldest castle on the Marchfeld, first mentioned in 1021. There are two tumuli quite close to the castle, one of them at the entrance to the park, and diggings have proved that the graves date from the time when the Huns were on the retreat before the armies of Charlemagne. The legend that Attila's grave is at Sachsengang is, of course, just that; there is another alleged site north of Obergrafendorf near St. Pölten. Attila the Hun can, however, be chalked up as an authentic presence.

The Battle of Dürnkrut in 1278 was one of the turning points in the history of Austria, immortalized by Franz Grillparzer in his play *König Ottokar's Glück und Ende*. After the death of King Ottokar Przemysl of Bohemia on the field of Dürnkrut, the danger that Austria might become and remain for all time a mere appendage of Bohemia, was dispelled, the supremacy of Rudolph of Habsburg was assured and the six hundred and thirty years' rule of the Habsburg dynasty began.

The next figure on the scene is Suleiman the Magnificent, marching south of the Danube past Bruck an der Leitha, fanning out towards Wiener Neustadt (both towns held out) to lay siege to Vienna in 1529. In 1683 the Grand Vizir Kara Mustapha set up his tent outside the city walls.

Aspern, where Napoleon experienced his first defeat on 21st and 22nd May 1809, lies within the present boundaries of Vienna, and the main surviving evidence of the battle is centred on the churchyard. (Napoleon's headquarters were in the Lobau.) But the battlefield of Wagram can have changed very little. The front extended all the way from Nussdorf above Vienna to Orth on the Danube, but after the French had crossed the Danube under cover of a violent thunderstorm which lasted most of the night (Sachsengang suffered badly in the advance on Grossenzersdorf) the brunt of the battle was taken by the Austrian left flank and centre between Deutsch-Wagram and Obersiebenbrunn. In the two-day battle in which Napoleon brought about 160,000 and Archduke Charles only about 100,000 men into action, the hamlet Aderklaa near Wagram was a crucial sector for some hours because of the presence of a strong contingent of Austrian artillery. 'Oh, that I had but been in possession of Aderklaa,' Napoleon was heard to exclaim, 'even for a few minutes!' The crux was the defence of the hill at Markgrafneusiedl with its old square tower above the stream, the Russbach, where the Austrians made a desperate stand, hoping for the arrival of Archduke Johann with reinforcements. But by the time his advance unit reached Obersiebenbrunn, the hill at Markgrafneusiedl had been taken by storm and Archduke Charles was making an orderly retreat towards the River Thaya.

From then on, foreign celebrities were seldom seen on the Marchfeld.

9

Burgenland

As it pottered along the western shore of the Neusiedlersee the local train had it vaguely in mind to drift over the frontier to Sopron. It was not the kind of train normally associated with inter-state travel, and while the frontier was undeniably there, it still presented the bland appearance of old, half-forgotten sins which, in 1939, were just gathering impetus for new wickedness. The engine driver was in no hurry, the indeterminate stops allowed time for refreshment, and now and again the train rested at halts marked by a shed like an overgrown dog kennel or even by nothing at all. The few passengers, who had nothing to do to pass the time apart from leaning out of the window and gazing idly across miles of reeds and grassy swamp, suddenly became aware that the quiet hiss of the engine had been infiltrated by a noise in which the carriages now formed an island. It was as though a million carving knives were being sharpened in expectation of a gargantuan feast. The ground was full of it and the middle and upper air: a hundred thousand or heaven knows how many frogs, all croaking away, hour by hour, day after day, high voices and low, pausing and resuming. In intention somehow urgent and hostile, the effect was nevertheless soporific.

There are more melodious sounds to be heard round the shores and among the swamps, moors and marshes of the Neusiedlersee, the largest steppe lake in Europe: the song of the cicada, for instance, and the fluting 'hoodley-hoo' of the golden oriole. This is an ornithologist's paradise, a unique phenomenon in which the balance of nature is desperately precarious, menaced as it is

204

by more subtle influences than the obvious perils of bungalow development, tourism, drainage and low-flying aircraft. But in the meantime the great colonies of rare resident species and the seasonal migrants persist in their timeless habits comparatively undeterred. There are quail, plover, redshank, avocet, glossy ibis, the purple, great white and squacco heron, and the little egret. There are bittern among the rushes and the great reed warbler. The names of the wild duck are like an incantation: gadwall, shoveller, garganey and shelduck, pintail, wigeon, goldeneye and teal, tufted and eider duck and velvet scoter. In spring clouds of grey and white migrants continually circle over the lake, and the air is filled with their clamour. September brings thousands of wild geese, and in December the laughing white-fronted geese bring up the rear, joined perhaps by a few of their 'lesser' relations, who, shyest of their kind, graze watchfully far out on the plains. They take no notice of that extraordinary bird which may become extinct in our lifetime, the great bustard, but the tired migrants resting on the lake and the whole chattering, clacking, nesting throng share an instinctive knowledge of a speck in the sky which, like the vultures of the Stubachtal, is watching for weaklings and stragglers: the sea eagle.

Icy winter winds sweep across the Seewinkel, bending the resilient reeds which will be harvested when the lake is frozen over, howl their way past Wulkaprodersdorf to Wiener Neustadt; villages by the dozen are cut off by snowdrifts. But the Leitha range gives shelter from the north, the Rosalien hills from the south-west, and southern Burgenland is less exposed altogether to this violence. In spring the Burgenland is transformed into a land of cherry, apricot, plum, almond and peach blossom, early vegetables will win the race to the markets or go straight into the canning and deep freezing factories. In the Rosaliengebirge a warm scent of sage hangs in the air. On lower ground, fields of strawberries are ripening, the grapes are swelling in a thousand vineyards. All the way down to Güssing, this is a land of extinct volcanoes, of hot springs and mineral waters.

Like everywhere else, the Burgenland has changed a good deal since the last war, and not wholly for the better: a time has now come when the distinctive character of the villages is disappearing so fast that soon nothing will be left but a few self-conscious corners. The storks may continue to return to their nests on the chimneys of Rust and Mörbisch regardless of what the building looks like under their feet, but there may be an end even to their patience. This problem is so well known that there is no need to labour it here. But in the Burgenland there is an unusual slant to it all in that, by European standards of antiquity, very few of the typical low gabled farms and cottages are much more than a hundred years old. How often have these villages been left a heap of smoking rubble, the inhabitants murdered or scattered? But the houses were rebuilt in the old way, and the villages laid out on the original medieval pattern. And now, it would be perfectly simple to build yet again in the old way, while modernizing the interiors.

Older in themselves are the *Kittinge*, small granaries built of timber and insulated with clay: ten still stand at Unterschützen, all scheduled as ancient monuments. They are dated between 1740 and 1793, but these are only the last survivals of an extremely effective method of storage which is believed to have originated in Asia Minor in the third century B.C.

The *Kittinge* will have been a familiar sight to the Roman army veterans who lived around Unterschützen and along the valley known as 'In der Wart' below Pinkafeld. And some will have known the characteristic wells on the Seewinkel heath with the pole and pylon mechanism, which have also survived in Finland to illustrate the common origins of the Hungarian and Finnish peoples. In northern Burgenland permanent settlements were built for retired legionaries, but they clearly made themselves at home all through the province. Only, however, in the plains, along main roads and in the spas: work in the forests was no part of their business. Seventy-five present-day Burgenland villages were lived in in Roman times, and while fifty towns and villages were inhabited at various prehistoric periods from the late stone age onwards, I find that in at least thirty-six cases the Romans were living where these earlier peoples had lived before them. This continuity is particularly strong west of the Neusiedlersee: at

Mörbisch, near the famous quarries at St. Margarethen where sculptors now possess a free, open-air studio, in the hamlets Oggau, Oslip and Zillingtal, and also below the Ödenburg hills at Deutschkreuz and Neckenmarkt. That was the golden age. A time came after the first major Turkish invasion in 1529, when the country was so depopulated that new settlers had to be looked for. This time, and to a limited extent after 1683 as well, they were found not among German-speaking, land-hungry farmers but among 'displaced persons' from the Austrian military frontier in Croatia. They gradually settled in five widely separated islands on the Wulka plain (Oberpullendorf), a few scattered villages towards the north, and down on the southern slope of the Günsergebirge. At the last census 28,242 people spoke Croatian as their mother tongue or were bilingual, which is 10·4 per cent of the Burgenland population.

This province was and would long remain 'German Western Hungary', lined with castles *contra teutonicos,* castles *contra ungaros*: the province never quite knew which way to look. Although part of Hungary, most of it was mortgaged to and therefore *de facto* in the possession of the Habsburg emperor. Forchtenstein, Kobersdorf and Landsee, Eisenstadt and Hornstein, Ödenburg/Sopron, Rechnitz, Schlaining, Bernstein, Güns and Theben: the Habsburgs held them in pawn, the Hungarian nobles schemed and struggled to get them back. Treaties were signed at intervals, the Hungarians did at least get their crown back, and in 1621 came the Peace of Nikolsburg which was largely brought about by the efforts of a landowner from Transylvania. As a reward for his diplomacy the mortgages on Forchtenstein and Eisenstadt castles, with their domains, were ceded to him. The Esterházys had arrived. In 1648 these estates became the property of Nikolaus Esterházy. At almost the same moment the Emperor bestowed on Eisenstadt the rights of a free town (which the town fathers bought at a high price). Since then there have been periods of calm, but if the Emperor had meant the two parties to get on each other's nerves right down to the 1970s, he could not have chosen a better way. The really decisive factor in the rise of the Esterházys however was the family's loyalty to the Habsburgs and the western cause at the time of the great siege of Vienna and during the hostilities in the early eighteenth century, when all the other Hungarian magnates in this area including a relation, Anton Esterházy, rose against the Emperor. In retrospect, the process whereby the small landowners were gradually bought out is not a very attractive sight. Many of them must have held their properties for centuries; in the early times, the kings of Hungary had granted lands, deliberately in small patches, on the sole criterion of personal loyalty. National antecedents were irrelevant. But many of these small squires and yeomen farmers were technically Austrians, and by Hungarian law they could be compelled to sell. Such large landowners as the Battyánys (Bernstein, Burg Schlaining, Güssing) were not affected. A complete list of purchases show Nikolaus II investing heavily in landed estate during the Napoleonic wars. He evidently foresaw the danger to money values as early as 1801, when he bought twenty-seven vineyards, and he was buying up land as hard as he could go for the next ten years. In the early spring of 1811 the purchases tailed off and by April they had almost ceased. On 20th February 1811 the Austrian state to all intents and purposes declared itself bankrupt, and the currency was reduced to one-fifth of its value.

There was nothing particularly evil about all this: it was an economic process for which a thousand parallels can be found. In the meantime, the splendour and the cultural achievements of the Esterházys were casting a nimbus around their name which only royal courts could overshadow. There had always been a pronounced talent for music in the family. To Paul Esterházy, who as Palatine of Hungary became prince regnant (*Fürst*) in 1687, concerts and the theatre in Vienna meant far more than an idle diversion for bored courtiers, and he maintained a small orchestra in Eisenstadt. Paul Anton, born in 1711, laid the foundations of the library of music which was to grow into a highly important collection, and it was he who filled the vacant post of assistant *kapellmeister* with the young candidate Joseph Haydn.

Haydn's name is so intimately linked with Eisenstadt that the significance of Eszterháza tends to be overlooked. Until Paul Anton died in 1762, his younger brother and heir Nikolaus lived in fairly modest style at Süttör, a country estate south of the Neusiedlersee. With almost unlimited means suddenly at his disposal 'Nikolaus the Magnificent' set about building a palatial shooting box at Süttör which included a library, a chapel and a *sala terrena,* and changed the name of the house to Eszterháza. The elderly *kapellmeister* Gregor Joseph Werner remained in Eisenstadt, but Haydn was put in charge at Eszterháza where his duties were to provide church and table music and two concerts per week. At that time his orchestra consisted of seven string instruments, a flute, two oboes, a bassoon and two alpine horns; not unusual for a minor court, that was only the start of it. Prince Nikolaus evidently spent about eight or nine months of the year at his country seat, and also kept up households in Vienna and Eisenstadt. The political, social and cultural centre of Hungary was Pressburg (Bratislava), where the Esterházy palace was the scene of brilliant entertaining. The premiere of Haydn's *La Canterina* was held there in 1767. Complete records were kept at Eszterháza from 1780 onwards, and if more than a thousand performances of seventy-one operas over a period of just ten years seems to be a remarkable achievement, such demands on a con-ductor-manager were common at that time. Even so, the record for 1786 is remarkable: Haydn put on sixteen new operas in 124 performances, and one must remember that he was also respon-sible for at least three, often five, public concerts a week. But it was the quality of the entertainment which dazzled his contem-poraries and brought music-lovers to Eszterháza from all over Europe. The standard in Vienna was no higher, and is thought to have been inferior to Haydn's performances: did not Maria Theresa say 'If I want to hear good opera I go to Eszterháza'? After the death of his first patron in 1790, the great days at Eszter-háza came to an end. But Haydn merely transferred his ensemble, now consisting of fifteen singers and an orchestra of twenty-two, to Eisenstadt.

The interests of Nikolaus II extended to the arts and natural sciences. This man whom his contemporaries compared to Lorenzo de Medici, assembled collections of pictures, prints, coins and geological specimens. He converted the park, in the fashion of the time, from the French to the English style, and rebuilt Schloss Esterházy in Eisenstadt in its present form, although by no means on the scale that the original plans foresaw. The work was in full swing on 1st September 1800 when Nelson was there with the Hamiltons, when Haydn gave Nelson his pen and received in exchange the watch which had ticked through Abukir and the Battle of the Nile.

One can imagine that, in some ways, Haydn's working life was simpler in Eisenstadt than it had been out in the country. At Eszterhaza, special housing was built for the orchestra and singers, but at Eisenstadt he could call on the resources of a town, and Vienna was close. He was able to perform *The Seasons* in 1801, and it was almost a matter of routine to put on operas with no skimping on personnel. A century and a half of intensive cultural patronage by the Esterhazys was, all the same, slowly coming to an end, and end it did in 1813. In the years after the Napoleonic wars even an Esterhazy could no longer carry the expense of staging plays and opera on a royal scale, while maintaining an orchestra which, under Johann Nepomuk Fuchs, amounted to forty-three persons, plus seven choirboys, a secretary, stage decorators and costumiers.

Close to the Iron Curtain stands a small farmhouse, and only a yard away from the barbed wire there is a brick bread oven. The farmer has had to build a wooden fence against the wire to protect his wife's clothes when she removes the bread. If there is one thing to be learnt from the writings of local historians in eastern Austria it is this: whenever, as so repeatedly happened, these populations were slaughtered, carried off to slavery and their villages which were simply farms laid side by side for protection, were fired and pillaged, the 'troubles' came, or were sent, from a long way away. (The total losses in Lower Austria at the time of the great siege were about 80,000, and the price of female slaves in the Middle Eastern markets dropped sharply.) But on this frontier the German-speaking Austrians, the Croats, Hungarians and the Slavs beyond the River March lived peacefully together.

Whether or not this mutual tolerance has any bearing on the history of the Burgenland Jews it is hard to judge. In the larger Austrian towns the picture is much as one would expect: tolerance in the interests of trade and finance alternating with bursts of superstitious panic. In the Vorarlberg, the Hohenems family protected 'their' Jews fairly consistently, and the Prince-Arch-bishops of Salzburg were in their way consistent too: between 1498, when Turnip Keutschach expelled them, and 1848 no Jews were allowed to live in Salzburg. Vienna blew hot and cold, and whenever it blew cold many fugitives found asylum in what is now the Burgenland. The worst moments were the *Wiener Gesera,* the great pogrom of 1421 which almost wiped out the flourishing medieval community, and the expulsion of five hundred families from the Leopoldstadt district (then known as the Untere Werd) in 1670. By 1700 the Emperor was so short of cash that Samuel Oppenheimer was invited to Vienna from Heidelberg, and Prince Eugene of Savoy was soon to owe such a debt of gratitude to Oppenheimer that he presented him with a valuable collection of books and manuscripts. (This Turkish booty was bought by the Bodleian Library in 1829.) Between the edict of toleration under Joseph II and freedom under Franz Joseph lay a period of com-promise when only those Jews might live in Vienna who could prove their value to the state. Among many other conditions of residence they were required to pray for the Chief of Police.

A series of letters patent had protected the Jews of Eisenstadt since 1296, but there is known to have been a synagogue there even earlier. The Mattersburg ghetto, one of the 'Seven Communities', existed since 1354; Forchtenstein Castle gave sanctuary in an emergency. Under the protection of the Esterhazys the Eisenstadt ghetto became a flourishing centre of Jewish tradition and scholar-ship. The most celebrated personality living there in the eighteenth century was the Chief Rabbi of Hungary and the Austrian crown lands, honorary Rabbi of Eisenstadt, Prague, Krakow, etc, etc, merchant and supplier by Imperial appointment to the Court and Ministry of War, Simson Wertheimer. In the Unterberg district of Eisenstadt, one of the very few places in Europe in which a Jewish community has been able to maintain an unbroken tradition for so long, Wertheimer's house is Nr. 6, Unterbergstrasse. The posts are still visible which supported chains for closing off the ghetto during the Sabbath.

Burgenland

This latest addition to Austria was the home of the Haydns, of Franz Liszt and Fanny Elssler. It is not fashionable, but in odd pockets, highly exclusive. The Burgenland is a conglomerate of cultures, languages, geological formations, alien plants and rare creatures. In all this it is very Austrian indeed.

10

Vienna

On 25th April 1870 the Viennese picked up their newspapers and read that the crown estates in the Vienna Woods, about 80,000 acres of forest, had been sold to the highest bidder and would be hacked down and sold. Born of the shortage of money after the Austro-Prussian war of 1866, this time-bomb had been ticking away in the Ministry of Finance for more than two years. The article in the *Neues Wiener Tagblatt* and others which followed set off an avalanche of protest, and a campaign was launched which ended at last in cancellation of the contract. It was perhaps the biggest scandal of the time. What would the country look like today if the protests and petitions had had no result? Part of the area would have been replanted, but the hard-pressed monasteries, Heiligenkreuz, Schottenstift, Klosterneuburg, might have sold out as well, and one can be certain that speculative builders would have latched on to the Tulbinger Kogel and the Sophienalpe, and would have built their villas among the primroses of Kaltenleutgeben. Bursts of controversy are fairly common. Recently, not for the first time, it was about increasing the proportion of conifers at the expense of the less economic beech trees. Taken as a whole, the Vienna Woods are still predominantly a beech forest, and from the look-out tower on the Tulbinger Kogel in autumn, deeper and lighter patches of purple, scarlet and yellow mark the presence of oak, elm, maple, poplar and aspen and the plantations of silver birch on the estates of the Schottenstift. There was wholesale felling after both world wars. But these losses have been made up, and the woods, culminating on the heights of the Kahlenberg and

Leopoldsberg, cradle the capital of Austria with a grace that very few urban settings can rival.

When, as the legend goes, James son of Zebedee preached in a clearing at Penzing near Schönbrunn, the forest may have consisted largely of oak; certainly it did in the Middle Ages when the Emperor Henry II granted the southern end to the Babenberg Margrave, Henry the Strong. It was still trackless primeval forest in the twelfth century when the French Cistercians founded their monastery at Heiligenkreuz and embarked on mixed farming, planting out orchards and vineyards, breeding horses, cattle and sheep. Here and there the oak woods came right up to the town walls of Vienna, and one tree evidently stood alone and was a bit of a landmark, so that it became the fashion for young craftsmen when they came to the city looking for work to hammer a nail into its trunk. But whether or not the core of an oak really is buried inside the 'Stock im Eisen' we shall never know.

Everything about Vienna has been said before, including this: that until a very late stage it was not only an imperial city but essentially an aristocratic town where the counterweight of a powerful, independent merchant class was unable to develop. The civic pride which is so obvious in most of the larger cities of western Europe, and even in Graz, Klagenfurt and Innsbruck, was stunted in Vienna by the demands of a particular situation. Defence against Islam, precise and impartial administration of an empire called for a willing, co-operative population, and although it might occasionally seem necessary to execute the mayor, and, as late as the turn of this century, to veto a mayoral election four times in succession, by and large the Viennese did what was expected of them. Over a great part of its history Vienna has been as international as New York, and the present all-pervading mediocrity is caused by a number of very obvious factors such as the end of the old magnetism which attracted talent from far afield, Austria's enormous casualties in the last war, the disappearance of the Jewish intellectuals, the persistent brain drain, and probably to some extent by non-participation of the aristocracy in public life.

The government, the Town Hall and the archdiocese are stuck

with the legacy of men who wore the crowns of the Holy Roman Empire and of Austria-Hungary, and who built accordingly, often with political ends in mind. The Babenberg dukes built grandly because they longed to become kings; even St. Stephen's Cathedral was not built solely to the glory of God; during the struggle for the Spanish succession religious orders were brought in from Spain but dropped like wet fish when the dream faded. And only if the Counter-Reformation is to be seen as a wholly religious phenomenon can politics be left entirely out of account where the new or restored early seventeenth-century churches are concerned: the Jesuitenkirche, Dominikanerkirche, Franziskanerkirche and the rest.

No one can get entirely lost in Vienna because of the triple ring of roads, or widening horseshoes, round the inner city. The Ring itself is followed by an outer layer which the Viennese vaguely call 'die Zweierlinie' after the trams which run along it, and finally there is the Gürtel, as useful as its surroundings are hideous.

Lanes are older than the houses to which they point and streets than the houses which line them: this adage is quite untrue of the ring roads but it is worth remembering while exploring the Innere Stadt. The original heart of Vienna was a very small plateau above an arm of the Danube, now the Danube canal, which then carried the main current of water. The bed of the Ottakringer Bach would later become the Tiefer Graben (home of dyers and tanners, pickpockets and pimps), and a spring welled up on the Graben and flowed down the Rotenturmstrasse. The town walls formed a square, flattened at one corner by the river. They lay along the edge of Am Hof above the Tiefer Graben, followed the cliff above the Danube close to the base of the steps of St. Maria am Gestade, past the Ruprechtskirche (which stands partly *on* this wall), along the Kramergasse and Rotgasse and back along the inside of the Graben. As we sit in our cars, stuck in the traffic jam where the Tuchlauben, Bognergasse and Naglergasse run on to the Kohlmarkt and the Graben, there is plenty of time to remember where we are: here was the Porta Decumana, and on its base grew the massive medieval gate, the Peilertor.

This was the Roman Vindobona, a secondary garrison town manned first by the XIII Legion and a regiment of British cavalry, and after about A.D. 115 by the X Legion which remained until Vindobona, and the whole of Pannonia I, was ceded to the Goths. From the Hoher Markt, which was not a market but a place of assembly and occasional camping ground, the troops could look across to the hill where one day Prince Eugène of Savoy would build his Belvedere, think hopefully of time-off and the prostitutes in the *municipium*, and compare their own lot with that of the civil population: pensioned legionaries with their wives and families, peasants, traders, craftsmen and all that went to make up a town numbering between fifteen and twenty thousand souls, extending all the way from the River Wien to the present Danube Canal. But if we imagine these legionaries as living during the accelerating decline of the Roman Empire, they were seeing a gradual infiltration of their *castrum* by civilians; they were allowed to marry while on active service; traders were settling within the gates. By almost imperceptible degrees, Vindobona was ceasing to be a *castrum* and becoming a town.

There were two main routes leading away from Vienna. The Via Principalis (in line with the Landskrongasse) ran straight down the middle of the camp, through the gate and on to the road towards Hungary. All the traffic which had no need or right to enter Vindobona used the main road, and this has never gone out of use—the Herrengasse, continuing along the Augustinerstrasse to the Rennweg. The two roads joined at that awkward junction of the Rennweg and Landstrasse which travellers to and from the airport at Schwechat may have noticed.

The break between Roman and Carolingian Vienna might seem to be complete; as far as we know, no medieval house stood on the foundations of a Roman building. The town on the Rennweg disappeared completely. What happened in Vienna in the interval before the arrival of Charlemagne? St. Peter's Church on the Graben gives a clue to the situation in Vienna at a time when there is little other evidence. Unlike St. Stephen's, which was built much later, the original Peterskirche was built inside the walls. We know that its floor was precisely on the level of the

Roman road at the end of the Tuchlauben, and that old barracks were cleared to make room for a church square which stretched as far as the Brandstätte. The impressive dimensions of the church (which faced the opposite way, with its back to the Graben) and its extensive precincts show that it served a large and presumably flourishing population, far more numerous than in Carolingian times when there were hardly five hundred all told. The first Peterskirche, in fact, was built not later than 433; the Goths, being Christians of the Arian persuasion, will have used it during their short tenure.

It was hundreds of years before the Viennese filled, let alone overflowed, old Vindobona. After the ebb and flow of the migrations, two clusters of houses developed near the Peterskirche and on the site of the later ghetto near the Hoher Markt; gradually the Tuchlauben came to life as a typical linear village with a triangular market place where it meets the Brandstätte. Although there is no absolute proof, it is accepted as a reasonable assumption that Samo, the mysterious Frankish merchant who founded an empire which died with him, made Vienna his capital. Whether or not he kept all his twelve wives there at the same time (they bore him twenty-two sons and twenty-five daughters) no one can say; the family would have made a brave show in the Almanach de Gotha.

We can only sketch in the following developments. Around 800 the 'ing' villages—Simmering, Hietzing, Ottakring, Grinzing, Sievering—were coming to life, taking their names from the military leaders of an armed peasantry. After the Hungarian interlude in the tenth century, the town came back to the German crown in 991, and in the decade between 1125 and 1135, Leopold III, whose residence was at Klosterneuburg, was allowed to take possession of Vienna.

The town now consisted of the southern half of the space within the Roman walls, forming a rectangle with its upper gate at the junction of Hoher Markt and Wipplingerstrasse, and the lower on the Lichtensteg just above the crossing half way down the Rotenturmstrasse. It now began rapidly to expand.

The first Babenberg to build a residence in Vienna was Heinrich, nicknamed 'Jasomirgott', who threw back the town walls to the cliff above the Tiefer Graben and round the parish of St. Stephen's church. The word *Hof* can mean a royal court, a courtyard or a farm, and Am Hof was a mixture of all three, probably with administrative offices thrown in. The greatest poet and minstrel of the middle ages, Walter von der Vogelweide, lived there at the time when the Babenberg court reached its apex of civilized living. On the Danube side of the town, the salt boats from the Traunsee were being unloaded on the Salzgries below Maria am Gestade; the Duke's head forester could still leave his house on the site of the Esterhazy palace in the Wallnerstrasse and take his dog out for a run among the blackberry bushes, and in the evening, wild duck still landed on the pond in that sharp drop below the Naglergasse where, later, merchants would sell flax. But by the end of the twelfth century the Graben had been filled in, the walls were moved out to the Herrengasse, enclosing St. Michael's church, and ran down the Plankengasse and Himmelpfortgasse to the Seilerstätte. In Klosterneuburg, the Master of Verdun was working on that unique creation of its time which would later be known as the Verdun Altar.

When Styria joined Austria, trade with Venice down across the Semmering became much easier. The result was that wealthy merchants built houses along the Kärntnerstrasse which became and has always remained the city's main artery. The Stock-im-Eisen-Platz beside the cemetery of St. Stephen's was now the heart of town. The Kärntnertor was the gate to the south and west as in the last wave of expansion which expressed the Babenbergs' never-to-be-realized ambition to wear a royal crown, Leopold the Glorious established the walls of Vienna where they would stand until the day came in 1857 when the Emperor Franz Josef signed the decree for their demolition.

The predecessor to the Gothic St. Stephen's was the outward sign of the Babenbergs' incessant supplications to Almighty God that he might take sides, since the Pope could not, in the running conflict with the Bishops of Salzburg and Passau who sat so heavily on their respective rights in Vienna. If one could be efficiently played off against the other (Passau's Stephanskirche, for instance, against Salzburg's Peterskirche), then Vienna might emerge at last, to the greater glory of the sovereign, as a diocese. But this did not happen until 1468, and not effectively until 1480.

These gnawing ambitions explain the immense size of Romanesque St. Stephen's. More than 250 feet long, such a church could and did rival the great German cathedrals; the fact that the entire population of Vienna and the surrounding villages could hardly fill the enormous nave and the broad aisles was of no importance. It had begun as the parish church of the village which grew outside the old gate on the Lichtensteg, a community of long-distance traders whose caravans loaded and unloaded on a lengthy open space between the Bäckerstrasse and Sonnenfelsgasse. The village had its own walls along the site of the Heiligenkreuzerhof and the Postgasse, and its moat ran down the Wollzeile. The priest lived just outside the walls of his parish, somewhere within the site of the Archbishop's Palace. But the man who pressed on with the Gothic St. Stephen's and who did more for the life and institutions of Vienna than anyone had done so far, was Rudolph IV, who was determined to build a city which could compete with the brilliance of his father-in-law's residence in Prague. Rudolph 'The Founder's' university in Vienna was the second (after Prague) in German-speaking lands.

Directly facing Am Hof, Die Freyung with its uneven shape and steep slope is still one of Vienna's most attractive squares, its name telling of the asylum granted to all fugitives who could make their way to the precincts of the Schotten Abbey. The original *Scoti*, actually of course Irish monks from Regensburg, were brought to Vienna by the indefatigable Heinrich Jasomirgott, and for well over eight hundred years the abbey has been involved in the history of Vienna and has educated a large number of its leading citizens and the nobility. It would be going too far to say that for two hundred and sixty years the Irish monks managed to live in Vienna and develop a wide range of activities without learning a word of German. Those who were obliged to, did so. But although the expense of bringing fresh recruits over from Ireland was almost prohibitive, they steadfastly refused to accept reinforcements from other nations. On one dreadful day in 1418 which the monks noted in their records as '*dies irae, calamitatis et miseriae*' the shrunken party of seven had to face a papal delegation. They would agree, they said at last, to measures of reform, but rather than admit alien men of God to their ranks they would shake the dust of the Freyung from their sandalled feet. And so they did. The mother house at Regensburg was far from pleased at this all too truculent display of Irish mettle, and a struggle to win back the valuable property began which dragged on for two hundred years. Mary, Queen of Scots took the matter up with the Emperor Rudolph II but was told through her ambassador to pipe down. Officially, the last humiliating words were spoken by Ferdinand II in 1624—they had been put into his mouth by the ruling Chapter of the Schottenstift—the *Scoti* could not be entrusted with the abbey owing to the unsuitability of their forebears in Vienna who, wanting in knowledge of the German tongue, had been incapable of properly performing their duties, whether it was in management, in the cure of souls, or, in the case of the abbots, in conference with fellow dignitaries.

Two celebrated pictures in the possession of the Schottenstift are a touchingly precise record of fifteenth-century Vienna. The Visitation shows Mary calling on Elizabeth at her house in the Kärntnerstrasse, while the background to the Flight into Egypt is the town seen from the south with a high reed fence round the inner suburbs. The great humanist Aeneas Silvio Piccolomini, who later became Pope Pius II, described the Vienna that he knew. 'The citizens' houses are tall and spacious, finely ornamented and well and strongly built. There are broad courtyards, and ample rooms which they call *Stuben* and which they heat, because the winter is very harsh. Everywhere are windows of glass, which permit light to enter from all sides, the gates are usually of iron. Birds sing in the *Stuben* and many and costly are the items of equipment which may be observed. Roomy stables await horses and all kinds of beasts of burden. The gables on the roofs are sheer, they are decorated with taste and magnificence, most are painted within and without. The walls of the houses are of stone. Whenever you visit a citizen, you will suppose yourself to be in the house of a prince. The cellars are so deep and so long, that the common saying is, there are two Viennas, one above and one below the ground.'

If this last remark in a letter dated April 1438 was true then, it is basically true now. Quite apart from the catacombs of St. Stephen's which are a phenomenon in themselves, the cellars of a large and perhaps unknown number of houses are several storeys deep, and when bombed sites were cleared after the last war, passages could be seen to lead off them. Most Viennese of the more prosperous classes used at one time to own a vineyard on the outskirts and could offer their own wine to visitors, but even so they could hardly have needed all that cellar space, and the labyrinthine network must have developed early. According to his own account, Evliya Celebi, writer of travellers' tales, was in Vienna in 1665. His description in *The Realm of the Golden Apple* contains a welter of fable and wild oriental hyperbole and it is not even certain that he was ever actually in the dream city and unattainable goal of the dying Ottoman empire. But a good deal of what he says is correct. And when he reports: 'The fortress itself contains an extensive network of low underground vaulted passages so that they can pass from one end to the other through hundreds of subterranean alleyways', this can, at least, be accepted as the opinion of the Turkish military engineers. There certainly were underground skirmishes during the siege, and I have been told of a tunnel which linked the beleaguered city with Klosterneuburg. A passage leads from the deep cellars beneath the Alte Hofapotheke to the catacombs under the Michaelerkirche, and during the last war it was possible to go underground in the Annagasse and emerge on the Hoher Markt. The current construction work on an underground railway in Vienna ought to bring to light a good deal more about this subterranean warren.

In the generation or two before the siege of 1529, Vienna, its suburbs and the surrounding countryside reached an absolute peak of beauty and distinction. Antonio Bonfini, court historian to King Matthias Corvinus, said that 'Vienna's whole territory is one splendid garden among hills crowned with vineyards and orchards. At their feet lie gay little foothills, dotted with the most delicious of country seats and bedecked with fish ponds, hunting lodges, houses and gardens, all catering to every need and to every heart's desire. The nearby heights delight the wanderer's eye beyond measure by means of the quantity of castles and aristocratic residences, the villages and flourishing homesteads.'

On the approach of Suleiman the Magnificent, the villages were destroyed to deprive his army of shelter and to give a clear view to the defenders. Some were far enough out for a few buildings to survive both Turkish sieges, but it is this scorched earth policy which accounts for the total lack of Romanesque and Gothic churches in these districts. The decaying churches were abandoned to the weather, there was little church building during the Reformation and the architects of the Counter-Reformation were indifferent to the merits of medieval arts and craftsmanship.

It evidently took a long time for the surroundings of Vienna to recover. Fynes Morison, tramping down from Moravia in 1593, eating grapes with his bread as he went, was not particularly enthusiastic about the town 'vulgarly called Wien'. He noted down one or two local legends including the one about the mortar between the stones of the Cathedral having been mixed with wine, and he was warned that it was dangerous to walk the streets at night 'for the great number of disordered people'. He then continued on his way across the 'wild plain' to Wiener Neustadt, into 'this country of Styria, where many men and women have big wens hanging down their throats by drinking the waters that run through the mines of mettals'.

In the countries which line the course of the Danube it is usual to build in the shape of square blocks, enclosing a womb-like area accessible to but entirely different in character from the world outside, and it is not too fanciful to see the microcosm in Vienna's older courtyards in the four-square farms of Upper and Lower Austria. One or two relics of these farms still stand in Mariahilf and Neubau, leftovers from the farm-villages among the vineyards which covered the hilly country between Gumpendorf and Grinzing. When they were not overcrowded, the flats around courtyards of a type such as the Deutschordenshof on the Singerstrasse were very pleasant to live in. But constriction was always endemic within the city and became unbearable in the years when the walls had become an anachronism but no one quite had the heart to pull them down. Lady Mary Wortley Montagu was saying in 1740 that they ought to go: it was extraordinary to her, the way rich and poor lived cheek by jowl, a palatial apartment on the *belétage* separated only by a thin wall from the slum next door. Noble stairways were shabby and sometimes filthy because they were used by all the *Hausparteien* (the Palais Liechtenstein in the Bankgasse was said to have two thousand occupants) and by tradesmen, hawkers and beggars; the contrast was startling between the mean approach and the blazing magnificence of the interiors.

The Viennese are a race of flat-dwellers, and their fortresses are locked at 9 p.m. A Viennese architect commented in 1906 that the late nineteenth-century 'Cottage' district in Döbling was planned on English lines in the hope that some citizens of the wealthier sort might be drawn to the idea of living in a house rather than a flat; admittedly, he said, to live in rooms which were placed on top of one another called for careful examination of the problems involved.

For most people (but not for the *canaille*) the way to escape from the stuffy air of the city was to go for a walk along the *courtines*, the broad town walls linking the spear-head bastions. Here and there, as we can see now on the Mölkerbastei, houses were built on the bastions. Poplars were planted all along the walls by Joseph II and an avenue ran round the city. Latterly, the most popular garden, with a smart restaurant, was the Paradeisgartel which lay roughly above the Volksgarten where the Empress Elisabeth memorial is now and across the extension of the Bankgasse beside the Burgtheater. Strollers along the walls had an unimpeded view of a panorama which could hardly be equalled in any other capital in Europe. Below the walls and, apart from the river sector, extending all round the city, lay the Glacis, a band of open ground which was extended from its original width, 330 feet, to about 1,900 feet—the range of the cannon of the day—in 1683. No building was allowed on this open space. The great architects of the late seventeenth and early eighteenth centuries, Fischer von Erlach the elder and younger, Lukas von Hildebrandt and the rest, built for their noble patrons a ring of palaces on the outer rim of the Glacis facing inwards towards the focus of their lives and fortunes, the Imperial Hofburg. By about 1730 the circle was complete. Schwarzenberg, planned by Prince Fondi to annoy Prince Eugène, Schönborn-Battyány, Trautsohn, Auersperg, the Liechtenstein palace in the Rossau where the draught horses which pulled ships and barges upstream used to graze: these are now the only survivors of a ring of palaces and country houses linked and backed by generously laid out parks and gardens. Behind them lay scores of others. On one side of the Landstrasser Hauptstrasse there was the Palais Rasumovsky; on the other ornamental gardens backed up to the Palais Althan and the Palais Harrach, built by Hildebrandt and Fischer von Erlach. Nothing is left of these two great town houses. Prince Kaunitz, growing more and more eccentric in later life, rode up and down the grounds of his palace in Mariahilf. Out at Neuwaldegg in the Vienna Woods, Fischer von Erlach built a *schlössl* for Count Franz Moritz von Lacy, one of that famous band of Irishmen who rose to the highest ranks in the Austrian army. Lacy, advised by Lord Grenville, spent his entire fortune on laying out an English park. Seventeen cabins built of rushes but exquisitely furnished and equipped, formed a *hameau* on top of the hill, and all around were ponds, statues, temples and groups of trees—a Rococo idyll as a means of escape from the over-civilized life at court. The grounds of the Augarten Palace led round to the Prater, to the south Prince Eugene's double residence was soon joined—the circle now ends—by Fondi's chateau which, half completed, was bought by that same resplendent Prince Johann Franz von Schwarzenberg who was shot dead in a shooting accident by the Emperor Charles VI. ('My life', murmured the dying prince, certainly without a hint of irony, 'was ever at the disposal of Your Supreme Majesty.') Only the treetops of Maria Theresa's Schönbrunn and perhaps the Gloriette will have been visible from the walls. Lady Mary saw all this at its best, because the pressure of industry and an expanding population soon turned some of the smaller country houses into factories and slowly encroached on the gardens. The Karlskirche was the most important feature of all, but it was originally meant to be seen in a way that is impossible today. It is not only that the gardens and the lanes, lined by avenues of trees, the hayfields and the 'flea market' which gradually softened the once inhospitable Glacis, as well as the River Wien flowing in its open bed at the feet of the church, have all disappeared leaving only the token Rössel Park in front of the College of Technology. The town houses between the Ring and the Karlsplatz interrupt the original view from the Hofburg and distort the perspective. Roughly a century and a half was to go by between the growth of this magic outer circle and the construction of the Ring, but when the walls were torn down at last and Vienna burst into the orgy of monumental building which preceded its extinction as the capital of a great power, the fundamental ground plan was there.

It would not easily strike anyone who stands on the Heldenplatz and tries to sort out what he is seeing, that the Messepalast, J. E. Fischer von Erlach's royal stables which he built to his father's plans in 1725, was meant to play a vital part in the grand design for a new Vienna. It faces Nobile's Burgtor and closes off the vista lined by the Museums of Art and Natural History; the axis is the Maria Theresa memorial. The original idea was much more ambitious, and we have to realize that the Neue Burg was to have been double the size, balanced by an equivalent block directly opposite to it. If the plan had been carried out in its entirety, the Heldenplatz, instead of being open on one side, would have been an enclosed space facing towards the Burgtor, leading the eye between the museums to the imperial stables. It is always said that the Austrians do everything by halves and fail to follow up their victories, but if the semicircle had been rounded off as it was meant to be, we should have been robbed of the view from the steps of the Hofburg across the trees to Parliament, Rathaus and Ballhausplatz.

The Viennese seem to feel a great nostalgia for the Ringstrasse era. They never stop writing about it, and as often as not writing very well indeed. But the generation which lived through it all took time to get used to the new feeling of space and freedom. Many people frankly hated the whole thing and felt almost indecently exposed. In theory, 'bliss was it in that dawn to be alive';

in fact, the Viennese were losing what they well knew to be one of the most beautiful town promenades in the world. It was also *gemütlich*. 'The walls of Vienna', Mrs. Trollope estimated, 'can be walked round by a party of ladies, chattering all the time, within the hour'—and if we reckon their pace at three miles an hour, she was about right. For some years the Viennese hardly knew what to do with their fine new boulevard, and it took one or two great occasions, in particular the fantastic, staggeringly opulent jubilee procession in 1879, designed by Hans Makart, to stimulate their imagination and show them what it was that they had been given.

Every stranger to Vienna is struck by the violent dissonance among the architectural styles along the sector between the twin museums and the Votivkirche. Many contemporaries had the same impression and they also thought that the Opera looked as though it had been screwed into the ground, lacking both elevation and a spacious foreground. But we only have to take one horrified look at the Arsenal beyond the Gürtel in the 3rd District, remembering that here the architects of the Ringstrasse practised techniques of monumental building which their fathers had all but forgotten, to realize how much we were spared.

The great virtue which the architects of the Ring shared was a sense of proportion. Whatever we may think about each individual structure, no one committed the mortal sin of building on the scale of, say, the Victor Emmanuel monument in Rome which throws the viewer's inner eye so completely off-balance that the entire city, and not merely the immediate surroundings, suffers from its presence. The Votivkirche is not really part of the Ring concept, as Heinrich von Ferstel, who was only twenty-five when his design won the competition, began work on it in 1856 while the town walls were still standing. It is not so much Neo-Gothic as plain imitation Gothic, and respectful indifference is the general attitude towards it. One does not love the Votivkirche, nor does one actually wish it would go away. The Rathaus is another matter. It was supposed to conjure up the usual associations of civic price and turtle soup respectability, of the merchants of Augsburg and the Hanseatic League. But if to be derivative was the intention, better models were available than megomaniac French Neo-Gothic at its most spikey. The House of Parliament, on the other hand, with its direct message about classical Greek democracy, is honest and has a certain nobility. It ought to have been possible to establish some link between Theophil Hansen's Parliament and Ferstel's University, which replaced the building (now the Academy of Sciences) on the Universitätsplatz.

We left Dr. Charles Burney floating dismally down the Danube on a raft, and we ought to gather him in. He did get to Vienna in the end, but it was a good fortnight before his books, innocuous though they were, got through the Customs. One thing about his stay is difficult to understand: how a musicologist of his standing, collecting material for a history of music, could spend the time that he did on interviewing nonentities. Could he not possibly have contacted Mozart? And although admittedly Eszterhaza was some way off, it would be nearly twenty years before, in London, he had another chance to meet Haydn. But he was received by Gluck, 'as formidable a character as Handel used to be: a very dragon, of whom all are in fear', and he wrote at length about Metastasio, who worked like a machine and 'never sets pen to paper except by compulsion'. (The librettist and Imperial poet laureate was probably marked for life by being forced to translate the whole of Homer into Italian verse before he was fourteen.)

Like most of his contemporaries Dr. Burney disliked Gothic architecture, but his description of St. Stephen's Cathedral was not altogether unjust: 'A dark, dirty and dismal old Gothic building, though richly ornamented; in it are hung all the trophies of war, taken from the Turks and other enemies of the House of Austria, for more than a century past, which gives it very much the appearance of an old wardrobe.'

Mrs. Trollope launched herself and her daughter in Viennese high society with surprising ease in view of her own lack of a title; foreigners could not be expected to grasp the life-enhancing properties, to an Englishwoman, of being well-connected. But she had good letters of introduction, and with button-eyed concentration and admirable thoroughness, Mrs. Trollope ploughed her way through the winter season of 1835 and the pre-Lenten carnival of 1836. She seldom got to bed before 4 a.m. She noticed the double windows, the cleanliness of the streets but also the distressing *odeur continentale* indoors, she studied the refined chic of the ladies of the aristocracy and thought that, by comparison, their equivalent in London looked like a band of shepherdesses. She had never seen such diamonds in her life.

Mrs. Trollope is not the only traveller to have noticed the 'indescribable impurity' of that 'black and vilely-smelling ditch', the River Wien: surely, she thought, Maria Theresa, 'whose days may be counted by the noble and beautiful works with which she adorned her empire', could never have permitted this noxious stream, emitting 'such vapours as nearly suffocated us yesterday', to flow between the wind and her regality? Mrs. Trollope felt persuaded that, 'before twenty-four hours had passed, five hundred diggers and delvers would have been seen deepening its shallow bed, and drawing from every brook that poured forth a wholesome current in the vicinity, wherewithal to supply such a stream as might be worthy of giving its name to imperial Vienna'; she appreciated, however, that 'in these days, when money is less easily obtained, and labour of high value', a spirit of very honourable and righteous economy must prevail.

This is all very well. But the Wien, having collected its load of suburban sewage, still had to pass through the Naschmarkt where it would pick up all the rotting vegetables that the stallholders, descendants according to legend of a defeated army of teutonic amazons whose brawny queen lies buried near the Spinnerin am Kreuz, cared to throw into it. Perhaps, after all, we should not be too nostalgic about the days when the Wien flowed through the meadows below the Karlskirche.

For all her protestations Mrs. Trollope was a bit of a ghoul. The scene as she describes it in the catacombs of the Cathedral, where not only stacked up skeletons but leathery semi-preserved corpses by the hundred lay around in impious, grinning abandon, could have been put straight into a mid-century Gothic novel, and perhaps it was. She was probably not exaggerating, because the catacombs were not finally tidied up until towards the end of the century, and a tendency for skeletons to burst out of their coffins owing to the combined weight of many lying one upon the other was noted by a Viennese writer in about 1910. It was interesting, Frances found, to be able to write home and say that a young murderer had been exhibited to the crowd for ten minutes on Am Hof square while his sentence was publicly proclaimed, and that he then sat at a table in police headquarters while a stream of visitors came to look at him, dropping into a plate coins which he could dispose of as he wished.

Mrs. Trollope's interest in Am Hof seems to have stopped at the murderer. She says nothing about the church—Carlo Carlone's façade is one of the finest of its period in Vienna—from the broad *terrazzo* of which Pope Pius VI blessed the crowd when he came to Vienna to beg Joseph II to call off or modify his sweeping reforms of church administration. In 1806, from the same terrace, Franz, first Emperor of Austria, abdicated as Emperor of the German Nation. She does not mention the old ghetto, nor the Zeughaus, which must be one of the oldest fire stations (1562) on record.

The rigidity of Austrian society astonished her. As a foreigner and particularly as an Englishwoman, she was able to move between two layers of gentility which co-existed but never met. Princes and counts were in the 'first society', banker-barons and industrialists, ennobled civil servants and officers made up the second, while the learned professions kept pretty much to themselves. (No one was in commerce, she noticed, they were all *bankers*.) The upper stratum managed to ignore the lower in a way that one would hardly think was possible in such a comparatively confined space, and Frances had many a poignant tale to tell about all this. The men did, when it suited them, move in lower (not necessarily more humble) circles; the women never. This system survived, of course, until the end of the monarchy and even trailed on, to some extent, into the republic.

Frances Trollope reluctantly came to the conclusion that bread and circuses worked. She had never, she felt certain, seen such a docile and yet gay and happy people. Exactly twelve years later the revolution broke out, Am Hof witnessed the ghastly scene of the lynching of the Minister of War, Latour, and the liberals, fighting for intellectual freedom, were astonished and shocked by the brutalized, almost inhuman appearance of the industrial proletariat which poured in from outside the city to join their cause.

The years between 1815 and 1848, from the Congress of Vienna to the largely abortive revolution, had a very long-lasting effect on the Viennese character. With the first breath that he draws, the Viennese is checking up on his pension rights, and his idea of hell is a country where absolutely anyone, without benefit of licence (*konzession*), can put up a notice on the door saying 'Gretl Schmidt, Dressmaker'. This mentality has a long history. In the twelfth century the town was granted privileges which compelled all goods approaching this crucial junction to be unloaded and offered for sale on the Vienna market. During the Crusades, it was in Vienna that the transfer was made from river to road transport. It was an effortless, not to say mildly parasitical way of making a living, unadventurous but safe. In course of time every trade and occupation came to be gripped in a corset of restrictive, monopolistic statutes; there was no free competition, and as the empire expanded, those who were not actually state employees tended to acquire the same habits of mind. Maria Theresa did her best to shake things up, but with little success. Nowadays, sharply etched personalities are very often to be found among the small tradesmen and craftsmen working on their own or in small family businesses: locksmiths, cobblers, printers, bookbinders, plumbers, house-painters, coal-dealers and so on—all that multitude of 'little men round the corner who fix things'. They have almost died out in West Germany but, thank God, they still hang on in Vienna. Economically, most of them are fighting a losing battle, they are independent, gay, witty and often generous.

Gluttony, sensuality and general frivolity are characteristics which we hear of again and again from the Middle Ages down to the present—they have been much overdrawn—combining with a tendency to melancholy and resignation. In the nineteenth century, in particular, the Viennese were so often accused of insincerity and mindless levity that a qualifying opinion must be quoted. The author Karl Postl, alias Charles Sealsfield, wrote in his *Austria As It Is* that although they were 'always reputed a sensual, thoughtless sort of beings . . . their honesty, kindness and sincerity were

proverbial'. In his blistering attack on the Metternich régime he
showed the effect of a police state on the character of a people.
'The ten thousand secret spies of Vienna have done their work.
Taken from the lower classes of society, tradesmen, servants,
mechanics, prostitutes, they form a confederacy in Vienna which
winds . . . through all the intricacies of social life. There is scarcely
a word spoken in Vienna which they do not hear. There is no
precaution possible, and even if you bring your own servants . . .
in less than a fortnight they will involuntarily prove your traitors.
The character of the Viennese has become what might be expected
in such circumstances. What they are, they have been made by their
masters; what is left them, is entirely their own—a kind heart, an
unbounded hospitality, and an obsequiousness which seems to
bespeak the consciousness of their own inferiority and degradation.'
As for the administrators of the empire, there they sat, 'in the
midst of gaiety and of sensual uproar, tied fast to their writing-
desks, working, watching—and watched'.

On the one hand, this was the Vienna of Ferdinand Raimund
and Johann Nestroy, but Grillparzer, whose plays were suppressed
or at best mangled by censorship at its most idiotic, put it on
record: 'Despotism has destroyed my life, at least the literary side
of it.'

The intellectual blight which lay over Vienna during the
Metternich era was not entirely swept away by the revolution—
the inevitable backlash saw to that—but the winds had begun to
blow, they blew down the walls of Vienna and carried away a
particular culture of exquisite delicacy and fragrance: bourgeois
Biedermeier, the world of Schubert, of Lanner and the Strauss
family, the world painted, all too idealistically, by Fendi, Dan-
hauser and Waldmüller.

Vienna's musical life was firmly rooted in royal patronage and
many of the Habsburgs, particularly in the eighteenth century,
were gifted performers. Vienna was a magnet for genius, and in
spite of individual distress and frustration so it remained, from the
days of Gluck on through Mozart and Haydn, Liszt, Beethoven,
Schubert, Brahms, Bruckner and Hugo Wolf, to Mahler and
Richard Strauss. There was something tangible about this tradi-

tion, something entirely personal, as when Mozart said of the sixteen-year-old Beethoven, 'Watch him, one day the world will be talking of him', or when Schubert, after Beethoven's funeral, drank 'to him, whom we have buried. And to the one who will follow him.' The line of personal contact has continued until now: Arnold Schönberg, Anton Webern, Alban Berg, Egon Wellesz.

From the downfall of Metternich until 1916: these sixty-eight years were spanned by the reign of Franz Josef, a tragic figure on the classical scale, absolute in his assumptions but no less in his self-dedication and discipline; a Canute. To all appearances the social scene changed very little. The Prater Corso, a traditional public parade of staggering dimensions, was joined by tributaries from every class of life. Into the main avenue of the Prater, the Hauptallee, now eerie in its emptiness, streamed the carriages of the aristocracy with their liveried coachmen and footmen, the landaus and cabriolets of celebrated actresses and *grandes horizontales,* of brewers and publicans: from the Emperor and Empress, the Archdukes and Archduchesses to the greengrocer, everyone was there who could raise four wheels to carry them and a nag to pull. Beside and between the tight ranks of the heterogeneous procession which might extend for four miles and in which no order of rank was involved, rode cavalry officers by the hundred, dazzlingly uniformed, impeccably mounted. So many travellers, from the 1820s to the early years of this century, have described the scene; in its essentials it hardly altered over eighty years and more.

What seems to be quite unaccountable is the eruption of genius which burst out in practically every field of learning and the arts in the last decades of the nineteenth century and swept through to 1914. This was the time when the Vienna school of medicine reached its zenith, the era of Arthur Schnitzler and of Siegmund Freud. The Secession, the Vienna Jugendstil, made their break-through in architecture, in building techniques, in painting, and in the crafts from textiles to bookbinding. Otto Wagner, Adolf Loos, Gustav Klimt, Egon Schiele, Rudolf Kassner, Ludwig Wittgen-stein, Hugo von Hofmannsthal, Robert Musil . . . any list is bound to be as broad as it is long, and the marvel of it all was the degree of intercommunication between the arts and sciences.

It was the ultimate paradox in the history of Vienna and the Austrians that an empire dying on its feet, a society set rigid from peak to base and about to fall into an all-but mortal political sickness, should have produced a cultural explosion such as had not been experienced for two hundred years and of which the ground waves, even now, have hardly come to rest.

Bibliography

Bahr, Hermann, *Salzburger Landschaft,* Innsbruck, 1937.

Berger, P. Wilibald, *Die Wiener Schotten,* Vienna, 1962.

Brentano, Josef (ed.), *Vorarlbergische Merkwürdigkeiten,* appr. 1780.

Brunner, Otto, *Kärntens Stellung in der deutschen Geschichte,* Klagenfurt, 1941.

— *Adeliges Landleben,* Salzburg, 1949.

Burney, Dr. Charles, *Continental Travels,* 1770–1772, London, 1927.

Cefarim, Rudolf, *Kärnten und die Freimaurerei,* Vienna, 1932.

Commenda, Hans, *Geschichten aus Österreich,* Linz, 1947.

Demus, Otto, *Kunst in Kärnten,* Klagenfurt, 1934.

Egger, Rudolf, *Der Ulrichsberg. Ein heiliger Berg Kärntens,* Klagenfurt, 1949.

Engels, Amélie, *Maria Anna, Erzherzogin von Österreich* (thesis in archives of the Nationalbibliothek), 1964.

Enzinger, Moriz, *Goethe in Tirol,* Innsbruck, 1932.

Eppel, Franz, *Ein weg zur Kunst,* Salzburg, 1965.

Fischnaler, Konrad, *Geschichts-, Kultur-, und Naturbilder aus Alttirol,* Innsbruck, 1936.

Frodl, W., *Die Romanische Waldmalerei in Kärnten,* Klagenfurt, 1942.

Fuhrmann, Franz. *Alte Gärten in Salzburg vom Barock zur Romantik,* Salzburg, 1958.

Fürlinger, Herbert Stefan, *Jagd in Österreich in Vergangenheit und heute,* Vienna, 1964.

Geschichte des Zollwesens, Verkehrs und Handels in Tirol und Vorarlberg, Innsbruck, 1953.

Ginhart, Karl, *Millstatt am See,* Klagenfurt, 1954.

Gleissner, Heinrich, *Das Salzkammergut,* Salzburg, 1961.

Grabher, Hubert. *Die Jagd in Vorarlberg,* Bregenz, 1937.

Bibliography

Görlich, Walter, *Die Geschichte des Schlosses Landskron in Kärnten,* Klagenfurt, 1958.

Griessmaier, Viktor, *Österreich, Landschaft und Kunst,* Vienna, 1950.

Groner, Richard, *Wien wie es war,* Vienna, many editions, 1900–1966.

Grüll, Georg, *Burgen und Schlösser im Salzkammergut und Alpenland,* Vienna, 1963.

Gugitz, Gustav, *Österreichs Gnadenstätten in Kunst und Brauch,* Vienna, 1955.

Halmer, Felix, *Niederösterreichs Burgen,* Vienna, 1956.

Hans, J., *Austria Between Two Wars,* Klagenfurt, 1946.

Harich, Johann, *Festgabe für Josef Haydn,* Eisenstadt, 1959.

Hartwagner, Siegfried, *Das Zollfeld, eine Kulturlandschaft.* Klagenfurt, 1957.

Henz, Rudolf, *Österreich,* Nürnberg, 1958.

Hietsch, Otto (ed.), *Österreich und die Angelsächsische Welt,* Vienna, 1961.

Hirn, Josef, *Welser Sagen. Ein Beitrag zur Geschichte der Sagenbildung,* Innsbruck, 1889.

— *Innsbrucks historischer Boden,* Innsbruck, 1896.

— *Englische Subsidien für Tirol und für Emigranten von* 1809, Innsbruck, 1912.

Ilg, Karl, *Vorarlberg: Landes- und Volkskunde, Geschichte, Wirtschaft und Kunst,* 4 vols., Innsbruck, 1961.

Kastner, Adolf, *Die Grafen von Montfort-Tettnang,* Constance, 1957.

Khevenhüller-Metsch, Graf Georg, *Die Burg Hochosterwitz in Kärnten,* Klagenfurt, 1953.

Klampfer, Josef, *Franz Liszt, Gedenkstätten,* Eisenstadt, 1961.

Klebel, Ernst, *Von den Edlingern in Kärnten,* Klagenfurt, 1942.

— *Der Lungau. Historisch-politische Untersuchung,* Salzburg, 1960.

Kortz, Paul, *Wien am Anfang des* 20. *Jahrhunderts,* Vienna, 1906.

Krause, P. Adalbert, O. S. B., *St. Hemma,* Mödling, 1948.

Kriechbaum, Eduard, *Die Städte Oberösterreichs,* Braunau, 1936.

Krobot, Walter, and others, *Schmalspurig durch Österreich,* Vienna, 1961.

Künstler, Gustav, *Kleiner Führer zur Alten Kunst und Kultur der Stadt Wien,* Vienna, 1942.

Bibliography

Lahnsteiner, Josef, *Oberpinzgau,* Hollersbach, 1956.

— *Unterpinzgau,* Hollersbach, 1960.

Langeder, Gertrud, *Die Beziehungen zwischen Juden und Grundherr-schaft im Burgenland* (Thesis in archives of the Nationalbibliothek), 1946.

Lechner, Karl, *Alte Kulturstätten Niederösterreichs,* Vienna, 1935.

Leeper, A. W. A., *A History of Medieval Austria,* Oxford, 1941.

Leitich, Ann Tizia, *Verklungenes Wien,* Vienna, 1942.

Lutterotti, Otto von, *Dürer's Reise durch Tirol,* Innsbruck, 1956.

Marboe, Ernst, *Österreich,* Vienna, 1948.

Matyas, Anton, *Österreichischer Bauernspiegel,* Vienna, 1959.

Moeser, K., and Dworschak, F., 'Erzherzog Siegmund der Münzreiche von Tirol', *Österreichs Münzwesen im Mittelalter,* vol. 7, Vienna, 1936.

Morison, Fynes, *Itinerary,* London, 1617, Glasgow, 1907.

Neumann, Alfred, *Die römischen Ruinen unter dem Hohen Markt,* Vienna, 1950.

Neumann, Wilhelm (ed.), *900 Jahre Villach,* Villach, 1960.

Nussbaumer, Erich, *Geistiges Kärnten,* Klagenfurt, 1956.

Oettinger, Karl, *Das Werden Wiens,* Vienna, 1951.

Österreich-Ungarische Monarchie in Wort und Bild, Die (relevant volumes), Vienna, 1886–92.

Paul, Hans, *Geschichte der Herrschaft Esterhazy in Eisenstadt,* Vienna, 1965.

Pfaundler, Wolfgang, *Tiroler Jungbürgerbuch,* Innsbruck, 1963.

Pick, Josef, *Jüdisch-geschichtliche Stätten in Wien und den Bundesländern,* Vienna, 1935.

Pirkhofer, A. M., *England-Tyrol. Vom Bild Tirols im englischen Schrifttum,* Innsbruck, 1950.

Plechl, Pia Maria, *Das Marchfeld,* Vienna, 1969.

Posch, Fritz (ed.), *Geschichtliche Wanderungen durch die steierischen Fremdenverkehrsgebiete,* Graz, 1967.

— *Flammende Grenze. Die Steiermark in den Kuruzzenstürmen,* Graz, 1969.

Rainalter, Erwin, *Mirabell—Der Roman einer Frau,* Vienna, 1941.

Roscher, Magda, *Geschichte der Zisterziensischen Abtei Viktring* (Thesis in the archives of the National Bibliothek), 1953.

Bibliography

Sauser, Gustav, *Die Ötztaler*, Innsbruck, 1938.

Schadelbauer, Karl, *Kulturhistorische Miniaturen aus Tirol*, Bozen, 1956.

Schmeller, Alfred, *Das Burgenland*, Salzburg, 1965.

Schönherr, David, *Die Heirat Jakobs III von England und die Entführung seiner Braut aus Innsbruck 1719*, Innsbruck, 1877.

Schultes, Anton, *Die Nachbarschaft der Deutschen und Slawen an der March*, Vienna, 1954.

Sealsfield, Charles, *Austria As It Is*, London, 1828.

Sieghardt, August, *Südostbayrische Burgen und Schlösser und die Salzburger Schlösser und Edelsitze*, Berchtesgaden, 1952.

Siegl, P. Heinrich, O. S. B., *Das Benediktinerstift Göttweig*, 1914.

Stickler, Michael, *Die Katakomben von St. Stephan*, Vienna, 1948.

Stifter, Adalbert, *Aus dem Alten Wien*, Vienna, 1940.

Steinacher, Hans, *Kärnten* (Centrum für österr. Dokumentation und Information), Klagenfurt, 1961.

Steurer, Maria, *Die Sechs Ehen der Anna Neumann*, Vienna, 1955.

Stüber, Eberhard (ed.), *Die Naturwissenschaftliche Erforschung Land Salzburgs, Stand, 1963*, Salzburg, 1963.

Swoboda, Hans, *Oberösterreich*, Vienna, 1964.

Tirol—Natur, Kunst, Volk, Leben, Landesverkehrsamt für Tirol, Innsbruck, Vol. 1, 1927, Vol. 2, 1931.

Tietz, Hans, *Alt-Wien in Wort und Bild*, Vienna, 1924.

Trollope, Frances, *Vienna and the Austrians*, London, 1837.

Travels Through the Raetian Alps, London, 1792.

Vaculnig, Gerlinde, *Die Burgen am Ostabfall des Wienerwaldes*, (Thesis in the archives of the Nationalbibliothek), 1954.

Varnhagen von Ense, *Sketches of German Life and Scenes from the War of Liberation in Germany*, ed. by Sir Alexander Duff Gordon, Bart, London, 1847.

Vorarlberg: Vierteljahreszeitschrift für Kultur, Bregenz, 1957.

Wachter, Christian, *Altes aus dem Montafon*, Bludenz, 1932.

Welti, Ludwig, *Merk Sittich und Wolf Dietrich von Ems*, Dornbirn, 1952.

— *Graf Kaspar von Hohenems*, Innsbruck, 1963.

Werner, Ernst, *Österreichs Wiege—der Amstettner Raum*, Amstetten, 1966.

Bibliography

Wickenburg, E. G., *Barock und Kaiserschmarrn,* Munich, 1961.

Wild, Friedrich, *Anglistische Studien,* Festschrift zum 70. Geburtstag, ed. by Karl Brunner and others, Vienna-Stuttgart, 1958.

Zandvoort, R. W., *Collected Papers,* Wolters, 1954.

Ziak, Karl (ed.), and others, *Unvergängliches Österreich,* Vienna, 1958.

Zöllner, Erich, *Österreich, sein Werden in der Geschichte,* Vienna, 1961.

Index

Index

Index

Index

Index

Index

Saalbach, 103
Saalfelden, 54, 94, 97
Sachs, Hans, 161
Sachsengang, 202
Sachsen-Hildburghausen, Prince
   Joseph, 200
Salamanca, Ferdinand von, Count
   Ortenburg, 113
Salm - Reiferscheidt - Krautheim,
   Count Franz Xavier, Bishop of
   Gurk, 118
Salzach, River, 27, 80, 94, 96
Salzberg, 152, 153
Salzburg, 25, 28, 33, 79–105, 106,
   126, 137, 138, 141, 147, 193, 211,
   219
Salzkammergut, 32, 151–3, 176
Samo, 125, 217
Saurau, Count, governor of Styria, 146
Schallaburg, 196
Schärding, 161–2
Schattenburg, 41, 44
Schauenburg, *see* Schaumburg
Schauenstein, 182
Schaumburg castle, 164
Scheibbs, 185
Scheuchenstein, 186
Schiele, Egon, 197, 232
Schlägl abbey, 167
Schlaining, 207, 208
Schlierbach, 177
Schlögen, 164
Schlosshof, 200–1
Schmittenhöhe, 98
Schneeberg, 28, 36
Schnitzler, Arthur, 232
Schönborn-Battyány, Palais, 224
Schönbühel, 194
Schottenstift, 213, 219–20
Schratt, Katharina, 158
Schrattenstein, 186
Schrems, 187, 188
Schruns, 46
Schuschnigg, Kurt von, 176
Schwarzenberg, Palais, 224
Schwarzenberg, Count Georg Lud-
   wig, 113

Schwarzenberg, Prince Johann
   Franz, 224
Schwarzensee, 147
Schwaz, 70, 71, 72
Scott, Sir Walter, 52
Sealsfield, Charles, 230
Seckau abbey, 85, 136
Seekirchen, 79, 80
Seewinkel, 205, 206
Selztal, 143
Semmering, 29, 190, 218
Sempach, Battle of, 40, 41
Septimus Severus, 105, 201
Sesselschreiber, Gilg, 61
Siegmund, Archduke (of Tyrol), 52,
   55, 70–1
Sievering, 198, 217
Silbertal, 47
Silvretta Alps, 37
Simmering, 199, 217
Sitticus, Marcus, Archbishop of
   Salzburg, 42, 43, 91
Skorzeny, Otto, 94
Slavs, the, 34, 35, 36, 78, 179
Smythe, F. S., 53
Sobiesky, Prince Jakob, 66
Sobiesky, Princess Maria Clementine,
   66–8
Soissons et Carignan, Comtesse
   Victoire de, 200
Sonntagberg, 183, 194
Sparberegg castle, 70
Spittal, 107–8
Splügen Pass, 27
Sponheim family, 108
St. Aurelia, 38
St. Boniface, 82, 84
St. Columban, 38
St. Domitian, 108–9
St. Florian, 173, 175, 183
St. Gotthard, 133
St. Hemma, 106–12
St. Johann in Tyrol, 54
St. Johann Nepomuk, 167
St. Margaret of Scotland, 84
St. Margarethen, 207
St. Martin's, Linz, 173

Index

Index